BYZANTIUM: *Greatness and Decline*

BYZANTIUM: *Greatness and Decline*   CHARLES DIEHL

Translated from the French by
NAOMI WALFORD

With Introduction and Bibliography by PETER CHARANIS
Professor of History, Rutgers, The State University
General Editor, The Rutgers Byzantine Series

RUTGERS UNIVERSITY PRESS
New Brunswick   *New Jersey*
1957

Contents

Contents

Contents

Contents

Illustrations

Note: The decorations and illustrations used in this book were assembled for use in the present translation. They did not appear in the French editions.

The text decorations for this book were designed by Fritz Kredel.

Illustrations

Introduction

One need no longer apologize for offering to the general public a book on Byzantium. We have gone far since the eighteenth century, when it was thought that the history of the Byzantine Empire "is nothing but a tissue of revolts, seditions, and perfidies" (Montesquieu), "a tedious and uniform tale of weakness and misery" (Gibbon), or "a monotonous story of the intrigues of priests, eunuchs, and women, of poisonings, of conspiracies, of uniform ingratitude, of perpetual fratricide" (Lecky). The meticulous work of hundreds of scholars, philologists, historians, archaeologists; our broadened conceptions of history; our ever-increasing familiarity with, and appreciation of, cultures other than our own; the rise into prominence of peoples whose cultural inspirations came from Byzantium; the Graeco-Roman roots of Byzantine civilization—all these have made us view Byzantium in terms quite different from those used in the eighteenth century.

That the Byzantine Empire was great both as a political and military power and as a center of civilization, there is today little doubt. It endured for over a thousand years, a fact which, when viewed in the light of the external pressure to which the Empire was continuously subjected, is by itself sufficient proof of its greatness. During the major part of this period, down to the end of the eleventh century, the Byzantine Empire was the center of civilization in Christendom. It produced great statesmen, soldiers, and diplomats, as well as reformers and renowned scholars. A highly developed system of law and a remarkable administrative machinery enabled it to maintain stability and order; at the same time, it was not adverse to change and more than once adjusted its institutions to changing conditions. Its powers of renewal were extraordinary, though in the end it became exhausted and finally succumbed. Heir to the great cultural tradition of the ancient

Introduction

Greeks and Romans, particularly of the Greeks, the Byzantine Empire had the will and vigor to study that tradition, preserve it, transmit it to posterity. In so doing, it was influenced by it.

Its own cultural forms, the Empire passed on to the surrounding barbarians and so brought these barbarians within the orbit of civilization. The eastern Slavs in particular owe virtually all their past to it. Byzantium, wrote a Czech historian, "moulded the undisciplined tribes of Serbs, Bulgars, Russians, Croats even, and made nations out of them; it gave to them its religion and institutions, taught their princes how to govern, transmitted to them the very principles of civilization—writing and literature." [1]

The Byzantine cultural achievement in many of its aspects compares favorably with any that history has to offer. It has been said of St. Sophia that it is and will remain one of the most remarkable works of architecture, sufficient in itself to classify the culture of Byzantium among the greatest. [2] Alfred N. Whitehead, perhaps with a little exaggeration, but certainly not without some basis in fact, has placed this culture on a level higher than that of the culture of the classical Romans. [3] And the noted English historian, F. M. Powicke, has said of Byzantium: "So far from being a moribund society of decadent voluptuaries and half-imbecile theologians, it was the greatest, most active and most enduring political organism that the world has yet seen, giving for centuries that opportunity for living which we associate with the spacious, but transitory peace of Augustus or Hadrian." [4]

There is, of course, another side to the picture. Byzantium had its weakness and failures. There is much in its culture which is obscure and lifeless. A great deal of its literature is characterized by empty form and meaningless rhetorical declamations. When there is substance and keenness of observation, as is often the case, archaisms in language and literary expression make this literature most difficult to read, and this difficulty has often discouraged study. In Byzantium's external relations all was not triumph and glory. There were times, even during the period of its greatness, when it suffered serious military reverses and losses of territory.

[1] F. Dvornik, *Les Slaves, Byzance et Rome au IXe siècle* (Paris, 1928), ii.
[2] F. Nansen, *L'Arménie et le proche Orient* (Paris, 1928), 31.
[3] A. N. Whitehead, *Adventure of Ideas* (New York, 1933), 104.
[4] F. M. Powicke, *Modern Historians and the Study of History. Essays and Papers* (London, 1955), 181.

Introduction

Later, in its declining years, it became a puppet in the hands of Venetians and Genoese and served the Ottoman Turks as vassal until it was finally destroyed by them. In its internal life acts of treachery and cruelty, revolts, social and religious strife were not uncommon. The internal strife in its various forms periodically weakened the Empire and in the end contributed greatly to its decline. Thus, Byzantine society reveals serious failings, but to put the emphasis upon the failings, as has often been done, is to draw a distorted picture of its history and civilization.

Among the hundreds of scholars whose work has made possible a reappraisal of the history and civilization of Byzantium, Charles Diehl (1859-1944) was one of the most distinguished. Trained in the classical tradition, Diehl early in his career turned his attention to Byzantium. His first great publication, issued in 1888, was on the exarchate of Ravenna, the Byzantine province in Italy which included Rome.[5] This was followed eight years later by another great book, the one on Byzantine Africa.[6] Both these books are still standard. In 1901 Diehl issued a general work on the sixth century which remained for many years the most comprehensive general account of the great age of Justinian.[7] Three years later he followed this by offering to the public a biographical essay on Theodora, the enigmatic and seductive wife of Justinian.[8] In 1905 he published a collection of studies, most of which had already appeared in different periodicals.[9] They covered a variety of subjects relating to Byzantine history and civilization, including, among others, institutions, central and provincial administration, literature and bibliography, monuments and problems relating to art, Byzantium's relations with the Papacy after the schism of 1054, the Venetian colony in Constantinople, and a plea for a more sympathetic approach to the study of Byzantine history.

Meanwhile he turned his attention to the study of Byzantine

[5] *Études sur l'administration byzantine dans l'exarchat de Ravenne* (Paris, 1888).

[6] *L'Afrique byzantine. Histoire de la domination byzantine en Afrique (533-709)* (Paris, 1896).

[7] *Justinien et la civilisation byzantine au VI siècle* (Paris, 1901).

[8] *Theodora, impératrice de Byzance* (Paris, 1904).

[9] *Études byzantines* (Paris, 1905).

Introduction

personalities and brought out two volumes, one in 1906,[10] the other in 1908,[11] of biographical essays, brilliant character sketches of significant or interesting Byzantine figures. The first of these two volumes, with some additional items, was translated into English in 1927,[12] the only work of Diehl's relating to Byzantium to appear in English except for two short essays,[13] a rather sketchy and superficial general history of Byzantium,[14] and the important chapters which he contributed to *The Cambridge Medieval History*.[15] Diehl also wrote an essay on *Digenis 'Akritas*, the Byzantine epic, and another on two medieval Greek romances, and these he included in the second volume of his biographical essays.

Venice, which played such an important role in the history of Byzantium, interested Diehl too. A study which he published in 1883 and included in his collection of 1905 covered the Venetian colony in Constantinople in the fourteenth century; a book which he put out in 1915 dealt with Venice itself.[16] The former is a substantial account of the Venetian colony in Constantinople, its internal organization, its relations with the Byzantine court, and its role as an instrument of Venetian policy; the latter is a penetrating essay on the growth, greatness, and decline of Venice. The study of Byzantine art was also a major preoccupation of Diehl's. His numerous studies in this domain prepared the way for the publication in 1910 of his *Manuel d'art byzantin*,[17] which, as revised in 1925-1926, has remained standard.

This summary listing, by no means complete, serves to illustrate

[10] *Figures byzantines*, 1st ser. (Paris, 1906).
[11] *Figures byzantines*, 2nd ser. (Paris, 1908).
[12] *Byzantine Portraits*, tr. by Harold Bell (New York, 1927).
[13] "The Byzantine Empire and the Crusades," tr. by C. H. C. Wright, *The International Monthly*, V (1902), 725-744; *The Emperor Who Lost His Nose*, tr. by Harold Bell (New York, 1927).
[14] *History of the Byzantine Empire*, tr. by George B. Ives (Princeton, 1925).
[15] *The Cambridge Medieval History*, 2 (Cambridge, 1913), ch. I: "Justinian. The Imperial Restoration in the West"; ch. II: "Justinian's Government in the East." *The Cambridge Medieval History*, 4 (Cambridge, 1923), ch. I: "Leo III and the Isaurian Dynasty (717-802)"; ch. II: "From Nicephorus I to the Fall of the Phrygian Dynasty"; ch. XIV: "The Fourth Crusade and the Latin Empire"; ch. XXII: "The Government and Administration of the Byzantine Empire"; ch. XXIV: "Byzantine Civilization."
[16] *Une République patricienne. Venise* (Paris, 1915).
[17] *Manuel d'art byzantin*, 2 vols. (Paris, 1925-26).

Introduction

the many-sided interests of Diehl. With the exception of formal theology, for which he apparently had no sympathy, Diehl had explored virtually every phase of Byzantine civilization. The variety of his studies necessarily meant delving into the different literary and documentary sources and studying in detail the monuments of art and archaeology. Thus, Diehl came to have firsthand knowledge of his materials, knowledge without which it is not possible to draw an integrated and meaningful picture of the past. But Diehl had something else. He had a flair for the general and a remarkable capacity for synthesis. This can be seen in virtually every one of his studies, no matter how limited the scope of its subject may be. But nowhere perhaps can it be seen more clearly than in the book which is being presented here for the first time to the English-reading public. *Byzance, grandeur et décadence* is an essay, rather than a formal history of Byzantium. But it is a sparkling essay, a penetrating analysis of Byzantine society, of the elements that made it strong and of those that made it weak, and of the services that it rendered to civilization. We see Byzantium in its grandeur and decadence, in its richness and misery, in its elegance and grossness, in its religiosity and worldliness. We learn of its institutions, its mixture of races, its military organization and diplomacy, its art and its literature, the greatness and the littleness of its people. We are given an analysis of Byzantine civilization, but at the same time also a synthesis, a picture whose various parts blend together into a fascinating whole.

Byzance, grandeur et décadence first came out in 1919. A second edition, but with virtually no changes, was issued in 1926. Much of its material was incorporated into another book called *Les grands problèmes de l'histoire byzantine*, which Diehl brought out in 1943, but here again there were no material changes. Thus, the book remains very much as it was in 1919 when it was first published. Since then significant advances have been made in the study of the different phases of Byzantine civilization. Some of the old views have been altered, and much that is new has been added to what was previously known. These advances necessitate some revisions in the details of Diehl's book; they do not, however, alter the general picture drawn by it.

Diehl's view concerning the work of the Iconoclastic Emperors, for instance, can no longer be accepted without some qualifications. No one, even today, denies the greatness of these emperors. Their reforming, legislative, and military activities were most significant. But the old view, which Diehl has not quite abandoned, that they transformed Byzantine society by abolishing the colonate and re-establishing the free village communities is no longer tenable. The colonate was never abolished, while the re-establishment of the free village communities and the consequent increase in number of free peasant proprietors was the work of Heraclius and his immediate successors. Iconoclasm itself was a complex phenomenon, in which theological and other religious factors played a greater role than Diehl is willing to concede, and in which the anti-monastic measures taken by the emperors were a consequence, rather than an original motive. And it is not accurate to say that the Iconoclastic Emperors "emerged triumphant from the tussle with the Church."

Indeed, Diehl's whole position on the matter of Church-State relations in Byzantium may be questioned. Diehl follows the traditional view that the Byzantine Church was subservient to the State even in the religious sphere, both with regard to dogma and practice. This view has some basis in fact, but the fact has been exaggerated beyond measure. In reality, this alleged subservience is less characteristic of the Byzantine Church than its dogged, obstinate determination to defend all that it considered fundamental among its beliefs, practices, and privileges. To be convinced of this, one need only recall its victory over the State when the latter tried to compromise with Monophysitism; its final triumph over Iconoclasm; and its successful resistance to all the efforts made by some emperors to subordinate it to Rome. As H. Grégoire has put it, "the religious history of Byzantium could be represented as a conflict between the Church and the State, a conflict from which the Church emerged unquestionably the victor." [18] Diehl, of course, analyses the different phases of this conflict and in so doing deviates somewhat from the traditional view, but he never abandons it.

Diehl's account of the separation of the Byzantine and the Roman churches also needs to be revised. One can no longer say,

[18] H. Grégoire, "The Byzantine Church," in N. H. Baynes and H. St. L. B. Moss, *Byzantium. An Introduction to East Roman Civilization* (Oxford, 1948), 130.

Introduction

as Diehl does, that "The West was gravely displeased by the re-installation of Photius on the patriarchal throne, by his haughty refusal to submit to the papal conditions, and by the way in which, at the Council of 879, he annulled and anathematized the acts of his adversaries. . . ." Underlying this statement is the traditional view concerning the Photian schism, that the Pope refused to recognize the reinstallation of Photius and denounced the acts of the Council of 879, acts which constituted a triumph for the Byzantine Patriarch. Recent researches, particularly those of Father Dvornik, have shown that there is no basis in fact for this view. The Pope did accept the reinstallation of Photius and did ratify the acts of the Council of 879, and as a consequence there was no renewal of the break which had occurred during the first patriarchate of Photius. Diehl also exaggerates when he puts virtually all the blame for the break of 1054 on Cerularius, the Byzantine Patriarch. That ambitious prelate did take the initial step in the controversy, but the violence which the quarrel assumed was due to the obstinacy and insolence of Cardinal Humbert, who headed the papal delegation sent to Constantinople in an effort to settle the differences which divided the two churches. What particularly irked the Byzantines was the arrogance with which Humbert insisted upon the doctrine of papal supremacy, which, as Diehl correctly observes, was the fundamental issue in the final break between the two churches.

Unacceptable also is Diehl's belief concerning the financial resources of the Empire. That money was one of the most important elements in the power of Byzantium has never been doubted. But the calculations of some scholars, including J. B. Bury, that the annual budget of Byzantium during its great days amounted to about 43,800,000 *nomismata* or 119,136,000 gold dollars, a figure which Diehl also accepts, is no doubt too high. E. Stein, whose estimate runs somewhere between 7,000,000 and 8,000,000 *nomismata* (19,040,000-21,760,000 gold dollars), is probably closer to the truth. It must be borne in mind, however, that the Byzantine Empire was a mediaeval state where, despite the money economy, prestations in kind were numerous.

Without laying claim to completeness, we have picked out certain premises in Diehl's book which need to be modified and indicated the direction that this revision must take. It should be made clear, however, that our observations do not reflect on the general accuracy of the book. The merit of Diehl's book lies in its penetrating analysis, the comprehensive picture that it draws, the feel that it gives of Byzantium. It is for these reasons that Naomi Walford offers it to the English-reading public.

The translation, made from the French text as it was printed in 1926, was carefully reviewed. It follows the original closely, except that here and there a few repetitious sentences have been omitted, and a few others have been recast for the sake of style, but without changing their meaning. The text itself has been altered only slightly. Two dates have been changed in order to have them conform with those generally accepted, and the figures, which Diehl gives as the equivalents in terms of the purchasing power of gold in modern times of certain Byzantine sums, have been eliminated. We eliminated these figures for two reasons. First, because they assume a purchasing power of the Byzantine *nomisma* five times that of its gold equivalent in modern times, and this is really too high; and second, because they are based on the purchasing power of gold as of 1914, and this makes them meaningless for us today.

PETER CHARANIS

Rutgers University

Book One

Evolution of Byzantine History

The history of the Byzantine Empire still remains the object
of stubborn prejudice. To many moderns it appears, as it did to
Montesquieu and Gibbon, as the continuation and decline of the
Roman Empire. Byzantium was, in fact, something very different.
It is true that its citizens liked to be regarded as the heirs of Rome,
that, to the last, its emperors called themselves "*basileis* of the
Romans," that their ambitions often turned towards the West,
and that they never relinquished their claims on the ancient
capital. Nevertheless Byzantium soon became and continued to
be an essentially Eastern realm, and should not be judged by the
standards of mighty Rome. It has been justly described as "a
mediaeval state on the boundary between Europe and Asiatic
barbarism," [1] and as such it was very great.

In the course of its thousand-year survival of the fall of Rome,
Byzantium did not suffer a steady decline. Often, after crises that
proved almost fatal, there followed periods of unparalleled splendour during which, in the words of a chronicler, "this old woman,
the Empire, appeared like a young girl, bedecked with gold and
precious stones." Byzantium lived for a thousand years, not by

[1] Alfred Rambaud, *L'Empire grec au Xe siècle* (Paris, 1870), vii.

some freak of fortune, but gloriously, governed and administered by great emperors, brilliant statesmen and diplomats, and fine generals, under whose guidance the Empire accomplished tremendous things.

Before the Crusades, Byzantium was the champion of Christendom against the infidel, and perhaps surpassed the Crusaders in tenacity of purpose; surrounded by barbarian neighbours, it developed a superb civilization, finer and more highly cultivated than any the Middle Ages knew for a long time. Byzantium was the tutor of the Slavic and Asiatic East, and its influence spread into the West, which learned more from the school of Constantinople than can well be estimated.

Certainly this Empire had its weaknesses, its faults, and vices; and in 1453 it crumbled at last beneath the hammer-blows of the Turks. Yet if a diagram were made of the course of its thousand years of history, it would not consist of a straight line running steadily downhill, but a series of rising and falling curves. This is something never to lose sight of in seeking to understand the Byzantine Empire and the deep-seated causes of its greatness and decline. Therefore, before beginning a closer study, a brief summary of the main events in its long history is necessary.

Courtesy of the Dumbarton Oaks Collection

Gold medallion of Constantius II (323-361). Actual size.

I. The Shaping of the Eastern Empire

1. THE EMPIRE FROM THE FOUNDATION OF
CONSTANTINOPLE TO THE BEGINNING OF
THE SIXTH CENTURY

On May 11, 330, the day Constantine founded Constantinople and made it the second capital of the Roman Empire, the Byzantine Empire was born. Situated as it was at the meeting-point of Europe and Asia, Constantinople formed a natural rallying-point for the Eastern world; and in addition, by its Hellenic traditions and even more by its Christianity, this young capital, New Rome, differed profoundly from the old and symbolized the new hopes and new character of the Orient. Therefore, although the Roman Empire survived until 476, and Roman traditions persisted even in the East up to the end of the sixth century, the eastern part of the monarchy gravitated about the city of Constantinople and became to some extent aware of its separate identity. Indeed, from the fourth century onwards, the two halves of the Empire were at times governed by different emperors; and when Theodosius the Great died in 395, bequeathing to his sons, Arcadius and Honorius, a divided succession to two empires, the rift that had long tended to separate East and West became clear-cut and permanent.

Between the years 330 and 518, two severe crises shook the Empire and gave to the eastern half its final, distinctive character. One was the barbarian invasion. At first it seemed as if Byzantium could withstand it no better than Rome; as if the successive shocks launched by Alaric's Visigoths, Attila's Huns, and Theodoric's Ostrogoths in the course of the fifth century would

Early Christian marble head, type of the Empress Flaccilla, wife of Theodosius I. Height: approx. 10″. Proto-Byzantine style. *Ca.* 350 A.D.

Courtesy of the Metropolitan Museum of Art

prove overwhelming. But events took a different course. While barbarian chieftains carved out kingdoms for themselves from the fragments of the Western Empire, and while the last Roman Emperor disappeared in 476, the invasion slid along the frontiers of the Eastern Empire and delivered only glancing blows; thus, the New Rome stood fast, the greater for the disaster that had overtaken the Old, and the centre of gravity shifted to the East.

The other crisis was that of religion. In the East arose the great heresies that troubled the Church in the fourth and fifth centuries: Arianism, Nestorianism, Monophysitism—all the complex arguments in which the Greek spirit, revelling in subtle theological metaphysics, clashed with the sober, lucid genius of the Latin world, and from which violent conflict arose between the Eastern episcopate—that supple servant of the Crown—and the haughty obduracy of the Roman pontiffs. In the fourth decade of the fifth century came the first schism, and in the days of Zeno and Anastasius there emerged ever more strongly the concept of a purely Eastern Empire, living a life of its own, a realm in which we can discern characteristics of what was to be the Byzantine Empire: an absolute monarchy, modelled on those of the East; a strongly centralized administration; and a Church whose language was Greek and which therefore tended to become an independent institution, while remaining closely bound to the State that ruled it. The eastward evolution of Byzantium seemed almost complete.

The Reign of Justinian (518-565)

The sixth century interrupted this seemingly natural and necessary process. The Emperor Justinian, whose powerful figure dominates this age, aspired to be a Roman Emperor, and he was indeed the last of the great rulers of Rome. This peasant from Macedonia was the embodiment of two great ideas, the imperial and the Christian; and it is for that that he is renowned. As heir of the Caesars, he was filled with recollections of Roman greatness; he was all pride, all ambition. He dreamed of restoring Roman unity and reaffirming the prescriptive rights which Byzantium as Rome's heir maintained over the barbarian kingdoms of the West. He reconquered Africa, Italy, Corsica, Sardinia, the Balearic Islands, and part of Spain, and the Frankish kings of Gaul recognized his suzerainty. Maintaining the traditions of the great emperors of Rome, he was, like them, the living law, the incarnation of absolute power. He was the supreme legislator, a reformer who set his heart on establishing good order within his realm; and he sought to surround the seat of majesty with fitting splendour. The Cathedral of St. Sophia which he so superbly rebuilt is the unrivalled monument to his reign and name. And even today, in the Church of S. Vitale in Ravenna, the mosaics glittering in the apse are a striking emblem of the magnificence that surrounded the Lords of the Sacred Palace of Byzantium.

Justinian's dreams went further. As Vicar of God on earth, he set himself to champion Orthodoxy and to propagate the true faith throughout the world. Theodora, herself of humble origin, was perhaps more clear-sighted than her imperial husband; for while Justinian, bemused with visions of the West, fancied he could hold together the reconstructed Roman Empire by the close alliance he had formed with the Papacy, she, with a keener and more realistic political sense, turned her eyes eastward. She would have liked to compose the quarrels that threatened the authority of the Empire, by timely concessions bring back into the fold dissident nationalities such as those of Syria and Egypt, and, even at the price of a breach with Rome, firmly reunite the Empire of the East.

It is an open question whether the more compact and homogeneous Empire of which she dreamed might not have offered stronger resistance to the Persians and Arabs, and whether Justinian's reign, by halting the natural evolution of the Eastern Empire and wearing out the sovereign in the pursuit of extravagant ambitions, may not have done more harm than good. The neglected East was to take terrible revenge.

2. REORGANIZATION OF THE EMPIRE OF THE EAST

Up to this time, however, despite the influence that inclined it towards the East, the Byzantine Empire still maintained apparent continuity with Rome. Strange as it may seem, Latin remained the official language; Roman tradition was all-powerful, and the administration preserved the titles and framework bequeathed by the Caesars. From the beginning of the seventh century to the middle of the ninth, the oriental trend was hastened and completed.

The Changes of the Seventh Century (610-717)

The Empire paid dearly for Justinian's ambitions, and his death was followed by a grim time of reckoning. Internally, from the financial and military point of view, the realm was exhausted, while abroad the Persian menace loomed larger. Worse still, the torrent of Arab invasion was soon to burst upon the Empire. Religious quarrels aggravated political anarchy. In all Byzantium's history, this period between 610 and 717 is one of the darkest: a time of acute crisis when the Empire's very survival seemed in doubt.

It is true that even then great men were not lacking. By his gallant and resolute efforts, Heraclius (610-641) halted and drove back the victorious Persians; at the head of legions fired by his enthusiasm, he carried the war into the heart of Asia. He triumphed at Nineveh and at the gates of Ctesiphon; he avenged Christendom for the insults it had suffered at the hands of the Persians and entered into legend as the first of the Crusaders. His religious policy complemented his military achievement, in an effort to bring spiritual unity to the regenerated realm. Yet even within his lifetime the Empire had begun to break up. The Arabs conquered Syria, Egypt, North Africa, and Armenia; and in Italy the Lombards were masters of more than half the peninsula. The imperial territories were now reduced to Asia Minor, the Balkan Peninsula, and the exarchate of Ravenna—a restricted domain, constantly threatened by Lombards, Slavs, Arabs, and Bulgars. Up to that time, the Empire had retained its Roman, universal character, but henceforth it was to become a truly Byzantine realm, of which the strength was centred about Constantinople.

These developments brought about important changes. The first of these was ethnographical. The Slavs settled in the Balkans: Serbs and Croats in the northwest, Bulgars in the northeast.

Byzantium: Greatness and Decline

There were administrative changes: in the interests of defence, all powers were gathered into the hands of the military leaders. The regime of *themes* was instituted and was to last as long as the Empire itself. Most important of all was the social change. The Hellenic elements came steadily to the fore: in speech, where Latin yielded to Greek; in literature, which was inspired by new ideas and modelled on new forms; and in manners and customs. At the same time, Christianity made itself more strongly felt, both in the part played by the Church in public affairs and in the steady development of monasticism. Lastly, there were political changes. Rivalry with Rome was embittered by continual conflict; the breach that was soon to separate Byzantium from the West had begun to appear, and therefore the attention of the rulers came to be concentrated more and more upon the East.

These changes, by which the Empire was almost radically renewed, were by no means always for the better. Increase of superstition went hand in hand with brutality of behaviour. Continuous military revolts testified to growing demoralization and lack of loyalty. Yet, notwithstanding the decay of the monarchy, weakened abroad, threatened on every frontier, and troubled at home by twenty years of anarchy (from 695 to 717), one important, indeed essential, fact emerges at the end of this perturbed and fateful period. The Byzantine Empire had come into existence, diminished indeed, but more compact, relieved of the dead weight of the West and of the danger of rifts in the East, an Empire capable of being strongly organized and, given firm guidance, of enduring.

The Isaurian Dynasty (717-867)

Such guidance was at hand. The Isaurian Emperors [1] were the builders of the new, permanent structure of the Empire.

The Iconoclast Emperors are often severely and mistakenly judged, being remembered chiefly for their religious policy, whose intention and scope are, in any case, imperfectly understood. We tend to forget the condition in which they found the

---

[1] The Isaurians occupied the throne from 717 to 802, but their successors (802-867) continued and completed their work.

Empire and the complete reorganization that was necessary. Leo III and Constantine V were very great emperors, violent, autocratic, passionate, and hard, but also great generals, who broke the force of Islam [2] and foiled the ambitions of the Bulgars. They were skilful administrators, and their achievements in the fields of legislation, government, and social reform were very considerable, as even their enemies have done them the justice to admit.

It is true that their policy had certain unfortunate results. At home, the controversy over icons and sacred pictures disturbed the East for a hundred and twenty years, from 726 until 842; abroad there were other disasters, such as the breach with Rome, the loss of Italy, and the re-establishment of the Western Empire under Charlemagne in 800, all of them events which turned Byzantium fully and finally towards the East. On the other hand, imperial power, having emerged triumphant from the tussle with the Church, was immeasurably strengthened; and despite external perils—such as the Bulgar threat to Constantinople itself, at the beginning of the ninth century, and the conquest of Crete by the Arabs in 826, which removed all security from the eastern seas—the Empire by the middle of the ninth century had achieved both lustre and might.

Under Emperor Theophilus, who reigned from 829 until 842, the Byzantine court rivalled the Baghdad of the Caliphs in the splendour of its architecture, the luxury of its Sacred Palace, and the brilliance of its culture. After a long period of unrest, literature and the arts revived; it was the prelude of a glorious renaissance. The University of Constantinople, reorganized by Caesar Bardas in about 850, became once more a great intellectual centre. Abroad, the influence of the Empire extended into the Slavic world, to which Cyril and Methodius, the "Apostles of the Slavs," brought not only its Orthodox faith, but also its alphabet and literary language. Lastly, since 843 religious unity had been re-established within the Empire, and the Greek Church was acquiring an ever more national character, stressed and defined by the schism of Photius.

---

[2] Their success here was greatly helped by the accession of the Abbasids, who transferred the capital of the Caliphs from Syria to the distant Euphrates, and also by the dissensions which disturbed and weakened the Arab empire during the second half of the eighth century.

Thus by the end of this period there existed a distinct Byzantine nationality which had taken shape slowly as a result of circumstance; and the now truly oriental Empire moved towards its zenith. From the end of the ninth century until the middle of the eleventh, there followed a hundred and fifty years of splendour, prosperity, and renown.

II. From Climax to Fall (867-1453)

1. THE MACEDONIAN DYNASTY (867-1081)

For a century and a half, from 867 until 1025, the Empire was at the height of its glory, and was ruled by sovereigns who, almost without exception, were men of outstanding quality: Basil I, founder of the line; Nicephorus Phocas and John Tzimisces, eminent usurpers who governed in the name of the legitimate rulers; and lastly Basil II, who reigned for half a century, from 976 until 1025. Not one of these was what is all too often thought of as a typical Byzantine emperor. They were stern and virile, often unscrupulous and without pity, strong-willed autocrats, who chose to be dreaded rather than loved; but they were also statesmen, passionately devoted to their country's glory; they were brilliant military leaders who spent their lives in camp among their soldiers, in whom they recognized—and loved—the strength of the Crown; they were able administrators, energetic, tenacious, and inflexible, and dauntless in the defence of the public good. Being intent on amassing wealth for the nation, they disliked needless expense; the luxury of the palace and the vain pomp of procession and ceremonial interested them only in so far as they served politics and maintained the sovereign's prestige. Jealous of their authority, these men had no favourites, their advisers being often men of obscure origin whom they employed and kept in their place. They were greedy of renown and filled with high ambition, and they strove to make their Empire the great power of the Eastern world, as well as the champion of Hellenism and Orthodoxy. By their feats of arms, the subtle skill of their diplomacy, and the vigour of their government, they realized their dream.

From the end of the ninth century and especially after the first three decades of the tenth, the Empire once more boldly took the offensive along all its frontiers. In Asia, the Arabs retreated from the line of the river Halys to the further side of the Euphrates, and the imperial armies overran Cilicia, Syria, and Palestine. John Tzimisces thrust forward his squadrons to the very gates of Jerusalem. In Europe, the mighty empire of the Bulgars, of which the Czars Symeon and Samuel had made a redoubtable rival to Byzantium, collapsed in blood before the onslaught of Basil II, and his subjects in their gratitude awarded him the grim surname of *Bulgaroctonus*, the Slayer of the Bulgars. Once more, Byzantine fleets patrolled the seas and checked the ravagings of Moslem corsairs. Even in distant Italy, the undying traditions of ancient Rome revived claims that had never been forgotten, and in defiance of the Caesars of the Germanic Holy Roman Empire, the Byzantine *basileis* haughtily maintained the rights and the prestige of their ancient majesty.

Their realm, larger now than at any time since the far-off days of Justinian, extended from Syria to the Danube, from annexed Armenia to reconquered southern Italy. And all round it, drawn in by astute diplomacy, was gathered a retinue of vassals, Italians and Slavs, Armenians and Caucasians, through whom Byzantine influence was spread through the world. Like the Rome of other days, Byzantium was now the great educator of barbarians; Croats, Serbs, Bulgars, and Russians owed their religion to it, their literary language, their arts, and their forms of government. Beneath the rays of Byzantine civilization they became gentler, more disciplined and scholarly. Constantinople at the time of the Macedonian Emperors was indeed the queen of cities, and held within her walls all the grace, all the refinements of art and luxury, and the subtle pleasures of the mind. There were to be found masterpieces of cunning craftsmanship and of architecture, as well as the entertainments of circus and theatre. This was "the Paris of the Middle Ages," whose wealth and splendour aroused the greedy admiration of the barbarian world.

Under the guidance of energetic rulers, order and security, pledges of prosperity, were re-established, the system of absolute power was consolidated, and the Macedonian Emperors, like Justinian, aspired to shine both as legislators and administrators. When Basil II died in 1025, the Byzantine Empire was at the peak of its power, prosperity, and glory. Its territory had been more than doubled, the pride of the great feudal barons had been humbled, and the treasury held reserves of 200,000 pounds of gold, or about 49 million gold dollars. Throughout the East, the Empire's prestige was enormous.

No more would have been needed to maintain this power and prestige ·than other such sovereigns, able to pursue the same strong and skilful policy. Unfortunately, the reins of government fell henceforth into the hands either of women or of inferior, negligent men, and this led to another period of crisis. Under this weaker rule, the aristocracy, hitherto subdued, raised its head, while the army was allowed to deteriorate for fear of military revolt. The government was now a civil body, composed of bureaucrats and intellectuals, and soon degenerated into anarchy. And anarchy was dangerous, for from without, two serious threats now arose on the horizon: in the West, the Normans, and in the East, the Seljuk Turks. Not that these foes were more to be dreaded than many others whom Byzantium had vanquished in the past; like them, they could have been Hellenized, brought under Byzantine influence, and adopted as vassals. But the Empire was weaker now; moreover, schism—the final break with the Roman Church—was an added cause of unrest. Yet the Byzantines seemed unconcerned. Court intrigue and civil war, revolution in the capital and anarchy in the provinces: such was the scene for nearly twenty-five years. In 1081 three emperors were competing for power, while the Turks, who defeated Romanus IV at Mantzikert in 1071, pitched their camp almost opposite Constantinople. Ruin seemed at hand.

2. RESURGENCE OF THE EMPIRE UNDER THE COMNENI (1081-1204)

Yet once again there was to be an unexpected recovery, achieved this time by the house of the Comneni (1081-1185). Like the Capetians of France, the Comneni were a great feudal family, and their accession seemed a triumph for the military aristocracy; like the Capetians, also, they succeeded in reestablishing the shaken authority of the Crown. Four outstanding rulers ascended the throne in turn: Alexius and John, great generals, clever administrators, and wily diplomats; then Manuel, the most attractive of the line, courageous to the point of rashness, a subtle theologian, a lover of feasting and display, and a man of letters, a remarkable blend of the knightly qualities of the West and the traditional spirit of Byzantium. He was perhaps the last of the great emperors, judged by the scope of his ambitions and the efforts he made to attain them. Lastly came Andronicus, the most intelligent of them all; the twelfth century rang with his escapades and vices, yet when once he was on the throne, his great qualities caused his contemporaries to reflect that "he might have been equal to the greatest." This forceful, picturesque figure, this corrupt genius, abominable tyrant, and eminent statesman, might have saved the Empire; instead he hastened its ruin.

Once again, then, strong men were not lacking in Byzantium. It was perhaps too late for the Comneni to restore the Empire to its past glory. The Turks were in Iconium, and there they remained. In the Balkans, supported by a rising Hungary, the

Mosaic portrait bust of John II Comnenus (St. Sophia).

Slavic peoples were forming almost independent states. Nevertheless the Comneni did bring to their realm a final burst of splendour, and during the following disastrous centuries, the people were often to look back on the Comnenian era as the happiest and most brilliant of all.

Once again, on all frontiers, the Byzantine armies were in action and often victorious; they repulsed the Normans of Italy, whose covetous eyes had turned eastward; they checked the Turks. That done, they rounded upon the Serbs and Hungarians and, further west, upon the Norman kings of Sicily and the German emperors. Imperial diplomacy spread wide its supple web of intrigue, from Iconium to Venice, and in Hungary, Germany, France, Italy, and Syria. In the twelfth-century world, Constantinople was one of the chief centres of European politics. At home, a great work of administrative reform was being accomplished. Byzantine society was unrivalled in its elegance, its interest in the things of the mind, and its love of the arts; Constantinople was a capital beyond compare. Travellers [1] described it in glowing terms and preserved a radiant memory of it ever afterwards. Such wealth was dangerous, however, because of the greed it aroused; a greed that was to prove the Empire's downfall.

One serious event marked the century of the Comneni when, through the Crusades, Byzantium came once more into direct contact with the West. For the Greek Empire, Christendom's struggle to regain possession of the Holy Sepulchre was positively harmful, since, in bringing together two worlds that were incapable of understanding one another, it embittered their relationship. When the riches of the Empire and the scope it offered for trade were revealed to the Western peoples, and in particular to the Venetians, their covetousness knew no bounds. The Greeks found themselves compelled to take precautions against their troublesome and hostile guests (for Godfrey of Bouillon, Louis VII, and Frederick Barbarossa each in turn thought of taking Constantinople by force), thus departing from their natural policy and becoming more vulnerable to the Turks;

[1] Among these were Odo of Deuil, Benjamin of Tudela, Robert of Clari, and Villehardouin.

and this abandonment of earlier, wiser courses was hastened by the stirring of old ambitions. The imperialism of Manuel Comnenus perturbed the Latins and taxed the forces of the Empire. Wealth joined to weakness was enough to attract Latin greed, while the disquieting rashness of imperial policy, which by offering violence to the West justified its hatred, did the rest.

Like Justinian, Manuel Comnenus had aimed too high, and once more the time of reckoning was calamitous. While Serbs and Bulgars awoke and reorganized themselves, Latin hostility increased, and to this was added the double threat of Papal claims and Venetian greed. At home, anarchy prevailed. The Comneni were succeeded by weak rulers of the house of Angelus, at whose hands the Empire decayed. The fatal consequence was the Fourth Crusade which, though undertaken to win back the Holy Sepulchre, ended in the capture of Constantinople. Venetian diplomacy, backed by the tacit connivance of the Pope, overthrew the Greek Empire and placed a Count of Flanders on the throne, amid the applause of Christendom.

3. THE EMPIRE UNDER THE PALAEOLOGI
(1261-1453)

The events of 1204 were a blow from which the Empire never recovered. It is true that Latin rule was of short duration, and in 1261 the Greeks re-entered their capital; yet the Latins retained a number of states in the East, where Venetians and Genoese were masters, and the West still kept its eyes fixed on Byzantium. And though the disaster of 1204 had stirred nationalist feelings in the Greeks, especially in the Nicaean Emperors

(1204-1261), yet the dynasty of the Palaeologi, which occupied the throne for the next two centuries, from 1261 to 1453, succeeded to an Empire that was territorially and financially reduced and was to be reduced still further as time went on.

The growing Christian states in the Balkans were by now conscious of their strength and bitter in disputing with Byzantium the hegemony of the Peninsula; these states were the second Bulgarian Empire in the thirteenth century and the Serbia of Stephen Dushan in the fourteenth. There were also the Turks, who were now lords of all Asia and whose capital, Brusa, lay opposite Constantinople. Later, in the middle of the fourteenth century, they set up their capital in Europe, at Adrianople. Of what avail then were even such men as John Cantacuzenus and Manuel Palaeologus, "who in better times would have saved the Empire, if the Empire could have been saved"? The Empire was past saving.

We have only to remember the conditions that prevailed. There was financial distress, aggravated by shameless Latin exploitation. There was civil strife, for which foreign aid was unblushingly sought, either from Serbs or Turks. There were class conflicts—rich against poor, aristocrats against plebeians— whose bitterness is revealed in the strange, tragic, bloody story of Thessalonica in the fourteenth century. Lastly, there were religious struggles. Greek national sentiment rebelled against the conciliatory policy of those emperors who desired to gain the support of the Papacy by negotiating the Union of the Churches. What strength remained to the nation was squandered in these clashes. There was no army left, no money, no patriotism. The Empire was shrinking daily. Constantinople, encircled on land, maintained only sea communications with its tattered territories. The time was coming when the whole Empire would be reduced to this one city, and thenceforth its fall was inevitable.

Yet such was the vitality of this civilization that the period of the Palaeologi was radiant with a superb revival in literature and the arts. The schools of Constantinople still flourished, and their many professors, philosophers, and orators were the forerunners of the great humanists of the Renaissance. Writers of merit appeared, as well as historians, moralists, poets, essayists, and even scientists, whose work was as valuable as that of Roger Bacon in the West. Once again Byzantine art was rekindled by contact with, or at least in emulation of, Italy; it was a vital, pictorial art, full of deep feeling, of drama, and of charm. Trebizond, Mistra, and Athos were the centres of this renaissance, besides Constantinople; and so once more Byzantine influence spread through the Eastern world, among Serbs, Russians, and Rumanians.

On May 29, 1453, Constantinople was captured by the Turks, and the last of the emperors met a hero's death, sword in hand, on the breached ramparts of his city. Is it not strange that on the very eve of final disaster, Hellenism should have rallied all its intellectual forces, as if to recall the glories of the past and to symbolize and herald the future? In dying Byzantium we hear again the great names of Pericles, Themistocles, and Epaminondas, and are reminded of all that these forebears once did "for the state, for the country." We find the most eminent men of the day urging the Emperor to discard the traditional, outworn title of "*Basileus* of the Romans" and adopt the new one of "King of the Hellenes," "which alone would suffice to ensure the preservation of free Hellenes and the liberation of their enslaved brethren." Such ideas appear senseless at a time when Mohammed II was at the gates; yet how striking is this resurgent Hellenism which refused to die and which at the very moment of catastrophe, groped, however dimly, towards a better future.

Such, in brief summary, is the history of Byzantium, from the founding of Constantinople in 330 to its fall in 1453. What glories there were in the eleven centuries that lay between! In the sixth century, under Justinian, the Roman Empire rises again for the last time, and the Mediterranean becomes once more a Roman lake. In the eighth century the Isaurians smash the headlong fury of Islam, and re-establish the principle of absolute monarchy. In the tenth century the great emperors of the Macedonian house make Byzantium the great power in the East. Under the Comneni in the twelfth century, the Greek Empire still shines upon the European world. It is therefore not enough to speak of decadence; greatness, too, must be our theme, and it will be worth while to seek the deep-seated causes of this greatness before studying the reasons for decline. Above all, let us never forget what was achieved by a civilization which was for a long time the most brilliant of any in the Middle Ages; let us see what East and West owe to the Byzantine Empire, and what heritage it has left us, even to this day.

Book Two

Elements of Power

To define the manifold causes, whether permanent or transient, of Byzantine decadence is relatively easy, and it has often
been attempted. It is harder to determine the reasons for Byzantium's greatness. Yet to endure and flourish for more than a thousand years, not without glory, the Empire must have contained
within itself certain elements of power, without which its continued existence would be inexplicable. What were the deep-
seated and persistent causes of this greatness? It is this question
that we shall try to answer here.

First—and this is fundamental—it had a strong and absolute
form of government: one of the most powerful conceptions of
monarchical authority ever known. This government was admi-
rably served: by a well-organized army which for a long time
was able to defend the monarchy; by a strictly centralized administration, competent to unify the Empire and to maintain it,
and constituting the basis and support of the Crown; and by
skilful diplomacy, which long continued to spread the influence
and uphold the prestige of Byzantium throughout the world.

There were other factors. The Empire had long enjoyed unprecedented economic prosperity, and it was the home of a bril-

liant intellectual culture; two things which made Constantinople one of the most magnificent and cultivated centres of civilized life. And to the splendour of its capital, the Empire added the qualities of vitality and strength, of which the provinces—Asia in particular—were for a long time the inexhaustible source.

No doubt the effectiveness of these factors varied with the period. There were times when the government was weak, the army disorganized, the administration slack and corrupt, and diplomacy rash and clumsy; though to counteract these temporary lapses there were not lacking positive and constructive elements. At last, economic prosperity declined, and the loss of Asia to the Turks had fateful consequences for the power and equilibrium of the Empire, two important events which paved the way for its incurable decadence, from the thirteenth century onwards. Yet up to the last, Constantinople commanded admiration as a centre of civilization and as a witness to the past grandeur of Byzantium, so that for a long time to come, the City was surrounded by the radiance of its former glory.

This, then, shall be the order of our study: Government, the Army, Diplomacy, Administration, and Economic Development. Like the two leaves of a diptych we shall see, on the one hand, Constantinople, home of wealth and culture, and on the other, the Asiatic Orient, the Empire's strength.

I. Government

Few rulers in the world have been more powerful than the Emperor of Byzantium. Few states, even in the Middle Ages, have had a more absolute conception of monarchical authority. And herein lay the great strength of the Empire.

1. ORIGINS AND NATURE OF IMPERIAL POWER

The Byzantine Emperor was a very great figure and one whose status, by its complexity, is not easy to define. As heir to the Caesars, he was like them *Imperator,* that is to say, at once the Commander-in-Chief and the Legislator. It was in his name that generals won victories; it was his sovereign and infallible will that made the law, of which he was the living expression. "What is there greater," wrote Justinian, "what more sacred than imperial majesty? Who so arrogant as to scorn the judgment of the Prince, when lawgivers themselves have precisely and clearly laid down that imperial decisions have the force of law?" Rome in its day had linked the glory of arms with that of law and on this dual foundation had based its monarchy. The Byzantine Emperor continued the Roman tradition. "Who should be capable

of solving the riddles of the law and revealing them to men,"
says Justinian, "if not he who alone has the right to make the

Mosaic panel, depicting Christ flanked by the Empress Zoë and her
third husband, Constantine IX Monomachus (St. Sophia).

law?" By definition, the imperial function conferred upon him
who assumed it absolute power and infallible authority.

Through contact with the East, the Byzantine Emperor became
something more: he was *Autocrator, Despotes*, and, with the
beginning of the seventh century, he became in the Hellenized

Government

Empire *Basileus:* that is to say, supreme Emperor, emulator of and successor to the Great King, whose humiliation and fall had lately been effected by the victory of Heraclius over the Persians. In the manner of Oriental rulers, from whom he had borrowed the fashion of his robes and of his diadem, the Emperor of Byzantium took his place above the rest of mankind; those beneath him were not subjects but slaves, and so they humbly described themselves. It was by prostrating themselves three times and devoutly kissing his hands and feet that those of even the highest rank approached their all-powerful master. The προσκύνησις of the protocol is, as the word denotes, an act of adoration.

To all this, Christianity added one further consecration. The Emperor was the Chosen of God, the Anointed of the Lord, the Vicar of God on earth, His lieutenant at the head of armies,[1] and, as they said in Byzantium, *isapostolos:* prince equal to the apostles. It was God who inspired the *Basileus* in every phase of government, who helped him and multiplied signs and wonders in his favour. "It is not in arms that we trust," wrote Justinian, "nor in soldiers, nor in generals, nor in our own genius; we set all our hopes on the providence of the Holy Trinity." Official acclamations proclaimed: "The Lord who giveth life shall lift up your heads, O Masters, above the whole universe; He will make of all peoples your slaves that they may bring gifts, even as the Magi of old, to Your Majesty." Champion of God on earth—his wars against the infidel bore the aspect of true holy wars—supreme head and defender of religion, King and Priest in one (ἀρχιερεὺς βασιλεύς, as is said of Justinian), the Byzantine Emperor was as absolute and infallible in the spiritual as in the temporal sphere.

From the combination of these elements, there emerged a power founded not merely on political authority, but sanctified and endued by God and the Church with transcendent sovereignty.

[1] John Comnenus declares that his soldiers fought "under God as their general and under me as His lieutenant."

2. EXTERNAL FORMS OF IMPERIAL AUTOCRACY

Outward appearances were designed to symbolize the nature of Imperial Majesty.

At every period of their history, the Byzantines pursued a policy of pomp and splendour; they regarded the surrounding peoples—somewhat naively, perhaps—as children to be easily dazzled, as credulous barbarians, impressed by spectacle, who could not fail to be awed by the sumptuousness of the imperial court. Display was always a favourite feature of Byzantine diplomacy, luxury, one of the mainsprings of policy. Byzantium was intent on presenting to the world a prince who ruled in glory, in apotheosis, less as a man than as a living manifestation of the divine.

It was to this end that magnificent titles were appended to the imperial name. Like Augustus and Trajan, Justinian was *Imperator, Caesar, Gothicus, Alemannicus, Francicus, Germanicus, Vandalicus, Africanus,* pious, happy, illustrious, victorious, triumphant, and always *Augustus.* In the Hellenized Empire his successors called themselves—as if the simpler terms summarized all earlier titles—faithful *Basileis* in Christ our Lord and Autocrats of the Romans. To this end, also, the gorgeous dress, the splendour of the imperial insignia, the privilege of the purple boots, and the tremendously elaborate setting of the festivals, in every one of which the Prince must appear in fresh array, brilliant in colour and flashing with gold and precious stones. Etiquette, ever ostentatious and somewhat childish, isolated the sovereign from common mortals and, to intensify their veneration for majesty, surrounded him with glory. "Beauty of ceremonial," wrote Constantine Porphyrogenitus who, in the tenth century, took delight in codifying the ritual, "renders imperial power more splendid, more glorious, and compels the admiration of both foreigners and subjects." For this reason, the imperial palace was the scene of daily ceremonies, solemn processions, and sumptuous banquets—

Courtesy of the Dumbarton Oaks Collection

Stone roundel representing a Byzantine emperor. Late 12th century.

where rules and precedence were governed by the strictest hier-archy—formal audiences, and strange, magnificent festivals. Many have described these spectacles, in which Byzantium appeared in a blaze of gold, and where, in luxurious tapestried and flower-strewn halls, the shifting colours of uniforms and the glitter of goldsmith's work mingled with such magical devices as roaring bronze lions, mechanical birds singing in golden plane trees, and an Emperor floating in mid-air, poised between heaven and earth. It is needless to describe these things again. And, at the heart of all this pomp, the sovereign himself, sheathed in gold, mag-nificent, dazzling, appeared upon his throne like a holy icon, like a god. Equally sacred was all that touched him, and art sets a halo about the heads of rulers—even of Theodora and Zoë—as it does about those of divine persons and the saints.

3. THE EXTENT OF IMPERIAL POWER

How real was this power?

Roman tradition, preserved by Byzantium, placed the Emperor above the law. (He was, as was said in the sixth century, *solutus legibus*.) He therefore exerted an absolute authority over things and people, over the army and the administration, over justice, finance, politics, and religion. He was in complete control. "Every-thing depends," wrote Leo VI, "on the personal supervision and direction of Imperial Majesty." The Emperor could regulate cus-toms, which he supervised and reformed, and even fashion; it was for him to select the manner of dress to be worn and to set bounds to its extravagance.

Government

The Emperor had military powers. He often led his armies in battle, and accounts exist of his triumphant returns to the capital after successful campaigns. The Emperor had civil powers: he made and unmade laws. From Justinian to the Comneni, the Byzantine Emperors were great legislators, as the Justinian Code, the *Ecloga*, the *Basilics*, and the great numbers of *Novels* promulgated by them all testify. He kept a close watch on administration —one has only to remember the great reforms of Justinian, of the Isaurians, and of Basil I—and corresponded directly with his provincial governors. He was the supreme judge, the imperial tribunal being a court of first instance as well as that of appeal. He had the great task of fiscal administration, so vital to the Empire. Justinian lays down that the citizen's first duty is to pay taxes punctually, regularly and in full, "with all devotion," for the State "is in greater need of money than ever," and it is the healthy condition of the Treasury that will bring about "fair and harmonious concord between governors and governed." Lastly he nominated and dismissed at will all officials, ministers, generals, and governors of provinces, and as freely promoted them in the complex hierarchy. Everything depended upon him, and Byzantine history is full of scandalous preferments and resounding falls from grace.

But the most characteristic feature of the Emperor's authority was the power he exercised in religious matters. "Your might, ye faithful Emperors in Christ and Chosen of God, truly proceeds from God and not from men," declared the official acclamations. Solemnly consecrated by the Patriarch in the *Ambo* of St. Sophia, the Emperor reigned by the grace of God and triumphed with the aid of Christ. His life mingled at every point with that of the priesthood; he alone was permitted to pass with the clergy beyond the sacred barrier of the *iconostasis*. He ruled the Church as he ruled the State, nominating bishops for election, consecrating them, and, if they proved insufficiently amenable to his will, dismissing them. He legislated in religious as in secular matters, summoning ecclesiastical councils, guiding their debates, confirming their canons, and carrying their resolutions into effect; and those who rebelled against the imperial will rebelled against God Himself. He drafted rules for ecclesiastical discipline and did not hesitate to fix dogmas; for within every Byzantine Emperor there dwelt a learned, subtle theologian with a taste and talent for disputation, who from the *Ambo* of St. Sophia delivered pious homilies and everywhere imposed his will. In religious matters he was the supreme justiciary, confirming or quashing the sentences of the ecclesiastical courts. He was the defender of the Church, active in fighting heresy and propagating Orthodoxy throughout the world (οἰκουμένη); but in return for his protection, the Church must obey his will. Before him the loftiest heads must bow: those of popes, whom he ill-treated or arrested, those of patriarchs, whom he beggared. In the sixth century the Patriarch Menas solemnly declared that "in the Most Holy Church nothing must be done against the counsel and commands of the Emperor." "The Emperor," says a prelate of the twelfth century, "is for the Churches the Master of Faiths," and Pope Gregory the Great himself acknowledged that God had bestowed upon the Emperor "dominion not only over soldiers but over priests."

4. THE LIMITS OF IMPERIAL POWER

The imperial power of Byzantium, then, was sacred and despotic. "Our souls," say the official acclamations, "have no duty but to look towards you, O Supreme Masters of the Universe" (δεσπόται τῆς οἰκουμένης). For the authority of the *Basileus* extended beyond the boundaries of his realm into all inhabited regions of the earth. Nothing in the Byzantine constitution balanced or modified this supreme power, which knew no limits or control. There were indeed, as in pagan Rome, the Senate and the people; and as in Rome, a constitutional fiction ascribed to them a rôle in the State which at times, even in the seventh and eighth centuries, seems to have had some reality.[2] In general, however, the Senate was nothing more than a Council of State: an assembly of high officials united in devotion to their prince. The senatorial nobility was merely a preserve from which were recruited the Empire's administrators. The people were a mob to be fed and amused, an unruly and factious mob which, despite the efforts made to tame it, sometimes broke out in rioting and bloody revolution.

In Christian Byzantium there was also the Church which, however submissive to imperial authority, attempted at least once, in the ninth century, to demand its freedom and came near to setting off another Investiture Struggle. And indeed this Church succeeded at last in compelling the Emperor to take a solemn oath at his coronation, by which he undertook to practise Orthodoxy, to respect the decrees of the seven oecumenical councils, and to abstain from interfering with ecclesiastical privilege. On occasion the Church could threaten him with the dreaded weapon of excommunication. In effect, however, even in this most Christian state, the Church counted for very little compared with the Emperor. Even those who criticized their Prince's interference in matters of religion, "as if he bore the Christ within himself and had been by Him divinely instructed in His mysteries," recognized in general the scope of his absolute authority. "The majority of the Emperors of the Romans," wrote Nicetas, "do not think it enough to rule as absolute masters, to be covered with gold, to use what belongs to the State as freely as if it were their own, to dispose of it how and to whom they choose, and to command free men as if they were slaves. Unless they be also venerated as sages resembling gods in form and heroes in strength; as beings inspired by God, like Solomon; as doctors of divinity; as canons more authentic than any canons—in a word, as infallible interpreters of things divine and human—they conceive themselves wronged. Thus, whereas they ought to punish the ignorant and the bold who introduce new dogmas into the Church, or

[2] In the seventh century one may discern the rudiments of parliamentary government in the Assembly of 687, at which the Emperor gathered together representatives of Church and Senate, officers of the Guard, and leaders of the people (*demarchs*); also representatives of the Army. But this institution seems not to have been developed.

else commit them to those whose function it is to know God and speak of Him, they esteem themselves even in this sphere inferior to none, and set themselves up as interpreters, judges and definers

Courtesy of The Byzantine Institute, Inc.

Emperor (Basil I or Leo VI) kneeling before Christ. Mosaic (St. Sophia).

of dogma, often punishing those who disagree with them." [3] It is interesting to note these adverse comments in the writings of a high official; they are an indication of how little the Church could in fact do to restrain the Emperor.

[3] Nicetas Acominatus, *Historia* (Bonn, 1835), 275.

Government

Only by force, then, could imperial power be held in check: the force of arms, manifesting itself in military revolt; the force emanating from the feudal aristocracy and expressed in attempts at usurpation; the force emanating from the people and exploding in riots. It has been justly said that in Byzantium, imperial power was an autocracy tempered by revolution and assassination.

The fact is that this absolute power had a weakness. Like Rome, Byzantium had no law of succession, at least until the end of the ninth century. Theoretically a man became Emperor either through election by Senate, people, and Army, or by the decree of the reigning Emperor, who, during his lifetime, designated and installed at his side a successor chosen by qualification of birth, adoption, or association. In fact, it was most often by brutal usurpation that emperors were made, and for a long time there was no reigning family or blood royal in Byzantium. It was for the emperors of the Macedonian line "to give imperial authority more powerful roots, that it might put forth the glorious branches of dynasty." [4] Thenceforward it was more difficult to overthrow so firmly rooted a tree; an imperial family now existed, whose members were given the name of *Porphyrogeniti*, and it is from this period that we may trace an increasing emphasis on legitimacy. Dynasties appeared: that of the Macedonians, lasting 189 years; that of the Comneni, who reigned for 104; and that of the Palaeologi, who held the throne for 192. Even usurpers respected the lawful dynasty, and among the people there grew up an attachment—a loyalist devotion—to the ruling house. Public opinion now held that "he who reigns in Constantinople is always victorious," which made usurpation not only criminal but, what was worse, foolish. In this Eastern monarchy, even women might ascend the throne—a thing unknown in the West—and those such as Irene, Theodora, and Zoë were popular.

[4] So expressed by Constantine VII in his life of his grandfather, Basil I. See Theophanes Continuatus, *Chronographia* (Bonn, 1838), 264.

5. THE LIFE OF AN EMPEROR

Lastly, to gain a clear idea of what a Byzantine Emperor was, let us briefly consider the life he led between his coronation in St. Sophia and his magnificent funeral in the Church of the Holy Apostles.

The Book of Ceremonies, written in the tenth century by Emperor Constantine VII, shows us a typical—and as it has been said, a truly "pontifical"—existence, through which the Emperor moved, a majestic figurehead, amid chants, rhythmic acclamations, processions, and solemnities. His every act, his every gesture was regulated by etiquette, and his days were filled with futile ceremonial, religious and secular feasts, audiences, and banquets. Every morning a solemn procession filed through the palace apartments; on certain days there were visits to churches, and at the beginning and end of the year came the splendid festivals of δωδεκαήμερον. And beneath this dazzling exterior one glimpses an extraordinary emptiness.

But all this was but a part—and the least part—of a Byzantine Emperor's life. Some rulers had a very different conception of their function. Among these were the warriors, who were always at the head of their troops: Heraclius and the first two Isaurians, Basil I, Phocas, Tzimisces, and the austere, luxury-hating Basil II, as well as Alexius, John, and Manuel Comnenus. There were Emperors who, even in the palace, led anything but idle lives. Justinian, despite his taste for pomp and formality, spent his nights working, and deserved his nickname of "the Emperor who never sleeps."

Government

6. THE STRENGTH OF THE IMPERIAL SYSTEM

Such men as these turned the imperial system into a source
of strength. It is true that in a state where everything is directly
dependent on the Emperor the sovereign's immediate entourage
is bound to exercise undue influence upon him, and because of
the position occupied by the palace in a realm of this sort the
regime may well become one of intrigue, directed by women and
favourites. It also offers a constant temptation to ambitious subjects to overthrow the monarchy, since revolution is the only
method of seizing power. Moreover in a state regulated by the
will of a single man, weakness or mediocrity in that man consti-
tutes a very real danger. Such are the drawbacks of absolute
monarchy. There are, however, the corresponding advantages
of undivided command, continuity of policy, and firmness of
conception and execution; and if the prince be a man of integrity
and strength of character, who knows how best to use the means
of government at his disposal—military, diplomatic, and administrative—his firm, untrammelled leadership is of immense benefit to the Empire. There were such sovereigns in Byzantium, and
more of them than is commonly believed; few states in history
have been ruled by a succession of such notable men. So long as
the Emperor was also a leader, fortune smiled upon his realm.

II. The Army and the Defence of the Monarchy

In every mediaeval state, the army played an essential part. In a state such as the Byzantine Empire, threatened ceaselessly on every frontier by formidable enemies, its rôle was even more important. As we shall see, military institutions formed the basis of the administrative machine; the two main preoccupations of the Emperor were the defence of his country and the welfare of his troops. So long as the army was large and strong, devoted to its duty and its master, the monarchy, despite all difficulties, survived; as military strength declined, so Byzantium decayed. Of all the factors of the Empire's greatness, therefore, the military organization must be reckoned among the first. "The Army is to the State what the head is to the body," said one Emperor. "Unless it be well cared for, the very existence of the Empire will be endangered."

1. COMPOSITION OF THE ARMY. RECRUITMENT

Just as in Roman times, the Army consisted partly of men recruited from among the citizens of the Empire. In principle, military service was required of every Roman citizen between the ages of 18 and 40, and whether conscripts or volunteers, they were regarded as the truest type of soldiers (στρατιῶται), not because they were better than the rest, but because they represented the nation—they were always known as 'Ρωμαῖοι—and were the heirs of the old Roman legions. Contrary to common belief, this national element long held a numerically important place in the Byzantine forces. However, the troops furnished by regional recruiting were of uneven quality. Though the rough peasants of Thrace and Macedonia and the sturdy mountain-dwellers of Cappadocia, Isauria, and Armenia made fine soldiers, others called to the colours were of poorer stuff, raw peasants, snatched from the plough, who knew nothing of fighting. For this reason the government soon came to accept money instead of service, and at times even encouraged those of military age to fulfil their obligations in this way. Exemptions seem to have been granted in a variety of cases, and to strengthen the forces mustered by recruiting, the Empire called more and more on mercenaries.

Mercenaries

From among the countless adventurers drifting along the frontiers and ever ready to sell their services, the Byzantine Crown had no difficulty in picking excellent soldiers. Levies were raised from foreigners settled within the Empire; these might be Vardariot Turks, Mardaites from the Lebanon, and Slavs from Macedonia or Opsikion. Others, called allies (σύμμαχοι), were foreign regiments, supplied by a friendly ruler and commanded by their own officers. Then there were those known as confederates: barbarians from a variety of places who sought service in the imperial army. Thus a positive mosaic of races met together under the Byzantine standards. Side by side in the armies of the sixth century we find Huns and Vandals, Goths and Lombards, Heruls and Gepids, Antae and Slavs, Persians, Armenians, Arabs from Syria, and Moors from Africa. In the tenth and eleventh centuries there were Khazars and Pechenegs, Phargans and Russians, Slavs, Iberians, Georgians, Mardaites of Lebanese descent, hillmen from the Caucasus, Arabs, Turks, Norsemen from Scandinavia, and Normans from Italy. The forces of the Comneni included Anglo-Saxons, Scandinavians, Italians, Germans, Latins from every Western country, Frenchmen from France, Normans from Sicily, and representatives of all the Eastern peoples, including Turks, who were known as *Turcopuls*. Later, the Palaeologi employed Catalans, Turks, Genoese or Venetian *condottieri*, and Serbian and Bulgarian auxiliaries. At no time in its history did the Empire lack foreign troops.

For the *Basileus* treated them liberally. Officers' pay was exceptionally good, calculated to tempt the needy nobles of Armenia and the Caucasus and arouse the greed of Scandinavian and Russian adventurers; and that of the men, too, was often very high. Moreover, the Emperor willingly bestowed land upon those who enlisted under his banner—land registered and protected by statute, inalienable and hereditary fiefs whose owners bore the title of knight (καβαλλάριοι). In addition to these advantages, they were held in special esteem. The Emperor placed more reliance on foreign soldiers than on his national troops, feeling that well-paid mercenaries were more surely his, and beyond the reach of anti-imperial influences. He therefore entrusted them with high commands and military dignities, and indeed the safety of his own person. One of the Guard regiments, the *Hetaeria*, consisted almost entirely of foreigners: Russians, Scandinavians, and Khazars. The famous Varangian Guard, originally composed of Russians, was later recruited in turn from Scandinavians of Russia, Norsemen of Iceland and Norway, and Anglo-Saxons. It was a picked corps, lavishly paid, and the exploits of its members, armed with a heavy axe, the *rhomphaia,* fill the pages of Byzantine history.

The result of this was a continual influx of foreigners from the barbarian world. In the tenth century bands of Russians and Scandinavians arrived at the capital in their long ships, and replenished the land and sea forces. These were magnificent soldiers, who preferred death to surrender. Armenian contingents were numerous at this time, and highly valued. Even prisoners did not hesitate to purchase their freedom by taking service in the imperial army; while Arabs allowed themselves to be converted so as to share in the Emperor's favours. In the twelfth century the Latins were the flower of the imperial forces, to the fierce resentment of the Greeks, who were jealous of the favour shown them by Manuel Comnenus. Sons of northern kings and the great barons of the West rejoiced in the romantic adventures to be met with and the fortunes to be won in the imperial service. And this composite army, in which so many separate peoples were represented, was unrivalled in steadiness and valour.

2. THE QUALITIES OF THE BYZANTINE ARMY AND ITS PLACE IN SOCIETY

We must not exaggerate the size of this army, despite the magnitude of its task. In the sixth century Belisarius reconquered Africa from the Vandals with a force of 15,000 at the very most, while 25 or 30,000 sufficed to destroy the kingdom of the Ostrogoths. In the tenth century the great expeditions launched against Crete employed a landing force of from 9 to 15,000. At this period an army of 5 or 6000 was a large one and accounted fully adequate to engage the enemy. It would be foolish to accept the statements of Arab writers, who estimate the armies of tenth-century emperors at 100 or 150,000. In the twelfth century not even the most powerful armies of the Comneni exceeded 50,000 men. The total number of Byzantine regulars forming the Army of Asia, who faced the Arabs in the tenth century, was about 70,000. This, together with the 24,000 men of the Imperial Guard and the regiments of the Army of Europe, brought the figure at that time to a maximum of 140,000.

But this army was a picked one. It consisted chiefly of cavalry —as in all mediaeval armies, this was the favourite branch of the service—and this cavalry, whether cuirassiers (*cataphracts*) or the light troopers of the *trapezitae,* was an arm of great strength and mobility. The men were kept in training by hard and continuous exercises, whose picturesque details are given in the treatises on tactics written between the sixth and the eleventh centuries. They were seasoned fighters, able to endure every sort of hardship and privation; and the continued improvements made in their fighting methods ensured an almost invariable superiority over their adversaries. These veteran horsemen, tested and tried in a hundred battles, were amazingly brave, and their valour was stiffened by the carefully instilled conviction that on the one hand, they were descendants of those Romans "who in bygone times overwhelmed all their adversaries by force of arms," while on the other, they were fighting in defence of Christendom. They fought under the protection of Christ and of the Virgin, who was the "invincible ally of the Emperor and shared his command"; they fought under the eyes of the great soldier-saints, who stood ready to direct their squadrons in battle. Whether on Asiatic and Bulgarian battlefields or overseas in Crete, Italy, and Africa, this army displayed unflagging courage and tenacity; and if it had faults, as we shall see, it nevertheless carried the imperial standard in triumph through the world. In the sixth century it overcame the barbarian kingdoms of the Vandals and the Ostrogoths; in the seventh it broke the power of the Persian Empire; it checked the onslaught of Islam in the eighth century; and in the tenth it re-established Byzantine prestige in Asia and drowned the great Bulgarian state in blood. Even as late as the twelfth century it succeeded in holding Normans, Hungarians, and Turks in check. Thus for more than six hundred years it served the Empire nobly and added glory to its flag.

And the Empire cared for its soldiers. A military work of the tenth century, in which the thoughts of the great warrior-emperors of the day are strikingly recorded, recommends that if the men are to set forth "joyously, with light and ardent hearts, to risk their lives for our holy emperors and for all Christendom," if they are to be "inspired with the boldness to attempt the impossible," then neither rewards nor privileges must be stinted. "They must receive all the consideration that is due to them," says this author. "The men who hazard their lives for the holy emperors and the freedom of all Christians must never be exposed to contempt and ill-treatment from base tax-collectors who render no service to the Empire." The soldier could be tried only by his officers, never by ordinary courts of justice; "men who are the defenders and, under God, the saviours of Christendom; men who in a sense die daily for the holy Emperors" must never be seen "chained like slaves and beaten with rods." The soldier had to be kept happy, contented, and keen; he would be the braver for it, and appear invincible, thus enabling the Emperor not only to defend his Empire but also to subdue the realms of his enemies.

In Byzantine society, then, no estate was held in higher esteem than that of the soldier. On his fief he and his household enjoyed many privileges, while in the state the military class (στρατιωτικὸς οἶκος) was superior to the civil one (πολιτικός). Defender of faith, emperor, and country (the phrase is to be found in another treatise of the tenth century), the soldier had the right to every privilege, every consideration. Indeed, one emperor even asked the Church to honour as martyrs the warriors who died devoutly, in combat with the infidel.

3. THE DEFECTS OF THE MILITARY ORGANIZATION

An army thus composed and occupying so high a position in the state naturally had, in addition to its good qualities, some very marked faults, that turned this fine instrument of war into a potential danger.

Troops acquired through recruitment within the Empire were often of poor quality. Not only were many of them unwarlike by nature, but relaxed discipline had allowed them to take up a variety of civil occupations in addition to their military duties. They were, in fact, less an army than a national guard, inadequately trained in warfare and often of questionable loyalty. We find evidence of this in the Army of Egypt, in the sixth and seventh centuries, which was thrown into confusion when faced by the Arabs. In provinces where the material was better, the regional recruiting system presented another danger. These troops were officered by members of the feudal nobility of the province, whom they knew, to whom they were bound as dependents or vassals, whom they obeyed blindly, and whose word carried more weight than the commands of a remote emperor. Any military leader with political ambitions found in his followers an instrument to serve him; and this accounts for the great number of military insurrections in which an army proclaimed its commander Emperor and more than once succeeded in setting him on the throne.

In an effort to remedy these ills, Byzantium reserved a large place in its forces for mercenaries; they were better soldiers and, it was hoped, more loyal. But this system, too, had its dangers. Belisarius said to his men, "You excel your adversaries in courage and bodily strength. You yield to them in one thing only: you do not know how to obey." Lack of discipline was the basic failing of Byzantine troops. These stateless adventurers, intent merely on lining their pockets, were a menace to their commander. They disputed orders, refused to march, and would even turn traitor in the heat of battle. They considered themselves above ordinary rules; they had to be reasoned with and humoured instead of punished. When they were discontented, they mutinied, and at all times they were the scourge of any country they passed through, whether friendly or hostile. Nor were their leaders much better; they were openly insubordinate; they thought only of enriching themselves and of profiting by the strength of their position and the weakness of the Empire to satisfy their personal ambitions. They were true *condottieri,* ever ready either to work for their own ends or to sell themselves to the highest bidder.

The Generals

Such being the rank and file, everything depended on the man who commanded them. If he inspired trust and affection and knew how to manage men, he could do what he liked with them. If he was unpopular, if he was considered too exacting or stern, his men refused to obey him, plotted against him, and forsook him on the battlefield. Fortunately for the Empire, it was served for much of its history by able and vigorous commanders, humane though firm, who, by their gallantry, their skill in war, their care for their men, and not least by their fiery eloquence, won the confidence and kindled the enthusiasm of their troops. In the sixth century there were Belisarius and Narses, in the seventh, Heraclius; in the eighth came the great Isaurian Emperors and in the tenth, John Curcuas—"another Trajan, another Belisarius"—while three generations of Phocas' family led the armies of the Empire to victory. There were the great Emperors of the tenth century—Nicephorus Phocas, Tzimisces, and Basil II—and later the Comneni, Manuel especially, who, valiant as a knight of chivalry, was long the idol of his men. Many more, whose glorious memory was cherished in Byzantium, might be mentioned. It was from these great leaders that, even after their death, the people implored help in time of crisis. In 813, when the Bulgars were at the gates of Constantinople, the mob surged into the Church of the Holy Apostles and threw themselves on the tomb of Constantine V, crying, "Rise! Come to the aid of the state, for it is dying." It was alleged that the great Emperor came forth mounted upon his charger, to give battle once again to the Bulgars whom he had so often vanquished in the past. When in 970 the Russians threatened Constantinople, and when in 986 the Bulgars overwhelmed the imperial army at the Trajan Gate (the Pass of Kapuln Derbend), Nicephorus Phocas was likewise implored to step forth from his tomb and take command of his victorious armies; his very name caused the Empire's enemies to tremble; he had "conquered all, save a woman, and his lion's roar alone could put his adversaries to flight." [1] And posterity, awarding to Manuel Comnenus the name of the most illustrious hero of the Byzantine epic, saluted him as "the new Akritas."

But once the Empire declined, once the flow of recruits dried up and great commanders were lacking, then the military instrument bent and broke. Henceforth there was mutiny in the camp, rebellion in the army, the pursuit of personal ambition among the officers, anarchy, and civil war. And as a result of this deterioration, the enemy prospered.

[1] From the poems of John Geometrus, *Migne Patrologia Graeca*, 106 (Paris, 1863), 920, 927.

4. FRONTIER FORCES AND DEFENCE

In addition to the mobile armies that fought the campaigns, Byzantium had another source of strength in its frontier forces.

Very early in their history, the Byzantines revived a Roman institution. They divided their frontiers into military sectors (*limites*) and grouped under the command of a few general officers (*magistri militum*) the special forces entrusted with defence. As dangers from without increased, this organization became the very basis of administration. To counter the threatening onslaught of Lombards and Berbers in the West, Persians, Arabs, and Bulgars in the East, *themes* were formed, each commanded by a *Strategus* in whom both military and civil powers were vested. Among these *themes,* those which lined the frontier (ἀκρίτικα) were of particular importance. Special troops were stationed here and in return for military service were allotted land on which they settled with their families, as farmer-soldiers. These were known as the soldiers of the frontier (*limitanei, akritai*), and their task was to man the strong points—the castles and fortresses—that covered the region. Rome had been content merely to establish a frontier guard; Byzantium threw up lines of fortifications one behind the other, in a series of barriers, and provided shelter for the local population in case of invasion. Thus all the country bristled with forts, which barred the roads, commanded all strategic points, blocked the defiles (κλεισοῦραι), and stood guard over the countryside. Sometimes, indeed, continuous walls, like that of Anastasius before Constantinople, were flung across a vast tract of territory. Fortresses were massive and scientifically built, and they withstood the shock of countless assaults. This network of *castella*, reaching from the steppes of Hodna and Tunisia to the banks of the Euphrates, from the mountains of Armenia to the Danube, was one of Justinian's mightiest achievements; by these, says Procopius, he saved the Empire. "Wishing to defend the line of the Danube," writes the historian, "Justinian bordered the river with numerous fortresses and set up guard-posts along the banks to prevent the barbarians from crossing. But when these structures were completed he reflected that should the enemy succeed in penetrating this barrier they would find themselves among defenceless inhabitants, whom they could carry off into slavery unhindered, having sacked their estates. He was not content, therefore, to ensure a general measure of safety by means of these river forts alone, but constructed great numbers of other defence-works all over the flat country, until every manor was either transformed into a fortress or was protected by a nearby fortified position." [2] This system was to be maintained through succeeding centuries. The Taurus Mountains, the Euphrates region, and Armenia were, like the Balkan Peninsula, covered with such forts. In eleventh-century Asia "there was nothing but fortresses." [3] Even today in many places, especially in Africa, the remains of these stout bastions may be found, and they provide the clearest evidence of the strength of the Empire and the scope of its military achievement.

Frontier Warfare

These fortresses were garrisoned by frontier troops who kept watch on the enemy, repulsed invasion, and defended the soil of their country in warfare that was both offensive and defensive. A curious tenth-century work on tactics gives a vivid description of the rough life and ceaseless battles of the frontier provinces, in the Taurus Mountains or on the borders of Cappadocia, under the continual threat of Arab invasion. It was skilled and difficult warfare, based on the necessity of holding an enterprising enemy in check with inferior numbers, a warfare of ambush and surprise attack, daring reconnaissance and bold action, wherein the light

[2] Procopius, *De Ædificiis*, ed. by J. Haury (Leipzig, 1913), 107.
[3] So expressed by George Cedrenus, the chronicler, *Chronographia* (Bonn, 1839), 2:590.

cavalry of the *trapezitae* excelled. The entire frontier zone was guarded by a network of small observation posts, linked to head-quarters by a system of signals. As soon as any enemy activity was reported, mounted patrols, carrying a day's rations and with their bright weapons dulled to be less conspicuous, rode forth in all directions. Behind this screen the main forces were mobil-ized. Infantry occupied the passes, the population of the plains poured into the fortresses, and the army was concentrated. In the orders issued nothing was left to chance: every detail was planned and provided for, whether it concerned the intelligence service, the victualling arrangements, troop movements, ambush and espionage, or night attack. Meanwhile bold raids were made into enemy territory to harass the rear of the assailants and pro-vide a useful diversion, while the Byzantine *Strategus* engaged the enemy, usually by an abrupt and unexpected attack and with a blend of daring and guile. This was rough fighting in which cavalry played the chief part; the defenders had to be ceaselessly on the alert to avoid being taken by surprise and to render blow for blow, raid for raid. It was fighting packed with brutal, chiv-alrous, heroic adventure, which tempered and toughened the spirits of those who took part in it.

The brave, free life of the men of the Asiatic marches is cele-brated in the poem of *Digenis Akritas,* defender of the frontier, "the pattern of brave men, the glory of the Greeks, the pacifier of Romania." Nowhere more than in Byzantine epic history is there revealed to us the knightly courage, vigour, and patriotism of these soldiers, and the proud consciousness of independence that inspired the great feudal barons who by their frontier guard ensured the safety of the realm. "When the cause is just," says the hero of the poem mentioned, "I fear not even the Emperor." Here is a characteristic touch that betrays a fatal weakness: the bad discipline of the Byzantine armies.

The Army and the Defence of the Monarchy

5. THE NAVY

In the sixth and seventh centuries and up to the beginning of the eighth, the fleet was a great element of strength in the Empire. It dominated the eastern seas, or rather—until the Arabs appeared on the scene in the middle of the seventh century—it was the only fleet in the Mediterranean. Even after the Omayyad Caliphs had built up their sea power it maintained the struggle, and by saving Constantinople in 717 it saved the Empire. Later, the navy appears to have been somewhat neglected, and Byzantium paid dearly for this in the ninth century, when the Moslem corsairs, lords of Crete, ravaged the coasts of the Archipelago for more than a hundred years. This menace brought about the overhauling of the navy in the tenth century; and until the beginning of the twelfth, Byzantium was again a great Mediterranean power and had command of the sea ($\vartheta\alpha\lambda\alpha\sigma\sigma\sigma\kappa\rho\alpha\tau\iota\alpha$) as far as the Pillars of Hercules. "Naval power," said Nicephorus Phocas in the tenth century, "is mine alone." And an eleventh-century writer declared, "the fleet is the glory of the Romans." And so it continued to be, until the day when Byzantium chose to entrust its naval operations to Pisans, Genoese, and, above all, Venetians.

To man the vessels, there were plenty of fine seamen along the Asiatic coasts, on the islands, and in Greece. The Byzantine shipbuilders built powerful warships, *dromons* with a complement of 300 men of whom 70 were soldiers, as well as lighter craft manned by 130 to 160 men, often Russian seamen. These vessels carried an excellent armament, which was made even more effective by the use of "Greek fire," invented in the seventh century by a Syrian engineer; this was used either in siphons or grenades and struck terror to the hearts of the enemy. Igor's Russians, overwhelmed before Constantinople in 941, said of it, "The Greeks have fire resembling lightning, and in hurling it against us they burned us; that is why we could not beat them."

Finally, like war on land, naval operations were conducted with tactical science, as we find from a number of special treatises that have come down to us. In the tenth century the imperial war fleet consisted of 180 vessels.

Thus on land and at sea Byzantium was a great power, and it maintained its strength as a military state until the end of the twelfth century.

III. Byzantine Diplomacy

Byzantium and the Barbarian World

Encircling the Empire were the peoples whom Byzantium, in its arrogance, grouped under the general heading of "barbarians," and who, indeed, for a long time were little more. They included. in the sixth and seventh centuries, the Germanic races —Vandals, Visigoths, Ostrogoths, Lombards, and Franks—who had carved kingdoms for themselves from the remnants of the Roman Empire, and those of Slavonic or Uralo-Altaic origin, Croats, Serbs, Bulgars, Huns, and Avars, who ebbed and flowed along the borders of the Empire. Later, in the tenth century, there were also the Khazars, Pechenegs, Hungarians, Russians, and others. Even in early times, some of these nations were more advanced than the rest, and among such we may mention the Persians and Arabs; while in the rest of Europe, barbarism gradually gave place to order and civilized life. Charlemagne's empire apart, in the tenth, eleventh, and twelfth centuries Germany, France, Venice, and the Norman kingdoms of Sicily were flourishing states. Nevertheless, the Byzantines persisted in regarding themselves as the only civilized nation. With the exception of the Persians and Arabs, for whom they always showed more regard, they continued to treat the rest of the world with condescension. Yet, proud though Byzantium might be as sole representative and lawful heir of Rome, loudly though it might boast of being the one state which for centuries possessed a strong and stable administration, nevertheless, these barbarians had to be lived with, reckoned with; their assaults had to be foreseen; they had to be made to serve the best interests of the Empire, to submit to Byzantine influence, and to accept the suzerainty of the *Basileus* as vassals and as subjects. This was the task of Byzantine diplomacy, which in its skill and ingenuity evolved a real "science of governing barbarians."

The study of the barbarian world was the constant care of the imperial court. Among the departments of the chancellery there was one called the Bureau of Barbarians in which, as in the offices of the *Logothete* of the *Dromus,* or minister for foreign affairs, information and memoranda relating to all foreign nations were carefully collated. The weakness and strength of each were known, as well as the best way of handling it, using it, or neutralizing it; notes were kept of its most influential families, of what presents pleased them best, which of their sentiments or interests might be most usefully cultivated, and what political or economic relations might be established with them. This taste for ingenious and subtle combinations was a very Byzantine characteristic, and Constantinople always preferred clever diplomacy to the cruder methods of violence. Adroitness, finesse, foresight, and good counsel—the εὔβουλα for which Byzantine writers like to praise their sovereigns—were held in high esteem by the Greeks, because through them the enemies of the Empire might be circumvented and brought under the dominion of the *Basileus* without bloodshed. And certainly the combination of political and religious action which throughout the Middle Ages was the ruling principle in the imperial chancellery produced excellent results. It was owing to the skill of its diplomats and the tireless activity of its missionaries that Byzantium withstood its assailants for so many centuries. And through them, too, it extended its civilization throughout the East and left an indelible mark upon the world.

Byzantine Diplomacy

1. INSTRUMENTS OF BYZANTINE DIPLOMACY

Political Action

The crudest, simplest, and most direct way of influencing foreign nations was by means of money. Money was always regarded by Byzantine diplomats as being an irresistible argument, and was used indiscriminately and sometimes unwisely, in and out of season. Justinian kept all the neighbouring barbarian kings in imperial pay; he granted annual subsidies and gave magnificent presents to the Hun princes of the Crimea, Arab emirs of the Syrian marches, Berber chieftains of North Africa, the rulers of far Abyssinia, of the Lombards, Gepids, Heruls and Avars, Iberians [modern Georgians] and Lazes. Six centuries later, Alexius Comnenus prided himself, not without reason, on having won the good will of the barons of the First Crusade by the same means; he fancied he had only to offer the right price to enlist them as his mercenaries. To serve the ends of his imperialist policy, Manuel Comnenus, too, poured rivers of gold into twelfth-century Italy, and the vast wealth displayed by the *Basileus* seems to have dazzled the entire West. It was a tenet of imperial diplomacy that every man had his price, were he a barbarian prince of the Utigur Huns, a Godfrey of Bouillon, or a Bohemond of Taranto. At times, however, the appeal to self-interest was made more discreetly, if no less effectively. To obtain the good will of the allied Venetians, Pisans, and Genoese, Byzantium tempted them with favourable trade agreements, as well as economic privileges for their nationals within the Empire. This squandering of resources and neglect of vital interests was more than once a matter of concern to observant and thoughtful men, from Procopius, who in the sixth century reproached Justinian for his prodigality to the barbarians, to Nicetas in the twelfth century, who hated to see Manuel Comnenus lavishing upon the Latins the money so painfully wrung from his subjects.

With the appeal to self-interest went the appeal to vanity. One of the most usual methods of securing the good will of foreign princes and other persons of importance was to confer upon them the orders and titles of the Byzantine court hierarchy. These barbarians were not a little proud to flaunt the title of *Magister, Patrician, Hypatus* or *Protospatharius,* for it seemed to make them half Romans, "with civilized manners and Latin gravity," as was the boast of a Berber chief of the sixth century. Even the Doge of Venice accepted eagerly and bore with pride the titles of *Patrician* or *Proedrus.* Many foreign princes were glad to receive at the Emperor's hands—as at an investiture—the tokens of their sovereignty: the golden crown, the silken robes embroidered with gold upon which appeared the likeness of the *Basileus,* like a badge of allegiance, and the portrait of the Emperor presented to them by each sovereign on his accession. To perpetuate Byzantine influence among these vassals, they were often given Greek women in marriage: members of the senatorial aristocracy and sometimes even kinswomen of the imperial house. It gratified the Byzantines to bind them thus indissolubly to the Empire, "like faithful slaves of imperial majesty."

By this carefully graded distribution of money and favours Byzantium was pursuing a further aim: to divide its opponents, to neutralize them by playing one off against another and to foment jealousies, grudges, and clashes between them. Nothing was easier than to sting the pride of simple barbarians and rouse them to fury. Justinian wrote to a Hun prince: "I directed my presents to the most powerful of your chieftains, intending them for you. Another has seized them, declaring himself the foremost among you all. Show him that you excel the rest; take back what has been filched from you, and be revenged. If you do not, it will be clear that he is the true leader; we shall then bestow our favour upon him and you will lose those benefits formerly received by you at our hands."

This was enough to stir up hatred and unleash savage wars.

Byzantine Diplomacy

Later, in an age when such crude methods had smaller chance of success, the same dread continued to haunt the emperors: that a coalition of the Western nations might sweep away the Empire, "like a torrent which swells into a flood and devastates the fields of the husbandman." Their sole policy was therefore to drive a wedge between the great Western states, by taking the part of Germany against France and the kingdom of Sicily, for instance, by supporting the Italian cities and the Papacy against Frederick Barbarossa, or Venice against the Normans, and by fostering political animosities with plentiful supplies of money.

Above all, Byzantium pursued a policy of pomp and prestige in its dealings with foreigners, designed to display the material resources and intellectual superiority of the realm. When ambassadors from abroad arrived in Constantinople, all its splendours were exhibited to impress and dazzle them. In the gilded apartments of the palace they beheld a pageantry of rich uniforms, priceless jewellery, and splendid tapestries—everything that could bear witness to wealth and power. In the imperial audience chamber a ceremonial etiquette was observed, where words and gestures were designed to emphasize the gulf that yawned between his Imperial Majesty and his humble worshippers, and where the childish vanity of the Byzantines found expression in somewhat absurd magical devices. They liked to invite foreign monarchs to Constantinople. During Justinian's reign there was a continual flow of such sovereigns, who, with wives, children, and exotically arrayed attendants, filled city and court with the buzz of every language in the world. Later came Russian princes and Turkish sultans, Armenian rulers and Latin barons from Syria, kings of France and emperors of Germany. They were assiduously courted; presents were lavished upon them all, and they were received with the fullest ceremony amid fanfares and flying standards, that they might carry away with them a dazzling memory of the power and majesty of the Empire. When in 957 Olga, Grand Princess of Kiev, came to visit Emperor Constantine VII, her hosts could not do enough to honour the first woman barbarian ruler ever to behold Byzantium. There were magnificent receptions at which she took her place beside the *Basileus;* the women's apartments rivalled the rest of the court in magnificence; there were sumptuous banquets—enlivened by singing, organ music, jesters, and ritual dances—where, however, Olga was not permitted to sit at the Emperor's table. There were gifts and the distribution of largesse, and finally the baptism, at which the Emperor craved the honour of being godfather to the converted pagan princess.

For all these guests, tours and visits were carefully arranged. They were shown fine churches, luxurious palaces, the wealth of the bazaars, the strength of the ramparts, and the excellent order maintained in the arsenal; but they were closely watched, lest their curiosity develop into indiscretion. Liutprand, Bishop of Cremona, in his famous report of his embassy to Constantinople in the tenth century, bitterly complained of the restrictions placed upon his movements and of the many minor vexations and humiliations to which he was exposed. This was just one more way of magnifying Byzantium in the eyes of foreigners: to snub them without ceremony when they grew too familiar. They were told, for instance, that the secret of Greek fire had been revealed to Emperor Constantine by an angel; that it was an angel who had brought him the jewels of his crown and that therefore they could never pass into barbarian hands; that the same Emperor had issued a decree forbidding the marriage of imperial princesses to barbarian kings. The reply to "such an absurd question" was that it would be "unseemly and insulting to the majesty of the Roman Empire" to unite women born in the imperial purple with "infidel and obscure men." The Byzantine court measured its courtesies by the importance of its guests, just as the imperial chancellery measured its phrases of welcome and the form of its letters. But all, ambassadors and sovereigns, returned from their visits to Constantinople dazzled and enchanted, convinced of the might of the Empire and the superhuman nature of its head, and happy to serve the *Basileus* who welcomed his loyal liegemen so warmly and rewarded them so liberally.

Religious Action

This was not all. To these methods, borrowed from old Rome, Byzantium added others no less effective which originated with its character of Christian State. A sixth-century poet writes:

Byzantine Diplomacy

Res romana Dei est: terrenis non eget armis.

This was a principle of imperial policy. It has already been noted that between the sixth and eleventh centuries, Christian propaganda—the work of conversion—marched hand in hand with conquest, reinforcing the soldier as the missionary reinforced the diplomat. In addition to the merchant, who on his long journeys spied out the land for the imperial chancellery and supplied it with necessary information, the priest performed an even more useful service in clearing a way for the politician, going before him into barbarian country, preaching, conquering souls for Christ, and seeking above all to win over the women, to whom the mysticism of the new faith chiefly appealed. It was the beauty of the Orthodox liturgy rather than the dogma that impressed these simple minds, as can be seen by what happened to the envoys of Prince Vladimir of Russia, on their arrival at Constantinople. There, beneath the golden cupolas of St. Sophia, bemused by the splendour of the ceremony, they seemed to behold amid the wreaths of incense and the radiance of candles young men, wonderfully arrayed, floating in the air above the heads of the priests and singing in triumph, "Holy, Holy, Holy is the Eternal." And on asking the meaning of this marvellous apparition they were answered, "If you were not ignorant of the Christian mysteries, you would know that the angels themselves descend from heaven to celebrate the Office with our priests." How resist a religion where such wonders were to be seen, "passing human understanding"? Vladimir's boyars could not, nor their master and his people. Many others before the Russians had embraced Orthodoxy, such as the Goths of the Crimea and the Abasgians of the Caucasus, Arabs from the land of Yemen and Ethiopians from the kingdom of Axum in the sixth century; and later Croats, Serbs, Moravians, Bulgars, and many others, who had, of course, received from Byzantium not only its faith, but also a whole world of ideas, sentiments, and customs, a whole new civilization which infused and kept alive in them the all-powerful influence of Byzantium.

2. THE RESULTS OF BYZANTINE DIPLOMACY

Already one may glimpse some of the results obtained by this diplomacy and understand how it contributed to the strength of the Empire.

First, it supplied the realm with soldiers. All the barbarian princes who received subsidies from the Emperor undertook to put a certain number of men at his disposal. Then along the whole length of the frontier, there were the vassals and allies, who formed a breastwork, a first line of defence against invasion. Valuable allies were secured by means of formal treaties, such as the one with Venice in the tenth century, against the Arabs and later the Normans; the treaty made with the Croats and Serbs against the Bulgars; the treaty with the Pechenegs, Khazars, and Russians, whose turbulent movements were watched from the observation-post of Cherson; while in Asia Minor there was the treaty concluded with the Armenians against the Arabs. At every period of its long history Byzantium contracted such alliances, and even in the twelfth century Constantinople was perhaps still the most active centre of European diplomacy.

And this was not all. Byzantium exerted political influence on her allies. The *Basileus* often reserved the right to dispose of their crowns, and kept at his court a whole staff of claimants to all the thrones in the world. The sons of many of these princes were brought up in Constantinople in the luxurious surroundings of the palace; the victims of civil war were also welcome there: unsuccessful pretenders and vanquished competitors. Thus the Emperor was able to hold his feudatories to their duty, and had instruments ready to hand with which to crush an enemy at the first sign of rebellion. In this the policy of Justinian coincides with that of the Macedonian Emperors and the Comneni; it was by such methods as these that Byzantium handled the barbarian vassal kings in Africa, Italy, and Spain in the sixth century, the Bulgars, Serbs, and Croats between the ninth and the eleventh centuries, and in the twelfth century the Serbs and Hungarians.

These vassals were by no means all equally loyal. Many of them rebelled more than once against Byzantium, or seceded from it. But two important things resulted from the diplomatic relations established between them and the Empire.

The first was that countless foreigners—soldiers, merchants, travellers, and pilgrims—came to Constantinople, and often remained for a considerable time. On such simple souls, the Byzantine capital made a staggering impression. They came as barbarians to this great melting-pot; in it they blended. They returned to their distant homes as semi-Greeks, to regale their countrymen with the marvels of the great city, of which they ever after preserved nostalgic memories. Tsarigrad, as the Russians called it— it was Miklagård to the Scandinavians—haunted the imagination of the barbarian world. By the fame of its wealth and splendour and by the admiration it aroused, it drew to itself the world's adventurers and made new men of them.

The other result was that by its diplomatic and religious missions, the Empire exerted a civilizing influence on all barbarian states. We shall see later to what extent Byzantium was the preceptor of the East, but it must be noted here that it created a universal pattern of thought and feeling, and was to the Slavic and Eastern world what Rome was to the world of the Germanic peoples and the West. This assimilation of barbarian peoples, or at least their close association with the Empire and the building of them into nations, was not the least of the achievements of Byzantine diplomacy.

Byzantium: Greatness and Decline

It cannot be denied that this policy had its dangers. The display of so much wealth and the granting of such lavish subsidies made the barbarians insatiable in their greed. Having once received, they returned for more, and with ever-increasing demands. Procopius wrote in the sixth century: "Once they had tasted the wealth of Byzantium it was impossible to get rid of them and make them forget the way thither." Justinian's historians severely criticized a diplomacy which consisted of loading barbarians with money, welcoming them too effusively, and bolstering their self-confidence, while exhausting the treasures of the Empire. As time went on their covetousness took different forms, less crude, perhaps, but no less dangerous. And when at last it became known that the nation's military strength was no longer adequate to defend its wealth, the fate of the Empire hung in the balance.

Yet another consequence was that the Byzantines too openly despised these foreigners, who in their eyes were all barbarians; they saw in them either mercenaries ready to sell themselves or vassals avid for bribes; and in treating them as such they wounded their pride. We know the story of the French baron in the First Crusade who, when in solemn audience with the enthroned Emperor, cried insolently, "There's a boor, to remain seated when so many great captains are standing!" This surly lord was no doubt mannerless and unused to court life; others had better grounds for resentment. The Byzantine *Basileus* reserved the title of Emperor for himself; the highest he would accord to others was that of King. Consequently Byzantium long declined to address Charlemagne as Emperor, and later made the same refusal to Otto the Great and Frederick Barbarossa. Nor would the court receive Conrad III of Germany or Louis VII of France save with outdated and haughty ceremony. Naturally such arrogance caused keen displeasure, and did nothing to win good will for Byzantium.

Rashly stimulated greed and wounded susceptibilities were two of the evils resulting from the manner in which the Byzantines conducted their foreign affairs, and they had therefore some bearing on the ultimate fall of the Empire. But for a long time this highly developed diplomacy was to remain a powerful instrument of the Crown.

IV. Administration

1. THE EVOLUTION OF BYZANTINE ADMINISTRATION

The Byzantine Empire long retained the Roman administrative system. Even in Justinian's day, despite the already predominantly Eastern character of the realm, Latin remained the official language—the language of government and of law—and, as the Emperor said, "the national tongue." Only condescendingly, and because more people understood it, did he occasionally consent to use "the vulgar tongue, which is Greek." Similarly, the heads of the various government departments bore the same titles as those of the Roman period: Praetorian Prefect, *Magister Militum, Quaestor Sacri Palatii, Comes Sacrarum, Comes Rerum Privatarum, Magister Officiorum,* and Prefect of the City. Above all, notwithstanding the great reforms brought in by Justinian to simplify the administrative machine and strengthen authority, the Byzantine Empire retained both the territorial divisions—a legacy of the Roman Empire—and the traditional separation of civil and military powers. In Africa and Italy, both of which Justinian reconquered, the Emperor had but one aim: to restore to those peoples the exact counterpart of Roman administration—"of the most prosperous Roman Empire"—such as they had formerly known.

Administration

As Byzantium became more Oriental in character, government and administration took on a new form. In the kingdoms that arose in the West as a result of barbarian invasion, the change from Roman institutions was abrupt. The Byzantine Empire was the only state in the world where the transition from the ancient to the mediaeval way of life was achieved smoothly, without upheavals, by slow and steady evolution; and this is not the least interesting feature of its history. The change was nonetheless profound. From the seventh century onwards, Greek became the official language: the language of imperial protocol and public acts. Ministers and high officials now bore Greek designations, such as *Logothete, Eparch, Strategus,* and *Drungarius.* Above all, a new administrative regime came into being, born of political necessity and the need to place national defence on a firmer footing. The civil provinces or eparchies, into which Rome had divided the realm, were replaced by military zones or *themes,* so named from a word which originally meant an army corps, and now by extension denoted also the area occupied by such a corps. Up to the last days of the Byzantine Empire this system of *themes,* inaugurated in the seventh century, extended and regularized in the eighth, remained the basis of the administrative system, its principle being the union of military, civil, and financial control under a single authority.

In spite of these fundamental changes, both the nature of Byzantine administration and its task remained unaltered. Let us now try to define and explain these permanent characteristics, to which the strength and duration of the Empire were so largely due.

Byzantium: Greatness and Decline

2. CENTRAL GOVERNMENT

Rarely has any administration been more strongly centralized or more ably run than that of Byzantium. In the capital, grouped about the head of the state, ministers and heads of departments directed the government and transmitted the Emperor's decrees throughout the Empire. The *Logothete* of the *Dromus* (this word, which basically means "running," here signifies transport and communications) was a most important figure, as he combined the offices of High Chancellor of the Empire, Minister of Police and the Interior, and Secretary of State for Foreign Affairs. He was later known simply as the Grand *Logothete*. There was the *Logothete* of the Treasury, or Finance Minister; the *Logothete* of the Military Chest, or Army Paymaster, and the *Logothete* of Flocks and Herds, who administered the Emperor's studs and crown estates. There was the *Sacellarius,* a kind of Comptroller-General; the *Quaestor,* or Minister of Justice; the Grand *Domestic*, Commander-in-Chief of the Army; and the Great *Drungarius*, Minister of the Navy. In addition to these there was the *Eparch*, the Prefect of Constantinople, a great personage whose task was to maintain order in the capital.

The majority of these dignitaries had seats in the Senate: a sort of Council of State which assisted the Emperor. It was small and had nothing in common with the Senate of ancient Rome, though it retained certain traditional constitutional privileges—perhaps more theoretical than real—and might, under a weak sovereign or one still a minor, invoke its former rights. The συγκλητος βουλή, as it was called, could intervene in political and religious matters; but the officials of which it was composed were meek servants and rarely ventured to oppose their master's will.

On a lower level were countless offices, known in the sixth century as *scrinia,* and later as *logothesia* or *secreta.* Just as Rome in the old days had ruled the world by the strength of its bureaucracy, so Byzantium owed its firm and integrated government to this crowd of obscure σεκρετικοί who formed the staff of the imperial chancellery and the ministries. Theirs was the task of examining matters of detail, formulating decrees and making them universally known. At certain periods this bureaucracy was powerful enough to direct the general policy of the Empire.

Administration

Provincial Government

Each province was ruled by a governor or *Strategus,* nominated by the Emperor and in direct communication with him. This high officer had authority over both local troops and local government; he also administered justice and controlled finance. Within his own district he was vice-emperor, and more than one *Strategus* was tempted—at least in earlier times, when *themes* were fewer and larger—to abuse his power. For this reason the central government placed beside him, though in a subordinate capacity, a representative of the civil interest: the *Protonotary* and judge of the *theme.* He, too, had the right to correspond directly with the Emperor, and was concerned chiefly with justice and finance. Nevertheless it was the military leader who was in command, and it is a fact worth noting that at every level of the administration, soldiers took precedence over civilians and exercised more real power. It was by virtue of this principle that Byzantium, for all its Roman descent, developed into a mediaeval state.

Administrative Centralization

The staff, from top to bottom of the administrative ladder, was directly dependent on the Emperor. It was he who nominated, promoted, and dismissed the highest officials in government employ, and conferred upon them the emblems of office. Their titles (*Magister, Proconsul, Patrician, Protospatharius, Spatherocandidatus, Spatharius,* etc.) formed the various grades of a kind of administrative aristocracy by which the hierarchy of Byzantine society was rigidly fixed. In Byzantium every official bore two titles, one honorary, marking his rank in the administrative nobility, the other indicating the actual office with which he had been invested; and between office and rank, there was a fixed relationship. (In this, as in many other respects, Imperial Russia based its administrative and social order on that of Byzantium.)

It was usually from among the great families, those known as the συγκλητικοί, that the Empire recruited its highest functionaries. Moreover, in order to ensure the supply of competent, experienced men for the public service, the imperial government provided special institutions where they might be trained. Such were the law schools founded by Justinian in Constantinople, Rome, and Beirut, and the law school reorganized in the capital in the middle of the eleventh century. These produced a corps of well-trained, disciplined, and devoted civil servants whose zeal was fanned throughout their careers by the hope of greater rewards and of promotion to a higher rung of the administrative and social ladder. Such promotions were entirely at the discretion of the Emperor; and though too often this made for intrigue and favouritism (there are instances of scandalously rapid advancement), more often it was an encouragement to efficient service. Moreover the central power kept a close watch on the activities of executive officers. The Emperor left them in no doubt of the dire consequences of failure or neglect of duty; he also encouraged his subjects to lay complaints against those in authority before the imperial tribunal; he urged bishops to watch the conduct of officials and denounce their faults; and he despatched special investigators to tour the provinces, examine accounts, invite petitions, and impose sanctions. No other administration, it seems, was more completely under the control of one master.

3. THE TASK OF BYZANTINE ADMINISTRATION

Finance

Financial problems were at all times a matter of grave concern to the Greek Empire. Expenditure was heavy. Upkeep of the army, incessant warfare, ruinous diplomatic practices, the extravagance of the court, and the magnificent buildings were all very costly, and Byzantium often found extreme difficulty in balancing its budget. Taxes, long modelled on the old Roman plan, were numerous and burdensome, and included head tax (*capitatio*), land tax, tax on buildings, tribute in kind, and dues and services of every sort, to say nothing of indirect taxation. Such levies were all the more exasperating because of the many exemptions allowed, such as those in the case of Church property and military fiefs, and because taxpayers, who were classified in cadastral and fiscal groups, were held collectively responsible. Thus the owners of cultivated, fertile land had to pay for barren and forsaken properties (ἐπιβολή), and those who were solvent had to pay the dues of defaulters (*allelengyon*). There were many added vexations, as when local officials, having purchased their appointment—as was customary—recouped themselves at the public's expense, and when the rich oppressed the poor. Moreover the authorities, in their effort to replenish the depleted treasury, had constantly to invent new forms of taxation. "For without money," said one emperor, "the State cannot be saved." One of the outstanding characteristics of the Byzantine Empire was its everlasting need of money and the discrepancy between its financial resources and its vast political schemes.

Tax-gathering was therefore the first duty of the administration. "To increase the revenues and devote every care to defending the interests of the Treasury," was the primary rule of conduct impressed by Justinian upon his officers. However, it was not the intention of any emperor that this principle should be carried to a point where it entailed hardship to his subjects. Every ruler was bent on protecting his people from needless annoyance, on reconciling public and private interest, and on sparing his subjects "all expense and distress, save for rents due to the State, and just and lawful taxes." And so we find a phrase often recurring in government instructions: agents must be scrupulously honest; they must have "pure hands." Justinian, like Basil I, urges them to do as they have sworn to do: to govern "without deceit or fraud," to protect the Emperor's subjects both from annoyance by subordinate employees and from extortion or violence of soldiers or the wealthy, and to maintain good order, security, and peace in the provinces. To ensure this, and to deprive the administration of any excuse for exploiting the taxpayer, provincial agents received high salaries which were often raised. Great care was also taken in choosing these men, and they were kept under the Emperor's constant supervision, to such effect that, as Constantine VII writes in his *Life of Basil I*, "the poor, formerly oppressed, could now revive, each tilling his soil and gathering the

Six gold coins (*solidi*) of Justinian I. Actual size.

fruit of his vine, without anyone seeking to rob him of the olive tree and the fig tree bequeathed to him by his forefathers; each might take his rest in the accustomed shade of the trees that were his heritage."

It is hardly necessary to say that this ideal was rarely attained. When money was needed, the government readily winked at the means used to obtain it, and, provided the sums were forthcoming, it overlooked extortion and the corruption of its officials and the harsh methods by which even the most honest of them col-

Administration

lected the taxes. This is as true of the sixth century as of the tenth or twelfth, and historians have much to say of the hardships inflicted on the people by these men, until, in the words of a sixth-century writer, "the Emperor seemed more to be dreaded than the barbarians." But if tax-gathering was always a major concern to the authorities, it must in fairness be admitted that their efforts were often successful—whatever may be thought of the means employed. At the beginning of the eleventh century the total revenues of the Empire amounted to about 119,136,000 gold dollars. At the death of Basil II there was a surplus of more than 49 million. Despite the burden of expenditure, the Empire's resources were real enough, and its efficient administrative system, for all its faults, gave unquestionably good results.

National Unity

Another, far more important, task was assigned to Byzantine administrators.

The Empire was without unity either of race or language. It was, as Rambaud has justly remarked, "a quite artificial creation governing twenty different nationalities and uniting them by the formula: 'one master, one faith.'" Syria and Egypt were always hostile to Hellenism, and were continually shaken by separatist movements. When not only they, but also almost all the Latin West were lost to the Empire, the Greek-speaking peoples of this now more compact realm were in the majority. In Asia Minor, in Constantinople itself, in Thrace, and all round the Archipelago, there existed a sturdy, homogeneous core of people of Hellenic race and culture. With these were mingled many other ethnic elements which had come in on the tide of invasion, immigration, or resettlement. In the European parts of the Empire there were Mardaites of Syrian origin, whom an emperor of the seventh century had settled along the shores of the Ionian Sea and in the Peloponnesus. There were Turks encamped on the River Vardar, Syrians and Armenians in Thrace and at Constantinople, Wallachians in the Balkans and the Pindus Mountains. And everywhere there were Slavs, whose settlements—*Sclavinias*, as they were called—were to be found in Macedonia, on the Strymon, and at the gates of Thessalonica, in Thessaly, in Greece, and right out to the extremity of the Peloponnesus. The Asiatic part of the

Empire, though less subject to invasion, contained other non-Hellenic elements, such as Lebanese Mardaites on the southern coast of Anatolia, Arab prisoners of war encamped in the region of the Euphrates, Slavs in Bithynia, and above all Armenians, who were very numerous and whose influence at times predominated in the Empire. It was no easy matter to govern and fuse together these varied races, who were long mutinously inclined towards imperial authority and at times ready to rise against it. The imperial administration had the tremendous task of absorbing these elements gradually, so bringing some sort of unity and cohesion to a state that had no nationality to hold it together. It was the solid framework supporting and strengthening the Empire. The work it did presents one of the most original aspects of Byzantine history and one of the best proofs of the power of expansion of its civilization.

By what means was this task accomplished? Partly by impressing upon all these alien elements a common stamp, that of Hellenism, and partly by uniting them in the common profession of the Orthodox faith.

Union Through Hellenism

It was a political principle in Byzantium never to ill-treat the conquered. "Any nation having customs and laws which differ from the rest," says a tenth-century emperor, "must be left in possession of its own." Certainly this rule of tolerance was broken at times; a portion of a conquered people might be forcibly transferred from one region to another, for instance, to make room for Greek-speaking colonies designed to ensure the predominance of Hellenic influence in that part of the world. In general, however, the nations annexed by conquest, or not yet absorbed into the Empire, were treated well. Their local customs were respected, room was made for them in provincial administration, and they were shown special consideration in the matter of tax reductions and so on, to reconcile them to their ruler. Thus, little by little, they were won over to the customs and culture of the Hellenized Empire.

"Greek, being the administrative, ecclesiastical, and literary language," says Rambaud, "seemed what it was not: a national language." Gradually all the foreign minorities learned to speak it; and such was the vitality of the Byzantine civilization that it assimilated and modified these apparently incompatible and rebellious groups without very much difficulty. "Byzantium," it has been said, "received these unlettered or savage aliens, and returned them to the great civilization of the Empire as scholars, scientists, theologians, able administrators, and conscientious officials." The élite of the subject races—Bulgars, Arabs, and Armenians—were admitted into the aristocracy by marriage with women of the Greek nobility, as were the élite among those others who came to seek their fortune in the imperial service: Italians, Frenchmen, Spaniards, and Scandinavians. They were promised and given large military commands and high administrative posts. Byzantium had generals of Armenian, Persian, or Slavic origin; Italian, Bulgarian, or Armenian government officials; while among its ministers were converted Turks and Arabs. In this cosmopolitan Empire, Greek was the common language, and foreigners in adopting it adopted also common customs and ways of life and thought, and came to bear something of the same stamp.

Union Through Orthodoxy

Profession of a common faith helped to draw together the clashing elements of which the Empire was composed. Religious propaganda was indeed no less active within the realm than it was outside, and its importance was even greater. "While beyond the frontiers it was essential to supremacy, within them it was essential to unity and almost to existence itself." At times, certainly, this propaganda took the brutal form of persecution, as in the ninth century against the Paulicians, in the eleventh against the Armenians, and against the Bogomils in the twelfth; indeed, thousands of heretics perished by steel and by fire. On the whole, however, the Byzantines displayed a wise tolerance in the winning of souls. Their missionaries evangelized and converted the Slavs of Macedonia and the Peloponnesus, the Turks of the Vardar, the pagan Mainotes, and the Arabs of Crete and the upper Euphrates. From the depths of Anatolia to the tip of Italy, numerous dioceses of the Greek rite were set up, whose bishops, under the authority of the Patriarch of Constantinople, were the finest and most faithful workers in the dissemination of Orthodoxy. The importance of the bond of religion in the Eastern world, even today, is common knowledge; the religious concept is still often confused with that of nationality. Here is nothing more than the lingering heritage of the Byzantine tradition, in which Orthodoxy took the place of national unity.

4. THE ASSIMILATION OF CONQUERED COUNTRIES

A few concrete examples may help to demonstrate the powers of expansion and absorption possessed by the Empire, and throw into relief the versatility as well as the ingenious variety of resources which imperial administrators brought to their task.

Bulgaria

When in 1018 Basil II brought about the submission of Bulgaria, his first care was to reorganize the wide territories which the protection of God, as the Emperor phrased it in an official decree, had once more reunited with the Roman Empire. The Byzantines approached their task in a remarkable spirit of gentleness and tolerance. By adroit distribution of titles, favours, and dignities, the government first wooed the Bulgarian aristocracy. The surviving members of the Bulgarian royal family took their place among the Byzantine nobility; the widow of the last Czar received one of the highest titles in the court hierarchy, while her sons, loaded with honours, followed distinguished careers as imperial administrators. Attempts were made by intermarriage to draw the two peoples closer together. A daughter of Czar Samuel married a Comnenus who later became Emperor. Another great Bulgarian lady became the wife of the first Greek governor of her conquered country, Duke Constantine Diogenes, and was to be the mother of another Emperor. At the same time the imperial government cleverly enlisted the support of the Church. The independent patriarchate of Bulgaria had, of course, to be abolished, but an autonomous body was set up in its place enabling the Bulgarian Church to remain independent of Constantinople; at the head of this Church was placed a Bulgar, who was none other than the former Patriarch, invested with a new title. Not only was he allowed to retain the jurisdiction that had been his during the Czar's reign, but all the episcopal sees, such as they had been at the height of the nation's power, were once more placed under his authority. Indeed, certain dioceses that had been usurped by Greek metropolitans were restored to him. The Bulgarian clergy retained all its privileges and immunities. The Byzantines were also careful never to encroach on any ancient right or interfere with time-honoured custom, and they allowed Bulgaria a large measure of self-government. Under the imperial High Commissioner—the *Pronoetes* or Duke charged with the administration of the province—native officials remained in office, and local customs were left undisturbed. The Bulgars were used to paying taxes in kind, in the proportion of one measure of wheat, one measure of millet, and one jar of wine for every owner of a team of oxen; and the wise Byzantines accepted this primitive form of tribute, so anxious were they to avoid offending the conquered race. This had been Basil II's purpose in commanding "that the old order of things should be everywhere preserved." And perhaps if his successors had been as wise—if they had not sought to set Greeks at the head of the Bulgarian Church or to substitute money payment for the old tribute in kind—Bulgaria would have submitted more willingly to the rule of her conquerors.

The Euphrates Region

There are even more characteristic examples of Byzantine administrative methods.

In eastern Cappadocia in Asia Minor, on the frontiers of the Arab world, there was a formerly thriving region which had been devastated and depopulated by war. At the beginning of the tenth century an Armenian adventurer named Mleh, or Melias, who had entered the imperial service, succeeded in reconquering this territory. He reorganized its defences by putting its old fortresses in order—those of Lykandos, Tzamandos, and Symposion—and in recognition of his services, he was appointed governor of this new province, with the titles of *Patrician* and *Strategus*. But the administrators' task did not end with mere occupation. In order to bind the country more firmly to the Empire, a great colonization scheme was undertaken. Melias summoned large numbers of his fellow-Armenians to people the region, which soon regained its former prosperity. The soil was fertile and well suited to the raising of livestock, and towns rose from their ruins and flourished again. Linked with this economic resurrection was a remarkable religious campaign, during which a number of new dioceses were established under the jurisdiction of the Metropolitan of Caesarea, to give the country the stamp of Orthodoxy.

Religious action and colonization worked together everywhere to incorporate annexed countries more completely with the Empire. At the beginning of the tenth century the imperial government created the *theme* of Mesopotamia on the upper Euphrates, its nucleus being lands ceded to the Empire by an Armenian prince; and at once the Church set up its authority there, to ensure the country's spiritual allegiance. Kamachos, one of the larger towns of the province, was chosen to be the metropolis, with jurisdiction over five bishoprics. Again, when the Empire annexed Melitene, the government established numerous colonies of Armenians, Syrians, and Iberians there, and hastened to found a series of Orthodox sees under the authority of the Metropolitan of Melitene. Even in places where Byzantine rule was only temporary, we find the same eagerness to use the power of the Church in the imperial interest. A metropolitan was installed at Samosata simultaneously with the government, while another took office in the Armenian country of Taron when its ruler ceded it to Byzantium. And when, at the beginning of the eleventh century, the whole of Armenia came under the direct authority of the Empire, the government's first care was to supply it with Orthodox bishops, who by the middle of the eleventh century numbered twenty-one, all suffragans of the Metropolitan of Keltzene (Erzinjan).

In the great work of Byzantine colonization, the Armenians seem to have played an important part. It was they who resettled

Administration

the areas won back from the Arabs, and from the end of the tenth century their activities extended into Cilicia, where the land they developed was later to become the kingdom of Little Armenia. It is for this reason that the exploits of Armenian adventurers in the tenth century, on the borders of the Arab world, are of greater historical importance than might at first be supposed.

Southern Italy

Yet further examples may be given of the powerful and effective way in which the Orthodox Church worked for the Empire. When one looks through the list of suffragan bishops appointed under the Metropolitans of Thessalonica, Larissa, Dyrrachium, Naupactus, and Philippopolis, in the tenth century, one is struck by the number of barbarian names that occur there. They bear witness to the advance of Orthodoxy among the converted Slavic peoples, and to the steady absorption of these into the Byzantine realm. An even more interesting indication of the Empire's way of extending its sphere of influence and authority is the case of southern Italy, which in the tenth and eleventh centuries was transformed into another Magna Graecia.

When at the end of the ninth century the Byzantines regained a foothold in Italy, the great aim of the imperial administration was to bind these Latin countries as firmly as possible to the Empire. To achieve this, it cleverly adapted itself to local life. The native aristocracy were allotted a part to play in provincial government, and to win them over more completely, resounding Byzantine titles were lavished upon them. By its tact and its respect for national customs, the administration won the good will of the peoples of Calabria and Apulia to a degree that aroused in them a steadfast and enduring loyalty to Byzantium and a readiness to adopt the Hellenic way of life. This was achieved partly by establishing colonies of people from the East, but chiefly by an astute religious policy, through which the Orthodox Church, with its own liturgy and ceremonial, came insensibly to prevail. Eight bishoprics were created in Calabria under the new metropolis of Santa Severina. In the province of Otranto there were five new bishoprics, the metropolis being in Otranto itself. A Greek prelate was installed in each, and all were subject to the Patriarch of Constantinople. The Latin clergy were drawn into the Byzantine ecclesiastical hierarchy, so far as this was possible, by the offer of a more independent charge and the title of Archbishop, as was done at Bari, Taranto, and Trani, in the hope of winning them over from Rome and turning them into loyal subjects of the Empire.

But the most active agents of Hellenism were the monks. Numbers of monastic houses were founded all over southern Italy, whose Greek members were tireless in proselytising and laboured as far afield as the Campagna and up to the gates of Rome. Local inhabitants clustered about convent, chapel, and hermitage, and through this association they came to learn the Greek language. Even today, southern Italy is full of their memorials, in the shape of hundreds of chapels adorned with paintings and inscriptions, in which both laymen and religious expressed themselves in Greek. So the language, ceremonial, and civilization of Byzantium were spread through Italy, while legal transactions were conducted according to its law. Greek became the official and unofficial language, and the Hellenic imprint was so deep that even after the collapse of Byzantine rule, as late as the fourteenth century, the Greek tongue and ceremonial were retained.

We have seen how ably the Byzantine administrators governed the Empire. Throughout its history, these administrators maintained the authority of the *Basileus* by an endless variety of methods. Under the guidance of the central government, they diplomatically left to local authorities the task of winning over their subordinates to the new regime. In subject nations they set the influence of the Church to work for the State, thereby disseminating both Orthodox ritual and Greek culture. And so this able, well-organized, and strongly centralized administration, following precise directives and ever conscious of the greatness of its task, did the Empire an outstanding service: to a state lacking unity either of race or language, it brought a unity born of a common culture and a common faith.

V. Economic Power

1. THE CAUSES OF ECONOMIC PROSPERITY

Trade Routes

By its geographical situation, the Byzantine Empire was destined to enjoy great economic prosperity. First of all, it lay at the meeting-point of Asia and Europe, East and West; and here the great, bustling trade routes of the world met or ended. In the Balkan Peninsula the routes from Constantinople and Thessalonica followed the rivers of Thrace and Macedonia towards the Danube Valley and its peoples, and passed beyond it into Hungary and Central Europe. Here, too, was the great road that followed the line of the ancient Via Egnatia, crossing the Peninsula from west to east, from Dyrrachium to Constantinople, and linking the Adriatic with the Bosphorus: a magnificent highway, open to Italy and the West. On the Black Sea, the Crimean ports were gateways to the river routes of the Dnieper and the Don, which penetrated deep into Southern Russia. At the other end of the Black Sea, in Lazica, the Colchis of the ancients, and later at Trebizond, the Empire commanded the roads that led by way of the Caucasus and the shores of the Caspian to the oases of Turkestan, Bokhara, Samarkand, Central Asia, and distant China. Syria marked the end of the caravan routes linking the Far East with the valley of the Euphrates and the Byzantine world, through

Persia, as well as those from the Persian Gulf that carried the produce of Ceylon, India, Indochina, and China itself. Lastly, Alexandria and the Red Sea ports were the terminals of the sea routes that led on the one hand to Ethiopia and the great port of Adulis, where caravans from Axum unloaded wares from the African interior, and on the other along the coasts of Arabia to Ceylon, the collecting-point of the wealth of India and the Far East.

It is true that parts of these great routes were in the hands of the Persians and later of the Arabs, so that the Byzantines, who rarely travelled to these remote lands to fetch merchandise for themselves, were dependent on intermediaries who were often enemies. That is why in the sixth century Justinian made every effort to establish direct relations with the Far East, and so relieve Byzantine traders from the burdens and restrictions of Persian monopoly. For the same reason, and in the same century, the Byzantines tried to negotiate with the Turks who occupied the oases of Turkestan. These attempts failed. Yet despite all such hindrances, Byzantine commerce prospered greatly, for the Empire controlled all the coasts where the great trade routes of the world debouched; its merchants gathered up and then distributed throughout the Mediterranean countries all that those routes brought in.

Ports

Byzantium possessed fine seaports all round the eastern Mediterranean, busy marts, to which came merchants and merchandise from all over the world. Up to the seventh century, Alexandria exported the rich produce of the Nile Valley to both Constantinople and Arabia, and imported by way of the Red Sea the produce of Ethiopia, Africa, Arabia Felix, India, and China: that is to say, spices, perfumes, precious stones, and rare metals. Until the seventh century likewise, Byzantium held the Syrian ports, to which caravans brought raw silk from China and the riches of the Orient, gathering in exchange the wares of Syria, such as enamelled glass, fine fabrics, embroidery, jewellery, coral, amber, jade, and wine, which they carried to the remotest corners of the Orient. There were also the ports of the Anatolian coast: Tarsus, Attalia, Ephesus, Smyrna, and Phocaea; and on the Black Sea,

Trebizond in the south, where big fairs were held, and in the north, Cherson, the great trading post for Pechenegs, Khazars, and Russians, who brought thither their pelts and furs, their caviar and wheat, in exchange for the products of Byzantine industries: fine jewellery and rich fabrics.

On the Greek coast there were the seaports of Nauplia, Corinth, Patras, Athens, and Negropont, where merchants came to buy

Formerly Adolph Loewi, Los Angeles

Ivory plaque with animals. 12″ x 4¾″.

the silks woven in the workshops of the Peloponnesus, of Corinth, and of Thebes. There were Durazzo, Avlona, and Corfu on the Ionian Sea. Above all, there was Thessalonica, the most important commercial centre in Europe after Constantinople, the necessary port of call for all trade between the Adriatic and the Bosphorus and the natural outlet for the exports of the Balkan Slavs. Each year, at the end of October, at the feast of St. Demetrius, a famous fair was held on the Vardar plain. In the wood-and-canvas town that sprang up on the river bank for those few days, Greeks, Slavs, Italians, Spaniards, "Celts from beyond the Alps," and people from the shores of the distant ocean all came together. Booths overflowed with precious wares: fabrics from Boeotia and the Peloponnesus; produce of Egypt and Phoenicia; goods brought by sea from the West, such as fabrics and wine

· 81 ·

from Italy, embroidered carpets from Spain, and those that arrived from the Black Sea via Constantinople: salt fish, furs, wax, caviar, and even slaves.

There were also the ports of the Thracian coast: Heraclea, Selymbria, and Rodosto. Above all, there was Constantinople.

Merchandise flowed into the capital from all parts of the world, and a sixth-century poet writes engagingly of the merchantmen sailing full of hope to the sovereign city, the very winds conspiring to bring thither the wares that will enrich her citizens. In every age, Constantinople was the great warehouse and market of the world. The bazaars along the great street of the Mese were unrivalled; here were heaped rich stuffs, brilliant in colour and embroidered with gold, fine goldsmith's work, jewellery, delicately carved ivory, bronzes inlaid with silver and gold and cloisonné enamel. In arcades and squares, countless craftsmen plied their trades: goldsmiths, leatherworkers, wax-chandlers, bakers, silk and linen drapers, and sellers of pigs, sheep, horses, or fish. Dealers in perfume displayed their wares in the square before the imperial palace, so that the fragrance of them might rise like incense to the image of Christ above the gateway. The great city was filled with a lively, noisy, cosmopolitan crowd of Syrians, Arabs, and Asiatics from Pontus and Cerasus, who brought cotton and linen stuffs to market; of traders from Chaldia and Trebizond with spice and scent; Russians with fish, salt, and furs for sale; Bulgars who brought flax and honey; people from Armenia and people from the West—Amalfians, Venetians, Genoese, and Pisans, some of whom had a specially reserved quarter on the Golden Horn where they lived and had their warehouses. The Russians who voyaged down the Dnieper every year in their dug-out canoes stayed at St. Mamas, the Beshkitash of today; the Venetians had the finest site on the Golden Horn, extending from the Great Bridge area to below the Suleiman Mosque; and the Genoese, who at first lodged beside their competitors, were later given the commanding position of Galata. The Bulgars, too, had their own depôts.

Constantinople appeared to all these foreigners as a miracle of wealth, splendour, and prosperity. "Here is the glory of Greece," said a twelfth-century Frenchman. "Her riches are renowned, and she is even wealthier than she is famed to be." Benjamin of Tudela called it "a great business city. Merchants come to it from every land, and save for Baghdad there is no city in the world to compare with it." It was said, according to Robert of Clari, "that two thirds of the world's goods were in Constantinople." And everyone knows Villehardouin's famous passage, in which he declares that "one could not believe there was so rich a city in all the world," and that at the sight of "those rich towers," "those rich palaces"—the word "rich" constantly recurs in his writing—he was absolutely dazzled by this "sovereign among cities."

The Navy and Economic Expansion

A factor contributing to Byzantine prosperity was the navy, which was for centuries the undisputed sovereign of the Mediterranean. Its vessels patrolled the sea, and the active and hardworking peoples of the realm took full advantage of this. The traders of Egypt, Syria, and Armenia extended their field of operations to the furthest limits of the Mediterranean; in the sixth and seventh centuries they were to be met with in Africa, Sicily, Italy, at the northern end of the Adriatic, in Ravenna; also in Spain and Gaul, in the ports of Marseilles, Bordeaux, and Narbonne, and even in Tours, Orleans, and Paris. These "Syrians," as they were called, established quite large colonies in some of the Western cities, to which they brought fabrics, tooled leather, Syrian wine, and Egyptian papyrus. On the Mediterranean, now a Byzantine sea, the Greeks had undisputed supremacy; and such was Byzantium's economic status that by the sixth century and for long afterwards, its currency was accepted in every market in the world. As late as the Crusades the "besant," as the Byzantine gold coin was called, was the most highly valued and widely used currency in the whole of the eastern Mediterranean.

It is true that the Arab conquest of Egypt and Syria in the seventh century was very damaging to Byzantine trade. The Empire lost the inexhaustible granary of the Nile Valley and the products of Syrian industry—since the previous century Syria had had almost a monopoly of the silk trade—as well as many fine and thriving ports. Byzantine prosperity was not seriously affected by this for long, however, though in the ninth and tenth centuries the alarming increase of Moslem piracy dealt a severe blow to trade by depriving eastern waters of their former security. But again these perils were overcome. More serious was the deterioration of the Byzantine navy. From the twelfth century onwards, the Greek pennant began to disappear from the Mediterranean, and the fleets of the great commercial cities of Italy—Pisa, Venice, and Genoa—gained an increasing monopoly of shipping and trade.

In spite of this, Constantinople continued up to the last days of the Empire to be one of the great commercial centres of the world, a huge market where people of every nation came together to do business. From this prosperity the crumbling realm finally ceased to benefit, the profits having passed to others, but its perdurability testifies, nonetheless, and in a significant manner, to all that Byzantium owed at the time of its greatness to the geographical position of its capital, which for centuries made it the economic centre of the Eastern world.

2. ARTICLES OF TRADE

A little book of the tenth century, discovered half a century and more ago, gives us quite a clear idea of some of the characteristic features of Byzantine industry. In the list—which is, however, incomplete—of the industrial guilds of the capital, we find one significant fact: the importance of the luxury trades. There were, of course, the staple trades of grocer, butcher, baker, fishmonger, pork butcher, and wine merchant, whose heavy task it was to victual the capital; there were the artisans and craftsmen employed in the building trade—joiners, locksmiths, painters, and stonemasons—who were naturally in demand in a city where much building was always going on. There were the bankers, whose numbers give evidence of the importance of the money

"The Rubens Vase." Honey-colored agate. *Ca.* 400 A.D.

market. But we find another group of guilds—perhaps the wealthiest and most thriving of all—consisting of the manufacturers of
luxury articles, for which Byzantium was renowned and admired
throughout the world. There were the goldsmiths, who dealt in
gold, silver, pearls, and precious stones; the weavers and importers
of silk, some of whom traded in raw silk, while others wove it,
and yet others held the monopoly of Byzantine fabrics or special-
ized in silks and garments imported from Baghdad or Syria. There
were the linen drapers, who came from the Struma, from Pontus
and Cerasus, the spice dealers whose spices and aromatic herbs—
so dear to mediaeval society—came to the capital by way of
Trebizond and Chaldia.

These few notes give a fair summary of what Byzantium had
to export. Gorgeous silks, dyed brilliant purple, dark violet, or
peachblossom, and embroidered with the figures of animals or
with scenes sacred and profane, were the monopoly and glory of
the Byzantine workshops. Thessalonica, Thebes, Corinth, and
Patras, as well as Constantinople, were famed for the position
they held in this industry. Then there was the goldsmith's work:
the jewellery sparkling with stones and pearls; plaques of cloisonné
enamel for the adornment of reliquaries and icons as well as
clothes; bronze inlaid with silver; specimens of all the arts of fire
and metal, of which Thessalonica, after Constantinople, was the
chief producer. There were the brocades, the cloth of gold, fine
lawn, glass, carved ivory, skins dyed in purple—in short, the fine
flower of all the luxury, craftsmanship, and beauty known to
mediaeval man.

Imports from all over the Eastern world included other precious
wares—which were then re-exported to the West through the
Byzantine markets—and also raw materials for the use of Byzantine craftsmen. Arabs brought silk from China, pearls and precious
stones from India, as well as spices and aromatic herbs. From
Baghdad and Syria came silken garments, fine wine, and rich
carpets. Damascus, Aleppo, and Antioch were the chief centres
for this Arab trade. The caravan routes that crossed Central Asia,
however, ended in Armenia, whose great city of Arzan was a
lively market, while the port of Trebizond provided an outlet for
goods destined for Constantinople. The rich regions of southern
Russia supplied the Empire with wheat, salt fish, salt, honey,

Byzantine treatment of Sasanian motive. Silk, in dark blue, green, yellow, ivory. 8th-9th century.

wax, caviar, furs and pelts from the North, amber, and slaves. Cherson was the great storehouse for these, and so to an even greater extent was Constantinople, which was frequented by many Russian merchants. From the Balkans came flax, honey, salt fish and the varied farm produce of the Serbs and Bulgars; these goods were delivered for the most part to Thessalonica.

All imported wares were re-exported, together with Byzantium's own products, throughout the West. The Empire carried on a lively trade with the Italian towns of Bari, Amalfi, Pisa, Genoa, Florence, and above all Venice. Through them it received Italian and German merchandise, metals wrought and unwrought, hemp and linen fabrics, wool and woollens, embroidered rugs from Spain, wine, and salt provisions.

From quite early times, the terms upon which this foreign commerce was to be conducted were formulated in trade agreements with the countries concerned. From the tenth century onwards, Byzantium signed treaties of this sort with Arabs, Russians, and Venetians; some of these documents have come down to us and make very curious reading. They are full of restrictions, stipulations, and exemptions, and give evidence of close supervision and irritating demands. They also enable us to deduce with some accuracy the economic policy of the Empire.

3. ECONOMIC POLICY

One rather remarkable point should be noted at once. In earlier centuries, Byzantium encouraged its nationals to trade with other countries, and as late as the eighth century it promoted the development of its merchant navy by the publication of the Nautical

Code. Yet gradually the Empire seems to have changed its ideas. Instead of importing goods direct from abroad, the Byzantines preferred to leave the task of fetching them to others; and rather than export their own products, they encouraged foreigners to come and buy them in the Byzantine markets. It flattered Greek pride to make Constantinople the hub of world trade and to show all the races that met on the shores of the Bosphorus the wealth of the capital, the scope of its interests, and the colossal quantity of precious merchandise poured into it by the whole world. The imperial government saw in this an enhancement of power and prestige; moreover—at any rate until the tenth or eleventh centuries—it despised the barbarian West too much to fear its competition. What more natural than that the world should come and fetch the goods of Byzantine manufacture, of which the Empire so jealously guarded the monopoly? Instead of seeking outlets for its trade, Byzantium waited loftily for customers, believing that in this way the same profit might be made with less trouble. This was a mistake that was to have serious consequences later on, when younger, more vigorous nations sought to cut out the Byzantines and make their own profits from the wealthy oriental markets of which the Empire had appointed itself the jealous guardian and broker.

Byzantium's economic policy was regulated entirely by these principles. It has been rightly said that mediaeval Constantinople was "the paradise of monopoly, privilege, and protectionism." Industry was meticulously controlled and supervised by the State. As in every mediaeval society, the organization of the guilds, each of which had its strictly defined field, left no room for independent work or individual initiative. The State fixed the quantity of purchases, the quality of manufacture, prices, and wage-rates. It exercised constant control, searching shops, inspecting ledgers, forbidding the export of this or that product, and in every way enforcing a sternly inquisitorial and protectionist regime. The policy regarding foreign traders was no less rigorous. Visiting merchants were closely watched, and were forbidden to import certain goods—soap from Marseilles, for instance—which might compete with national industries; they were also forbidden to send certain others out of the country, especially purple silks, for these were reserved exclusively for the use of the imperial court.

There was a whole range of materials called "prohibited articles" (τὰ κεκωλύμενα), which might not on any account be sold to foreigners. The imperial customs authority ensured compliance with these rules by careful inspection, and before any fabrics were exported they had to be marked with the seal of the prefect of the city, both buyer and seller who contravened the regulations being liable to severe penalties: fine, flogging, or confiscation of goods. Fraud and smuggling were sternly punished. Other heavy dues were imposed, such as export and import duty, sales tax, and purchase tax. A troublesome, niggling bureau saw to the enforcement of all these measures. At ports and at the entry into the Straits, customs officers examined cargoes and rummaged through passengers' baggage with an unpleasing thoroughness that aroused the indignation of Bishop Liutprand of Cremona; the imperial excisemen showed scant respect for his diplomatic privilege. Maritime tribunals, presided over by the *Parathalassite*, were rigorous in imposing sanctions on offenders.

These vexations were offset by a system of privilege and exemption, according to the general policy of the day, in the case of certain favoured nations. Venice in particular obtained special treatment from quite early times, and so came to enjoy a unique status in the Byzantine East.

Despite the drawbacks of this grudging system, there is no denying that it brought in a considerable revenue. It has been calculated that in the twelfth century, in Constantinople alone, shop rents and market and customs duties together furnished the Emperor with a sum of 7,300,000 gold besants, or about twenty million gold dollars. This one figure is enough to show the great importance of commercial prosperity for the power and the financial stability of the Empire, and explains why the development of trade was one of the constant cares of the imperial government. Close attention to economic problems would have been necessary in any case, if only to keep the capital supplied with provisions and avoid arousing discontent among its turbulent population; and one of the main duties of the prefect of the city was to fix, according to the quantity of imports, the prices of bread, wine, fish, and meat.

Economic Power

4. AGRICULTURE

Another source of national wealth was agriculture. "Two things are essential to the State," wrote a tenth-century emperor, "agriculture, which feeds the soldiers, and the art of war, which protects the farmers. All other professions are inferior to these." He therefore urged provincial governors to be vigilant in protecting workers on the land from hardship or loss.

The Land System

The Byzantine Empire, like that of Rome, was founded on agriculture. The great majority of the inhabitants of the provinces worked on the land, and the estate tax was one of the most fruitful sources of national revenue. Yet it is not easy to determine the exact position of agriculture in the Empire, the system on which it was run or the condition of the country people. Here, as in all mediaeval states, we can trace a somewhat disturbing dual evolution, tending on the one hand to abolish small, independent estates, which were absorbed by usurping landlords into the larger properties, and on the other to regiment the free peasants into farming communities and merge them with those who were hereditarily bound to the soil of their masters. We also find proof of a constant effort on the part of the government to oppose this dual trend, either by protecting the small holdings of the poor against the inroads of the powerful, as was done by the sixth-, eighth-, and tenth-century emperors, or, as the Iconoclast Emperors sought to do in the eighth century, through the promulgation of their Rural Code, by improving the condition of the farm workers and developing groups of villages accorded a greater measure of freedom. But these efforts were only partially successful. The wealthy merely increased their encroachments, the tie binding serf to soil was strengthened, and the number of serfs grew steadily larger. As will be seen, the social problem was acute, and often threatened the peace and welfare of the State.

The government's fiscal policy bore hard on agriculture. A tenth-century emperor wrote, "The great number of peasants is a sign that public needs are being met, through payment of taxes and the fulfilment of military duties; both of these would fail were the large rural population to disappear." To ensure an adequate supply of recruits for the army, and to balance the budget, the government made every effort to maintain this "large rural population." But the dwindling of taxable property and the dread of losing the revenues derived from it often induced the administration to adopt regrettable measures, such as, for instance, the troublesome system of collective responsibility. Continually torn between praiseworthy reluctance to lay intolerable burdens on the small taxpayer and urgent need of money, the Byzantine government pursued a somewhat vacillating financial policy, to the great detriment of agriculture.

The Condition of Agriculture

The consequences of this state of affairs may easily be imagined. In addition, there were the miseries of war, the insecurity of the countryside, and the vexations of administration; as early as the sixth century the countryside was becoming depopulated, farming languished, the provinces were "virtually uninhabitable," and people were drifting to the great cities, to such a degree that, as one historian puts it, "the tax-gatherers could collect no money, as there was no one left to pay it." In tenth-century documents, constant mention is made of the distress of the poor and the insatiable greed of the wealthy, who, "like gangrene, seize upon village communities to achieve their ruin." In the twelfth century, peasants forsook their fields and took refuge in the towns; many, to escape the fiscal tyranny, went abroad. Indeed, the list of dues, charges, and exactions that might be heaped upon the unhappy peasant was endless, as may be seen from the exemptions granted to the monastery of Patmos. And since the great estates were often only indifferently cultivated and contained a large proportion of barren land, the revenue that might have been expected from them dwindled still further.

This being so, it is difficult to see what in fact agriculture could contribute towards the strength of the Empire. There is reason to believe, however, that in certain regions production remained at a high level. The plains of Thrace yielded an abundance of wheat, which helped to supply Constantinople, while many provinces in Asia Minor seem to have been very fertile. Certain texts mention magnificent estates in the Cilician plain and the *theme* of the Thracesians; while Cappadocia, where there were many winegrowers and cattle breeders, was apparently no less rich. But at this distance of time we don't know the details; all we can say is that when the reins of government were in the hands of an energetic ruler, strong enough to protect the weak and with administrative ability, the national economic structure based on both trade and agriculture seems on the whole to have been satisfactory. In the eleventh century the total revenue amounted, as we have seen, to 120 million gold dollars,[1] and at the death of Basil II there was a reserve fund of more than 49 million. It must, therefore, be acknowledged that despite the burden of expenditure, the Empire's resources were vast and its economic position sound, and that for a long time this constituted an unquestionable element of power. The Empire's most flourishing periods correspond fairly exactly—and here we have proof of the importance of its agriculture—with the periods when the government was at pains to protect the small estates.

[1] Other figures are no less significant. At the beginning of the sixth century Emperor Anastasius was able to build up a reserve of about 63 million gold dollars, and in the middle of the ninth century Theophilus and Theodora left a fund of more than 22 million.

VI. Constantinople

Constantinople occupied an extraordinary and indeed unique place in the vast Empire of which it was the capital. It was the political and administrative centre, the religious and economic centre, and the centre of literature and the arts. It was the queen city, on which the eyes of the world were turned, the magnetic pole for both foreigners and subjects. Constantinople was more than an ordinary town; for the Byzantine it was "the city guarded by God," or more simply, "The City." Whereas most of the great cities of the West were at that time no more than squalid, overgrown villages, Constantinople was of sovereign elegance, the hub of the civilized world, and, as has been neatly said, "the Paris of the Middle Ages." But that was not all. More than once in the course of its long history, it was in itself all that remained of the Empire. More than once it rebuilt the realm, and from the disaster which seemed to have overwhelmed it, it thrust forth new shoots in a vigorous renaissance that proved its salvation.

"At the time of Romanus Lecapenus and Symeon," writes A. Rambaud, "[Constantinople] was almost all that remained of the Empire's possessions in Europe. Under both the Heraclids and the Comneni it was almost all that remained of its Asiatic provinces. But when the opportunity arose, it hit back, now against the Bulgars, now against the Arabs and the Seljuk Turks. By its policy, Constantinople re-created the Empire both east and west of the Bosphorus. So long as this tremendous fortress stood fast, all was well; the Empire stood with it, and could again thrust back its frontiers to the Danube and the Euphrates. When at last the Ottomans seized all, Constantinople was itself the State. Byzantium survived the Byzantine Empire by nearly a century." [1]

And indeed the great capital was in many respects a microcosm of the entire realm, in everything, that is to say, that for so many centuries was its power, its prestige, its pride: military strength, worldly magnificence, wealth, piety, and literary and artistic glory. But Constantinople was not the whole of Byzantium, and side by side with the rich, cultured, elegant, turbulent, cruel, and corrupt capital, there was another simpler, cruder, more robust, more serious-minded Byzantium: the Byzantium of the provinces. Though less well known to us than the first, it was as great a source of strength. The two are inseparable, and if we are to understand this vanished world, we must never forget the dual aspect of Byzantine society: capital and province are two leaves of a diptych, and despite their profound contrast, it was the union of the two that gave the realm its power.

1. THE MILITARY CITY

From the beginning of the fifth century, when Emperor Theodosius II extended the boundaries of Constantine's city and built

---

[1] Rambaud, *op. cit.*, 540.

the splendid ramparts—extant to this day—running from the shores of the Marmara to the tip of the Golden Horn, Constantinople became a great military stronghold, an impregnable fortress. This

Cyril Mango

Land Walls of Constantinople.

great wall with its triple line of defences rising one behind the other was carefully maintained, restored, and completed through many centuries. Heraclius modified its plan to include the quarter of the Blachernae; the Comneni fortified the palace sector with splendid towers. It still remains one of the finest examples of military architecture of all time. On the sea side and along the

Constantinople

Golden Horn, few traces remain of the single wall. But on the landward side, for a distance of nearly five miles, the triple enclosure remains, battered by time indeed, but so ingenious and scientific in plan that it protected Constantinople for centuries. Seen from the top of the Fortress of the Seven Towers, the mighty line of ramparts rising and falling with the ground and vanishing in the shades of Eyoub is one of the grandest sights in the world. A nearer view is yet more stirring. There is incomparable grandeur in these walls and crenellated towers, massive against the blue sky, gilded by the centuries, and enriched by a luxuriant growth of ivy, wild vine, and Judas trees—a green cloak to clothe breaches and ruins. Few roads are of a more haunting beauty than the one, paved with huge flagstones, that runs for miles between walls and cemeteries, where each step evokes a memory of the past.

On one of the gates may be read this inscription: "Christ our God, guard thy city from all disturbances and wars. Break victoriously the force of the enemy." For a long time this pious prayer was answered. Against these walls, all manner of barbarians dashed themselves in vain: Huns and Avars, Bulgars, Russians, Pechenegs, Arabs from the East, and Crusaders from the West. More impressive than Carcassonne and Aigues-Mortes, more poetic than Avignon, grander than Rome, the ancient wall of Theodosius II is one of the wonders of Constantinople and one of the monuments most steeped in history.

Other buildings contributed to the military character of the great city. On the Golden Horn, at the foot of the Acropolis, stood the great arsenal of the Mangana where the war-engines were kept and whose library contained books on ballistics. Protected by the chain stretched, in time of war, from the Mangana tower to the tip of Galata, lay the harbour of the Golden Horn, where the imperial fleet was stationed and where lay the naval dockyards of Neorion. There were the barracks of the Guards regiments, those 24,000 men who formed the regular garrison of Constantinople. On the very eve of final disaster, men still sang the praises of the military might of the capital and of "this crown of ramparts which yield nothing to those of Babylon."

2. THE WORLDLY CITY

Sheltered within these mighty walls lay a huge and splendid city.

In its tenth- or twelfth-century aspect, for instance, which many eyewitnesses have described, Constantinople was essentially an Oriental town. In contrast to the uproarious, overcrowded quarters where the rabble lived, there were serene and solitary districts where monasteries and quiet churches, schools and hospitals stood in the shade of gardens. In contrast to lordly palaces and wide roads lined with arcades, there were vaulted alleyways where the sun seldom penetrated, where squalid humanity seethed and swarmed in low, cramped houses. Beside squares adorned with fine monuments, columns, and statues, ran filthy, stinking streets, where mud lay so deep that men and beasts were often bogged in it. At night no lamps relieved the darkness, and the alleys were given over to stray curs and to robbers, of whom there were "almost as many as there were poor" and whom the police usually left alone. A twelfth-century writer has neatly summarized these contrasts: "If Constantinople is superior in wealth to all other cities, it is also their superior in vice." But such as it was, it made a tremendous impression on all who came.

Monuments

Constantinople was unmatched in the beauty of its setting, in the grandeur of its public monuments—where the classic style survived—in the number of antique statues adorning the wide squares and streets, and in the splendour of its palaces and churches. A tenth-century poet praised "the illustrious and venerable city that dominates the world, radiant with a multitude of marvels: the splendour of tall buildings and superb churches, the long galleries and porticoes, the soaring columns." Constantinople alone could show seven wonders of the world, "in which she arrayed herself," said one writer, "as in as many stars."

The square of the Augustum, "the Piazza S. Marco of Constantinople," was surrounded by colonnades and bounded on the north, south, and west by St. Sophia, the imperial palace, and the palace of the Senate. From this square, the great street of the Mese led to the Forum of Constantine, one of the most beautiful parts of the city, where there were palaces with huge domes and with walls decorated with mosaics and precious medallions, and where, beneath marble colonnades, the masterpieces of Greek sculpture were assembled. Further on came the great Taurus square, where, in front of the Capitol, the lofty column of Theodosius soared to the sky. There were other squares, other fine streets, of which traces can still be found in the Istanbul of today, as well as monumental columns rising from the sea of houses and palaces; there were the domes of countless churches, and statues that made the city the richest of museums.

The imperial palaces, above all, were of unrivalled splendour. On the slopes running down from the Atmeidan to the Sea of Marmara, numberless terraced buildings formed the Sacred Palace, a city within a city, where from the days of Constantine until the eleventh century almost each successive emperor took pride in adding to the huge residence. It was a complex agglomeration of every sort of building: reception halls, pavilions buried in greenery, palaces, barracks, baths and libraries, churches and prisons, long galleries and terraces commanding views far across the Bosphorus and the Sea of Marmara, stairs, towers, and gardens arranged without symmetry or general plan, but with the charm of the fantastic and with an unprecedented magnificence. Others have described it all, and we need not speak in detail of the great halls, splendid with marble and golden mosaics, the gorgeous costumes, the processions, ceremonies, solemn audiences, formal banquets—all the pomp accompanying every act of the Emperor's life—all the enchantments, worthy of the Arabian Nights, with which Byzantium loved to dazzle foreigners.

Byzantium: Greatness and Decline

In the twelfth century the Comneni moved from the old imperial residence to a no less splendid one in the quarter of the Blachernae, at one end of the Golden Horn. Foreigners admitted to this palace have left us dazzling descriptions of it. Gold and

Cyril Mango

One of the few standing examples of Byzantine palace architecture, in the vicinity of the Blachernae palace. Probably early 14th century.

jewels were everywhere, and a contemporary remarks that it was hard to tell "which added more to its costliness and beauty: the workmanship or the value of the materials." The brilliant, fashionable court delighted in feasts, music, and tournaments, as well as intrigue and adventures, all of which lent great fascination to the city. Travellers to Constantinople declared that "nothing like it was to be found in any other country"; and the sight of Byzantium's wonders reminded them of the legendary marvels of Susa and Ecbatana.

The Religious City

Constantinople was also a great religious city. Constantinople contained, said Benjamin of Tudela, "as many churches as there

Gaspare Fossati, Aya Sofia, Constantinople, *London, 1852*

St. Sophia from the northeast.

are days in the year." Countless monasteries and houses of meditation and retreat had been built there by devout princes and wealthy private citizens; and relics, which mediaeval men valued far above "gold and precious stones," were preserved there in such numbers that, as a thirteenth-century emperor wrote, "the whole Latin world does not possess so many." For pilgrims, visits to the shrines of Constantinople were almost as meritorious as those to the Holy Places, and many aspects of an active and forceful religious life found outward expression in the capital.

St. Sophia, or the Great Church, as it was most often called, was the wonder of Constantinople, as it is today. With its lofty dome—so light and ethereal that it seemed, in Procopius' phrase, "to be suspended from the heavens by a golden chain"—with its spaciousness, its exquisite proportions, its fine marbles and blazing mosaics, and the magnificent goldsmith's work adorning *iconostasis, ambo,* and altar, the church filled all comers alike with admiration. Justinian's successors took pride in maintaining and adorning it, and throughout the centuries we catch the echo of its praise on every lip. A man of the fourteenth century said, "One can find no words worthy of it; and having spoken of it, one can speak of nothing else."

But Constantinople boasted many other famous churches. There was that of the Holy Apostles with its five domes: a masterpiece of sixth-century architecture, later to be imitated in St. Mark's of Venice. Here an artist of genius had portrayed in mosaic episodes from the life of Christ; here lay ten generations of emperors in sarcophagi of porphyry and marble. There was the New Church, a basilica, built in the ninth century, and those beautiful ones built by the Comneni, of which the most famous was the Pantocrator, with its crown of domes; from the twelfth century onwards this was the St. Denis of the Empire. There were many others, of which some charming examples survive in the vastness of present-day Istanbul: St. Irene and little St. Sophia, dating from the sixth century; the Theotokos (Kilissé-Jāmĭ), apparently eleventh-century, an incomparably graceful example of classical Byzantine church architecture. We must also mention Fetihiye-Jāmĭ and Kariye-Jāmĭ, built in the twelfth and thirteenth centuries respectively, in the second of which, one of the most exquisite Byzantine mosaics yet remaining to us is preserved.

In all these churches, Orthodoxy displayed its ritual pageantry. In St. Sophia, above all, processions and imperial progresses added to the solemnity of the sacred acts. Here were performed the ceremonies of councils and coronations. On feast days the

Gaspare Fossati, Aya Sofia,
Constantinople, *London, 1852*

Interior of St. Sophia, looking east. This represents the building after
its restoration in 1847-1848, when it was still being used as a mosque.

night offices were celebrated by the light of silver hanging lamps, by lanterns suspended from the base of the cupola, and by the flowerlike flames of candelabra, so that the Great Church seemed splendidly on fire. "Luminous night," says a poet, "took on the hues of the rose." Beneath the great dome, candles burned and incense wreathed before the silver *iconostasis*, and silver organs accompanied the voices of the choir. Against this setting moved the glories of ritual processions and the mystic acts of the divine sacrifice, so moving, so enthralling in their beauty, that barbarians seemed to behold angels coming down from heaven to officiate with the priests.

Elsewhere, in still and solitary places adjoining the Petrion cliffs and the green Vale of Lycus that lay at the foot of the Great Wall, stood many monasteries. These were little cities in themselves: cities of silence and contemplation where in the shade of the conventual church, through green courts and gardens, passed the long-haired monks, in their dark habits and tall, black hats, a population of devout men who had renounced the world. Within the encircling wall, building succeeded building: the refectory, the dormitory, the residence of the *hegumen*, the granaries and the wine cellars, workshops, library, guesthouse for wayfarers, infirmary, old men's home, and often schools, which, said a thirteenth-century writer, "filled the neighbourhood of the church with a murmur of childish voices that was like birdsong."

Monasteries played a very important part in the social life of the capital. Being less strictly shut off from the world than the religious houses of the West, they could exert great influence on lay society. The monks were directors of conscience and were consulted chiefly by pious ladies. The holy images possessed by many houses were associated with miracles and were objects of awe and veneration. The fanatical army of monks more than once disturbed the streets by uproarious demonstrations, and carried their protests to the Sacred Palace itself.

The City of Industry and Trade

As we have already seen, Constantinople was a great industrial and commercial centre. Between the squares of the Augustum and the Taurus, the bazaar quarter ran the whole length of the great street of the Mese, its stalls being set up under por-

Constantinople

ticoes. Here were workbenches where goldsmiths carried on their
craft in the open; money-changers' tables, covered with coin;
booths of provision merchants, who sold meat, salt fish, flour,
cheese, vegetables, oil, butter, and honey; and those of the
perfume sellers, who had their stands in the square before the
palace. These bazaars, like the whole of Istanbul today, were
Oriental in character. In the neighbourhood of the Long Portico, between the Taurus and the Forum of Constantine, the
sellers of silks and cottons had their allotted places. There was
also the House of Lamps, corresponding more or less to the
Bezesten in the great bazaar of the modern city. In the Taurus
and the Strategion, sheep and pigs were sold; in the Amastrianon,
horses; while the fish market was on the quays of the Golden
Horn. In addition to all these, under close State supervision and
control, closed guilds manufactured the luxury articles that were
the glory and renown of Byzantium.

So much buying and selling made no little bustle in the great
city. The harbour, both along the Golden Horn and on the shores
of the Propontis, swarmed from morning till night with a cosmopolitan crowd, as if the whole world had arranged to meet
here. Hooknosed Asiatics with pointed beards and black hair
falling to the shoulder; turbaned traders from Babylon, Syria,
Egypt, or Persia; shaven, dirty Bulgars, wearing an iron chain
round their waists by way of belt; Russians with long, drooping
moustaches, green-eyed, snub-nosed, and dressed all in furs;
Khazars and Pechenegs; men from Spain and Lombardy; merchants from Pisa and Amalfi, Genoa and Venice, who had their
own quarter—with its quays, warehouses, and churches—on the
Golden Horn; all races, languages, and religions met and mingled here. Storehouses were crammed with precious merchandise
from all over the world. Bargaining was tremendously lively, and
marvelling visitors noted that "merchants from all over the world
came to Constantinople by land and sea."

The City of Scholarship and the Arts

Constantinople was, besides, a great intellectual city. The University of Constantinople, founded in the fifth century by Emperor Theodosius II, reorganized by Caesar Bardas in the ninth
century, and carefully protected by the emperors of the tenth,

· 105 ·

was an excellent school of philosophy and science. Students came from all parts of the Empire—from the distant West as well as from the Arab world—to sit at the feet of such famous masters as Leo of Thessalonica, Psellus, John Italus, and later the great

Courtesy of the Dumbarton Oaks Collection

Silver paten. The Communion of the Apostles. Late 6th century.

professors of the period of the Palaeologi. As in the great universities of the West, the *trivium* and *quadrivium* formed the essential matter of the teaching. Rhetoricians, who were at once grammarians, philologists, and humanists, commented on texts of the poets, historians, and orators of ancient Greece. The philosophers studied Aristotle and Plato and, from the eleventh century onwards, initiated the Platonic renaissance that was to be the glory of fifteenth-century Italy. The men of science—mathematicians, astronomers, and naturalists—are said on good authority to have done as much for the East as Roger Bacon did for the West. The law school that flourished in the time of Justinian was reorganized in the eleventh century. In the field of medicine there was much informed research. From the ninth century to the fourteenth, the schools of Constantinople were celebrated throughout the world and influenced both the Arab East and the Latin West. A thirteenth-century writer has left us a telling sketch of their vitality, which resembled that of the Moslem universities of today; he describes the school of the Holy Apostles, where all day long crowds thronged the porticoes: students, grammarians, and dialecticians disputing subtle problems; physicians discoursing near the great basin in the atrium and chirping "like sparrows endowed with reason"; mathematicians and musicians. All day long there were unending discussions, enlivened with shouts and insults, in which the spirit of philosophy was often lacking and knowledge of natural laws rare; and the imperial commissioner, or Proctor of the University, often had difficulty in restoring order.

Constantinople was also a city of the arts. Squares, palaces, and churches were full of antique and Byzantine masterpieces. We know the far-reaching influence exerted by the capital on the development of art both in the Slavic world and further west. To this we shall return later. Its churches became the pattern for those in Russia and Italy, while its iconography inspired both Serbian and Tuscan art. The Middle Ages turned to it for masters and for fine workmanship: bronze doors, cloisonné enamel, ivory, fabrics, and illuminated manuscripts. For centuries Byzantine art was the "regulating art" of Europe, and in mediaeval times only Gothic was capable of so wide and so prolific a development.

Byzantium: Greatness and Decline

The City of Pleasure

In addition to its other aspects, Constantinople was a city of diversions and amusements. The Hippodrome, no less than the Sacred Palace and St. Sophia, was a focus of Byzantine life, and

Robert Walsh, Constantinople and the scenery of the seven churches of Asia Minor. Illustrated . . . by Thomas Allom, *London, n.d.*

The Hippodrome as it looked in the early 19th century, when it was still used for equestrian exercises.

until the twelfth century, races and circus performances were the most popular entertainments with subjects and foreigners alike. "All entertainments that could rejoice the ear and the eye" were to be found in the great city; and the emperors, ever anxious to amuse the people, spared no effort to increase the variety and the magnificence of the displays. Chariot races, hunts, fights of wild beasts, mimes, acrobatic feats, and theatrical shows—especially farces and clowning acts—exhibitions of freaks, and later tournaments and mystery plays: all these were necessary to the Byzantines, for without them, says a grave historian, "life would have been virtually joyless." They provided one more attraction that, added to beauty of setting, wealth, and intellectual eminence, made Constantinople indeed a "sovereign city."

3. THE PEOPLE AND THE STREETS ·

The population of this great city was enormous. People streamed in from every province, from every country, either on commercial and legal business, or for pleasure. Streets and squares were thronged from morning till night with colourful, cosmopolitan crowds. Anyone who has visited the city will remember the Great Bridge. The same variety of type, dress, trade, and condition was to be seen there then. Citizens gorgeously clad in gold-embroidered silks, mounted on fine horses, and "looking like princes" jostled merchants from all over the world. Slav adventurers rubbed shoulders with Armenian and Scandinavian fortune hunters, soldiers in gaudy uniforms, Varangian guardsmen "tall as palm trees," Khazars, Russians, soldiers of the Negro Guard, Latin mercenaries wearing the long sword, who "looked like figures of bronze," beautifully dressed women, jewelled and painted, moving along on foot or in litters, and pedlars crying their wares.

All these gave life and colour to the streets, and an ever-changing pageantry. There were imperial progresses when the *Basileus*, attended by a magnificent escort, crossed the city on horseback to attend one or another of the famous churches. There were triumphal entries when the streets were hung with tapestries, radiant with lights, and strewn with flowers, and the brilliance of uniforms and weapons mingled with the blaze of purple and gold. When a son was born to the Emperor there followed seven days of rejoicing, and in every square one might eat and drink at the Emperor's expense. When he married or was crowned there were other great displays. From year's end to year's end, the capital was the scene of ceremonial and of curious or splendid spectacle. Travellers took away with them a dazzling impression of the Byzantine street scene.

It is true that this huge population caused the government much anxiety. It was no easy matter to keep the peace among this excitable, uproarious, and factious mob, which passed abruptly from cheers to execration, from merrymaking to rioting, from exaltation to despair. In this crowd of idle loungers, always agog for some fresh excitement, the newsmongers found an eager audience. During the sixth century their headquarters was beneath the galleries of the Royal Portico, in the booksellers' arcades, where they held forth on every subject—philosophy, politics, medicine, religion—in a cocksure and dogmatic manner that impressed the vulgar. Their hearers marvelled at the wonderful tales they told and the authority with which they proclaimed their news and their opinions.

Constantinople was also a favourite meeting-place of soothsayers and fortune-tellers; the credulous, superstitious, timid masses accepted the miraculous without question and often gave way to frenzied and unaccountable panics. At such times they would storm the churches, believing that the last day was come, and fill streets and squares with prayers, chants, and lamentations.

It is needless to speak at length of the vices that infected the capital: of the houses of ill fame established under the very shadow of the churches, of the blasphemies, the gambling fever, and the wineshops that were closed by order of the police at seven in the evening, to prevent those who had spent the day there from returning to pass the night "and, under the influence of drink, give themselves up to brawls, riots and quarrels." We have seen how unsafe the streets were at night, when robbers had a free hand. It was a desperate task to keep order in a rabble ever ready to carry its resentment and rage to the very steps of the throne, ever ready for riot and revolution, a rabble that had to be fed, amused, and subdued.

In spite of this, Constantinople impressed all visitors with its beauty, wealth, and power, and throughout the known world its prestige was enormous. Men of the Middle Ages dreamed of Constantinople as a city of marvels, glimpsed through a haze of gold. They dreamed of it among the cold fogs of Norway and along the Russian rivers, by which northern adventurers travelled down to wondrous Tsarigrad. They dreamed of it in the castles of the West, where troubadours told tales of the imperial palace: the bronze children that blew horns, the room that swung round with the sea breeze, and the blazing carbuncle that lit the apartments by night. They dreamed of it in the banking houses of Venice, as they calculated the huge annual revenues drawn by the Emperor from his capital. Up to its last days, its ruins notwithstanding, Constantinople continued to be one of the loveliest and most illustrious cities of the world. And because of this, because it was the centre and jewel of the Empire, the home of unrivalled wealth and culture and the glory of the Crown, Constantinople was one of the chief elements of the Empire's might.

VII. Asia, the Empire's Strength

Throughout the ages, in Byzantine administrative and military organization, more importance was attached to the Asiatic part of the realm than to the European. The greatest number of troops—and the best—were concentrated in the *themes* of Anatolia. In the hierarchic list of administrators, the governors of Asiatic provinces held a rank far superior to those of provinces in Europe, and their salaries were correspondingly higher. These facts are significant: they show that in the eyes of the imperial government the East—which included for purposes of administration the rich European provinces of Thrace and Macedonia— was of far greater value than the poorer possessions in the West. In Asia, local governments were responsible for vast areas of territory; we may mention those of the Anatolics, Armeniacs, Thracesians, Opsicians, and Bucellarians. These were fertile, well-populated regions, peaceful and law-abiding on the whole, and punctual in the payment of taxes. On the seaward side they were guarded by the imperial fleet, and along the frontier by an unbroken series of mighty fortresses; and they were inhabited by a fairly homogeneous people of Hellenic origin, interested in trade, industry, and farming, and preserving traces of their old civilization. "These provinces," it has been said, "formed in fact the Roman Empire,"[1] Constantinople being no more than "a sort of bridgehead on the European shore."[2] If in contrast to the glittering capital, the provinces present an earthier, sturdier character, it is above all in Anatolia that these qualities make themselves felt. It was with the loss of Asia Minor that the Empire's decadence set in.

1. POPULATION OF ANATOLIA

The ethnic groups of Anatolia had altered little since ancient times. The predominant race and tongue were always Greek. The Anatolian peninsula had suffered much less from barbarian invasion than had the Balkans, and despite moments of acute crisis, it withstood the shock of Arab assault with some success until the end of the eleventh century. As a result of wars and civil disturbances, Anatolia became impoverished and diminished indeed; but ethnographically there was little change. Time brought with it a certain influx of foreigners, in the shape of Germanic or Slavic mercenaries and Syrian, Arab, or Armenian colonists; but on the whole, Greek Asia, with its fine cities and great memories, endured. This proved more than an integrating, stiffening force; for "by their religious and monarchical spirit, by their tradition, and above all by their need of peace and good order, so necessary to trade, the Hellenic countries set a good example to other races."

[1] Rambaud, op. cit., 235.
[2] Carl Neumann, "La situation mondiale de l'empire byzantin avant les croisades," tr. by E. Renauld, Revue de l'Orient latin, 10 (1905), 65.

Anatolia supplied the Empire with its best soldiers, while from the coastal *themes* of Samos and the Cibyrrhaeot were recruited most of the crews for the imperial fleet. Inland, the tough mountain-dwellers of Isauria, Lycaonia, and Taurus, the sturdy peasants of Cappadocia, and the needy, valiant nobility of the Armenian districts were valuable additions to the army. It was chiefly in Anatolia that those hereditary military fiefs existed, where life was shaped and coloured by training in war. Here, too, was the belligerent race of *akritai*, guardians of the frontier, who fought their incessant battles along the Euphrates and Taurus borders with unflagging energy and zeal.

From early times, great estates were founded in Asia Minor, whose lords led an entirely feudal life among their tenants, vassals, and men-at-arms. The flower of the Byzantine aristocracy was of Eastern origin, and from Anatolia came the great families of Phocas, Skleros, Maniakes, Dalassenes, Diogenes, Botaniates, Ducas, and Comnenus, whose illustrious names fill the pages of Byzantine history. These Asiatic barons considered themselves greatly superior to the aristocracy of the European provinces; and indeed they justified their claim by the great services they rendered to the Empire. From their ranks came the finest leaders and commanders. Their presence among the Asiatic troops ensured an unrivalled steadiness and cohesion of forces. Having been brought up as soldiers from their earliest youth, these great lords were superbly trained and skilled in warfare. The system of regional recruitment furnished them with men who knew them; men familiar with their military prowess and their wealth; men who in civilian life were often bound to them by ties of dependence or vassalage. These followers held them in respect and devotion, their loyalty being stimulated by liberal treatment and the hope of favours to come. The Anatolian regiments, therefore, were ever ready to follow their commanders with unshakable loyalty.

The Empire also drew its finest civil servants from this great Anatolian aristocracy. Anatolia, Georgia, and Armenia—both subject and independent Armenia—were breeding-grounds of potential high-ranking officials and army commanders; from here, soldiers of fortune hastened to the capital to storm the heights of military rank and court appointment. The great feudal lords of Asia made it a point of honour that they and every member of their families should serve the government of the Empire. In the ninth and tenth centuries, court and army were full of Armenians; the dynasty called Macedonian was in fact of Armenian origin, and the Emperor Romanus Lecapenus was born in the Armeniac *theme*. The most illustrious generals, Curcuas, Phocas, Skleros, Maniakes, and many others, belonged to the Anatolian nobility, which also gave the Empire some of its most renowned emperors, such as Nicephorus Phocas, John Tzimisces, Romanus Diogenes, and the princes of the house of Comnenus. There is a note of disdain in the distinction made by an eleventh-century writer between an emperor springing from the eastern aristocracy (ἐκ τῆς ἑῷας εὐπατρίδης) and a noble from the western provinces, whom by comparison he regards as a man without family or breeding.

2. PROVINCIAL LIFE IN ASIA MINOR

Anatolia, then, was a reservoir of strength and vitality: qualities largely due, so far as we can discover, to the people's way of life.

Stories of Asiatic saints show us the vigour of Anatolian farming life in both the eighth and tenth centuries. Whether in the Bucellarian *theme* or in that of the Thracesians, whether in the Miletus region or in Paphlagonia, we hear of fertile lands tilled by sturdy farmers. Some passages indicate the extent of this cultivation. The property of one man—a man of importance in his village, no doubt, but one of simple country stock and no great lord—comprised some fifty farms spread over a considerable area of well-cultivated, well-irrigated land, producing a high yield. With this went 600 head of cattle, 100 draught oxen, 800 horses out at grass, 80 draught horses and mules, and 12,000 sheep. Many farm servants lived on the estate with their wives and families. The manor house was large and handsome, with reception rooms and a finely decorated *triclinium*, with its huge, round, ivory table, which could accommodate 36 people. There was also the *gynaeceum*, where the women of the household dwelt beyond the range of indiscreet eyes, and from which they seldom emerged.

There were, of course, lesser properties, consisting perhaps of a house, a few fields, a pair of oxen, a horse and a donkey, a cow with her calf, and a couple of hundred beehives; here a man and a girl would do all the work. Life was hard. Often the working animals had to be bought on credit, and loans were necessary to support the usually numerous family. But everyone, from top to bottom of the social ladder, seems to have led an arduous, simple, and hardy life. The man of the house ran the farm, often toiling in the fields himself with plough and oxen, while his wife, with the aid of a servant girl, cooked, cleaned, and kept house. When guests came they were waited on by the children. The whole family lived under one roof—parents, sons, daughters, and daughters' children—in a close-knit, affectionate community. Their hospitality and charity were liberal, their piety simple and deep. Asiatic society seems to have abounded in solid virtues.

There were others. A passage in the writings of Leo the Deacon, a historian, shows us how strong were the ties of devotion and loyalty between the great Asiatic barons and the people of their native province. Bardas Phocas, nephew of Emperor Nicephorus, patrician and duke of the *theme* of Chaldia, fell into disgrace on the death of his uncle and was interned in Amasia. With the aid of two cousins he escaped and hastened straight to Caesarea in Cappadocia, where his family had property, where he himself had his feudal castle, and where the name of Phocas was known and loved. At once he found the support and men he needed for rebellion. "All those bound to him by ties of blood or friendship rallied round him," the historian tells us. His cousins supplied him with troops; his father, who had escaped from exile in Lesbos, brought him Macedonian mercenaries; and crowds of other supporters were drawn to him by his name and fame, his wealth, his generosity, and the great hopes they cherished of his success. One of whom Leo the Deacon speaks was a strange character. His name was Symeon, and he bore the surname of Ampelas because of his many vineyards. His wealth was famous throughout Anatolia, and though not of noble birth, he was a match for any knight in strength and valour. A natural partisanship inclined him to side with Phocas, for all the great *archons* of Asia were allied not only by marriage, but by common interests and sympathies, which welded them into a fierce, proud, loyal, and devoted caste.

Other factors helped to develop and maintain the energetic character of the Anatolians. From the shores of the Black Sea to the banks of the Euphrates and the Taurus Mountains, Asia Minor bordered on Arab countries. In these frontier provinces, peopled with soldiers and bristling with forts, where every day brought renewed threats of Moslem raids and renewed retaliation, life was rough, hazardous, and heroic. A little book written in the tenth century, the *Treatise on Tactics* preserved under the name of Nicephorus Phocas, gives us a vivid picture of the perils and brutalities of life on the Cilician border and the marches of Cappadocia. Alertness and vigilance were needed to watch the movements and circumvent the plans of a tireless and elusive enemy; swords must be kept drawn and horses saddled, and men be ever ready to dash into action and beat back the invader. This warfare was chronicled in Byzantine ballads, and the song of *Digenis Akritas* shows us what this border country was, the country where the great feudal lords, heroes of chivalry, maintained an endless struggle against the infidel in the name of the Emperor. It was the country of *akritai,* or guardians of the marches; the country of *apelates,* brigand knights ever in quest of adventure; the country of swordsmanship, single combat, kidnapping, looting, surprise attack, and massacre, of adventures in war and love.

Popular imagination no doubt endowed chivalry with graces it never had, and its heroes with legendary glamour; indeed, in this poem, Digenis Akritas appears as a true paladin. But beneath this idealization we glimpse the enduring characteristics of savagery and cruelty. Among these people might was right and cold steel was king; they were a race of ruthless, bloodthirsty warriors whose life was perpetual battle and whose one aim was to fight splendidly, joyously, in defence of faith and Empire and for the love of glory, women, and gold.

The men of the Asiatic provinces, then, were steeled to life and combat. Their land was rich. The countries of Cilicia and Cappadocia as well as the Thracesian and Bucellarian *themes* seem to have been exceptionally fertile and well cultivated. In Anatolia there were numbers of great cities, of which many, up to the twelfth century, seem to have been prosperous: Caesarea, Ancyra, Amorion, Amasia, Chonae, Pergamum, Philadelphia, and Nicaea. The ports were centres of brisk trade: Adana, Tarsus, Adalia, Ephesus, Smyrna, Phocaea, Cerasus, Sinope, and Trebizond. The life of the great Asiatic barons, as seen in history and epic, was one of luxury. The palace of Digenis Akritas, set among wonderful gardens on the banks of the Euphrates, sparkled with gold and jewels, and its walls were lit with mosaics depicting the feats of Samson and David, Achilles and Alexander, and the adventures of Ulysses side by side with the story of Joshua. The banquets held in these manors were sumptuous indeed; we hear of silver plate, jewellery, splendidly embroidered silks, exquisite enamels, and tapestries, of processions, gorgeous robes, and superb weapons. And if legend has somewhat exaggerated these wonders, the wealth was real enough and contributed to the might of the Empire.

3. DANGERS OF PROVINCIAL POWER

As we shall see, the strength that Asia contributed to the Empire was not without its dangers. The Anatolian nobility, so proud of its origins, its wealth and power, was of markedly independent temper. Loyal subjects though these feudatories were, they lacked discipline; they treated the Emperor almost as an equal; they felt entitled to offer him advice and were surprised when he dared decline it. Within their own domains, among vassals and men-at-arms, they were kings. When the *Basileus* travelled through Asia and entered the border provinces, he left the greater part of his court behind him; it was the privilege of the *akritai* to provide an escort for him and ensure his safety.

One may imagine the dangers inherent in such a state of affairs, and the temptations it offered the Asiatic nobles to express their discontent or their ambition by rising against the imperial government. Nearly all the big insurrections that shook the Empire broke out in Asia Minor, and most of the usurpers who coveted the throne were governors of eastern *themes* or feudal barons of Anatolia. The central power was therefore inclined to mistrust these lords, with their excessive wealth, influence, and military strength, and while making use of them as soldiers, spared no effort to restrict their power. And it may be that these sometimes ill-judged efforts did less harm to the leaders they were designed to curb than to the Empire as a whole, by weakening its defences.

Byzantine Patriotism

For it is a fact that for all its haughty, independent spirit, the Asiatic nobility had a profound sense of its duty to the Crown, and its genuine Byzantine patriotism is usually underestimated. There is a curious polemical work of the tenth century with the significant title of "The Patriot" (*Philopatris*). The *chanson de geste* of *Digenis Akritas* gives vivid expression to the same sentiments. Its hero is presented as the defender of the Empire and the Christian faith; it is as much for this as for his valour that the Emperor praises him; and indeed in the mind of Digenis, Romania and Orthodoxy are inseparable concepts, two aspects of the same fealty. To maintain the defence of the frontier, subjugate the infidel, and enable the Roman and Orthodox realm to live at peace, secure from attack—such is the ideal he strives for, the service he performs and desires to perform for the Empire. The poet's awareness of Byzantine nationality is very marked, and we have every reason to believe that he faithfully interprets the spirit that animated the Anatolian people. These were more homogeneous than the rest of the Empire, more Greek in race and language, more deeply imbued with the spirit of religion and monarchy; and this was another source of imperial strength.

Provincial Life in Europe

Asia Minor had no monopoly of robust energy, devotion, and patriotism. There is a curious little book by a feudal lord of the eleventh century, Cecaumenus, who with realistic and somewhat disillusioned wisdom summarizes the lessons of long experience. He shows us that the European provinces were not unlike those of the East.[3] There, too, was a class of rich landowners who lived on their estates and were ever eager to increase their wealth. As in Asia, they devoted most of their life when at home to the cultivation of the soil. Cecaumenus says, "There is no better life than that of husbandry. Produce wheat and wine, raise crops and stock, and you will be happy." When he did consent to leave his native province and enter public life, he would serve nowhere but in the army, loyally and faithfully indeed, but from a sense of duty rather than with enthusiasm. By choice he lived on his own estates, where he was independent and respected, far from the humiliations, the precarious favour, and the perils of the court, far from the over-elegant and sophisticated capital, which in his rustic wisdom he regarded with inveterate contempt.

But though the spirit may have been the same in both Europe and Asia, the western *themes* were on the whole of insufficient importance to allow the nobles who lived there—the Bryennii, Melissenes and Cantacuzeni—to carry much weight in the destinies of the Empire. The strength of the realm did not lie here, as history clearly shows. So long as Byzantium possessed the coasts of Anatolia, whence its finest seamen were recruited, its fleets ruled the eastern waters. The loss of them in the eleventh century spelt the ruin of a navy that had long been "the glory of Romania," as a writer says. So long as Byzantium ruled the eastern *themes*, which supplied not only tough soldiers but the

[3] See Charles Diehl, *Dans l'Orient byzantin* (Paris, 1917), the chapter entitled "La sagesse de Cecaumenos."

best officers, the army was enormously strong. When the Seljuk Turks won the decisive battle of Mantzikert in 1071 and founded the Sultanate of Roum in the heart of Anatolia, the Empire suffered a blow from which it never recovered. So long as Byzantium retained the rich, fertile provinces with their prosperous cities and busy ports, it had no difficulty in raising revenue. When they were lost, the sources of wealth dried up; and from the end of the eleventh century, ravaged, depopulated, war-weary Asia—including the regions remaining or temporarily reverting to the Empire—ceased to be an asset. The Comneni were the last of the great Anatolian families whose names appear in history. In the thirteenth century, and even more in the fourteenth, Hellenism in Asia had pitifully decayed. The eleventh century, which was for the Anatolian provinces what the fifteenth was for those of Europe, deprived the Byzantine Empire of most of its military and economic strength.

Book Three

Elements of Weakness

Having considered the causes of the greatness and certainly the long duration of the Byzantine Empire, we must now discover the nature of the weaknesses that led to its decline and fall.

These weaknesses were numerous and varied. Some were perennial, and affected the fortunes of the Empire in every age to a greater or lesser degree. These included political demoralization—an all too frequent source of revolution and anarchy—and the even more pernicious social corruption, arising from the peculiar character and mentality unhappily associated with the word Byzantine. There were also transient factors that did their part in undermining the Empire.

There was the social problem, present in quite early times, which from the ninth to the eleventh century became acute, owing to the rise of a powerful landed aristocracy. This seriously weakened and troubled the realm.

Next came religious unrest, born of the relationship of Church and State and expressed in the ninth century by the Church's efforts to shake off its temporal fetters. At times it took the form of patriarchal ambition and the resulting schisms of the ninth and eleventh centuries; and often, as in the eighth, tenth, and fourteenth centuries, it was expressed in an excessive development of monasticism and in the agitation stirred up and maintained by the monks.

In addition there was extreme imperialism. Byzantium's extravagant ambitions were out of all proportion to its resources. Justinian, Basil I, and Manuel Comnenus, fired by the memory of old Rome, turned to Italy and the West; while others exhausted the realm in endless battles with the Bulgarian Empire or with the Serbia of the Nemanjas, in an effort to win the hegemony of the Balkans.

These varied causes were to have serious effects. Increasing financial difficulties together with the decline of trade in the twelfth century resulted in economic distress. Linked to this was the deterioration of military strength; territorial losses reduced the size of the Empire, and bit by bit, it crumbled away. By the end of the eleventh century Asia was as good as lost, and in the thirteenth the Western provinces began to disintegrate. Economically and territorially depleted and militarily weakened, Byzantium was ripe for its inevitable fall.

One last factor tipped the scale. The Empire might have been saved, even at the eleventh hour, by Western intervention. But the West, for various reasons, was implacably hostile. The Papacy had been antagonized by religious differences. Political and economic considerations impelled the Latins to exploit the East; while the contact of East and West during the Crusades had produced nothing but hatred and mistrust.

Byzantium succumbed, then, for many different reasons; and it is these reasons that we shall now try to analyse in detail.

I. Political Demoralization

1. CAUSES OF POLITICAL ANARCHY

Like Rome, the Byzantine Empire suffered for a long time from a serious defect in its constitution, namely the lack of any law of succession; and it was not until fairly late in its history that it adopted the idea of dynastic legitimacy. In this seemingly absolute monarchy there was one entirely democratic principle. There being no blood royal, no family with an inherited and acknowledged right to the throne, anyone might aspire to rule: "Everyone had the stuff of an emperor in him." [1] The acquisition of a crown was one of the commonest predictions of soothsayers and astrologers. Like Macbeth, every Byzantine at one time or another met someone who said to him, "Thou shalt be king." Byzantine history is full of these predictions, and of their fulfilment: the accession of countless upstarts. Justin, a rough Macedonian peasant; Phocas, a centurion; Leo the Isaurian, who began life as a poor artisan; Basil I, a peasant, also of Armenian origin, and many others. The success of some encouraged all. "The dis-

[1] Montesquieu observes: "Fortune having chosen emperors from every walk of life, no man was of too low birth or too slender merit to cherish hopes." *Considerations sur les causes de la grandeur des Romains et de leur décadence*, ch. XXI.

ease of the purple" was endemic, and a scourge. Nor did the frightful torments inflicted on would-be emperors deter them. "The horrors enacted in the Forum Amastrianon and the Hippodrome taught the people nothing. Conspirators were merely the more determined to mete out the same treatment to the reigning sovereign and his family when they were deposed." [2]

Some of the forces that, as we have seen, tended to restrict imperial authority were powerful enough to support these ambitions. The population of the capital was excitable and unruly and ever ready for riot and revolt; it was also able to make or overthrow an emperor. The Church, too, through its moral ascendancy over the people, could unleash tremendous storms, and the support of the Patriarch was a trump card in a pretender's hand. Last but not least, there was the army. It was in the camps that most of the usurpers were proclaimed Emperor, and the devotion of the soldiers placed many a general on the throne.

No sovereign was safe, therefore, and the Crown, however secure it might seem, was always at the mercy of revolution. Of the 107 sovereigns that occupied the throne between 395 and 1453, only 34 died in their beds, and 8 in war or by accident; the rest either abdicated—willingly or unwillingly—or died violent deaths by poison, smothering, strangulation, stabbing, or mutilation. In the space of those 1058 years we can count, therefore, 65 revolutions, in palace, streets, or barracks. Even when the pretenders failed to achieve their goal—and failures far exceed successes—the result of these ceaseless turmoils was no less damaging to the State. When the Crown was weak, when imperial authority seemed to slip through the hands that held it, rivals sprang up on all sides, and anarchy prevailed. At the end of the seventh century and the beginning of the eighth, after the fall of the Heraclian dynasty, six or seven emperors succeeded one another by means of as many revolutions, within the space of twenty years. At the beginning of the ninth century, after the Isaurians, three or four revolutions occurred, again within a score of years. In the second half of the eleventh, after the Macedonians, yet another twenty years of disturbance ensued, during which we find three or four aspirants competing with each other to de-

[2] Rambaud, *op. cit.*, 29.

pose the rightful sovereign and assume the purple. Anarchy re-curred at the end of the twelfth century, when the line of the Comneni was at an end, and again during the fourteenth century, under the weak rulers of the house of the Palaeologi. We can easily surmise the cost of these disturbances and disasters to the Empire.

2. FORMS OF POLITICAL ANARCHY

Popular Revolt

Revolutions were of different kinds. First, there were the revo-lutions originating among the people. We have already seen something of the plebeians of the capital; as in other great cities, they included numbers of vagabonds, adventurers, thieves, and beggars. They were credulous, excitable, impressionable, and noisy people, ever on the verge of panic or sedition; they loved bloodshed; the sight of pain fascinated them; they were foul-mouthed and uproarious, passionate and fierce. They claimed to be the heirs of the ancient Romans, and if they no longer cast their votes in the Forum, or elected tribunes and consuls, they reserved the right to demonstrate in the Hippodrome: to execrate or applaud, to howl or to cheer, until, indeed, the circus seemed "the final refuge of public liberties." They were armed, too. The famous factions known as the Blues and the Greens were not merely racing associations; they had a political and military or-ganization which turned the people of Constantinople into a sort of urban militia, and enabled them to intervene in public affairs. This they did with an enthusiasm in which survived, perhaps, something of the democratic spirit of the ancient Greeks—to the grave danger of the State.

The Nika Insurrection

The terrible revolt known as the Nika Insurrection, which in January 532 came near to overthrowing Justinian's throne, is a telling example of the people's power. It began with a violent scene at the circus, when the mob addressed the Emperor directly, with howls, insults, and protests, in mingled wrath and derision. Uproar spread through the town; in one of the most beautiful quarters fires raged for a week, while furious men—and women, too—routed the Emperor's troops, proclaimed a new sovereign in the Hippodrome, and made ready to storm the palace. A contemporary declared that "the Empire seemed on the eve of its downfall." We know how Theodora's energy stiffened the courage of Justinian and his advisers, and how in the Hippodrome Belisarius crushed the rebels and strewed the arena with more than 30,000 corpses. This bloody execution subdued popular passion for some years, although often during the rest of the sixth century fights and plots disturbed the capital. But this frightful insurrection, which filled Byzantium with fire and ruin, gives abundant proof of what the many-headed monster could do.

The Revolt of 1042

The rioting of April 19, 1042, is another example, rendered especially interesting through an eyewitness account by Psellus. Few pages in Byzantine history are more vivid. We know the cause of the rebellion. Emperor Michael V had just dispossessed the popular old Empress Zoë and shut her up in a convent; and in Psellus' account we can follow the whole course of the revolt. He describes in memorable terms the mounting roar in the city, the sudden cessation of all business, the groups muttering in the streets, and the crowds of both sexes and all ages, murmuring at first, then menacing, while "a dark veil of pain and wrath sank over the city, as in times of great national disaster." In the squares there were pamphlets and protests; elsewhere, vociferous outcry. The women especially were in a state of fierce excitement. Even the most retiring of them—those who until then had seldom left the *gynaeceum*—mingled unveiled with the mob "like furies,

Political Demoralization

huddled in a howling mass and uttering hideous imprecations."
Soon the rabble were organized and armed, each snatching up
whatever came to hand: axes, swords, cudgels, stones. They broke
open the prisons and then headed for the palace "as if moved
by some unseen power." "They stampeded in their thousands,
feeling their strength increased tenfold. Their eyes flashed fires
of resentment and rage." The homes of the Emperor's kinsmen
were sacked and demolished. The palace itself was invaded and
despoiled, precious objects in the Treasury broken, tax registers
torn up, and money stolen. The Emperor fled.

Delirious joy and triumph followed; there was dancing in the
streets and the singing of songs improvised for the occasion. Then
came the final act of the drama. In the religious house of the
Studium, where they had sought refuge and now clung desper-
ately to the altar, the Emperor and his uncle were surrounded
by the mob. "All those wild beasts threatened to tear them to
pieces." Agonized and half dead with terror, they begged and
pleaded. They were torn from the sanctuary and dragged by the
heels into the square amid yells, savage songs, and taunts, hoisted
on to a mule and led to the executioner, who was waiting to put
out their eyes. Contemporaries were profoundly shocked by the
atrocities of that day, and by the mighty and mysterious unleash-
ing of the mob soul, μέγα καὶ δημοσιώτατον μυστήριον, as Psellus
wrote. Their reflections on the transience of worldly power are
expressed in terms reminiscent of Bossuet. And indeed, few events
bear such striking witness to the hideous brutality of a Byzantine
mob when goaded to frenzy.

Church Revolutions. The Event of 963

The people did not always act alone, but sought support either
from the Church or from the army. In August 963 Nicephorus
Phocas, the Empire's most illustrious general, had just proclaimed
himself Emperor at Caesarea in Cappadocia. His troops were at
the gates of the capital, where the excitement was intense. The
chief minister, the all-powerful Bringas, was attempting to or-
ganize defence, and had outlawed the kinsmen and supporters
of Nicephorus. Bardas, the father of the pretender, had had no
time to escape; he sought refuge in St. Sophia, where the Patri-
arch Polyeuctes received him. The people, who took his part,

Courtesy of The Byzantine Institute, Inc.

Mosaic bust of Empress Zoë (St. Sophia).

Mosaic bust of Constantine IX (St. Sophia).

rushed to the Great Church and threatened and reviled the soldiers of the regent, who were trying to drag the fugitive from the sanctuary by force. In vain did Bringas order the Patriarch to deliver Bardas to him; in vain did the "abusive, haughty man" harangue the crowd, threatening to starve them by denying them bread unless they yielded; in vain did he compel Bardas to leave St. Sophia and return to his house. For when the people attending afternoon service—it was Sunday—found the fugitive no longer in the Great Church, they raised such an uproar against the Patriarch and the clergy who had let him go that Polyeuctes had hastily to invite him back. And when Bardas hesitated, they took steps to protect him by mounting guard round the palace all night. Soon the rebels armed themselves and attacked the government troops; and in this street-fighting, women did their share, hurling missiles from above. A leader had been found: the *Paracoemomenus*, Basil, natural son of Emperor Romanus Lecapenus. Arming the men of his household—he had more than 3000 people at his command—he plunged boldly into the struggle. At his instigation, the people broke into the palaces of the chief minister and his friends, looting, sacking, and razing the buildings to the ground. Fighting continued in the city for three days; the infuriated mob arrested and imprisoned people of high rank on the smallest pretext. Plundering and destruction were frenzied. The arsenal was captured and the fleet handed over to Nicephorus; and while Bringas, deserted by everyone, fled in his turn to St. Sophia, his victim, Bardas, took possession of the imperial palace until such time as his victorious son should make his triumphal entry into Constantinople.

The Revolution of 1057

An even more active part was played by another patriarch in the revolution that carried Isaac Comnenus to the throne in 1057. At first, Michael Cerularius left the disaffected generals to plot together in St. Sophia, and when they departed, he was aware of their intention to proclaim Isaac Emperor. Informed men regarded him from that moment as master of the situation. And indeed, while the insurgents were pitching camp at the gates of Constantinople, it was he who took charge in the capital and prepared the revolt. On the morning of August 31, 1057, a crowd

gathered outside the Great Church, loudly demanding the Patriarch. Having allowed them to wait some little time, Cerularius
appeared in full canonicals, and in the crowded church listened
to what the insurgents had to say. But soon voices were heard
acclaiming Comnenus, and the Patriarch made no protest. On the
contrary, he soon openly assumed leadership of the revolutionary
movement, compelled the Emperor to abdicate, set up a pro-
visional government with himself at the head, and unleashed
rebellion and bloodshed in Constantinople. Once master of the
city, he handed it over to Isaac Comnenus. On this occasion it
was the Patriarch who made the Emperor.

Military Revolts

The army, however, was the mightiest force of all, and in any
really serious situation it was to the soldier that Byzantium turned
for succour. Military *pronunciamentos* raised many fine emperors
to the throne: Heraclius, who delivered the realm from the tyranny of Phocas; Leo the Isaurian, who put an end to the frightful
anarchy at the beginning of the eighth century; Nicephorus
Phocas, who in the tenth brought such glory to the Empire;
Alexius Comnenus, who saved it from disaster at the end of the
eleventh. This does not include the pretenders, such as George
Maniakes, Bardas Phocas, Bardas Skleros, and countless others,
who felt sure enough of their soldiers to assume the imperial
crown and the purple boots, and who, less fortunate, never attained their goal. It was in camp amid their devoted troops that
ambitious malcontents, as well as those who in critical times strove
to uphold the might of the Crown, sought and found support.
More than once, indeed, it was the soldiers who coerced their
hesitant leaders. It was thus that Nicephorus Phocas was proclaimed Emperor, in his camp at Caesarea in July 963. Sword in
hand, the high officers surrounded their general's tent and amid
acclamation greeted him as Autocrat of the Romans. Nicephorus
protested and refused, spoke of family bereavements that had
drained him of all ambition, and declared that he had but one
duty, one desire: to carry on the war against the infidel. Heedless
of this, they dragged him from his tent and raised him shoulder-
high. He yielded—not too unwillingly. Girded with his sword and
leaning on his lance, he stood on a mound and addressed his

soldiers for the first time; those soldiers who, says the historian to whom we owe this account, "loved him marvellously (δαιμονίως) and were proud to receive his praise."

All who feared for their lives in Constantinople sought refuge in the camps. When in 1057 Michael VI—"The Old," as his adversaries called him—was unwise enough to displease the leading army commanders and to reply to their representations with smooth words and jests, the generals did not hesitate to plot against him, being sure that the whole army would follow them; and from their conspiracy resulted the proclamation of Isaac Comnenus. Again in 1081, when Alexius Comnenus learned the evil designs of Botaniates' ministers, he fled with his adherents to the troops of whose loyalty he was assured, and marched resolutely on Constantinople. Rarely did the capital resist the military forces of usurpers for long; and as we have seen, there was always a party within the walls ready to serve them.

Palace Revolutions

We know how important a place the palace occupied in Byzantine life, and how strong was the Empress's influence there. Within those walls and in the seclusion of the women's apartments, among women, eunuchs, and courtiers, many plots and counterplots were woven to secure the succession to the throne. The Sacred Palace of Byzantium is full of grim stories. There the devout Irene had her son Constantine VI blinded, in the very room in which he had been born. There in 820, in St. Stephen's Chapel, Leo V the Armenian was assassinated by murderers lurking among the choristers while, according to his custom, he was conducting the singing. There Basil the Macedonian and his friends slew Michael III; and there also, one December night, Theophano had her husband, Nicephorus Phocas, assassinated and from a window displayed to the soldiers of the guard the severed, dripping head of their master.

Political Demoralization

3. CONSEQUENCES OF POLITICAL ANARCHY

In the face of the constant threat of revolt, of plots, risings, and intrigues, the position of the Crown, however secure in appearance, was in fact precarious. It is true that the government was often able to foil conspiracy and crush rebellion, and it punished any attack upon its authority with relentless cruelty. But though many attempts failed, a great number succeeded. It has been rightly said that Byzantine monarchy was absolutism tempered by assassination. In these conditions few emperors were sure of the morrow, at least during the earlier centuries, when the right of succession was virtually unrecognized. Although Justinian ruled for nearly half a century, first in the name of Justin, his uncle, and then in his own, he was an exception. Between the fifth and the ninth centuries we find few such examples; Heraclius may be mentioned, with his 31 years, and Constantine V with 35. Basil II occupied the throne for 49 years—the longest reign of any in Byzantine history—while the Comneni ruled for 37, 25, and 37 years respectively. But by that time, the concept of legitimate succession had somewhat reduced the risk of revolution. Nevertheless, the Crown was never out of danger.

Another consequence of these ever-recurring disturbances was that the Empire was constantly ravaged by civil war, often at a time when danger from without was most imminent. Weakness in the government, which encouraged internal strife, almost always coincided with disasters abroad and was often a result of them. Yet instead of making a united stand against a common enemy, revolutionaries had no scruples in profiting by the situation to further their own aims. It did sometimes happen that in crises that threatened to destroy the Empire, the evil itself produced a saviour, as happened in the cases of Leo the Isaurian, Basil I, and Alexius Comnenus. Yet one circumstance was always a formidable danger: civil war opened the gates to the enemy, to whom both sides appealed—to the greatest possible detriment of the realm. During the second half of the eleventh century Pechenegs and Turks intervened in internal quarrels and supported all the claimants to the throne against the lawful sovereign. In the fourteenth century it was even worse. In the endless struggle between Andronicus the Young and his grandfather, Andronicus II, and in the conflict that raged for so many years between John Cantacuzenus and John Palaeologus, their adversaries appealed to Bulgars, Serbs, and Turks, and to all the Empire's foes. Byzantium suffered very greatly by these practices. A throne shaken by revolution, a nation torn by civil war and delivered into the hands of those who plotted its ruin by men who should have defended it—such were some of the effects of political demoralization, which was the permanent underlying weakness of Byzantium.

II. Social Demoralization

More serious even than political demoralization, social demoralization was one of the main causes of Byzantium's decline and fall. During the eleven centuries of its history we encounter a great variety of types: proud, honest men as well as shifty scoundrels. Often in the same character we find a mixture of oddly contrasting qualities: outstanding intellect, perhaps, and bold, original thinking, allied to a base and servile nature. From among so many complex and contradictory figures, it is by no means easy to pick out the common denominators in the Byzantine character; to do it—to explain the mentality of the mediaeval Greeks—we must first try to define their tastes.

1. THE TASTES OF BYZANTINE SOCIETY

Without claiming that the whole of Byzantine history is summed up in the quarrels of the Greens and the Blues, we can be certain that until the twelfth century, circus events were the chief delight of the Byzantine world. Indeed, it has been fairly said that the Hippodrome seemed to be a "mirror of Greek society in the Middle Ages." From the Emperor to the meanest of his subjects,

Emperor, with bodyguard and courtiers, watching games in the Hippodrome. Relief on base of the Egyptian obelisk in the Hippodrome.
390 A.D.

Byzantines were passionately interested in all that concerned the circus, and women were as eager as men to watch the displays, chariot races, and contests. A sixth-century writer remarked upon the tremendous enthusiasm "that inflames men's souls to inordinate heights of passion. Should the green charioteer take the lead, some are in despair; should the blue overtake him, half the city is in mourning. People with no personal interest in the matter utter frantic imprecations; those who have suffered nothing feel grievously wounded, and for a mere trifle, they fly at each other's throats as if the Empire's safety was at stake." The most serious men declared that without theatre or Hippodrome life would have been "virtually joyless," and an emperor said that shows were necessary to amuse the people.

This meant that displays and festivals became an instrument of government, and since the Emperor himself took sides in the contests as passionately as anyone, circus rivalries often assumed a political colour. The people were not content to admire the thousand and one varieties of shows offered them by the generosity of the Emperor: the chariot races, hunts, fights of men and wild beasts, acrobats, and clowns; they were not satisfied with solemn pageants, in which victorious generals paraded, followed by the spoils of conquest, nor with the executions that glutted their lust for cruelty and blood. The circus replaced the Forum of ancient times; it was a focus of public life, the place where the people could express their feelings, their rebellious and factious temper. It was here that a new emperor met his subjects for the first time and made over them the ritual sign of the cross. Here also, as we have seen, more sombre encounters took place between sovereign and subjects, and here sometimes a dethroned and tortured emperor might end his life, amid the yells and execrations of the mob.

Religion

Religion, also, played an essential part in the Byzantine world. It was not only that these people, avid as they were for spectacle, took delight in the magnificence of the ritual, or that in their credulity they attributed miraculous virtues to the holy icons—those "images not made with hands." Nor was it merely that they sought to discern the divine will in every event and endowed every monument with mystic significance. There was more to it than this. Every Byzantine of whatever walk of life took a fierce delight in theological disputation.

It would, of course, be foolish to assert that the interminable wrangles over dogma and the deep-seated unrest resulting from

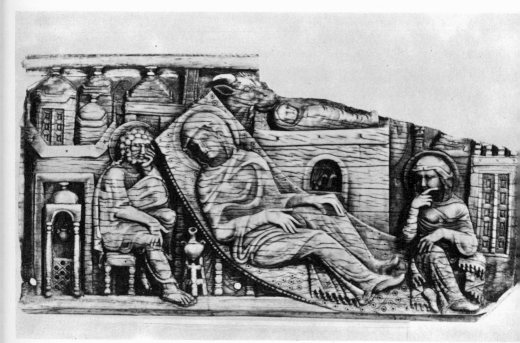

Courtesy of the Dumbarton Oaks Collection

The Nativity. Ivory, probably from Alexandria. 6th-7th century.

them arose solely from the national love of controversy, the mania for argument, the subtlety of the Greek mind and—in the case of statesmen—the sterile pleasure of laying down the law. Heresy often masked political opposition, and reasons of state rather than a desire to introduce new doctrines influenced many an emperor's conduct. But there was another aspect to this interest in religion and its mystic attraction for so many souls. Many found in it an illusion of intellectual superiority that flattered their pride; it seemed to them a mark of qualities above the ordinary, and of deeper culture. There was a certain nobility in this, and it explains the attraction of the cloister for so many Byzantines; weariness of the world and a need of renunciation and peace led many bruised and disappointed spirits to the monastery. It explains the profound respect in which monks were held; those men who had left the temporal world to become "citizens of heaven," and wrought for the Empire's salvation by prayer and penance. It also accounts for the influence they exerted on people's consciences, particularly those of women. Religious studies held an important place in the education of every Byzantine, and in this, too, the emperors set an example. Moreover, by tradition, devout practices were closely bound up with daily life. It has been shrewdly observed that Church and Hippodrome were the only public meeting-places this society possessed. Church festivals and court ceremony were so intermingled that the Emperor's life was sacerdotal in character. Lastly, a true and sincere piety burned in many souls, and Orthodoxy was so stout a support for the Empire that even those of lukewarm faith rarely ventured to discard the mask imposed upon them by universal custom and government intolerance.

Intrigue and Court Life

Although circus entertainment and religion were the two main interests in the life of every Byzantine, his taste for intrigue was no less marked. We have seen the importance of the court in the Byzantine world. Where monarchy was absolute and everything depended on the ruler's favour, the palace was the hub of the State; and naturally in the struggle to win or keep this favour those at court engaged in continual intrigue. Intrigue was everywhere in this household of eunuchs, women, and idle dignitaries; everyone elbowed and jostled his way forward and sought to bring down the favourite of the moment; all means were acceptable, whether flattery, calumny, bribery, or murder. In such an atmosphere there was room for every sort of baseness and betrayal. Moral standards were low in the imperial palace, which was the scene of many glaring scandals; while the taste for intrigue, so necessary to climbers at court, spread outward and downward into every class of society.

Byzantium: Greatness and Decline

The Hippodrome, St. Sophia, and the Sacred Palace: these were the poles round which Byzantine life gravitated; and from this we may perhaps deduce a few of the principal traits of the Byzantine character.

2. THE BYZANTINE CHARACTER

The Stamp of the East

To whatever social category he might belong, the Byzantine was, generally speaking, high-strung, impressionable, devout, superstitious, and fiery. He loved pleasure and display and found them in the games of the arena, in court ceremonies, or church festivals. If what he beheld was savage and bloodthirsty, so much the better. Being in part Oriental, he had a cruel streak in him, which was inflamed at the sight of torture, suffering, and bloodshed. Punishments were of appalling ferocity. Noses were cut off, eyes put out, and ears torn away; and execution of the death sentence was preceded by prolonged agony. Refined tortures were inflicted by the mob on its victims, and I need cite only one example, the ghastly end of Emperor Andronicus Comnenus: a spectacle which, says a contemporary, "ought to have drawn floods of tears from every eye." The fallen sovereign was given over to the mob. They broke his teeth and tore out his beard and hair, while women in particular belaboured the unfortunate with their fists. Then they put out one eye and dragged him, almost naked, through the streets of Constantinople on the back of a mangy camel. "Some," says Nicetas, "beat him on the head with sticks; others pushed dung into his nostrils; others again squeezed sponges soaked in excrement over his face. Some thrust at his ribs with spits, some stoned him, and a courtesan fetched a jar of boiling water from a kitchen and emptied it into his face." Finally he was taken to the Hippodrome and there suspended by the feet from a beam placed across two columns. A spectator ran a sword into his mouth and by a great effort thrust it up into his vitals. Soldiers amused themselves by testing the keenness of their swords on his body and seeing who could deliver the best strokes. Even his dead and mutilated body was viciously attacked.

And all this was in the twelfth century, in the refined and elegant Byzantium of the Comneni.

It is needless to quote further examples, though they are plentiful. These people were voluptuaries with a taste for blood and death, pitiless and unscrupulous when their passions were aroused and their hatred unleashed against religious and political opponents. In this they strongly resembled the Turk of today, and like him displayed in their calmer moods sound qualities and virtues. Among both the middle class and the aristocracy we find examples of united family life, where the father is honest and hard-working and the mother orderly in her ways, staid and discreet in behaviour, charitable, sincerely pious, and conscientious in bringing up her children. Yet even in such excellent people as these, we find an element of hardness, while the powerful hold that their religion had over them resulted in a lack of balance and a certain mystical exaltation that are quite disquieting.

The Stamp of Hellenism

But although they were in some degree Orientals, the Byzantines were also Greeks, charmed by the things of the mind, eager in research and the study of subtleties, and, as a rule, keenly intelligent. Therefore they delighted in the finer points of argument, and approached theological questions with fervour and according to the methods of ancient sophistry. Controversy attracted and excited them, and eloquence was to them the supreme virtue. Like the good Greeks they were, they loved words, they loved gossip, as well as mockery and invective, whether coarse or witty. But if in that they were the heirs of Aristophanes, Christianity had given a new turn to their character. The Byzantine was pious, indeed devout, and very superstitious. He believed in miracles, divinations, magic, and astrology; he lived in an atmosphere of mystical exaltation; and he was ready to sacrifice anything—even his country—for the sake of being in the right and getting the best of an argument.

Contrasts in the Byzantine Character

None of this strengthened his moral sense. The Byzantine was fond of luxury, whether in dress, jewellery, food, and furniture or in the quality of his horses and carriages. He loved pleasure, and despite the apparently strict seclusion in which women were kept, loose living was not uncommon.

He was fond of money, too. The administration, though it did great service to the State, was riddled with corruption. Appointments were bought; favour, protection, and justice sold. A man bent on advancement and a fortune relied less on his own merit than on adroit string-pulling, plots, and sedition. There were exceptions, but in the main the members of the ruling class, whether pushing or servile by nature, were unscrupulous men, capable of any baseness or treachery.

There emerges from all this a somewhat confused image of Byzantium: an image of sumptuousness, of refinement both in culture and vice, and, amid a fairyland décor, men of weak, inferior character, dominated by a handful of evil geniuses with power in their hands.

Yet in their best moments—and they were many—they were capable of courage, sensitivity, and devoted loyalty, and in high and low alike we find examples of sound and chivalrous qualities. Nevertheless there was a strangely passionate side to their temperament, whether for good or evil; and if their intellect was often of a high order, their character seldom matched it. They were unprincipled and ruthless in self-seeking, whether in the pursuit of pleasure, adventure, wealth, or power. In personal relationships they were unreliable; the wily Byzantine took too much delight in strokes of cunning and nicely calculated betrayals not to indulge in them freely. And this explains why, for all its good qualities, Byzantine society so rapidly degenerated; why, despite very real virtues, these subtle Greeks always disconcerted the blunt, straightforward Latins. Lastly, while the greatness of their

Empire bears witness to the merits and the vitality of those who built it, it explains how the term Byzantine has acquired such unpleasing associations.

A few examples will enable us to appreciate more fully the complex and baffling Byzantine character, with its blend of vileness and excellence.

Michael Psellus

Michael Psellus, who lived in the eleventh century, was one of the most remarkable men that Byzantium ever produced. He was of outstanding intellect; he was learned, talented, and versatile. He had studied everything and wrote about everything with equal interest and ability. His encyclopaedic knowledge reminds us of the men of the Renaissance, and so do his classical attainments and his passion for Plato. He was a writer of the first order, full of humour and verve; he was also a fine teacher and a fluent orator, with breadth of mind and vision. If fate had allotted him some quiet employment, far from court, where he might have dedicated himself entirely to scholarship, he would have been a man of merit and integrity. Politics were his undoing, and brought out in him the shabbiest characteristics of the Byzantine. He was self-satisfied, proud of owing his fine career to no one but himself, and of limitless ambitions. He was preoccupied with his own advancement and careful never to compromise himself; and when circumstances led him to court and a position of power, his conduct was abominable. In the course of twenty years he served under four emperors as minister, and showed himself ready at all times to stoop to any task, however mean or base. He could deliver fine speeches and write eloquent letters, but he lacked moral courage and integrity and chose to trim his sails to every wind. Intoxicated by his power at court, he could not bring himself to leave it, and became the lackey of every regime. Tossed into a world of intrigue, he intrigued with the worst. It has been said of him that he was a professional journalist "who knew that his pen was a weapon, and sold it." It is certain that he preferred charges against his old friends when so ordered; that he yielded without protest to the revolution that beggared his pupil; that having loaded Romanus Diogenes with flattery, he formed one of the party that overthrew him, and that he had the impudence to write letters of commiseration to the man he had betrayed. He was mean, cowardly, and corrupt: a perfect example of the Byzantine courtier, in whom a contemptible nature was combined with a first-class brain.

John Cantacuzenus

John Cantacuzenus of the fourteenth century offers us a similar example—on a slightly different social level—of the highest intelligence allied to thorough unscrupulousness, of a total lack of moral sense and at the same time a mystical leaning towards the monastic life and a passion for theology. He came of a great and distinguished family; he had been given an excellent upbringing by his mother, and was well instructed in all subjects; he was an astute politician and a fine soldier, a good speaker and a diplomat of ability, as well as a talented writer. He lacked nothing that could bring him success—and he stopped at nothing to gain his ends. To seize and hold the throne, he did not shrink from touching off a civil war that ravaged the Empire for five and a half years, nor from appealing to a foreign country for aid and sharing out among his Turkish allies the treasures of Christian churches. Yet he governed well and showed himself a conscientious administrator, with a sincere desire to raise up the Empire he had so grievously troubled. His nature was full of contrasts: fiery ambition and a somewhat ostentatious contempt for dignities; lack of principle and a real concern for religious matters and indeed a mystical desire for renunciation that led him to the cloister. To all this was added the impulse to paint a fine picture of himself in his memoirs, for the benefit of posterity. John Cantacuzenus, in short, was one of those passionate, mystical Byzantines who carried everything to extremes, but in whom character fell far short of intellect.

The Family of the Comneni

We find similar characteristics in the members of the great house of the Comneni. They all had certain things in common: they were of high lineage, they were intelligent, adventurous, and passionate; they threw themselves into every enterprise with tremendous ardour and were extremists, both in worldly ambition and religious fervour, in the pursuit of pleasure and the love of intrigue. Isaac, the brother of Emperor John Comnenus, an excitable, conspiratorial character, made no bones about approaching the Turks when he had quarrelled with his brother; yet this did not prevent him from founding hospitals and religious houses, or from being a patron of letters, a writer of some merit, and an excellent soldier. His son was the famous Andronicus Comnenus, a typical Byzantine, with all the characteristic qualities, good and bad. He was an accomplished horseman and an unusually intelligent and well-informed man, cheerful, witty, and full of charm. Yet he was of violent and stormy temperament, and where the attainment of some ambition, desire, or whim was concerned, nothing restrained him, neither moral considerations nor the sense of duty or gratitude. Plots, betrayals, and perjury were sport to him, and no means came amiss, whether cold steel, poison, intrigue, or force. Similarly in affairs of love, neither public opinion nor convention was allowed to stand in his way. For thirty years the Byzantine world re-echoed to his outrageous escapades. He was a true actor, capable of playing any part, however vile; yet on his accession, even his foes admitted he could be "equal to the greatest," and there was a certain dark grandeur about him, even in his debauchery and crime. Genius and tyrant as he was, he could have been the saviour of the Empire; but he used his great gifts merely to serve his passions and vices. He exemplifies the characteristic defect: an evil nature combined with intellectual power.

Naturally these examples do not typify all Byzantines. There were men of great integrity among them—men such as Nicetas

Acominatus, Eustathius of Thessalonica, and many others—and both aristocracy and middle class yielded, as we know, a rich harvest of positive qualities and sound virtues. Yet certain traits recur in the best of them: impulsiveness, enthusiasm, a high-strung, impressionable temperament, inordinate ambition, and a love of subtlety and intrigue; all of which resulted in conduct that too often smacked of unscrupulousness and double-dealing, and above all of a weakness of character in contrast to strength of intellect. We feel that the race bore the burden of too weighty a past, that their energies were quickly dissipated, and that their character lacked moral foundations.

We can well understand, then, that court life produced many men who—genius apart—bore a strange resemblance to Psellus, and that politics and public life bred numbers who, in a humbler way, were of the same stamp as Andronicus Comnenus and John Cantacuzenus. In this connection, we may recall the natures of otherwise eminent men like Photius or Michael Cerularius. Nor is it surprising that the same traits should appear among the provincials, blurred and overlaid, perhaps, but always discernible.

Cecaumenus

By way of example, I need only turn to a curious little book that is unsurpassed in its portrayal of the Byzantine character. In it, that great Thessalian lord of the eleventh century, Cecaumenus, of whom we have already heard, summarizes the lessons of experience and lays down certain rules of conduct as a guide to his children. The dominant note is one of prosaic common sense, together with a practical, cautious, sceptical, and somewhat dis-illusioned attitude to life. Cecaumenus knew the slippery ways of the court; he knew how carefully one had to pick one's way and choose one's words. He knew the humiliations, back-bitings, and disgrace that lay in wait for all who frequented the capital. "If you serve the Emperor," he says, "beware! Have constantly before you the vision of your downfall. You do not know what is being plotted behind your back."

Cecaumenus also knew something of the imperial administration and the perils of being connected with it. He knew what effect money had on the outcome of deliberations; he knew when to offer bribes and when to accept them; and in recommending as a general rule never to accept, he does so less because it was wrong than because it was dangerous. Similarly, in private life he had learnt to avoid quarrels and to keep on good terms with powerful neighbours without becoming too familiar or in any way committing himself; above all, he attached great importance to economy and good management, to the diligent amassing of wealth and the avoidance of either borrowing or lending. Lastly, he says, a cautious man will put his trust in no one; neither in his friends, of whom he can never be sure and who may prove troublesome or indiscreet, nor in women, whom he finds strangely disquieting; in particular he should never trust his wife, and the author recommends that she should be kept safely under lock and key. Cecaumenus had many other prejudices; he disliked physicians, actors, flatterers, idlers—anyone, in short, who seemed to him useless.

Altogether, the garnered wisdom of this provincial land-owner—so economical, prudent, mistrustful, cautious, and scep-tical—though certainly unattractive, is instructive, in that it re-veals so much of the Byzantine mind and character. It enables us to learn something of provincial ways—less elegant and pol-ished than those of the capital, and also less degenerate—but in which, as in Constantinople, we find the same traits: prudence and guile uncurbed by scruple; keen intellect divorced from moral principles. And when we remember that it was chiefly among the ruling class that these defects appeared, we can see how it was that despite the sturdy virtues and fine qualities that built the Empire, social demoralization was rapid and did more than any-thing to hasten its fall.

III. Elements of Dissolution. Feudal Peril and Class Warfare

1. ORIGINS OF FEUDALISM IN THE EAST

Both in the Byzantine East and the Latin West, from a quite early period, a dual process gave rise to the feudal system: namely, the disappearance of freemen and the swallowing-up of small independent estates. In troubled times, the humbler people liked to seek the protection of some wealthy, influential neighbour; they begged his "patronage" (*patrocinium*), they "commended themselves to him," as the phrase went; and in exchange for his protection they renounced their freedom and became the servants and vassals of their master, often acknowledging his right of ownership to their land. At the same time, big landowners used their power to round off their domains at the expense of the small-holder. Either by intimidation or by force, they took possession of their poorer neighbours' land by compelling them to sell at a low price, or by annexation. Thus, while close bonds of dependence were being forged between man and man, huge estates were growing up for the enrichment of all-powerful lords.

This dual process in the East can be seen during the last period of the Roman Empire, and even more in the days of Justinian. In the imperial *Novels* of the sixth century there is continual mention of great landowners, these powerful lords, true tyrants, whose assaults upon persons and property gravely disturbed the peace of the realm, especially in the Asiatic provinces. These overlords, with their vast domains and numberless dependents, maintained troops of men-at-arms at their own charge. Ruthlessly and without fear, they ravaged the countryside, harried and oppressed the people, and seized what lands they chose, including those belonging to the Church and even to the Emperor himself; they defied law, they defied the helpless governors, they wrought perpetual havoc through the provinces and were an ever-present danger to the State. The countryside was laid waste by these raids on goods and property, of which local administrators often took their share; the inhabitants fled, agriculture ceased, and revenues dwindled; while on their estates, the barons openly resisted the authority of the Crown.

Justinian strove in vain to remedy the evil. He could do nothing. In vain his successors, the Isaurians, by their great work of reorganization, tried to prevent thefts of land and forbid patronage, as their Rural Code shows. The abuses continued, the power of the landed aristocracy increased, and feudalism became more widely established. In the ninth century, the situation came to a head. A real social problem had arisen between two classes, the powerful and the poor, and constituted so grave a danger to the State that tenth-century emperors were compelled to put forth their utmost efforts to prevent the depredations of the barons.

Eastern Feudalism in the Tenth Century

Contemporary documents show us what this feudal nobility was. It was made up, according to one text, of "those whom God had appointed to rule; of those who in riches and renown excelled the common run of men." Another passage tells us that it comprised "those who had been appointed to a high command and honoured by civil and military distinctions." Thus the power of the landed aristocracy was enhanced by the dignity of State appointments, while salaries and gifts added to the wealth they derived from their estates. It was mostly from the great feudal families that the Emperor chose his officials and generals, and their wealth and power accumulated from generation to generation. They were insubordinate subjects; they dictated to the gov-

ernment and laid down the law to the Emperor, and when their
sovereign chose to disregard their advice, they stirred up formidable insurrections.

All these great men—civilians and soldiers, laymen and ecclesiastics alike—flouted the law and strove by every means in their
power to enlarge their estates at the expense of the poor. "They
regard the poor as their prey; they fret when they cannot seize
their goods." They are savage in despoiling them; they swoop
upon them "like a plague." They "tyrannize over the inhabitants,"
subjecting them to "the heavy yoke of physical and mental op-
pression." Such are the words of the imperial *Novels* of the tenth
century; and they describe the barons as eager "to devour the
goods of the poor," buying their lands at a beggarly price, exacting them as a gift or bequest, or annexing them with the promise
of a good rent which they have no intention of paying; and they
exploit their official position to enlarge their domains and to extort
gifts from the sovereign. "Hence all is thrown into confusion,"
says a contemporary document, "hence countless injustices, hence
the bitter and enduring misery of the poor and their long groan-
ing, whose echo awakens the Lord." Hence, also, a yet graver
danger to the State. "To all those who can understand," runs the
forcible phrase of a tenth-century law, "the power of these lords
will bring irreparable disaster to the realm."

The point is clearly explained in another text. The disappearance of the free peasant meant the disappearance of the taxable
property so indispensable to the exchequer. Were all the military
fiefs, the basis of recruitment, to be annexed, the army must lack
soldiers: "everything collapses when numbers fail." More than
that: the barons were a national danger. Not only did they possess
vast estates, where they ensconced themselves in impregnable
castles; not only were they surrounded by a horde of serfs and
vassals who knew their lineage, respected their wealth and their
prowess, and appreciated their liberality and the value of their
protection. Owing to the system of regional recruitment, they held
the army itself in their hands. Lastly, they were bound together
by common interests as well as by intermarriage, and their alliance was daily strengthened and renewed by shared adventure.

The Macedonian Emperors were fully alive to this peril, and
struggled manfully with the great families of Phocas, Maleinus,

and others, who from generation to generation amassed wealth and clung to vast possessions that had been wrongfully acquired. "Shall we not oppose these people's enterprises?" wrote Basil II. "Are we to leave in their hands the possessions of those whom they have basely robbed and despoiled?" Such was not the emperors' will.

2. CENTRAL POWER AND FEUDAL ARISTOCRACY

Imperial Policy

From the day of his accession, Basil I took up the fight. Henceforth "the poor should cease to be oppressed by the rich"; he intended to put an end to the depredations of "those greedy hands, ever clutching at the goods of others." He strove to reestablish the small estates and, in the words of a contemporary historian, "restore life to the bodies of the poor, so lamentably weakened before his coming." All through the tenth century his successors, Romanus Lecapenus, Constantine VII, Nicephorus Phocas, and Basil II, carried on his work, forbidding powerful men to acquire land from the poor on any pretext whatever; annulling the contracts of illegal sales and compelling the buyer to make restitution; abolishing the prescription which, after a period of forty years, confirmed the fraudulent purchaser's title to property; forbidding patronage and upholding the inalienable rights of the State in the face of all usurpers.

It is necessary to read the imperial *Novels* to appreciate the intense bitterness of the struggle and the withering strictures on those who, "instead of showing pity and humanity" to the poor, speculated in distress so as to "buy the property of the wretched cheaply, and who founded their fortunes on the misery of the destitute." There is hatred and indignation in the words of Tzimisces as he sees the State deprived of its finest domains, and the exertions of the imperial army serving the turn of a few individuals. The same bitterness flows from the pen of Basil II, who in the name of the public good and the security of the realm, inveighed against the "terrible evil of cupidity."

Another proof of the violence of the struggle, and of its necessity, is found in the great feudal revolts of the second half of the tenth century: the Asiatic rebellion that so troubled the reign of Tzimisces and the minority of Basil II, and in which some of the great figures of this Byzantine aristocracy are thrown into strong and colourful relief.

The Great Feudal Insurrections of the Tenth Century

As has already been described, in 971 the whole of feudal Anatolia rallied round Bardas Phocas. The insurrection of Bardas Skleros some years later was no less typical. Like Phocas, whom he fought and conquered, Bardas Skleros had the soul of a conspirator. He had won glory and distinction in the past, he was enormously rich and adored by his men; and when in 976 he fell into unmerited disgrace, he rose in rebellion. As in the case of Phocas, Asia Minor supplied him with everything he needed. He had once held command in the Euphrates region, and won fame there by his feats of arms. "The whole army loved him," says a chronicler. He had only to appear in camp, therefore, for men to flock to his standard. Officers and soldiers alike agreed to proclaim him Emperor. To obtain the necessary funds he seized the tax money from the imperial collectors and levied large sums from the landowners. But many people with faith in his star voluntarily contributed their private fortunes, in the hope of hundredfold reward. His renown brought him allies from every quarter: Arab emirs from Amida and Maiphergat sent him money and horsemen, and so did the petty princes of Armenia. Adventurers, malcontents, all who hoped to gain by revolution rallied round the pretender. Within a few weeks Skleros was the master of all Asia, and as he marched forward in triumph, the leaders of the imperial army—who had orders to arrest him, but who were

secretly in sympathy with the cause of a feudal baron like themselves—left their own forces to swell his. The government, remem-
bering how it had once disorganized the troops of Phocas, tried
in vain to undermine the loyalty of Skleros' friends by promises
of money, titles, and honours. These offers were regarded as signs
of weakness, and merely added to the prestige of the usurper.
Soon Skleros captured Nicaea and marched on Constantinople,
which was also threatened by his fleet.

For three whole years this insurrection troubled the realm. To
crush it, the Crown had to appeal to the vanquished Bardas
Phocas, and oppose one baron with another, who alone, by the
prestige of his name and family, was able to reverse the fortunes
of Asia. On March 24, 979, the adversaries met in a dramatic
engagement. The battle was fought on the plain of Pankalia, and
just as the imperial forces were wavering, Phocas sprang forward
and challenged Skleros to single combat. The fighting ceased, so
"beautiful and moving was the encounter of these two men, who
matched one another in daring and resolution." With a stroke of
his sword Skleros sliced the ear from Phocas' charger; but Phocas
brought down his mighty iron club on Skleros' head, dashing
both man and mount to the ground with the force of the blow.
While Phocas set spurs to his horse and rallied his men, Skleros'
squires lifted their unconscious master and carried him to a
nearby fountain; but in the confusion his horse bolted across the
battlefield; his men recognized it, and seeing it covered with
blood they believed their leader dead. They scattered, and the
rebellion was crushed. Skleros was forced to seek refuge among
the Arabs and was interned for seven years in Baghdad.

Eight years later the two adversaries met again, this time as
allies against the Emperor. In 987 the army leaders were angry
because Basil II refused to be guided by them, and at Charsian,
on the domains of a great Asiatic lord, the generals proclaimed
an emperor of their own choice: Bardas Phocas. All Asia took his
part. He rallied Cappadocia without difficulty, for his family
came from there, and also the most influential members of the
Anatolian aristocracy. Skleros himself, who had escaped from
Baghdad, joined his onetime rival, and they agreed to divide the
Empire between them. Constantinople was soon blockaded by sea
and land. In this desperate crisis all Basil II's great energy was

needed to save the Crown. The decisive battle was fought in 989 on the plain of Abydos. Again, as at Pankalia, the fiery Phocas challenged the Emperor to single combat, "preferring a glorious death to the shame of defeat." He charged at a mad gallop, "like clouds swept by the storm," towards the imperial forces; then suddenly he was seen to swerve aside and urge his horse on to some high ground. There he fell to the earth, the victim of a stroke. The rebellion was at an end.

But Skleros remained. Having been thrust aside and imprisoned by Phocas, he came once more upon the scene and for months carried on a stubborn guerrilla war, intercepting convoys, capturing vessels, destroying all traffic in Anatolia, and starving Constantinople; and not one of his soldiers so much as thought of disloyalty. "There were never any deserters," wrote Psellus, "for he well knew how to attach them to himself by his rough kindness and hold them by largesse, and how to keep them in good humour, living and eating with them and drinking from the same glass, knowing each man by name and never speaking to them but with friendliness."

To put an end to the struggle, Basil II adopted a lenient policy. He offered Skleros a pardon and the sonorous title of *Curopalates,* as well as restitution of property and honours for him and his allies. The meeting of Emperor and baron was dramatic. The rebel, old, very fat, crippled, and nearly blind, hobbled painfully to the imperial tent; and Basil exulted: "Behold the man I have so dreaded! The man who made us all tremble! He comes to me as a suppliant, and has one to lead him by the hand." Nevertheless, he received the defeated man cordially, and a long conversation ensued, during which Skleros explained the causes of the rebellion. Basil listened with deference and asked his advice. And here, according to Psellus, is what Skleros replied: "He counselled him never to tolerate powerful officials or to allow military leaders to acquire excessive wealth, but to lay heavy burdens and exactions on them, thus obliging them to devote all their time to private affairs and preventing them from becoming powerful or dangerous." Basil was not to forget this advice. The *Novel* of 996 is inspired by long and bitter memories of revolt, and is the most savage of all the edicts issued by the imperial government against feudal abuses. It was the Crown's revenge on the Anatolian rebels. The greed of the great lords now seemed to have been curbed forever; for not only were future acquisitions forbidden, but a strict enquiry was made into all those of the past. Titles to property were closely scrutinized and wrongs redressed, including concessions unlawfully made in the Emperor's name. The central power seemed to have triumphed.

3. THE TRIUMPH OF THE FEUDAL SYSTEM OVER THE CENTRAL POWER. ELEVENTH CENTURY

The victory was to be of short duration.

The utmost efforts of even so energetic a ruler as Basil II were needed to tame these powerful lords, who were undaunted by misfortune and were loyally supported in their struggle against the Crown. In the years that followed he taxed them unmercifully, and when travelling through the Empire he ruthlessly chastised those who seemed to him too powerful and rich, especially Eustathius Maleinus, on whose territory Bardas Phocas had been proclaimed Emperor in 987, and whose too lavish hospitality disturbed and offended his sovereign. The Emperor had already confiscated the enormous fortune of *Paracoemomenus* Basil, that formidable minister, a fortune amassed at the expense of the State and of private individuals. But the feudal aristocracy was too strong to be thus subdued, as became evident after the Emperor's death, when sovereign power passed to weaker hands.

Yet the same rigorous policy was maintained and even intensified. Regional recruitment was discontinued in order to reduce the barons' authority over their troops, a special tax was substituted for military service, and the national forces were replaced by mercenaries, in the hope that these would prove more loyal. In a vain effort to prevent military *pronunciamentos,* the army was disorganized, funds depleted, generals impoverished and kept under surveillance, and a firm policy of peace pursued. To lessen the influence of the aristocracy, appointments equalling theirs in importance were allotted to civil servants and men about the court. Officials were chosen from among civilians, and the Senate was democratized; it was impressed upon all that the time had come, in the words of a contemporary historian, for soldiers "to lay aside their arms and become lawyers or jurists."

It was all in vain. Generals were indignant; discontent among the troops increased, and with it their jealousy of the civil power. Nothing came of these measures but fresh disturbances.

In 1057 the feudal and military aristocracy took its revenge. On Easter Day the generals, led by Isaac Comnenus and Cecaumenus Catacalon, sought to gain the ear of Michael VI. The Emperor replied by insulting Cecaumenus and accusing him of being concerned solely with his own enrichment, and by snubbing the other leaders who tried to defend him. Their response was what one might expect: they plotted insurrection. Soon, at their call, the Army of Asia arose to put an end to civil rule, and the proclamation of Isaac Comnenus as Emperor set the seal upon the victory of the military and feudal forces. It is true that Isaac's tenure was brief. But later, under the rule of his weak successors, the triumphs of Turks and Normans and the appalling anarchy prevailing in the Empire give striking proof of the services rendered to the realm by these feudal lords, these army commanders and architects of victory. It was to them that the nation appealed in the chaos of 1081, and it was they who saved it. The accession of Alexius Comnenus, like that of the Capets in France, marked the triumph of feudal aristocracy: the victory of soldiers over civilians, of province over capital. More important still, it proved that despite the efforts of the Crown, feudalism remained all-powerful in the realm.

Elements of Dissolution. Feudal Peril, Class Warfare

4. EASTERN FEUDALISM OF THE THIRTEENTH AND FOURTEENTH CENTURIES

In the tenth century, Western and Byzantine forms of feudalism differed greatly, and they continued to do so. In the East there was never the strict hierarchy that made European feudal society a connected chain of lords and vassals. Yet the existence of this powerful provincial aristocracy had results similar to those in the mediaeval states of the West, and whenever the central power was weak it became a source of unrest and disintegration.

This is shown by the anarchy that followed the end of the Comnenian dynasty—the succession of the Angeli was aristocracy's revenge on the Crown—and in the dislocation of the Empire resulting from the Fourth Crusade. Aristocracy everywhere was raising its head. By the end of the twelfth century, Trebizond was establishing itself under the noble house of Gabras as an independent feudal principality. At the beginning of the thirteenth century, Leo Sgaurus ruled Nauplia, Argus, Corinth, and for a time even Athens, as a true overlord. Everywhere we find huge estates whose owners lived like princes, supported by their own army and backed by undisputed territorial authority. So striking was the analogy that it deeply impressed the Latins, who conquered the Byzantine Empire in the thirteenth century. "French barons found in the Morea a system similar to the one they had left. At the bottom of the ladder were the peasants and serfs, to whom they quite naturally gave the name of villeins, while at the top were the nobles and military leaders, landowners and owners of fiefs, whom equally naturally they called lords (*gentilshommes*)." [1] They got on well with these *archons;* they allowed them to keep their privileges and made room for them in the ranks of the Latin nobility. Men such as Villehardouin and La Roche were good friends with the Melisseni, Cantacuzeni, and other Greek lords of the Morea; they had the same ideas and customs, and together formed a single caste.

Right up to the last days of the Empire this feudal aristocracy survived and was an intermittent source of trouble. The fourteenth century was full of class struggles between aristocracy and a rising democracy, which could not forgive the tyranny it had so long endured. Cantacuzenus, in a curious passage of his memoirs, describes the wind of revolution blowing through the Empire, and all the cities, following the example of Adrianople, rising against the δυνατοί and seething with unrest, pillage, and murder. Of these passionate struggles, the most notable and dramatic was that known as the revolution of the Zealots in Thessalonica, which for seven years filled the town with uproar and bloodshed. Here again, though in a different way, the landed aristocracy proved itself an element of dissolution in the realm. That the feudal system could wield such power under a seemingly absolute monarchy is not the least curious feature of Byzantine history.

[1] Rambaud, *op. cit.*, 259.

IV. Elements of Dissolution. The Religious Peril

1. THE CHURCH'S PLACE IN BYZANTINE SOCIETY

The Patriarchate

In a society where religion played so great a part, the Church naturally wielded considerable power. The Patriarch of Constantinople, its head, was a very great figure; in the tenth century his ecclesiastical jurisdiction comprised no fewer than 57 metropolises, 49 archiepiscopal sees, and 514 bishoprics. He had risen steadily above the other eastern patriarchs, and the Council of Chalcedon had made him the equal of the Roman pontiff; in the sixth century, despite papal protest, he took the title of Oecumenical Patriarch, and when the Arab Conquest of the seventh century separated the patriarchates of Alexandria, Jerusalem, and Antioch from the Empire, he became the sole head of the Byzantine Church, the true Pope of the East. His position in the State was no less important. It was he who consecrated the Emperor and administered the oath by which the new sovereign undertook to defend Orthodoxy and respect ecclesiastical privileges. He was very rich, and he controlled the vast resources of the Church which, in times of emergency, formed a reserve fund for the State. His power derived as much from his authority over the innumerable monks of Constantinople as from his influence on the laity, and he was able to render great services to the government. For the same reasons he was also in a position to defy the Emperor, either by threatening him with the interdict and excommunication, and so imposing his will in the name of God, or by resorting to the more mundane methods of fomenting or suppressing riots, and of revolution, by which emperors could be made or broken.

"The Patriarch," says Montesquieu, "was always, albeit indirectly, the arbiter of public affairs." Emperor, head of the State, dealt with Patriarch, head of the Church, as one great power with another; and it was a matter of no little concern to the sovereign to be able to trust his Patriarch.

Monasticism

The regular Church played no less a part in Byzantine life than the secular. From early times the monastic life was held in honour. The people venerated the stern-faced, black-habited monks who had renounced the world to become "citizens of heaven." The cloister held great attractions for all classes of society. Some entered it devoutly, feeling the need for humility and penitence and because they were discouraged and weary of the world. Others sought there a refuge from disgrace, an escape from the crushing burden of public life, or a way of attaining high ecclesiastical rank. Even the seemingly indifferent cherished the ideal of dying in the venerated habit and so ensuring their eternal salvation. All were eager to found religious houses and endow them lavishly; and the law favoured such works, and the resulting increase in monastic wealth.

Constantinople was full of monasteries. In Egypt, Syria, Palestine, Mesopotamia, and even the remote Sinai Peninsula, monasteries sprang up and flourished during the fifth and sixth centuries. Later, Olympus in Bithynia, the mountainous region of Latros near Miletus, the solitudes of Cappadocia, and above all, from the tenth century onwards, Mount Athos, became centres of large religious communities, and vast tracts of land came into the possession of the monks.

Such wealth was a danger to the State, both politically and socially. Not only did the development of monasticism deprive agriculture of its labour, but monastic property was largely exempt from taxation. Also, neither monks nor their tenants were

Elements of Dissolution. The Religious Peril

liable to military service, and their wealth gave them enormous power. Moreover, the monks had great influence on the people, owing to the miraculous and prophetic powers attributed to them, and to the ancient relics and holy icons preserved in their monasteries. For all these reasons, and because, to the annoyance of the secular clergy, they were active as spiritual directors; because, also, many charitable works were closely associated with the monasteries, monks were extremely popular. This fact, together with their intolerance, fanaticism, and independent spirit, made them very troublesome to the State; and for the Emperor they were, like the Patriarch, a factor to be reckoned with. Byzantine history is full of their demonstrations and violent interventions in political and religious affairs; and more than once the State found itself compelled to yield to their demands.

Church and State in Byzantium

The nature of the relationship between Church and State tended, it might seem, to lessen these dangers. We know the scope of the Emperor's authority in matters of religion; we know how, in exchange for his protection, he claimed supreme leadership in the Church and reserved the right to dictate discipline and dogma and to exact its obedience to his will. We know, too, how savagely the Byzantine State could crush opposition. To ensure the appointment of a loyal patriarch, the Emperor indicated to the electors the candidate of whom he approved, "and the metropolitans," says one text, "bow to the Emperor's choice, as is fitting." Similarly, if the Patriarch failed to please him, the sovereign either compelled him to abdicate or instructed a synod to depose him. The Emperor presided at ecclesiastical councils, at the Patriarch's side; he guided debates, formulated articles of faith, and argued with bishops and also with heretics, for whom he reserved the ultimate argument of the stake. Lastly, he confirmed and implemented the canons adopted in council, and charged those who opposed him, not only with the crime of *lèse-majesté*, but with being enemies of the faith and of God. High rank was no safeguard; dismissal, imprisonment, exile, and corporal punishment were the customary means of dealing with ecclesiastics; not even Popes escaped his violence and tyranny.

The Eastern Church submitted on the whole patiently to imperial intervention. "Nothing must be done in the Church that is contrary to the will and commands of the Emperor," said one sixth-century patriarch. The bishops about the court—suave, pliant men, accessible to discreet marks of favour and adroit bar-

Courtesy of The Byzantine Institute, Inc.

Mosaic panel, depicting the Virgin and Child flanked by the Emperor John II Comnenus and his wife, the Empress Irene (St. Sophia).

gaining—protested as a rule as little as their superior. Nevertheless, certain undercurrents of opposition persisted (mostly among the monks, who were more intransigent and perhaps surer of their power) and often broke out in open revolt. The Eastern Church, like that of the West, tried at least once to throw off the burden of State control, though with small success; and the wealth and the fanaticism of the monks as well as the inordinate ambitions of the patriarchs were a recurrent source of disturbance in the Empire.

Elements of Dissolution. The Religious Peril

2. MONASTICISM AND THE EMPIRE

The Iconoclastic Controversy and the Church's Struggle for Freedom

At the beginning of the eighth century, the Iconoclast Emperors undertook their great work of religious and social reform, known to us as the Iconoclastic Controversy, a strangely inadequate term. In this, the Emperors' fiercest adversaries were the monks, whose influence was directly threatened; for in proscribing icons, the Isaurian Emperors were attacking the excessive wealth and power of monasticism, icons being among the monks' most effective instruments. The struggle rocked the Empire for more than a century. By order of the Emperor, monasteries were closed, secularized, and turned into barracks or given to laymen of high rank. Monastic property was confiscated, religious communities dissolved, and monks arrested, imprisoned, exiled, beaten with rods, and sometimes condemned to death. More often, they were exposed to the mockery of the mob, as on that day in 765 when a grotesque procession of monks, each holding a nun by the hand, was driven through the Hippodrome amid taunts and jeers; or as at the assembly at Ephesus, when all the religious of the province had to make their choice on the spot between marriage and torture. It seemed, as a contemporary said, as if "the government's intention was to exterminate the monastic order altogether."

The monks responded to these ruthless measures by equal violence. Not only did they take the legitimate course of defending Orthodoxy, and pride themselves on "suffering for Justice and Truth," but in the heat of the struggle and the excitement of the triumph permitted them by Empress Irene's government, the monks and their devout and fanatical supporters went too far: they turned a blind eye to any faults or crimes committed by the Orthodox, and shunned the conciliatory gestures made by emperor-reformers or opportunist patriarchs. They acclaimed the death of Emperor Nicephorus with joy, when he was slain in defending the Empire against the Bulgarian invasion; they were jubilant at the fall of "the new Ahab" who had persecuted the faithful. They sought support from Rome against the Crown, bowing before the Pope as their "Apostolic Head," and were ready to acknowledge Roman supremacy and the right of the Roman Church to pronounce final judgment in all ecclesiastical difficulties, provided this would enable them to liberate the Eastern Church from imperial dictatorship. This was the last and most interesting form taken by monastic opposition—this stupendous effort to secure the Church's independence of lay authority and set the relationship between Church and State on new foundations.

Already in the eighth century Gregory II and John of Damascus, and before them the seventh-century Fathers, disputed the Emperor's right to interfere in Church matters. Ninth-century monks were even more insistent. Theodore of Studium wrote to Leo V, "Ecclesiastical matters are the province of priests and doctors; to the Emperor belongs the administration of external affairs. The former alone have the right to make decisions touching faith and dogma; your duty is to obey them, and not to usurp their place." In words of even greater import, since they contravened the famous principle of *princeps legibus solutus est,* the same man wrote, "Unless the Emperor be subject to the law, there are but two possible hypotheses: either he is God, for divinity alone transcends law; or nothing remains but anarchy and revolution."

These were entirely new ideas. The monks of the monastery of St. John of Studium defended them with tireless energy. Neither persecution nor exile could induce them to "hold their tongues captive and be silent as to the truth." For twenty years they maintained obdurately that, although kings "have power to judge human and temporal affairs," yet in questions of "divine dogma," "their part is to give support and approval to what has been decreed" by the priests. "They have been given no power over divine doctrines; if they exert it, it will not endure." By such resolute faith and high moral purpose, the Studites contributed in no small measure to the final triumph of the pro-icon party. But although in its long struggle with the State, the Church won the battle of the images, it was not able to secure its liberty and free itself from the ancient tradition of monarchy based on religion. The end of the Iconoclastic Controversy left the Church more dependent on the Crown than ever, and the only result of this barren conflict carried on by the monks had been a long period of unrest.

Development of Monastic Estates

Monasticism disturbed the Empire in other ways, too. The monks were acquisitive, and because of the vast tracts of land they came to possess, they joined the ranks of the "powerful men" whom tenth-century emperors regarded as being so formidable a danger to the health of the social order. Nicephorus Phocas, though a most pious ruler and a founder of religious houses, and in no way to be suspected of hostility to the monastic order, was extremely forthright in his description of the monkish practices of his day: "The monks possess none of the evangelical virtues; they think of nothing save the acquisition of land, the erecting of huge buildings and the purchase of vast numbers of horses, cattle, camels, and every kind of livestock. All their energies are devoted to their own enrichment, so that their life in no way differs from that of people living in the world." "What a contrast there is between this frivolous existence and the lives of the holy religious who in past centuries dwelt in Egypt, Palestine, and Alexandria, those whose almost immaterialized existence was more that of angels than of men."

The Emperor decreed that thenceforth monks should live more remote from the world, and to enforce this he adopted drastic measures. There were to be no new foundations, and no further grants were to be made to those that existed; and no property whatever was to be acquired at the expense of the poor. Nicephorus, good soldier and administrator as he was, well knew how much the monasteries cost the treasury and the army, and he did not hesitate to strike hard.

Religious feudalism was as powerful and predatory as the lay kind, and could be dealt with no more successfully. The government gave way before the displeasure of the Church and abrogated the law. This was in 988, twenty-four years after the edict of Nicephorus. The Empire was passing through a great crisis: Phocas had risen in revolt and was at the gates of Constantinople; the help of the Church was needed, and Basil II did not hesitate. "Our Majesty," runs the preamble to his edict, "has heard it stated by many venerable religious who have given proof of their piety and virtue, and also by other worthy persons, that the edicts of our predecessor, the Lord Nicephorus, relating to holy monasteries and pious foundations have been the origin and cause of the evils from which the Empire is now suffering, for those laws were an offence not only against these most pious monasteries, but against God Himself. Our own experience has convinced us of the truth of these allegations, for since those laws came into force we have not known a moment's happiness. Therefore, by this present chrysobull, signed by our own hand, we declare that those regulations are abrogated, and we command that they be no longer given the force of law."

This was a severe check to imperial authority; it demonstrates the power of the monastic party and the pressure it could bring to bear on the government.

Decay of Monastic Institutions

Up to the last days of the Byzantine Empire, monasticism was a source of disturbance. The works of the period of the Comneni show to what a state of moral decay and corruption the monastic institutions had fallen since the end of the eleventh century. The monks were more covetous than ever of money and estates, and the *hegumens* were more concerned to expound the principles of efficient husbandry than to save souls. Worldly life invaded the monasteries; seclusion, communal life, discipline—all had gone. Like the great barons, abbots rode, hunted, and lavishly entertained, and the country was full of vagabond monks who infested the roads, ravaged the countryside, and robbed wayfarers. Of intellectual culture, no trace remained. "The monastery," it was said, "has no need of letters"; and the libraries were sold. So long as a man wore a somewhat ragged habit and had a shaven head, a long, unkempt beard, and bare, dirty feet, so long as he walked slowly with his eyes downcast, his edifying appearance was enough to make him a good monk. It was in vain that Christodulus of Patmos at the end of the eleventh century and Eustathius of Thessalonica at the end of the twelfth tried to introduce necessary reforms. Vainly, too, Manuel Comnenus brought back into force the *Novel* of Nicephorus and, as Christodulus had done in Patmos, founded a model monastery on the Bosphorus. "Perceiving that the possession of land and preoccupation with business caused the monks to lose their serenity of soul and forget their duty to God," says Nicetas, the Emperor included no land in his endowment, but merely allowed them the money necessary to maintain the community. He further commanded that religious foundations should be situated far from the world, in mountains and deserts, and that the monks should avoid Constantinople "as Ulysses resisted the song of the sirens." It was all in vain. When they were not distressing pious souls by their demoralized behaviour, they disturbed them by profitless disputes. The fourteenth-century Hesychast quarrel, born of the mystical dreams of the monks of Athos, troubled the Byzantine world for nearly fifteen years. It was a strange affair, a passionate conflict between Latin Scholasticism and Oriental mysticism; and its repercussions on the political struggles of the day show how closely Church matters were bound up with affairs of State, and how much disturbance could be caused by the monastic party.

Byzantium: Greatness and Decline

3. THE PATRIARCHATE AND THE EMPIRE

The secular Church was equally troublesome.

Like the abbots of the monasteries, the bishops were among the "powerful men" who robbed the poor, and a tenth-century emperor rebuked them severely for their maladministration of Church revenues, "intended for the poor," he said, "and benefiting only the clergy." The political danger was worse than the social one, however. The patriarchal throne of Constantinople was often occupied by exceedingly ambitious men who, for all their apparent dependence on imperial authority, kindled war between Church and State and, not content with their omnipotence in the Church, aspired to play an important rôle in politics, either as prime ministers or revolutionary agitators.

It was bad enough when the head of the Church forbade the Emperor to enter St. Sophia because of some question of ecclesiastical discipline, as did Nicholas to Leo VI, and Polyeuctes to Nicephorus Phocas; or when he laid a penance upon his sovereign, as did Cosmas on Alexius Comnenus; or when he forced him, on pain of excommunication, to withdraw measures contrary to ecclesiastical privilege, as did Polyeuctes with John Tzimisces. More serious still, and more significant, was the sight of a patriarch treating the Crown with disdain and questioning the commands of the *Basileus*. Nicholas wrote: "If the Emperor, inspired by the devil, should order something contrary to the law of God, no obedience is due to him; an impious command from an impious man must be held to be null and void." Michael Cerularius declared: "Between Patriarchate and Empire there is little or no difference; and as regards the honours due to them, the Patriarchate has a superior claim."

If we bear in mind how proud these prelates were of their power, and how vast was the wealth that they could place at the service of the State, as Sergius did for Heraclius; if we remember that they often conceived themselves to be potential statesmen, we can well understand how they dared oppose the Emperor, especially when the Emperor was weak.

Elements of Dissolution. The Religious Peril

Michael Cerularius

The conflict that set the Patriarch Nicholas [1] at odds with Emperor Leo VI at the beginning of the tenth century will suffice to show the part that the head of the Eastern Church could play in the State, and the ambitions that might spur him on. The story of Michael Cerularius in the eleventh century is perhaps even more typical. He, too, having attained the patriarchate, aimed higher; he ensconced himself, as Psellus puts it, "as in a fortress," so as to seize an all-powerful position in the State. Proud, haughty, utterly self-assured, "seeming in his demeanour like a god pacing across the heavens," intelligent, too, and with wide interests, he was rigid and uncompromising, but courageous, tenacious of purpose, and implacable in hatred. Though he made bitter enemies, he had loyal and devoted friends, and his strong personality impressed itself deeply on the people of the capital. We may imagine how much such a man could accomplish in the reign of a weak emperor. Indeed, in the desire for self-aggrandisement he fomented the schism with Rome in 1054 and compelled the Emperor to accept it, under threat of rebellion. Intoxicated by this victory, he was for five years the supreme authority in public affairs. It was he who in 1056 set Michael VI on the throne and consolidated his power, and he who a year later forced the same Emperor to abdicate and brought to a successful conclusion the revolution that carried Isaac Comnenus to the throne. Full of the "love of power and the desire for universal command," and claiming as Psellus says "to move heaven and Olympus with his frown," Cerularius meant to dominate the new master—the Emperor he had made—as he had dominated his predecessor. He has been accused of wishing to "combine royalty with priesthood," of "issuing imperial decrees," and of coveting the supreme power. However this may be, he made bold to wear purple sandals, the traditional insignia of supreme authority, "declaring it to be a priestly privilege." Battle was joined between Patriarchate and Empire. Cerularius, aware that by the breach with Rome he had won the people's support, threatened, demanded, and resorted to violence. "He foretold the Emperor's fall in commonplace, vul-

[1] See Charles Diehl, *Figures byzantines*, 1st ser. (Paris, 1906), ch. VIII: "Les quatre mariages de l'empereur Léon le Sage."

gar language, saying, 'I raised you up, you imbecile; but I'll break you.'" This was too much. Isaac Comnenus had him arrested, imprisoned, and sent to Imbros, and took steps to depose him. There was no time. Exhausted by his sufferings, Cerularius died before he could confront his judges; but he died unyielding. The whole Empire venerated him as saint and martyr; and Psellus, who had accused him so abusively in life but who never boggled at a recantation, delivered his funeral oration in fine and solemn style.

These examples show us how much trouble the Patriarch of Constantinople could cause in the State, and how boldly he could outface the Emperor. It would be easy to find other instances of ambitious prelates who, in the phrase of a fourteenth-century historian, "had nothing about them of the priest save the pastoral staff and the habit." And though we must note that in the end the Crown always won, it is no less true that ambitious princes of the Church who attained the See of Constantinople caused continual trouble by their taste for politics, their intrigues and plots, and the rebellions they fomented and supported.

It is true that the patriarchal throne was occupied at other times by a very different order of men: ascetics and saints; or prudent politicians, drawn generally from the ranks of the imperial administration and raised abruptly from a lay appointment to the summit of the ecclesiastical hierarchy; or again, amenable men on whom the Emperor could rely. But antagonism between priesthood and Empire prevailed most frequently, and the Crown had often to reckon with bishops who, whatever their private virtues, were politicians of marked ability, capable of outfacing both Emperor and Pope.

The Patriarchate and the Papacy

We shall see later how Photius in the ninth century and Cerularius in the eleventh took advantage of the long-standing hostility between the Greek Church and Rome to unleash schism and break with the West, and how much this breach cost the Empire. But it should be noted at this point how the ambitions and encroachments of the Patriarchs contributed to the weakening of the monarchy. The struggle between Church and State was never as bitter in Byzantium as it was in the West, and on the whole the State maintained its authority over the Church in the manner laid down by Constantine and Justinian. Nevertheless the Empire was often conscious of its own weakness in the face of monastic and patriarchal danger, and despite vigorous resistance it was sometimes defeated. Thus religious unrest was not the least of the causes of the Empire's decline.

V. Byzantine Imperialism

At every period of their history, the Byzantines considered themselves the heirs of Rome and never gave up the idea of restoring the ancient Roman Empire. From Justinian to the Comneni, the *basileis* regarded both the barbarian kings, who carved out kingdoms for themselves from the remnants of the Roman Empire, and the successors of Charlemagne, who ruled over the reconstructed Western Empire, as usurpers. They were inferiors, provisionally entitled to hold certain portions of Byzantine territory either by powers delegated by the *Basileus* or by lawless annexation. To all of them, even the greatest, Byzantine sovereigns refused the title of Emperor, and called them Kings (ῥῆγες), reserving the imperial status for themselves alone. They dreamed continually of reconquering these territories and of making Rome their second capital; and more than once they attempted to make the dream come true. Such vast ambitions were out of all proportion to the national resources, and their most marked effect was to involve the Empire in tremendous conflicts, and so weaken it.

Byzantine Imperialism

1. BYZANTINE IMPERIALISM IN THE WEST

Justinian's Policy

It was a principle of the Byzantine Chancellery never to admit the loss of any territory. The list of its domains included provinces that had either been lost altogether or were represented by a few towns at most. The *basileis* never looked upon these regions as permanently lost, and proudly maintained their historic right to them. When, in the second half of the fifth century, the Roman Empire collapsed, Byzantium refused to regard the barbarian kings installed in Africa, Italy, and Gaul as anything but the Emperor's representatives: they were his deputies and servants. It was the same in Justinian's day. Imperial rights were deemed valid in the barbarian kingdoms of the West, and when the Emperor judged the time ripe to reclaim them, it was a matter not of conquest, but of restitution. His right, or rather his duty, was to re-absorb into his realm all that had been conquered in the past by the ancient Romans and lost by the negligence of their rulers. Not one of his contemporaries could have conceived of his renouncing this obligation save by outright abdication. "It is the natural desire of a noble-minded emperor," wrote Procopius, "to enlarge the Empire and render it more glorious."

Strangely enough, the barbarians themselves accepted the principle. Eager to win the titles and insignia of Roman dignity and proud to govern their people as the Emperor's lieutenants, they bowed before the "master," received his commands and rebukes with humility, appealed to him as supreme judge and, dazzled by the prestige of the Roman tradition, almost understood and acknowledged the legitimacy of the imperial claims. Theodoric's successors, like those of Genseric, readily consented to be the tributaries and vassals of the Emperor; kings of the Burgundians and Franks received imperial instructions "with devotion," and were proud to address the *Basileus* as master and father. To all these barbarian rulers, Constantinople was the capital of the universe, and the sovereign there enthroned was the universal Emperor, for whose majesty prayers were offered in the remotest churches of the West. Can we wonder, then, at the tone used by Justinian when he told the Ostrogoths "that it has seemed fit to him to bring them back into the bosom of the Empire, and that he believes this will content them"?

We know the results of the great military enterprise that Justinian undertook in accordance with these principles. Dalmatia, Italy, a large part of North Africa, southern Spain, and the islands of the western Mediterranean—Sicily, Corsica, Sardinia, and the Balearics—re-entered the Empire. By the occupation of Septum, the Emperor's power was extended to the Pillars of Hercules, and the Mediterranean became once more a Roman lake. Carthage, Rome, and Ravenna came under imperial authority again, the former for more than a hundred years and the last two for over two centuries. As a result of these conquests, the area of the Empire was almost doubled. Justinian could assume the resounding titles of "most happy, most illustrious Emperor, victorious and triumphant" and, as in the finest days of the Roman Empire, could call himself *"Africanus, Vandalicus, Alemannicus, Germanicus, Gothicus,* and *Francicus."* He believed that in the reconquered provinces it would be easy to restore that perfect peace and good order which, in his eyes, were the mark of a truly civilized state, and that he could give back to the inhabitants a replica of the Roman Empire they had known in the past. Exalted by his triumphs, which brought the riches of Carthage and the treasures of Theodoric before the dazzled eyes of his people; proud to commemorate in medals and splendid mosaics "the glory of the Romans," he never doubted "that God would permit him to take back the other countries once possessed by the ancient Romans, to the very bounds of the two oceans." "He aspired to conquer the whole world," said one of his historians.

We know how much these dreams and inordinate ambitions cost the Empire, and the price paid in the East for conquests in the West. The brilliant victories over Vandals and Ostrogoths were offset by Persian, Slav, and Hun invasions and by the frightful devastation and depopulation of Illyricum, Thrace, and Macedonia. Worst of all, the Empire emerged from this huge imperialist enterprise financially and militarily exhausted. By the end of Justinian's reign, an official document tells us, the treasury "was reduced to the last degree of penury," and the army was "so completely disbanded that the state was exposed to incessant invasion and barbarian insolence."

Byzantine Imperialism

The conception of rebuilding the Roman Empire was grandiose indeed, and the task most resolutely attempted; but the discrepancy between aims and means was too great, and the aftermath bore heavily on Justinian's successors. The results obtained, though spectacular, could not last. For two centuries the government's attention had been diverted from its proper sphere, upon which its policy was based, and focussed upon the reconquered West. Because of this, and also because the expansion was not commensurate with the resources of the Empire, these great schemes did more harm than good, despite the renewed prestige and glory they brought to the Crown.

2. THE IMPERIALIST POLICY OF THE MACEDONIAN EMPERORS

Yet the Byzantines never gave up their rash and extravagant ambitions. By the end of the eighth century, only fragments of Justinian's conquests were left; in 812 the Empire had to recognize the new order established in the West, and with it Charlemagne's right to the title of Emperor; nevertheless, such concessions were regarded as purely temporary, and the Byzantines seized every opportunity of affirming their historic rights. The weakness of Charlemagne's successors encouraged the Macedonian house to revive Justinian's ambitions. Basil I sharply rebuked Louis II, Charlemagne's great-grandson, for calling himself Augustus and Emperor of the Romans, and in the name of "eternal principles and the rules laid down by the old emperors," he declared that only the sovereign reigning in Constantinople could claim the title of *Basileus*. Other sovereigns could be no more than kings, especially those Frankish princes who were altogether unworthy of the Empire which their ancestor had usurped. In vain Louis retorted that the Greeks had long abandoned the ancient imperial capital, forsaken the people, and forgotten the language of the Romans; Byzantium remained inexorable.

It maintained its claims no less vigorously against the powerful Germanic emperors of the tenth century. The representatives of Nicephorus Phocas, in addressing the ambassadors of Otto the Great, declared that Otto was not entitled to be called Emperor, but only King; that the power he wielded over Rome was tyrannical, based on force and violence, and that the territories he claimed in Italy were an integral part of the Byzantine Empire. They therefore demanded the restitution of Ravenna and Rome, with all the territory lying between those cities and the Greek frontier. Since the day Constantine transferred the capital of the Empire to the East, they said, and with it the Senate and the aristocracy of Rome, those who remained were inferior people, plebeians, slaves. It was a scandal that the Pope, in proclaiming himself the head of that base multitude, dared to dispose of the Empire, and that a king of barbarian Saxony dared to accept the imperial title at his hands.

Acting on these principles, the sovereigns of Byzantium boldly attempted to regain a foothold in Italy. From the end of the ninth century until the beginning of the eleventh, Basil I and Nicephorus Phocas, John Tzimisces and Basil II strove to re-establish imperial authority in the Peninsula. In practice, no doubt, they carried out their Western policy with skill and prudence, restricting their aims to within practicable limits; and by their undoubted success in Italy, they established their power and influence from the southern tip of the country to the very gates of Rome. Yet in theory, the haunting ambition to reconquer the whole of the West survived in the minds of the *basileis;* thus the smallest incident sufficed to involve the Empire in conflict and grave danger.

3. THE IMPERIALIST POLICY OF THE COMNENI

This could be clearly seen at the time of the Crusades. When these great enterprises brought Greeks and Latins into direct contact, Byzantine imperialist theories contributed in no small measure to the embittering of relations between the two worlds. Alexius Comnenus refused to regard the great barons who led the crusading armies as anything but mercenaries ready to sell themselves, or as vassals willing to swear allegiance to him and do him homage. His successors took the same haughty and disdainful attitude toward the kings of France and Germany and also the Emperor Frederick Barbarossa, persistently treating them as inferiors and thus deeply wounding their pride. The Latin princes who had acquired states in Syria received no better treatment, and everything was done to force Byzantine suzerainty upon them.

It was above all in Italy, Rome, and the West that the Byzantines pressed their claims. The great—and mistaken—ambition of Manuel Comnenus was to make the forgotten past a reality, and this in the twelfth century.

A curious passage by the historian Cinnamus, which seems to reflect the mind of the Emperor, shows the ideas that were current in the Byzantium of the Comneni. In the writer's view, the rulers of Italy had never at any time been more than deputies of the *Basileus:* mere kings, who wrongfully called themselves Emperors, forgetting that since the fall of Rome, this title belonged to the sovereign of Byzantium alone. In deriding both the unlawful Emperor and the Pope who presumed to consecrate him, Cinnamus made a laughingstock of these odd rulers, who humiliated the Crown by making themselves the squires of the Roman pontiff, and of the Popes who, forgetting that they owed all they were to Constantine, fancied themselves competent to confer imperial rank, whereas it was for the Emperor alone to create the supreme pontiff. "Your Pope is an emperor and no bishop," said an outraged Byzantine ambassador of the twelfth century, indicating thereby that Byzantium denied the Pope any but religious powers.

For twenty-five years it was Manuel Comnenus' steadfast ambition and the aim of Byzantine diplomacy to make the Emperor the protector of the Papacy; to re-establish unity of empire, destroyed by Charlemagne's usurpation; to make Rome once more the capital and to bring down the Western Empire of Frederick Barbarossa. And at one time—in the days of both Adrian IV and Alexander III—the Papacy was so gravely threatened by the Germanic Emperor that the reconciliation dreamed of in Constantinople appeared to have some chance of success. Did not the papal ambassadors at the court of Byzantium declare that the Western emperors were nothing but usurpers, tyrants, barbarians, and that the Pope and the Roman people would be happy to submit, body and soul, to the authority of the *Basileus*?

The way seemed clear for the Emperor to claim "ancient Rome and all Italy," as in the days of Justinian. To smooth the process he proposed the healing of the schism and the union of the Churches, if in return the Pope would confer the imperial crown upon him and proclaim the re-establishment of the one and only ancient Roman Empire. Yet Manuel failed, and could not but fail. The Pope is said to have stipulated that the Emperor should henceforth live in Rome; moreover, Alexander III evidently took refuge behind "the decisions of the Fathers" in refusing to pronounce upon "such high and complex questions" as were raised by the imperial demand. Agreement was unattainable. The Comneni, aiming at universal Empire, would, if ever they had become masters of Rome, have turned the Papacy into an ordinary Byzantine see; and to this the Papacy could never consent, for it, too, aimed at world dominion and its theocratic claims extended to the control of the Byzantine Church and the Greek Empire. The two conceptions were incompatible. The enmity between the

Byzantine Imperialism

Papacy and Germany did indeed bring about a temporary *rapprochement*, but when it became clear that the Greek Emperor meant to take the place of the German, a breach was inevitable; the more so as the Orthodox clergy, by refusing to recognize Roman primacy, made any attempt at union far more difficult.

The Emperor sought other means of destroying the Hohenstaufen empire. He flooded Italy with gold to encourage Barbarossa's enemies and add to their number. At the very moment when Manuel was asking Alexander III to re-establish imperial unity in his favour, he was helping to reform the Lombard League, negotiating with Ancona and Pisa, Genoa and Venice, and preparing to engage in open conflict with the German sovereign in Italy. Documents of the day make frequent mention of the "infinite riches" and "prodigal gifts" that the Greek Emperor, "the most opulent of kings," was bestowing on the states of the peninsula. But here again, despite the skill of the diplomats and the intrigues carried on in Italy as in Germany, and despite armed intervention, Manuel failed. His restless ambition not only exasperated Barbarossa, but caused anxiety in the Italian cities, especially Venice. The breach with the Most Serene Republic in 1171 and the peace concluded six years later between the Pope and the German Emperor, through the mediation of Venice, marked the end of Manuel's ambitious dreams for Italy.

The West was now uniting against Byzantium, and Frederick Barbarossa took the offensive on the very soil where he had been provoked. In a curious letter of his, addressed somewhat insolently to "the noble and illustrious King of the Greeks," he declared that he inherited from his predecessors, the glorious Roman Emperors, the right not only to govern the Roman Empire, but also to administer "the Kingdom of Greece" at his own pleasure. Rome was "the head of the world," and in consequence Byzantium must both recognize the temporal authority of the Roman Empire of the West and submit to the spiritual authority of the Papacy. Barbarossa treated the Greek Emperor haughtily, as he would have treated a vassal and subject; and this was the bitterest humiliation that could be inflicted on Byzantine imperialism.

In this case, too, the effort made by the Byzantine Empire was out of all proportion to its means. The idea was boldly conceived, but its fulfilment was impossible; Manuel Comnenus perhaps failed to appreciate the inherent contradictions in his policy, which could only result in disaster. At any rate, he could not conciliate the Latins, who were alarmed by his ambitions and offended by his arrogance; and despite the dissension that he sought to sow among the great Western powers, they formed a coalition against him. At the same time he displeased the Greeks by his display of good will to the Latins and by his lavish distribution among them of imperial funds. In the end, he exhausted the realm's resources by the huge sacrifices he demanded of it, and his Italian policy so gravely compromised the safety of Byzantium in the East that by the end of his reign the Empire was having difficulty in defending itself against the Moslems in Asia Minor; while in Cilicia and Syria its influence dwindled daily. Like Justinian, Manuel chose to add to his title—by a significant breach of contemporary protocol—a long list of resounding designations borrowed from the names of once-conquered peoples; like Justinian, he proclaimed himself "heir to the crown of Constantine the Great" and to "all the rights that belonged to him," although, he added, "certain of them have since been removed from our authority." As was the case after Justinian's death, the liquidation of Manuel's work was a difficult and calamitous one for the Empire; the more so as by the end of the twelfth century the West was incomparably stronger and better organized than it had been at the end of the sixth. Those who had been disturbed by Byzantine imperialism or outraged by Byzantine arrogance— whether the Holy Roman Empire or the Papacy, Venice or the Norman kingdom of Sicily—never forgave. Immediately after Manuel's death, the Normans attacked the East and devastated Thessalonica (1185). A little later, Barbarossa thought seriously of taking Constantinople (1190). And the Crusade of 1204, which placed a Latin emperor on the throne of the Comneni, was the West's dramatic revenge on Byzantine imperialism.

Byzantine Imperialism

4. BYZANTINE IMPERIALISM IN THE EAST

As heirs of the Caesars, Byzantine emperors dreamed of restoring the ancient Roman Empire. The Christian character of the realm imposed other obligations and inspired them with other ambitions.

It was firmly believed in Byzantium that the *Basileus* was charged with the mission of spreading the true faith throughout the world; and since according to prophecy the whole earth was the Lord's, the whole earth belonged by divine right to the sovereign of Byzantium. "One God is announced to all," wrote Eusebius in the fourth century. "One Empire stands ready to receive and contain them: that is, the Roman Empire. By divine will two seeds have sprouted; they have thrust up from the soil and covered the earth with their shadow. They are the Roman Empire and the Christian faith, and they are destined to unite the entire human race in the bonds of concord."

To embrace the world in one imperial and Christian whole: such was the vast prospect revealed to imperial ambitions by religion. All, princes and commoners, were one in believing in this sacred mission and were convinced that the duty of the *Basileus* was, as a sixth-century writer said, "not to allow the Christian world to diminish, but to extend it indefinitely." We know that religious missions were a characteristic instrument of Byzantine diplomacy; we know how the spread of Christianity was bound up with that of Byzantine influence and civilization, "even into lands whose very names were before unknown," as Justinian wrote. But although in this way Byzantium drew many barbarian nations into its sphere of action, particularly the Slavs —Serbs, Croats, and Bulgars—who from the seventh century onwards were established in the Balkan Peninsula, and although it often succeeded in making them its vassals, yet at the same time, its claims to universal empire clashed violently with these people's national aspirations, as soon as they had formed themselves into organized states. Between the end of the ninth century and the beginning of the eleventh, the first Bulgarian empire, as we know, felt equal to competing with Byzantium for the hegemony of the Balkans; we know what seas of blood were shed by such men as Romanus Lecapenus, John Tzimisces, and Basil II in attempts to destroy the realm of the great Czars Symeon and Samuel. We know, too, how at the end of the twelfth century the stubborn Bulgars built up their new empire, which had one century of glory, and which neither Latin nor Greek emperors could overthrow. The same was true of the Croats and Serbs; they, too, strove to break the shackles that bound them to Byzantium. In the second half of the eleventh century the Croat state was at the peak of its power, and its head appealed to Gregory VII in Rome for the royal crown that would free it from Constantinople. In the twelfth century, during the reign of Stephen Nemanja, Serbia—long a vassal, but ever seething and ready for revolt— laid the foundations of complete independence and future greatness. In the thirteenth century the Serbian state prospered so well that in the fourteenth its leader, Stephen Dushan, was able to dispute the hegemony of the Balkans with Byzantium; and although he did not succeed in capturing Constantinople, the Byzantine Empire, now in a state of decadence, was equally incapable of subduing the powerful state that the Nemanjas had founded.

But Byzantine ambitions reached far beyond the Danube and the Balkan Peninsula. From the tenth century, Byzantium had Hungarians as neighbours and tried to convert them to Orthodoxy, so as to bring them under its influence; but they were not to be seduced from Rome. Nevertheless the Greeks never gave up trying to bring the Hungarian kingdom into the Byzantine sphere of influence. The Comneni seized every opportunity of intervening in Hungarian affairs, of forming their own party within the kingdom and setting princes of their choice upon the throne, who should be vassals of the Greek Empire. At one time this was the mainspring of Manuel Comnenus' policy; he fancied he could replace German influence by Greek and secure one more ally against Barbarossa. His dreams went further: by marrying his only daughter to the heir to the Hungarian throne, he was apparently planning to annex the kingdom and to place upon the head of his son-in-law the united crowns of the Empire and of St. Stephen. He did at least succeed in setting the man of his choice upon the Hungarian throne, and found in him a faithful ally.

By the end of the tenth century, Byzantium had converted the Russians to Orthodoxy. Advantage was taken of this, as usual, to attempt to keep the princes of Kiev under Greek influence. Manuel Comnenus strove to uphold the prestige of the Empire in this quarter and to prevent the Russian Slavs, like those of Serbia, from exchanging Byzantine protection for that offered by Hungary.

Elsewhere, in Armenia, Cilicia, and the Latin states of Syria, we note the same struggle to maintain the suzerainty of the Most Christian Empire. But for all its successes, Byzantium exhausted itself by these efforts, and in the end was to be broken by them. Its imperialism had aroused the anxiety of the West; it had also disquieted the young Balkan peoples by hindering their national development. In attempting to maintain the Balkan hegemony and dominion over the European and Asiatic East, Byzantium made enemies. The stupendous ambitions of the emperors had prevented them from achieving harmony with other Christian peoples in the Peninsula, whom they dreamed only of subjugating. Thus the Byzantine Empire, exhausted by its struggles and too weak to dominate its rivals, found itself alone in its hour of greatest peril. The capture of Constantinople by the Turks in 1453 completed what had been begun in 1204 with the capture of Constantinople by the Latins.

VI. Economic Decay

The Byzantine Empire was rich and prosperous; yet even in its most golden days, the financial situation was often unstable and difficult. The burden of expenditure was heavy. War and diplomacy, the vast and intricate machinery of public administration, the splendour of the court and of public buildings, and the numbers of religious and hospitable foundations—in short, all the magnificence required by tradition not only to satisfy the people of Constantinople, but to impress foreigners, was extremely costly. Revenue already inadequate for so many requirements was further diminished by the greed and corruption of officials. Thus at every period of Byzantine history, taxation was a crushing burden on all citizens, and the budget was always exceedingly difficult to balance. The situation became even worse when the sources of revenue dwindled and at last dried up altogether.

1. THE DECAY OF AGRICULTURE

Agriculture, as we have seen, was one of these sources. The causes of its decline increased with the centuries. The Turkish conquest at the end of the eleventh century deprived Byzantium of some of its richest provinces, in particular, the major part of Asia Minor, which was the Empire's strength. Even the territories that the emperors were able to hold were in a permanent state of insecurity and misery, owing to war and incessant raids by Ottomans, Serbs, and Bulgars, to say nothing of the ravages of the Byzantine army itself—so much so, that at the beginning of the fourteenth century, Constantinople was reduced to relying for its very existence on cargoes of grain and fish from the Black Sea, the fertile plains of Thrace and Macedonia having been devastated by Catalans and Turks. On the other hand, government measures to prevent the continuous growth of the large estates and to stop the usurpations of the strong fell more and more into oblivion; by the middle of the fourteenth century they were an antiquated notion to which no one paid any attention. The free peasant disappeared with the independent small holding, and the commonest form of labour between the thirteenth and fifteenth centuries was that of the πάροιϰοι: men bound to their master's land and liable to him for numerous dues and duties.

During the Empire's final period, communities of free peasants became more and more rare. A great part of the land belonged to the Emperor or the treasury; they employed πάροιϰοι to work it or leased it to others. Churches and religious houses, too, owned great numbers of estates, which were cultivated by the monks and their πάροιϰοι, and although in theory these properties were liable to land tax, in fact they were often exempt; and in any case they were free of any supplementary charges. The remainder was private property. It consisted firstly of large estates belonging to the nobility, who cultivated them by the labour of their own πάροιϰοι or leased part of them; secondly of military fiefs, from whose owners only military service was required; and finally of rural communities and farms. These last were the fewest and most heavily burdened; for, besides countless taxes, they owed certain obligations to the local lord whose patronage they had willingly or unwillingly accepted. The occupiers of such holdings were known as "the poor"—and so indeed they were.

The consequences of such a state of affairs may be imagined. The preponderance of large estates and the manner of their cultivation resulted in an inferior yield. The hardship to which the πάροικοι were subjected brought destitution and the abandonment of the countryside, and aroused universal discontent among the lower classes. In the fourteenth century especially, a social situation of great and increasing tension arose. The many exemptions enjoyed by the big landowners diminished the revenue from land tax and, by causing the greater part of the burden to fall on the poor, added to the people's distress and goaded them to rebellion. This state of affairs was aggravated by increased exactions to meet the deficit and by the extortionate methods used, and peasants were made to pay six or even twelve times the amount they owed.

In the nation's agony, the rural population had nothing to look forward to but a change of masters; and it was natural that, as in the last days of the Roman Empire, the peasants regarded the coming of a new lord almost as a deliverance. As early as the eleventh century, provincials sometimes appealed to the enemy or joined forces with rebels; often, to escape the fiscal tyranny, they fled into the mountains or went abroad, and vast tracts of country lay deserted. In the fourteenth and fifteenth centuries the situation was far worse, and the disappearance of taxable property left the nation's finances in a desperate state.

2. DECAY OF TRADE

The Greek Empire had recovered without too much difficulty from the Arab conquest in the seventh century, which resulted in the loss of the rich provinces of Egypt and Syria and their thriving ports. It bore less easily the eleventh-century Turkish occupation of some of its wealthiest regions. Yet in the twelfth century trade still flourished, as is shown by the prosperity of Constantinople and Thessalonica at that time. The primary causes of the subsequent decline in this prosperity must be sought elsewhere, and mainly in the mistaken economic policy of the Byzantines, who neglected their navy and allowed themselves to be ousted from eastern markets.

Merchants in the commercial cities of Italy soon perceived the profits to be made by exploiting the Byzantine Empire, and seized every opportunity of doing so. From the middle of the tenth century, Bari, Amalfi, and, above all, Venice were foremost in maintaining close relations with the Empire, not only by lawful trade, but also in the smuggling of prohibited articles. The Venetians soon wanted more, and as the Greek government often needed their help and their shipping, it allowed them many exemptions and privileges. The treaty of 992, the first of a series that was to make Venice's fortune in the East, allowed Venetian merchants considerable reductions in import and export duty payable at the Dardanelles, as well as guarantees against molestation by Byzantine officials. The treaty of 1082, renewed, confirmed, and amplified during the twelfth century, increased these privileges. Thenceforth Venetian merchants could buy and sell in every part of the Empire, free of duty or customs examination. Many ports were opened and vast territories made accessible to them for free trade. These unheard-of concessions gave them a pre-eminent position in eastern waters. On the coasts of the Peloponnesus, the Archipelago, and Thrace, and in the Sea of Marmara, they found all the ports they needed to establish communication with the distant East. In Constantinople they had their own quarter, situated at the finest point on the Golden Horn. Their vessels sailed into the Black Sea, to the Crimea, and to the end of the Sea of Azov, to fetch wheat from south Russia and the precious wares that came along the trade routes from Central Asia. The ports of Asia Minor lay open to them; Crete, Rhodes, and Cyprus offered fine harbours for the Syrian eastern route. At last their activities extended into the interior, as far as Adrianople and Philippopolis in Europe, and in Asia as far as Philadelphia. Thus the Venetians found foothold and enjoyed privileged treatment throughout the Greek Empire; they became the necessary intermediary for all traffic between East and West, and their Italian rivals of Bari, Amalfi, and even Genoa, less privileged than they, had difficulty in competing. The decay of the Byzantine merchant navy helped them to keep the monopoly they had won.

Throughout the twelfth century their hold upon the East was strengthened. Being exempt from the taxes and dues imposed on others, the Venetians settled on Greek territory and founded thriving colonies; in 1171 that of Constantinople numbered over 10,000. Indeed, a Byzantine emperor wrote that he regarded them "not as foreigners but as Greeks by birth," while Nicetas said of them that they had become "the compatriots and best friends of the Romans." They wormed their way in everywhere—even the ships' companies of the imperial fleet were full of Venetian seamen—and were so intoxicated by their good fortune that they forgot they were not at home and behaved as if in a conquered country. They made no effort to disguise their mercenary greed or their arrogance and treated not only the lower classes with insolent disdain, but also those of high rank; even the Emperor himself was not spared their insults. "They treated citizens like slaves," said a twelfth-century Greek chronicler. "Their boldness and impudence increased with their wealth," wrote Nicetas, "until they not only detested the Romans but even defied the threats and commands of the Emperor." In time they became altogether insufferable.

The Greeks, justly uneasy at the rapid success of the Venetians and their ill-disguised ambitions, tried to hold them in check. In return for the privileges they enjoyed, Emperor Manuel Comnenus tried to impose upon the Latins some of the obligations of Greek citizens, such as military service and the payment of certain taxes. At other times, as in 1122, Byzantine sovereigns refused to renew the treaties or resorted to sterner measures, as in 1171, arresting all Venetians established in the East, confiscating their property, and seizing their ships. Or again, as in 1182, they allowed the population of the capital to storm the Latin quarter and massacre the inhabitants. Venice retaliated by war, and the good will of earlier times gave place to smouldering hostility. Gradually the idea was borne in upon the Republic that if it was to retain its monopoly of the eastern trade and continue to profit by the fine markets of the Greek Empire, one course alone lay open to it: to conquer Byzantium and lay the foundations of a Venetian colonial empire upon its ruins.

Pisans and Genoese had also settled in the East. "Maritime Italy," said Nicetas, "entered the imperial city under full sail." It is true that the first treaties concluded with Pisa and Genoa were less advantageous than those with Venice; yet in the course of the twelfth century the Greek emperors sought to check the Venetians by favouring their competitors. These, too, had their own quarter and colony in Constantinople—in 1162 there were a thousand Pisans in the capital—and they were allowed customs concessions and free access to all the ports of the Empire. But they often caused anxiety to the government, which at times withdrew its permission for them to settle in Constantinople itself and made them move outside, or allowed the populace to attack and rob them. Nevertheless, their alliance was necessary to Greek policy, so that in the end they always received satisfaction, to the great annoyance of the Venetians—who were jealous of any competition—and to the detriment of the Empire, since the number of its exploiters was hereby increased.

The Fourth Crusade—born of Venetian ambitions and the Venetian desire to secure the monopoly of eastern trade against all comers—dealt a decisive blow to the economic prosperity of the Greek Empire. In the partitioning of the Empire, the Republic seized the best of the Byzantine possessions: fertile lands, coastal territory, the most useful ports, and the most important strategic points. Venetian patricians settled in the Archipelago, and for Venice their domains were so many friendly states, open to a profitable trade. And although the fall of the short-lived Latin empire and the return of the Greeks to Constantinople was for a time very damaging to this prosperity, it did not benefit the Byzantine Empire. To check the Venetians, the Palaeologi favoured the Genoese, giving them complete customs exemption, handing over to them the important site of Galata for their colony, and allowing them to settle on the coast of Asia Minor and at Caffa on the Black Sea, where they might claim the monopoly of all trade in those waters.

This was merely to change masters. The historian Pachymeres records, "The Genoese closed all maritime trade routes to the Romans." And as Venice was still mistress of the Archipelago and firmly entrenched in Euboea and Crete, Byzantium found itself even more at the mercy of exploiting foreigners than before, especially as Michael Palaeologus soon allowed Venetians and Pisans the concessions which at first he had reserved for the Genoese.

By the beginning of the fourteenth century, all the eastern seas were surrounded by Latin colonies. The Genoese were masters of Phocaea, Chios, Lesbos, and Aenos on the Thracian coast; they colonized Caffa, Tana, and Trebizond; they were lords of Galata, and in 1348 they made so bold as to build a naval station on the Bosphorus itself and denied entry into the Black Sea to any Venetian or even Greek ship without their express permission. The Venetians on their part held the islands of the Archipelago: Naxos, Andros, Paros, Tinos, Santorini, Cerigo, Coron, and Modon in the Morea, also Negropont and Crete; while their colonists had quickly returned to Constantinople and Thessalonica, despite the hostility of the Greeks and the obstacles placed in their way by the imperial government. Rivalry between the two cities was very bitter; at the end of the thirteenth century and throughout the fourteenth it broke out periodically in open warfare, the Empire being the battlefield and the victim.

To protect his capital, Michael Palaeologus attempted to neutralize the waters lying between the entry of the Dardanelles and the outlet of the Bosphorus, and here forbade any naval engagement. In defiance of this, the fleets of Venice and Genoa joined battle in the Bosphorus, before Constantinople, and in the Golden Horn itself; colonists from both cities fought in the streets of the capital, and the weak rulers of the house of the Palaeologi were toys in the hands of the Latins. In 1292 Roger Morosini arrived before Constantinople with a fleet of 75 sail, in defiance of the Emperor. In 1305 a Venetian fleet sacked the Princes' Islands and forced the Emperor to renew his treaties with the Republic. In 1351 a Venetian squadron compelled the *Basileus* to abandon his neutrality and side with Venice against Genoa. In 1375 Venice made the Byzantines cede the important position of Tenedos, which commanded the Dardanelles; whereupon the Genoese retaliated by touching off a palace revolution in Constantinople and overthrowing John V Palaeologus. All was violence and insolence, in things great or small. For instance, it was the custom for every Latin vessel passing Constantinople to heave to before the imperial palace, in order to salute and acclaim the Emperor. Genoese and Venetians constantly omitted this courtesy, by which Byzantine vanity set great store. In 1348, when John Cantacuzenus was planning to refit the Byzantine navy and, in order to restore activity in the port of Constantinople, proposed to lower the customs duties collected there, the Genoese expressed their disapproval of measures so damaging to their trade by attacking Constantinople, destroying the vessels under construction and repair, and burning the merchantmen stationed in the Golden Horn.

The Greek people protested loudly at "Italian pride and arrogance," and at the disdain shown by the Latins for the *Basileus* of the Romans. But the emperors put a good face upon it; they usually received insults with a smile and confined themselves to making courteous representations. Or, if they did venture upon any gesture of resistance or reprisal, they gave in in the end, conscious of the hopeless weakness of their position. "The naval power of Byzantium had long vanished," said a Greek historian at the end of the thirteenth century. Upkeep of the fleet seemed to the Greeks to entail unnecessary expense, and apart from the few ships moored in the Golden Horn, all the vessels that had once constituted the strength and wealth of Byzantium lay empty and unrigged, or rotted on the bottom. As Nicephorus Gregoras wrote in the fourteenth century, "While the Latins steadily increased their profits and their power, the Greeks grew weaker, and every day added fresh calamity to past misfortune."

Genoa and Venice took advantage of this situation to exploit the Empire. Genoa created the powerful trade association known as "Mahone of Chios" which from the produce of this island and the yield of the Phocaean alum mines drew an annual revenue of from 60 to 80,000 florins. In contrast to declining Constantinople, the Genoese port of Pera was tremendously active. And whereas by the fourteenth century the Constantinople customs authority collected no more than 30,000 *hyperpera* annually, that of Galata brought in over 200,000. Even the few restrictions imposed on certain articles by the economic policy of the emperors were ineffectual, owing to clever smuggling, which still further diminished what was left of the Empire's resources.

Venice meanwhile was carrying on an immensely profitable

trade throughout the East, from the Black Sea to Egypt, and from Syria to the Ionian Sea. By the beginning of the fifteenth century the day seemed near when, in the words of Doge Mocenigo, Venice was to become "mistress of the gold of all Christendom." Times had indeed changed since the day when Robert of Clari declared that "Two thirds of the world's riches were in Constantinople."

Yet Constantinople still remained the finest and busiest port in the East. Pisa, Florence, Ancona, Ragusa, Barcelona, Marseilles, Montpellier, and Narbonne had flourishing colonies there, as well as Venice and Genoa; merchants came from Cadiz and Seville, and even from Bruges and London. Similarly, the Greek ports that were outlets of the great trade routes were still extremely busy. But the Byzantines did not benefit. Nicephorus Gregoras wrote in the fourteenth century, "The Latins have taken possession not only of all the wealth of the Byzantines, and almost all the revenues from the sea, but also of all the resources that replenish the sovereign's treasury." The Greeks could not even collect the harbour dues and the excise and customs duties from their astute rivals, the Venetians and Genoese, who had been exempted too long from such payments.

3. FINANCIAL DISTRESS

Henceforth Byzantium's financial ruin was inevitable. The two principal sources of revenue were the land tax and customs duties, and strictly though payment was enforced, the former now brought in a quite inadequate sum, while the latter were rapidly dwindling. And since the Byzantine government clung to its tradition of magnificence and display—so long the basis of its policy—and was determined to keep up appearances, it found increasing difficulty in balancing revenue and.expenditure. Attempts were made to economize, regardless of the Empire's safety. Thus from the end of the thirteenth century the fleet, which Michael Palaeologus had tried to keep in good order, was allowed to decay, on the pretext that its upkeep was a needless expense, and "a greater burden on the imperial treasury than anything else." Other essentials such as fortresses and armaments were likewise pared away. Army estimates were reduced, regardless of the fact that by leaving the way open to invasion and piracy and by necessitating the bribery of Serbs and Turks, economic distress was aggravated and the Empire plunged further into ruin.

By these means, however, the imperial government was able to save some money for the upkeep of the court and the ostentation to which the Byzantines attached so much importance and by which they liked to think they still dazzled the world as in bygone times. There is something very pitiable about the treatise on ceremonial drawn up about the middle of the fourteenth century, containing long descriptions of the uniforms of court dignitaries, of their variously coloured hats, their different sorts of shoes, their insignia, and their hierarchic and ceremonial rank. To read this little book, one would suppose that Byzantium was still resplendent in jewels, purple, and gold, and more preoccupied than ever with luxury, banqueting, and ceremonial etiquette. But what were the facts?

In the middle of the fourteenth century Emperor John Cantacuzenus declared, "There is no more money anywhere. Reserves are exhausted, the imperial jewels have been sold, and taxes bring in nothing, as the country is ruined." The wife of this same sovereign noted that the Empire had been reduced to nothing and fallen to the lowest degree of poverty, "so that I dare not speak of it, lest I blush before my hearers." Another still more significant fact was that the court itself, where every effort was made to keep up an appearance of splendour, was henceforth unable to conceal its penury. At the marriage of John V Palaeologus in 1347, the wedding feast was served in vessels of earthenware and pewter, and not one item of gold or silver appeared on the table.

Byzantium: Greatness and Decline

Clothes and crowns were adorned with coloured glass instead of gems, and gilded leather took the place of gold. Nicephorus Gregoras, who tells this tale, rightly remarks, "Anyone with any knowledge of custom will understand by this and by other breaches of etiquette how intolerable was the burden of distress."

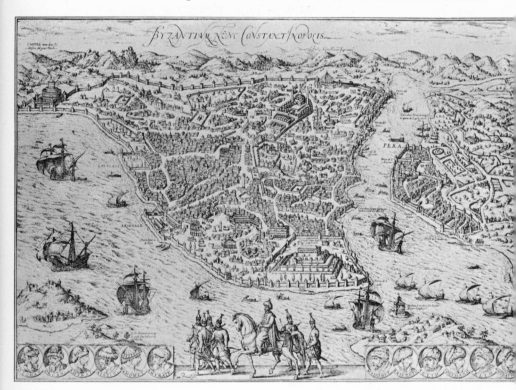

Pieter Coeck van Aelst, The Turks in MDXXXIII, *London and Edinburgh, 1873*

General view of Constantinople. *Ca.* 1500.

He ends sadly, "The bygone splendour and prosperity of Byzantium were dissipated and gone, and it is not without shame that I relate it." For the Byzantine court to consent to such humiliation, the financial situation must have been desperate indeed. The treasury was empty. "Nothing was to be found there," says Gregoras, "but air and dust."

And so the last of the Palaeologi were reduced to dire expedients. John V pawned the Crown Jewels and sold some territory for a few thousand ducats. The *Basileus* became the prey of usurers and—most humiliating incident of all—while on a journey in the West, he was arrested for debt in Venice and detained there until he paid his creditors. When we recall how transcendent a figure the Emperor of Byzantium had once been, we can appreciate the full poignancy of this account.

Everything bore witness to the same distress. In 1423 the Empire was forced to sell Thessalonica—its second city—to the Venetians for 50,000 ducats. By the beginning of the fifteenth century, the loveliest quarter of Constantinople lay in ruins, and even for the upkeep of St. Sophia money was not always forthcoming. Stripped of its ancient glories and greatly diminished in population—"there is more emptiness than fullness here," said a fifteenth-century traveller—the dying capital seemed in mourning for the Empire; and although it still held a proud place in the world and attracted crowds of travellers and traders, foreigners alone won profit from its fine situation and from all that for so long had made it wealthy.

VII. Military Decay and Territorial Disintegration

Serious though these causes of decadence were, the Byzantine Empire might yet have endured, had it been able to maintain the sturdy institutions on which its military strength was founded, and the army that had so often carried it to victory. One of the main causes of collapse was certainly the progressive dwindling and final exhaustion of military power, and it will be well to discover exactly how this came about.

1. DIMINUTION IN NUMBERS

First we notice that, as time went on, the army shrank. Loss of territory was naturally accompanied by a falling-off in regional recruitment; in the eleventh century, for instance, the Turks conquered Asia Minor, which had always supplied the Empire with its best troops. In 1204 the Fourth Crusade brought dislocation, and the Palaeologi rebuilt the realm only very imperfectly, and on diminished territory. Lastly, in the fourteenth century, Ottomans and Serbs seized the greater part of the European provinces, notably Thrace and Macedonia, which for centuries had given the army fine soldiers. At the last, the imperial government was often at its wits' end to find the necessary troops.

Military Decay and Territorial Disintegration

The system of military fiefs had long provided a firm basis for recruitment, and it seems to have been continued up to the last days of the Empire. But the loss of the Asiatic provinces, whose feudatories have been estimated at 36,000, greatly impaired the efficacy of this system, while usurping lords had been no more sparing of military properties than of small holdings, so that, despite legislation, the number of these fiefs had declined on that account also. This was serious, because military fiefs were primarily responsible for the defence of the frontier.

Lastly, as we have seen, the dangers inherent in regional recruitment soon induced the government to replace military service by a tax; and this resulted in a profound change in the attitude of the public as well as in the make-up of the army. Provincials lost their taste for fighting, and the Byzantine troops contained a growing proportion of mercenaries. It is true that up to the last days of the Empire provincial levies were used, though with poor results. Pachymeres tells us that in 1302 what national troops there were dispersed at once on learning that their native provinces were threatened, and hurried home to protect their own property. Gregoras notes that in 1329 the imperial army—if we except 2000 picked horsemen—consisted entirely of shopkeepers and artisans, whose one concern was to discover how best to run away. It can hardly be wondered at, then, if the government ceased to count seriously on these "Roman" contingents (on whom, as a historian says, "the divine wrath was clearly visited") and pinned more faith on mercenary soldiers.

But here the emperors encountered another difficulty. There is no doubt that in the thirteenth and fourteenth centuries, as in preceding ages, there were hosts of adventurers willing to sell their services to the highest bidder. Alans, Serbs, Bulgars, Catalans, Turks, Italians, and Germans were ready to flock to the Byzantine colours in their thousands. But the *Basileus* was no longer as rich as he had been, and mercenaries expected high pay, so much so that the emperors often boggled at their demands, "reckoning that the expense would be great," as a historian said, "and burdensome to the public funds, which were at a lower ebb than ever."

The imperial troops were therefore not very numerous. It would be a mistake to accept the statements of fourteenth-century

Byzantine historians literally when they speak—in rather vague terms—of the large forces mobilized by the emperors, or to believe the swaggerings of Ramon Muntaner when he describes— no doubt to enhance their glory—his Catalan compatriots at grips with 50 or 100,000 Greeks. If we consider the precise figures given by historians, we soon find that at this time a few thousand men represented a considerable force. The biggest expeditions were undertaken by 10 or 12,000 men at most; indeed at the beginning of the fourteenth century the 6 or 7000 men of the Great Catalan Company arrived, amid the confusion of the imperial troops, as saviours for whom no reward was too high. The advent of 10,000 Alans, asking to serve the *Basileus,* was an event of major importance, "so diseased and reduced was the Empire," says a historian. A reinforcement of 7000 Serbian auxiliaries and 6 or 10,000 Turkish cavalry seems to have been enough to alter the whole course of events and ensure victory to those they came to help. And indeed the enemy were no more numerous; in 1329 the "innumerable army" of Sultan Orkhan consisted of barely 8000 men. Many of these incessant wars—except for the large-scale attacks on Constantinople—were minor engagements; Byzantium was only able to put small armies in the field, and of these the mercenaries alone retained any vestiges of courage or discipline.

Diminution in Quality

Even the mercenaries had lost some of their old virtues. The imperial government, being weaker and poorer than before, had less control over the auxiliaries it employed, and all the faults inherent in mercenary forces came naturally to the fore. Less disciplined, more grasping than ever, these redoubtable troops were now a greater danger to the Empire than to the enemy. They lived off the country; they looted and laid waste everything in their path, and even on the day of battle were quick to forsake the imperial cause, if they were displeased with their leader or thought they had more to gain by fighting on the other side. Often they demanded their discharge after only a few months of service, saying that they could not endure the fatigues of a long campaign and wanted peace in which to enjoy the fruits of their victories; and when their request was refused, they mutinied and murdered the generals who had urged them to return to duty.

Military Decay and Territorial Disintegration

This was not all. There was perpetual rivalry and jealousy between the various groups of mercenaries, arising from differences in pay or privilege, and ill feeling often erupted in fighting and bloodshed. The Emperor's generals had only very precarious authority over these men. Cantacuzenus writes, "As the Turkish auxiliaries were too numerous for the Romans to control, they went into action on their own initiative, wherever there was hope of gain." Such fickle servants often became the Empire's enemies, the more dangerous in that they knew its weaknesses and could exploit them. They thought of nothing but their own advantage; the men were intent on plunder, while their officers sought high positions, wealth and honours, and the chance to snatch duchies and principalities from imperial territory. The defence of the Empire was a minor consideration.

A case in point is the strange tale of the Norman *condottieri* at the end of the eleventh century: Hervé, Robert Crispin, and Roussel de Bailleul, for instance, who sought their fortunes amid the chaos of the Empire and came near to founding a Normandy in Asia Minor, as was being done in England and Sicily at about this time. The history of the Great Catalan Company at the beginning of the fourteenth century was even more characteristic. In 1302 Emperor Andronicus II engaged 6 or 7000 Spanish mercenaries who were then unemployed as a result of the peace recently concluded between the King of Aragon and Charles of Anjou. To gain the support of these tough, splendid soldiers, the *Basileus* promised them twice the sum which the Empire usually offered to mercenaries, while their leader, Roger de Flor, was to receive the rank of Grand Duke and the hand of an imperial princess. Byzantium paid dearly for its rash liberality. On the very day after their arrival in the East, the Catalans set the streets of Constantinople in an uproar by a violent and bloody affray with the Genoese of Galata. Later they were sent to Asia, where they quarrelled with the Alan mercenaries with whom they had been associated, and the two forces came to blows. When stationed at Cyzicus, the Catalans lived off the country and were guilty of every kind of excess, "worse than the enemy would have committed," says a chronicler. When they were brought back to Europe, Roger de Flor had fresh demands to make: he insisted upon and received enormous sums for his men—more than a million besants in all—and for himself the title of Caesar and the promise of a principality in Asia. His men behaved as if in conquered enemy country, carrying away crops, slaughtering beasts, seizing horses and money, raping women, and slaying any who ventured to resist them. The insolence of their leaders was unbounded. Berenger d'Entença kept the gold and silver dishes in which the Emperor had sent him food from the imperial kitchens; he despatched his ships in single line past the Blachernae Palace without deigning to salute the *Basileus,* and in the presence of high officers of the court amused himself by dredging up sea water in his ceremonial mantle, the token of his newly bestowed grand dukedom. The Byzantines finally lost all patience, and Roger de Flor was assassinated at Adrianople. Thereupon the enraged Catalans declared war on the Emperor. They entrenched themselves at Gallipoli and for two whole years blockaded Constantinople, repulsing the imperial troops sent to dislodge them, winning over the Turkish mercenaries from the Emperor's service to their own, ravaging Thrace, and making forays up to the very gates of Constantinople. No longer recognizing any authority, they styled themselves "the Army of the Franks ruling the Kingdom of Macedonia," while their leader proudly assumed the title of: "By the grace of God, Grand Duke of Romania, Lord of Anatolia and the Islands of the Archipelago." The Emperor could only look on, his helplessness a manifest sign of the decay of the Empire.

When Thrace was stripped bare, the Company left for Macedonia, where it remained for another two years, ravaging the countryside as before. Thessalonica nearly fell into Catalan hands, and the monasteries of Athos received unwelcome visits. Next they went to Thessaly and afterwards entered the service of the Frankish Duke of Athens. However, they soon quarrelled with him, and their long and colourful odyssey ended somewhat unexpectedly with their crushing victory over the Frankish cavalry on the shores of Lake Kopais and the establishment of a Catalan duchy at the foot of the Acropolis.

The Empire suffered almost as severely from the Turkish mercenaries, whom sovereigns of the middle of the fourteenth century were so ready to employ. According to contemporary testimony, they were admirable soldiers. But they were terrible allies.

Emperor John Cantacuzenus, who constantly sought their aid, said of them, "For the Turks, killing is a delight, and the taking and enslaving of prisoners gives them more pleasure than any plunder. They have no mercy, no pity for the unfortunate, for owing to the profound difference in religion, they are the natural enemies of the Romans." "How many acts of pillage and enslavement the Turks have perpetrated on Christians," says Gregoras, "how many insolent acts of aggression they have committed against consecrated places, it is impossible to relate." And elsewhere: "As a result of the habitual tyranny of the Turks, the state of the Empire was more diseased than usual." Yet this did not prevent John Cantacuzenus from begging Sultan Orkhan, his son-in-law—for the Most Christian Emperor had not blushed to marry his daughter to an infidel—for 10,000 horsemen in 1348 and 20,000 in 1349 and another 10,000 in 1353; nor did Empress Anna hesitate to send for 6000 more from other Moslem princes of Asia. Both sides made shameless use of infidels; in the imperial palace itself the Turks were treated as friends and took every kind of liberty. To the great scandal of the Christians, they disturbed the sacred offices by their dancing and singing, and already they felt themselves masters of the Empire.

The Army Command

As may be imagined, Byzantine generals had some difficulty in handling soldiers of this sort, especially as mercenaries, who were always commanded by men of their own race, obeyed these rather than the Emperor's representatives. Moreover the Greeks often refused to serve alongside foreigners and threatened to desert if forced into such unwelcome contact. Outstanding leadership was needed to control so many undisciplined and incompatible elements; but Byzantium could no longer find such men as those of old, whose renown and personal influence had so strongly impressed the troops under their command. Whether the reason for this must be sought in the undoubted weakening of the military spirit among the Byzantines, or in the impossibility of winning wars with scanty and ill-disciplined armies, the fact remains that after the great emperors of the house of Comnenus, few if any great leaders are to be heard of at the head of the imperial armies. If we except John Vatatzes and Michael Palae-

ologus in the thirteenth century, John Cantacuzenus in the fourteenth, and the last Emperor of Byzantium, Constantine Dragases,
who perished heroically in 1453, no illustrious names are to be
found in the military annals of the Empire. Those who maintained
the defence of Constantinople at the beginning of the fifteenth
century were Frenchmen—Boucicault and Châteaumorand—and
it was they who lent a final, illusive glory to the dying Empire
of the Palaeologi.

Consequences of Military Decay

This undisciplined, indifferently commanded, and numerically
weak army was no longer adequate to defend the Empire. Moreover, the network of fortresses that had so long and so sturdily
protected the frontiers had by now almost entirely disappeared.
There remained, indeed, many strongholds garrisoned by forces
great and small; but often such places were isolated in the midst
of enemy-held territory. Among these we may cite Philadelphia
and Magnesia in Asia, at the beginning of the fourteenth century; and later in the same century, Didymotica and Thessalonica in Europe. However heroic the stand made by the garri-
sons of these citadels, their efforts, being no longer co-ordinated
from above, were insufficient to guard the frontiers and assure
the safety of the surrounding country. Serbs, Turks, and Bulgars
penetrated to the heart of the Empire, unhindered by any serious
obstacle. The imperial forces, cowering behind the ramparts of
the towns, scarcely dared engage the enemy; and these towns
defended themselves independently of each other, as best they
might. "When only inferior armies were left," wrote Montesquieu,
"or none at all, the frontier no longer protected the interior,
which had to be fortified; and this meant more strongholds and
less strength; more retreats and less safety."

Vainly the emperors strove to reorganize both army and navy.
Events seemed to frustrate every attempt. In the twelfth century
the Comneni had made a great and successful effort to restore
military power. Because of the Crusades, however, not all the results hoped for were obtained; the twelfth-century emperors were
more than once compelled to withdraw their attention from the
enemy at the frontier and focus it on the countless armies march-
ing in from the West. Their progress through the provinces had

to be controlled and Constantinople protected from their greed. The need for reserving troops to fight the Latins, should they prove hostile, too often diverted the newly reconstituted army from its true purpose. Later, the long civil wars of the fourteenth century impaired discipline and fostered deplorable habits of desertion and treachery; they brought large numbers of dangerous auxiliaries into the army and opened the gates to the enemy. John Cantacuzenus tried in vain to rebuild the fleet, reinforce the army, and replenish his arsenal, but in the face of Genoese threats he had to abandon a great part of his plans. A little later, the Sultan Bayazid obliged Emperor John V to demolish the ramparts he was building for the better defence of Constantinople. The Empire was caught in a vicious circle; it was too weak to defy the orders of its enemies, and those orders removed all possibility of regaining the strength that might have saved it. So the realm moved steadily towards ruin, and the Byzantines looked on helplessly as the territories of their Empire crumbled away.

2. TERRITORIAL DISINTEGRATION OF THE EMPIRE

Despite the territorial losses it sustained at various times during the seventh and eighth centuries, the Empire remained a great power in the world until the beginning of the eleventh century. At the end of Basil II's reign, the realm extended from the Danube to the Euphrates, and from Syria and Armenia to the tip of Italy. After the middle of the eleventh century, events took another course, and subsequent losses were never to be made good.

Byzantium: Greatness and Decline

The Loss of Asia

The arrival of the Seljuk Turks in Asia Minor dealt the first severe blow to the Empire. They were led by three outstanding men, Tughril-Beg, Alp-Arslan, and Malik-Shāh, and little by little made themselves masters of almost the whole of Anatolia. In 1054 they crossed the Euphrates; in 1064 they took Ani, the last refuge of Armenian independence; in 1069 they occupied Melitene and arrived in Caesarea; and in 1070 they reached Iconium. The defeat of Romanus Diogenes at Mantzikert in 1071 completed the loss of Asia. The Sultanate of Roum was founded in the middle of Anatolia, and the Turks pressed on in all directions, capturing Antioch in the south, Neo-Caesarea and Sebaste in the northeast, Philadelphia and Smyrna in the west, and Cyzicus and Nicaea in the north. By the end of the eleventh century nothing of Asia remained to the Greeks except the northern provinces: Heraclea Pontica, Paphlagonia, and Trebizond. The Comneni did succeed in taking back part of Asia in the twelfth century and reconquering nearly all the Anatolian coast; they also pressed eastward beyond the Halys and southward as far as the valley of the Meander, and narrowed the corner of Moslem territory lying between this river and the southern coast of Anatolia. But they could not prevent the Sultans of Roum from enlarging their domains at the expense either of their Moslem neighbours or of the Empire, and the deadly defeat suffered by Manuel Comnenus at Myriocephalon in 1176 lost in one day all that had been gained and put an end to Byzantine domination in Anatolia for all time. By the end of the twelfth century Byzantium possessed no more of Asia Minor—so long its reservoir of strength—than a narrow strip of territory along the shores of the Black Sea and in the northwest of Anatolia. Thus the Greek Empire, in being thrust back upon its European provinces, was thrown off its balance and deprived of its strongest support.

Dislocation of the Empire in the Thirteenth Century

The capture of Constantinople in 1204 by the Crusaders, and the resulting partition of the realm, marked the second stage in the dislocation of the Byzantine Empire. From the end of the twelfth century, Stephen Nemanja's reconstitution of an independent Serbia and the foundation of the Vlacho-Bulgarian Empire under the Asen dynasty had deprived Byzantium of the entire northern part of the Balkan Peninsula. Shortly afterwards, as a result of the Fourth Crusade, a swarm of little states, both Greek and Latin, sprang up amid the ruins of the Empire. There were now an empire of Trebizond, an empire of Nicaea, a despotat of Epirus, and principalities of Philadelphia and Rhodes; these were Greek. Those of the Latins included the empire of Constantinople, the kingdom of Thessalonica, the duchy of Athens, the principality of Achaia, and the Venetian seignories of the Archipelago. Although many of these states existed for only a short time, a great number of provinces that had once formed an integral part of the Empire lost the tradition of imperial unity forever. When in 1261 the Palaeologi re-entered Constantinople and re-established the monarchy, they lacked the power to reclaim the territories once subject to the Comneni. Their Empire comprised no more than the northwest of Asia, Constantinople, Thrace, part of Macedonia, including Thessalonica, a few islands in the northern Archipelago, and part of the Greek mainland. It was now flanked by the empire of Trebizond, which occupied the whole of the Black Sea coast from Heraclea to the Caucasus, by the despotat of Epirus, and, in Thessaly, the principality of Great Wallachia; there were Venetian possessions in the Peloponnesus, in Corfu, Cerigo, and Crete; there were Venetian baronies in all the islands of the Archipelago, Genoese possessions on the Anatolian coast and the large islands adjoining it, Chios and Lesbos; lastly, there was a duchy of Athens in central Greece, and a principality of Achaia in the Peloponnesus. Twenty states sprang up in what had been the Greek Empire; and the realm now known by that name was weaker than ever.

The Ruin of the Empire under the Palaeologi

The coming of the Ottoman Turks in the fourteenth century was to complete its ruin. In the north, the young Balkan states were growing at the expense of the old Empire; Stephen Dushan conquered nearly the whole of Macedonia in the middle of the fourteenth century and proclaimed himself "Czar of the Serbs and Romans," and at the same time Bulgaria was spreading into Thrace. Meanwhile the Ottomans completed the conquest of Asia.

They took Brusa, which in 1326 became the Sultan's capital, Nicomedia, and Nicaea. In 1340 the Empire possessed scarcely more than Philadelphia in all Asia; this city remained Greek until 1391. In 1354 the Turks moved into Europe and settled at Gallipoli. In 1360 they took Adrianople and made it their capital. Soon the whole of Thrace was in their hands. Constantinople, isolated from the rest of the Empire together with Selymbria, Rodosto, and Heraclea, formed no more than an enclave in the middle of the Turkish State and had great difficulty in maintaining sea communications with its remaining territories: Thessalonica, Thessaly, and the despotat of the Morea. The Emperor, hemmed in and blockaded in his capital, was obliged to pay tribute to the Sultan and furnish him with a military contingent. In 1397 Bayazid subjugated Thessaly, in 1430 the Turks took Thessalonica, and in 1446 Murad II overran the Morea. Constantinople itself was now almost all that remained of the Empire.

Yet it fought on. In 1397 and 1422 it succeeded in repulsing the Ottoman attack. But the city was at the end of its tether. When in 1453 Mohammed II launched the final assault, there were barely 8000 men to defend it, and the best of them were foreigners. Out of 30 or 35,000 inhabitants able to bear arms less than 5000 Greeks—4973 to be exact—were willing to fight for their country. The other 3000 combatants were Genoese and Venetians and a few Cretans and Spaniards, to whom may be added the 2000 seamen forming the ships' companies of vessels massed in the Golden Horn. This was a small enough force to defend the city against 160,000 Turks with their terrific artillery and huge fleet; yet they held out for eight heroic weeks—from April 6 until May 29, 1453—and their glorious action shed grandeur and beauty on the dying Empire. But indeed the Empire had been dead for nearly a century when Constantinople fell; and the causes of its death were financial ruin and the decline of military strength.

VIII. Byzantium and the West

It has sometimes been asked whether Western intervention might have saved Byzantium from ruin, and whether the Latins, by dissociating themselves from its destiny, hastened its fall and were blind to the interests of Christendom. To say that Western help could have revived the exhausted realm would be an overstatement. The decadence of the Eastern Empire can be fully accounted for, as we have seen, by exclusively Eastern factors. But it is also true that the Latins, through their greed and enduring enmity, contributed in a great measure to its downfall; and it will be useful to examine the many reasons for this enmity and find out how much harm it did to the Empire.

1. RELIGIOUS REASONS

Relations between the Greek Church and the Papacy were strained almost from the beginning. The ambitious Patriarchs of Constantinople, in their obvious desire to be on an equal footing with the Popes, disturbed and offended the Romans. In the fifth century Pope Leo the Great protested energetically against the canon of the Council of Chalcedon, which allowed the bishop of the imperial city the same honorific prerogatives as the bishop of ancient Rome. In the sixth century Gregory the Great protested with even greater vigour—and no more success—against the title of Oecumenical Patriarch which, with the Emperor's consent, was assumed by the leader of the Byzantine Church. Conversely, the right claimed by the successors of St. Peter to subject the Eastern Church to Roman primacy deeply affronted the independent spirit of the Byzantine clergy and above all aroused misgivings in the hearts of patriotic Greeks.

But a more fundamental difference separated the two worlds and helped to render each incomprehensible to the other. To Oriental prelates, who were erudite, astute, subtle, and skilled in disputation, the Western Church seemed singularly ignorant and uncouth. Its servants understood less and less Greek as time went on; they grasped nothing of the complicated heresies for which the Byzantines had such a passion, and in their straightforward, simple faith they regarded these dangerous Oriental notions with deep anxiety and some contempt. An instinctive aversion existed between the two, and in the fourth century eminent men on each side treated one another with remarkable severity. Later, Gregory the Great said to the Greeks, "We have not your finesse, but neither have we your falseness," and by the sixth century the Greeks were regarded throughout the West as being wily and untrustworthy people.

A yet more serious question set East and West at loggerheads. As we know, the Emperor of Byzantium claimed absolute authority in religious matters; and whereas Eastern bishops, being courtiers and men of the world, and anxious to win the prince's aid and favour, meekly accepted the commands of the *Basileus*, the Popes regarded State interference as intolerable, and refused to be made the instruments of the sovereign's will. In opposition to the Greek Emperor, self-proclaimed king and priest, the Roman pontiff declared himself sole judge of conscience and sole defender of divine interests. Whereas the Byzantines placed the Church at the service of the Empire, Popes Gelasius and Symmachus in the fifth century formulated the Roman theory, in which imperial claims were haughtily dismissed. Between two such disparate conceptions conflict was inevitable, and this was to have the gravest consequences for the relationship between Byzantium and Rome.

The Political Rift between Byzantium and Rome

From the end of the fifth century Eastern and Western Churches were divided by schism for more than thirty years as a result of the religious policy of Emperors Zeno and Anastasius. The situation grew even more tense when Justinian's conquests, by bringing Italy back under Byzantine authority, made the Pope the Emperor's subject. Accustomed to the meekness of Eastern patriarchs, the *basileis* from the sixth to the eighth century expected similar obedience from the bishops of the West. To obtain it, no measure seemed to them too stern, no punishment too harsh. For two centuries everything possible was done to break papal resistance; some Popes were deposed, others arrested, forcibly transported to Constantinople, imprisoned, and ill-treated. Martin I was condemned and died in exile. Others were plotted against or openly attacked by imperial officers; the papal palace was invaded more than once, the treasures of the Church stolen, and the Pope's life threatened. But this policy, always so successful in the East, had no effect in Italy; the Papacy had become a power in its own right, aware of its influence in the peninsula and of its moral authority throughout the West. In the course of the seventh and eighth centuries the Popes felt their power increasing. They saw their authority gradually ousting that of the Byzantine administration; they saw officers of the Crown beginning to ask and take their advice. The *basileis* accepted their intervention in the conduct of political affairs and more than once begged their support. Above all, the Italian peoples took every opportunity of showing their attachment to this Church, which was their only shield against the barbarians, and they were ready to take up arms in its defence. Increased in stature by memories of old Rome and encouraged by the distance separating them from the Emperors, the Popes stood forth boldly as defenders of Orthodoxy against Eastern heresies; undaunted and unyielding, they opposed and condemned the Monothelites in the seventh century and the Iconoclasts in the eighth; and although for a long time their religious opposition did not shake their fidelity to the Empire, yet in the end the struggle began imperceptibly to shift into the sphere of politics.

In the seventh century, in the course of legal proceedings against Martin I, the Pope was charged with having betrayed the Empire, and his supporters were accused of being the enemies of the State. Abbot Maximus was asked the significant question: "Why do you love the Romans and hate the Greeks?" In Constantinople it was felt that Italy was becoming increasingly disaffected and discontented. By the end of the seventh century this discontent had begun to break out in insurrection. The people rallied to Rome; they acquired the habit of listening to the Popes' advice, and they rose in their defence. There was a not ill-founded fear that the Bishops of Rome, who by now reigned almost as sovereigns in the papal city, would be tempted to dissociate themselves from the heretical and tyrannical Emperor and look elsewhere for protection. For a long time the Popes hesitated to cause an open breach, as that would have run counter to all their traditions. But in 751 Byzantine rule in Italy succumbed to the Lombard assault, and help from distant Byzantium was no longer to be hoped for. The Popes, having done all they could to save Ravenna and the Empire, were reduced to begging help from the Franks to save Rome from the Lombards. At the hands of the victorious Pepin, Stephen II accepted in 754 the once Byzantine territory constituting the papal domains, thus becoming an independent sovereign. The breach between Rome and Constantinople was now a fact. In the eyes of the Greeks, the Pope was a rebellious, faithless subject who had wrongfully seized imperial territory and, ignoring the Emperor, his master, had made himself his heir by unlawful means. But the days of imperial authority in Italy were over. In 774, Charlemagne solemnly confirmed Pepin's gift; in 787 the Popes ceased to date their official acts by the years of the Eastern Emperors. And in placing the crown of the re-established Western Empire on the head of Charlemagne, on December 25, 800, Leo III put the finishing touch to the political breach between Rome and Byzantium and rendered permanent the situation created by the events of 754.

Byzantium and the West

The Religious Breach

The West had thus dealt a blow to both the real power and the moral prestige of the Greek Empire, and for a long time the Byzantines cherished a fierce grudge against the Papacy. Other factors were soon to embitter relations between the two Churches. Apart from the support demanded of Rome by the adversaries of the Iconoclasts, and their declarations in favour of Roman primacy—conduct which understandably displeased the imperial government and caused anxiety to the leaders of the Eastern Church—the rivalry between Byzantium and Rome in the ninth century in the matter of converting the heathen soon gave rise to further friction. In Moravia, German bishops savagely resisted and finally defeated the mission of Cyril and Methodius. In Croatia, and on the Dalmatian coast, Rome brought under its jurisdiction the Slavic peoples whom the Greeks had just converted to the Orthodox faith. In Bulgaria, which had been converted by Byzantium, Pope Nicholas I warmly welcomed Czar Boris's overtures, and at his request sent him Roman priests. Such incursions into the allegedly Greek sphere of influence exasperated the Byzantines, who resented these blatant attempts to impose Roman primacy on the East. Photius was particularly clever at exploiting this discontent and at turning his own private cause into a national issue.

On the one hand, there was Nicholas I, charging his legates to enquire into the dismissal of Ignatius and claiming the right to be supreme judge of the dispute; on the other, the ambitious Patriarch of Constantinople, who affirmed the independence of his episcopal see and, in terms of courtesy and deference, negotiated with the Pope as with an equal. He retorted to the excommunication pronounced upon him by Nicholas I in 863 by anathematizing the Pope in 867; he denounced his unlawful interference in the Eastern Church's affairs, and his claims to universal dominion. The root of the trouble lay there, rather than in the minor differences of dogma, liturgy, or discipline—the *filioque* clause or the use of unleavened bread—advanced by Byzantine polemicists in justification of the schism. By virtue of the privileges of the Apostolic See, "planted and rooted by God Himself," the Pope claimed "plenitude of omnipotence, the guidance of all the lambs of Christ." It was this claim that neither Photius, the Greek Church, nor the imperial government could stomach. The schism was of short duration, and so was Photius' triumph. The accession of Basil I brought about the Patriarch's dismissal and his conviction at the Council of 869. But at this assembly it could be seen that, in opposing Rome, Photius had interpreted the national feeling. When the question arose as to which Church would have jurisdiction over Bulgaria, the Emperor and the East in general were unanimous in rejecting the Roman claim, and Patriarch Ignatius himself, in consecrating a Greek archbishop for Bulgaria, was merely continuing the Photian tradition. In such circumstances friction was bound to increase. The West was gravely displeased by the reinstallation of Photius on the patriarchal throne, by his haughty refusal to submit to the papal conditions and by the way in which, at the Council of 879, he annulled and anathematized the acts of his adversaries and proclaimed himself "the supreme pontiff, holding his authority from God Himself." Although peace was re-established later, the patriarchs' hostility to Rome revived at the end of the tenth century, and in 1054 the ill-timed, haughty obstinacy of Leo IX and his legates gave the ambitious Michael Cerularius the pretext he had hoped for to confirm the breach.

From that time onward Rome and Byzantium were permanently divided, and this was to have serious consequences. In the eyes of the West, the Greeks were now merely schismatics, to whom neither consideration nor tolerance was due, and whom there was every reason to distrust. The constant aim of papal policy was to achieve, either amicably or by compulsion, the reunion of the Churches. Meanwhile the Byzantines maintained a steady polemical activity against the heretical Latins, which exacerbated misunderstanding, resentment, and hatred. In the end, political parties came to be classified according to their attitude to the West; to be λατινόφρων, as it was called—to feel and show sympathy for the Latins—was to be a traitor to one's country. Religious antagonism, inflaming mutual enmity to the point of frenzy, did more than anything else to deepen the gulf between the two worlds.

Byzantium and the West

2. POLITICAL FACTORS

From the second half of the eleventh century, Western ambitions were focussed on the Eastern world. The enterprises of Robert Guiscard had alarmed the Greeks, and with good reason, while the contact resulting from the Crusades aggravated mistrust and hatred. To the elegant, sophisticated society of Byzantium, the Latins appeared somewhat boorish. Westerners, on their part, were contemptuous of the schismatic Greeks and had lost the respect so long felt for the imperial city. In their blustering conceit, they grasped nothing of the subtleties and fine shades of Oriental politeness, and were often offended by what seemed to them discourtesy. They were also excited by the prodigious wealth of the Greek capital and did not conceal their covetousness. The Greeks had good reason to be uneasy.

The Crusaders put little faith in them; indeed, they complained bitterly of the ingratitude, double-dealing, and treachery of the emperors and their subjects. Certainly the Byzantines, exasperated by the brutal behaviour of the Western peoples, often took mean advantage of them and treated them badly. Even in the First Crusade, the basic antagonism that held the two civilizations apart gave rise to mutual suspicion, constant friction, and conflict.

The emperors, indeed, did all they could to smooth out the difficulties and promote harmony between these clashing worlds. But they never understood the great surge of enthusiasm that swept the West into the Holy Land for its deliverance, and saw the Crusade as a purely political move. Like their subjects, they could not rid themselves of the fear of some attack on Constantinople, and suspected the great Latin lords of "dreaming of the Empire of Byzantium." The emperors were first and foremost Greeks, and regarded the foreigners who overran their provinces as mercenaries ready to sell their services to the *Basileus*, at a price, or as potential vassals willing to do homage and swear fidelity to the Lord of Byzantium. These assumptions stung Latin pride and emphasized the distance at which the Greeks held their inconvenient guests. The almost inexhaustible patience of the *Basileus* was often sorely tried by the tactless, proud, grasping Latins, who, said Anna Comnena, were "by nature brazen-faced and insolent, greedy for money, incapable of resisting any whim, and above all more talkative than any other men on earth." In such circumstances no agreement between the two could ever be sincere or lasting. The emperors had every reason to complain of the Crusaders' forgetfulness in fulfilling their obligations and to dread the dangers to which the Crusades exposed their realm. The Latins, on the other hand, justly resented the hostile measures taken against them, the sometimes treacherous methods used to get rid of them, and the undercurrent of enmity of which they were continually aware.

Throughout the twelfth century this antagonism increased with every encounter, and it was not long before the men of the West conceived the idea of solving the Byzantine question by force, believing it to be the best and most profitable way of dealing with these shifty Greeks, who were doing the Crusade more harm than good.

The policy of the twelfth-century emperors only made things worse. The expeditions of the Comneni against the Latin principalities in Syria and their desire to establish suzerainty over the Frankish states that sprang up as a result of the Crusades disquieted the West. From the beginning of the twelfth century, Bohemond, Prince of Antioch, preached the Crusade, not now against Moslems, but against the Greek Empire. Displeasure deepened when John Comnenus laid hands on Antioch, when Manuel Comnenus forced humiliating submission on Renaud de Châtillon and treated the Latin kings of Jerusalem as vassals. But when the imperialist policy of Manuel Comnenus threatened the West, in aiming at the recapture of Italy and the destruction of the Germanic Holy Roman Empire, Western anger knew no bounds. Such enterprises were to bring down thunderbolts upon the Empire. We know how arrogantly Frederick Barbarossa replied to Manuel's claims. Ten years later, during the Third Crusade, the German Emperor openly announced his intention of subjugating "all Romania." For his proposed capture of Constantinople he sought help from all the seacoast towns of Italy, and invited the Pope to preach the Crusade against the Greeks. The situation went from bad to worse when his son, Henry VI, ascended the throne.

Henry had inherited the ambitions of the Norman kings of Sicily, and so began by demanding from Isaac Angelus all that part of the Greek Empire once conquered by his predecessors, from Dyrrachium to Thessalonica; he also claimed satisfaction not only for the obstacles placed in his father's way by the Greeks, but for the intrigues by which Manuel Comnenus had detached the Papacy from the Empire and attempted to chase Barbarossa from Italy. As if he had been, in the words of a Greek chronicler, "lord of lords and king of kings," Henry VI laid down the law to Constantinople and dreamed already of placing the crown of the *basileis* upon his head. He had compelled the kingdoms of Armenia and Cyprus to become his vassals, and he now prepared to enter Syria, hoping to conquer Constantinople from there and unite East and West in a single empire. Nicetas, in a curious and significant passage, tells how the German Emperor's demands were received in Constantinople. Alexius Angelus was resigned— "a thing he had never been before," remarks the historian—to the purchase of peace for gold. But, recalling the old methods of Byzantine diplomacy, he fancied he could dazzle the German ambassadors by a display of wealth; and for Christmas 1196 he organized a splendid reception at the palace, at which the whole court appeared in brilliant array. Nicetas himself considered the idea ill-timed and somewhat ridiculous; and so it proved. The Germans were unimpressed by all the magnificence; the sight of it merely put an edge to their covetousness and their desire to begin fighting these effeminate, gold-bedecked Greeks as soon as possible. In vain the Byzantines invited them to admire "the jewelled splendour of the Emperor, and to taste the vernal delights showered upon them in the depths of winter." The ambassadors retorted rudely that soon the Greeks would have to replace gold by iron, to fight "men who do not shine with the brilliance of precious stones, nor boast of Orient pearls or of the fire of jewels mingled with purple and gold, but who, like true sons of Mars, bear flames of fury in their eyes, more brilliant than the fire of gems, and the drops of whose sweat are fairer than pearls." The time had long passed when Western barbarians stood in awe and admiration of Byzantium. The Crusades had taught them both the wealth and the weakness of the Empire and sown anti-Greek prejudice throughout the Latin world. Few things, indeed, did Byzantium more harm than the Crusades.

3. COMMERCIAL FACTORS

The commercial ambitions of Italian maritime cities further complicated a very tense situation.

We have already seen something of the grasping policy of these cities: how in the eleventh century and even more in the twelfth, they—especially Venice—were intent on turning to account the rich markets that lay open to their enterprise. We have also seen how the Greeks protested at the greed and insolence of these foreigners. The Constantinople of the Comneni was full of Latins; Eustathius of Thessalonica reports that towards the end of Manuel's reign there were no fewer than 60,000 of them in the capital. The favour shown them by the Emperor drew them in multitudes to the East, and not only merchants. The army was full of soldiers from the West: Lombards, Frenchmen, Englishmen, and Germans; and Manuel had even rearmed his cavalry in the Latin fashion. In administration and diplomacy, too, Latins held important positions. "Despising his little Greeks as weak and effeminate," says William of Tyre, "Manuel entrusted affairs of importance to Latins alone, rightly relying upon their fidelity and strength." Such blatant favouritism displeased the Greeks as much as did the arrogance and cupidity of the Italian traders. Nicetas complained loudly of the trust the Emperor placed in these foreigners, who were ignorant of the Greek language and culture, "and who spat better than they spoke." He complained that they were treated as the Empire's best and most faithful servants; that they were entrusted with the most difficult missions and the most exalted posts; and, above all, that they were laden with money that had been painfully wrung from the Emperor's subjects. He noted, too, that these things resulted in unpopularity for the *Basileus.*

Above all, they resulted in an increase of hostility to the exploiters. The unruly population of Constantinople and the clergy who swayed it felt fierce hatred for the people of the West, which sometimes broke out in wild nationalist explosions. This happened in 1182. Andronicus Comnenus had only to spread the rumour that the Latins in the capital were planning to attack the Greeks, for the citizens to besiege the Latin quarter of Constantinople. They sacked and burned and massacred both clergy and laity, women and children, and even the aged and the sick in the hospitals. Three years later the Normans took Thessalonica in ruthless retaliation. These reciprocal acts of violence deepened the gulf between Byzantium and the West.

The Fourth Crusade and Its Consequences

The Fourth Crusade was the logical outcome of religious antipathy, political ambition, economic greed, and incurable antagonism between two races and two worlds. In overthrowing the Byzantine Empire, with the tacit connivance of the Papacy and the universal applause of Western Christendom, in setting a Count of Flanders on the imperial throne, and in dismembering the realm for the benefit of the Venetians, the Latins dealt a blow to Byzantium from which it never recovered, and exacerbated the Greeks' hatred of the West. Byzantine patriotism burned more fiercely than ever. Nevertheless, from this continual contact, inimical though it often was, there emerged an intellectual and social exchange. If Latins living in the East learned to reflect upon many things that before had hardly occurred to them, Byzantine society also changed under the impact of Western ideas, though few outside the élite were affected—and then only superficially—by Latin ways and habits. The masses remained implacable in their loathing and mistrust of foreigners, and with them the Greek Church, which was always disturbed by Roman ambitions and was outraged, as by sacrilege, at the thought of any closer relationship with the Papacy. The Byzantium of the Palaeologi, even more than that of the Comneni, kept its eyes upon the West, but the two worlds remained enemies. In their overweening pride, the Byzantines, "Romans, sons of Romans," as they sometimes called themselves, refused stubbornly to see the Latins as anything but barbarians and felt only contempt for the new spirit blowing from the West. Western peoples on their part could not but detest the schismatic, faithless Greeks. Agreement in such circumstances was impossible.

4. BYZANTIUM AND THE WEST IN THE PERIOD OF THE PALAEOLOGI

The restoration of the Greek Empire by the Palaeologi made the relationship of East and West more difficult. The West was set upon re-establishing the shattered Latin empire; it was the ambition of all the European princes, from Manfred Hohenstaufen to Charles of Anjou, to extend their dominion into the Eastern world, for whose wealth Venice and Genoa competed. Meanwhile the Papacy dreamed of achieving the Union of the Churches by hook or by crook, and more than once in the fourteenth century it favoured the attempts made to conquer the

Greek Empire. The Byzantines, therefore, were hardly mistaken in saying that in every act, whether openly hostile or seemingly disinterested, the Western peoples had but one aim: "the destruction of the Greek city, race, and name."

Some emperors had the political sense to see that in order to save the Greek Empire, they must maintain peace with the West at all costs and appease the Papacy by assenting to the Union of the Churches. To protect his realm against Charles of Anjou and pursue his policy of restoration undisturbed, Michael VIII came to terms with Gregory X, at the Council of Lyon in 1274, and placed the Byzantine Church once more under Roman authority. When the Empire stood at bay against the Turks, John VIII made a similar desperate effort at the eleventh hour and came to an agreement with Eugene IV, at the Council of Florence in 1439, by which union with Rome was re-established. Both in the thirteenth and fifteenth centuries these praiseworthy attempts— which were of a purely political character—were defeated by the savage intransigence and stupidity of the Greek clergy and people. The Union of Lyon touched off so alarming a crisis in the Empire that on the death of Michael VIII, eight years later, his successor's first care was to denounce it. Nor was the Florentine agreement given a warmer welcome. The people of Constantinople hooted at and insulted the prelates who had signed the convention, accusing them of having "sold their Church and their country for a little gold." When the Emperor tried to bring the treaty into force, the roar of riot was heard beneath the very roof of St. Sophia. "We would rather see the Turkish turban reigning in Constantinople than the Latin mitre," cried the frenzied fanatics, though their city was even then under the threat of Ottoman attack. It must be admitted that however fiery and passionate this hatred of the West may have been, it was not blind. The imminent danger of Turkish invasion had taught the West nothing, nor had it altered its anti-Byzantine policy. When Byzantium was facing its doom, the West was thinking less of how to defend it than of how to profit by its distress and so conquer it.

The Latins made their greatest mistake in never trying to allay this rancour and hatred. To help the Empire effectively, the West would have had to make up its mind to one great, united, and disinterested effort. At times it seemed to perceive this and to realize that in the interests of Christianity itself, the Turks should be beaten off and Constantinople saved at all costs. But the realization came too late and too imperfectly. The Crusade of Nicopolis in 1396 failed as lamentably as that of Varna in 1444; and apart from these two attempts, the Latins confined themselves to giving a flattering welcome and empty promises to the emperors who begged their help: namely John V, Manuel II, and John VIII. With the Palaeologi, the West pursued a selfish policy throughout, intent only on taking advantage of their distress in order to exploit the Empire and gain religious and political ascendancy over it. Western Christendom allowed Constantinople to sink beneath the Turkish assault and, less concerned with present needs than with old enmity, basely abandoned the Greek Empire to its fate.

For 350 years, from the end of the eleventh century to the middle of the fifteenth, the establishment of a *modus vivendi* between East and West was one of the essential problems of European politics; it was indeed, as has been said, the mediaeval Eastern Question. Greeks and Latins were alike powerless to solve it because of their mutual mistrust and their vindictiveness. Even today something of that hatred lingers in the prejudice of Western minds in contemplating the memory of Byzantium.

Book Four

Byzantium's Contribution to
the World

I. Byzantine Civilization

For almost a thousand years, from the end of the sixth century until the middle of the fifteenth, the Byzantine Empire was the seat of a civilization that outshone all others, a civilization as brilliant as any in the Middle Ages and perhaps the only

Gold pectoral cross. Height: 2³⁄₁₆″. 10th-11th century.

one known to Europe between the end of the fifth century and
the beginning of the eleventh. While the barbarian states of the
West were struggling to assemble the elements of a new culture
from scanty memories of Rome, and while the Carolingian renaissance of the ninth century and the Ottonian renaissance of the
tenth were painfully emerging—and both were noteworthy only
by comparison with the night of the preceding ages—Byzantium
was all grace, all elegance, and the centre of outstanding development both in thought and art. Because of the marked superiority
of its civilization, it was to exert a deep and lasting influence on
East and West, thereby leaving its mark on history and doing
great service to the world. We shall consider the nature of this
influence and service later; first we must define the essential character of Byzantine civilization and analyse the different forms in
which it appeared.

1. THE CLASSICAL TRADITION

Nowhere in the mediaeval world was the antique tradition more
completely preserved than in Byzantium; nowhere was direct
contact with Hellenism better maintained. Though politically
the Empire could claim to be the descendant and heir of Rome,
intellectually, it was firmly rooted in ancient Greece. All the
famed capitals of Hellenism lay within its boundaries: Athens,
Alexandria, and Antioch. And Byzantium itself, the new capital,
was essentially a Greek city. The peoples of the realm were for
the most part of Greek blood, or at least Hellenized, and the
majority spoke Greek; therefore they had a keener understanding
and appreciation of classical literature than other nations. For
the rest of mediaeval Europe, Greek was a difficult foreign language, which even the best brains were long incapable of understanding. In Byzantium Greek was the national tongue; and that
alone was enough to give Byzantine culture a character altogether
different from that of other mediaeval civilizations. For the
Greeks, no rediscovery of ancient Greece was ever necessary.

Whereas the manuscripts of most Greek writers reached the
Western world rather late, and in relatively small numbers, Byzantine libraries were stocked with all the riches of Greek literature, and many works were to be found there of which only the

Porphyry head of a man in a Phrygian cap. Height: 7½". Early 4th
century (?).

titles and the memory remain. The manuscripts of classical authors were regarded as precious treasures; they were copied with care and eagerly read and annotated. And although between the seventh and ninth centuries, neglect born of the misery of the times—or sometimes religious intolerance—caused the destruction of many ancient texts, although the capture of Constantinople by the Crusaders in 1204 and by the Turks in 1453 proved no less fatal to many of these treasures, yet the fact remains that Byzantium preserved and studied the principal masterpieces of Hellenic literature.

We do not know what was in the great library of the Basilica, except that besides works of "divine wisdom" it contained those of "profane wisdom," and that its volumes totalled more than 30,000. In the ninth century the Sacred Palace also possessed a great library, and Constantine Porphyrogenitus devoted a scholar's zeal to its enrichment. The patriarchate had its library, too.

Our knowledge of certain private collections enables us to surmise what these great public ones contained. For instance, the library of Patriarch Photius was immensely rich. Among the 280 books that he analysed with such critical discrimination in his *Myriobiblion,* the classical texts of historians, orators, grammarians, physicians, and even writers of fiction greatly outnumbered ecclesiastical authors; and although neither great philosophers, such as Aristotle and Plato, nor great historians, like Thucydides, Polybius, and Plutarch, figure in this collection, and although the poets are entirely absent, it would be wrong to conclude that Photius did not possess them. No doubt in the circle of intellectuals with whom he discussed his reading, he took pride and delight in dealing with works not read by everyone. In the course of his professional career he wrote commentaries on Aristotle, the Neo-Platonists, and Plato himself; and it is clear that a man who owned the complete works—which we no longer have—of Ctesias and Theopompus, Diodorus and Dionysius of Halicarnassus, Appian, Arrian, Dio Cassius, and Hesychius of Miletus, is the more likely to have possessed the great works of classical literature.

Let us consider Bessarion's collection, which became the nucleus of the celebrated St. Mark's library of Venice. Of the 500 or so Greek manuscripts that it contained, more than 300 were

ΕΥΑΓΓΕΛΙΟΝΚΤΑΜ

ρχὴ τοῦ λα ττελίονιῦ χῦ ἰ̅υ τοῦ οὖ ὡς γέ
γραπται ἐν τοῖς προφήταις · ἰδοὺ ἐγὼ ἀπο
στέλλω τὸν ἄγγελόν μου πρὸ προσώπου σου
ὃς κατασκευάσει τὴν ὁδόν σου ἔμπροσθέν
σου φωνὴ βοῶντος ἐν τῇ ἐρήμῳ · ἑτοιμά
σατε τὴν ὁδὸν κ̅υ̅ εὐθείας ποιεῖτε τὰς τρί
βους αὐτοῦ · ἐγένετο Ἰωάννης βαπτίζων
ἐν τῇ ἐρήμῳ · καὶ κηρύσσων βάπτισμα με
τανοίας · εἰς ἄφεσιν ἁμαρτιῶν · καὶ ἐξεπο
ρεύετο πρὸς αὐτόν · πᾶσα ἡ ἰουδαία χώρα
καὶ οἱ ἱεροσολυμῖται · καὶ ἐβαπτίζοντο πάντες
ἐν τῷ ἰορδάνῃ ποταμῷ ὑπ' αὐτοῦ ἐξομολο
γούμενοι τὰς ἁμαρτίας αὐτῶν ·

The Cleveland Museum of Art, J. H. Wade Collection

Headpiece from the Four Gospels. Illuminated manuscript. 11th century.

the works of secular authors: orators, such as Demosthenes, Isocrates, and Lysias; historians, like Herodotus and Thucydides, Plutarch, Diodorus Siculus, Dio Cassius, and Strabo; philosophers, like Aristotle, Plato, Plotinus, and Proclus; poets, like Homer, Hesiod, Sophocles, Euripides, Aristophanes, Pindar, Apollonius Rhodius, and Lycophron; also, physicians, such as Hippocrates and Galen; and mathematicians, of whom Ptolemy was one. These writers were to be found even in monastic libraries, among countless patriotic and sacred works. The ancient catalogue of Patmos (1201) is strangely deficient in secular authors, though it includes Aristotle's *Categories* and a volume by Josephus. That of 1355 indicates less caution and a wider curiosity; we find there the manuscripts of Diodorus Siculus, Xenophon's *Cyropaedia*, and Plato's *Dialogues*. Histories, too, seem to have been remarkably popular. In the library of the Graeco-Italian monastery of St. Nicholas of Casole we find Aristotle and Aristophanes, while the great religious houses of Studium and Athos contained a number of works by secular authors.

A still better proof of the Byzantines' intimate knowledge of Greek literature is the nature and extent of their reading, as indicated in what they wrote. We have seen how much a man like Photius read, in the ninth century. If we glance at the Lexicon of tenth-century Suidas, we note that, although some part of the texts quoted may have been taken from anthologies, the author had a wide knowledge of ancient literature. He had read Homer, Hesiod, Pindar, Sophocles, Aristophanes, Herodotus, Thucydides, Xenophon, Polybius, Lucian, and many others. Psellus, in the eleventh century, was a passionate admirer of Greek antiquity, and his encyclopaedic knowledge neglected nothing of it that survived. He loved the great philosophers of classical Greece, Aristotle and the Neo-Platonists; and he loved Plato even more. He commented upon the poets—Homer in particular—with keen and subtle curiosity; he read Pindar and Epicharmus, Aeschylus, Sophocles, Euripides, Archilochus, Sappho, Aristophanes, and Menander, and the great orators and historians. He had a profound sense of the charm of Greek poetry and the Greek language. In the twelfth century John Tzetzes read all there was to be read: Homer, Hesiod, Pindar, the tragic authors, Aristophanes, Theocritus, Apollonius Rhodius, Lycophron, Herodotus, Diodorus,

Plutarch, Arrian, Dio Cassius, Lysias, Demosthenes, Aeschines, Plato, Aristotle, Strabo, and Lucian. Theodore Metochites, of the early fourteenth century, read no less widely. His studies included Aristotle, Plato, Xenophon, Josephus, Plutarch, Dio Chrysostom, Ptolemy, and many others. Further examples could be cited, but these are enough to show with what care and also to what extent Byzantium had preserved the heritage of ancient Greece.

Greek literature, indeed, formed the very basis of Byzantine education. Much of this consisted of the study of sacred books, of the works of the Fathers and lives of the saints; but every man of culture knew Homer, "the all-wise Homer," as Tzetzes called him, "the sea of discourse." With Homer went Hesiod and Pindar, a few of the tragedies, Aristophanes, Theocritus, Lycophron, Thucydides, some of the works of Demosthenes, Plato and Aristotle, Plutarch's *Lives*, Libanius, and Lucian. We have seen what Psellus knew at the age of twenty, and how Anna Comnena, too, had read Homer and the lyricists, the tragic authors and Aristophanes, historians—Thucydides and Polybius, orators—Isocrates and Demosthenes, the treatises of Aristotle and Plato's *Dialogues;* she had learnt the history of ancient Greece and its mythology, the beautiful legends of Hellad, and also the art of speaking. She had penetrated, as she herself said, "to the end of the end of Hellenism." At the University of Constantinople the "consuls of the philosophers" and the "masters of the rhetoricians" drew their inspiration from ancient tradition. In the school founded in the ninth century by Caesar Bardas, philosophy and grammar took first place, and by the latter was meant all that today we call philology, that is, not only grammar, metre, and lexicography, but commentary and often the critical study of all the ancient texts. From the ninth century to the fifteenth this teaching remained unaltered. In the eleventh century Psellus expounded the classics with an enthusiasm for Athens which is expressed in striking terms. He taught Platonic philosophy with brilliant success, and his disciples, including John Italus, carried on the tradition into the twelfth century. During the period of the Comneni, Eustathius of Thessalonica wrote commentaries on Homer and Pindar and gathered a group of eminent students about his professorial chair. Even in the time of the Palaeologi the great professors of the University of Constantinople—Planudes, Moschopulus and Triclinius—were fine philologists; they tried their hand at textual criticism and were untiring in the interpretation or translation of classical authors. Homer, Hesiod, Pindar, Theocritus, Aeschylus, Sophocles, Euripides, and Aristophanes were in turn the object of their studies; and their works, imbued with the spirit of humanism, made no small contribution to the great awakening of the Renaissance.

We find the same love of classical letters among private individuals. A prince of the imperial family, Isaac Comnenus, the brother of Emperor John, devoted his leisure to writing commentaries on Homer. The wife of Manuel Comnenus, though of German birth, took pride in teaching the beauties of Greek literature, and asked Tzetzes to comment upon the Iliad especially for her. Her grammarian described her as "a lady very fond of Homer."

We can appreciate, then, to what extent Byzantine society was pervaded by the spirit of the antique. Besides the spoken language, which came to resemble vernacular Greek, there was the written one, as used by the majority of the great Byzantine writers: a learned, almost artificial language, modelled on the classics. From Procopius and Agathias in the sixth century to Psellus, Anna Comnena, and Nicetas Acominatus in the eleventh and twelfth, and after them the writers of the period of the Palaeologi, Byzantine authors aspired to imitate the most illustrious of the Greek masters and delighted in affecting the sober Attic grace of style, though the result was apt to be somewhat mannered. In the same way, they went in for antique forms: they composed witty epigrams in the manner of the Alexandrians of the Anthology and wrote ingenious essays in the style of Lucian. And just as their way of writing was an imitation of the antique, so their thought was moulded on classical ideas. They amused themselves by disguising the identity of the new peoples they met with ancient names: they called Arabs Persians, Serbians Triballians, Bulgars Mysians, Alans Massagetae, and Hungarians or Russians Scythians. Their minds were full of Hellenic history and mythology. It has already been noted that on the eve of final disaster, Byzantium sought solace in the classics; and to rouse and spur on the flagging spirits of their people, fifteenth-century writers evoked the glorious names of Pericles, Epaminondas, Themis-

Silver dish from the "Cyprus Treasure." David slaying the lion. 7th century.

tocles, and Leonidas; they found in eternal Greece the sole path of salvation for the dying Empire.

Similarly, as we shall see, Byzantine art was steeped in the Hellenic tradition; subjects borrowed from antiquity abounded, while the imitation or copying of ancient manuscripts was a regular practice. At the time of the Macedonian Emperors and of the Comneni, ancient Greek culture inspired the renaissance of the arts as strongly as it inspired that of thought.

The Stamp of Christianity

But the Byzantines were more than the heirs of ancient Greece and, as it were, the curators of the great works it bequeathed to them. Other elements went to make up their civilization and gave it its original and individual character.

The triumph of Christianity as a State religion had brought the Church into very close touch with the public and private life of Byzantium. Protected by the public authorities and indebted to imperial favour for its ever-increasing importance, the Church placed itself at the service of the sovereign and became one of the instruments of government. It held a no less important place in the society it claimed to guide. We know of the religious fervour and mysticism of the Byzantines and of their inclination to asceticism and the solitude of the monastic life; we know how deeply impressed they were by the magnificence of the Orthodox liturgy, how passionately they believed in miracles and the marvellous virtues of relics and images; we know their trustful admiration of the monks and with what joy all of them, both men and women, looked up to these venerable men as their spiritual directors. Study of the Scriptures and of Patristic writings occupied an important place in education, as is shown by innumerable manuscripts that have come down to us, including those of St. Basil, St. Gregory of Nazianzus, St. Gregory of Nyssa, St. John Chrysostom, and St. John of Damascus. And although Anna Comnena declared that so much abstract and subtle theology "sometimes made her dizzy," few Byzantines could resist the charm of these books. Emperors, too, and not only for reasons of policy, took singular pleasure in discussing religious questions, and many did so with a remarkable grasp of their subject.

In all classes of Byzantine society we find the same passion for

† ΥΠΟΜΝΗΜΑ ΕΙΣ ΤΟΝ ΑΓΙΟΝ ΚΑΙ ΕΝΔΟΞΟΝ ΠΡΟΦΗΤΗΝ ΜΙΧΑΙΑΝ·

προφήτης τοῦ θεοῦ Μιχαίας οὖτος ἦν ἐκ τῆς ἰουδαίων μὲν χώρας· ὁ αὐτὸς δ' ἦν ὁ προτῆξ τῶν ἐλάχιστος· ἐκ δὲ τῆς φυλῆς ἐφραὶμ ὁρμώμενος. ἡμῖν παραδέδοται. καὶ τὸ σὺν τῇ δόξῃ περὶ αὐτὸν ὀφθῆναι τοῖς οἰκείοις προπάτορσιν. ὥστε μικροῦ καὶ τινι αὐτῷ προσγενομένην κατηγορίαν· οἱ αὖ δὴ παρατρησαν τι κ τὸν τοῦ ῥόμον

Ζυγὸν ἄτι καὶ σαν τι· τὸ σὺν τὴν ὅρι τι τῆς ἀρετῆς αὐ πολέγεται· ἡ μᾶλλον αὐ τῶν δεῖξαι τῶν οἰκείων· ἀπορο τῆς τοῦ μ τῷ καὶ ἀσπαράμιλ λον. ὅσα μὲν τοῖς μὲν γὰρ. καὶ οἱ παρὰ πατρός· οἱ αὐτῶν κληρονομήσαν τὴν ὅρι τῆν ἐκ δ' ἐξαίρετοι καὶ ταύ την εἰς τὸ πλέος φυλάξαι τῶν· ὁ δὲ ἐκ προσηγορίας τῷ τρόπῳ δὴ κατὰ τῶν ὁμοίων ὅτι ὁ πολῖτος ἀσθαι διὰ δὲ τῶν πρὸς τὰ καλὰ τῶν ἀσθενῶν. καὶ τὸ τοῦ ἤθους δὴ μισοπόνηρον. τῷ

theological disputation, both in public places and in the scholar's study. "When you ask someone to change some money," writes a Church Father, not without irony, "he treats you to a dissertation on the difference between the Father and the Son; when you want to know the price of bread, the seller will reply that the Father is greater than the Son; and when you ask if your bath is ready, you are told that the Son was born of nothing."

If a nation's thought finds fullest expression in its literature, the fact that theology alone produced at least half of all Byzantine literature is significant indeed. Few writers, even among the laity, did not at some time and at some point touch upon theology. It is no less remarkable that Byzantine art—though it was not, as is sometimes thought, of an exclusively religious character—placed itself at the service of the Church, which found in it a mighty instrument for instructing and edifying the faithful. Byzantine iconography was an essentially Church-inspired branch of art.

Contact with the East

Byzantium's proximity to the Orient brought other influences to bear. At the time when the Greek Empire was formed, Persia, reconstituted under the Sassanid dynasty, was becoming the scene of a true national renaissance; from the great cities of Meso-potamia traditions of the ancient Eastern civilizations were revived, and they spread through the Hellenic world. Later, the Empire maintained close political and commercial ties with the Moslems and the sumptuous courts of Damascus and Baghdad, and conceived a boundless admiration for the products of their exquisite craftsmanship. We have already noted the profound influence exerted by Eastern monarchies on the Byzantine conception of imperial authority and of its outward attributes. We know, too, that in the Byzantine character, Hellenic traits were blended with much that was purely Oriental. During the early centuries of the Empire, the eastern provinces—Syria and Egypt—took first place in religious, economic, and social life. Later, Constantinople was full of Orientals; in the higher ranks of the administration and the army there were great numbers of Armenians, and contemporary artists loved to portray their dark faces, hooked noses, and pointed beards, and the black hair falling to the shoulder. Baghdad and Byzantium were alike in their love of splendour and ceremonial, in the important place occupied by the palace and its intrigues in the political life of the State, in the abrupt ups and downs of personal fortunes, and in the frequency of military revolts. They resembled each other also in the strict seclusion

Courtesy of The Walters Art Gallery, Baltimore

Ivory panel from a casket. Adam meditating near a palm tree. 12th century.

of their women (the Christian *gynaeceum* being similar to the Moslem harem), in their love of display and fine clothes, in their preoccupation with stately attitudes, as well as in their taste for cruelty and bloodshed. Throughout the history of Byzantium an Eastern current flows through its civilization, its literature, and its art. From the East came many of its stories, proverbs, and popular beliefs, its liturgical and political movements, its ideas and its art forms. It was from the ancient East that Byzantium drew its monarchical tradition; there the Church found the pattern for many

Silver dish from the "Cyprus Treasure." David anointed by Samuel.
Early 7th century.

· 240 ·

of its ceremonies, and there artists learned that art's true function was to glorify God and the Emperor. This blend of two spirits, two rival traditions, Hellenic and Oriental, explains the mingled fantasy and immobility of Byzantine art and the combination of noble, simple, almost abstract beauty with vital realism.

So Hellenism, Christianity, and the East met and united to form the Byzantine civilization; Byzantium was therefore something more than the continuation of ancient Greece and, contrary to what is still too often believed, was capable of originality and creativeness. We have only to consider the wealth and variety of its literature, the flowering of its art, the refinements of its material life, and the complexity of its life of the mind, to observe in them all certain peculiarly Byzantine forms which gave this civilization a place apart in the history of the Middle Ages.

2. TRENDS OF THOUGHT

It is unnecessary—and would be tedious—to summarize here the whole history of Byzantine literature, and we will do no more than note and define the principal trends of thought.

History

History was the favourite form of expression and, together with religious poetry, is certainly the most striking aspect of the Byzantine genius. If we compare the great historians of the sixth century, Procopius, Agathias, Menander, and later Psellus, Cinnamus, and Nicetas, with their Latin contemporaries, we find that the Greeks were on a higher intellectual level. They were superior in political intelligence, in acuity of psychology, and in the sense of composition and style. We can feel that they had a long tradition behind them, and indeed in no other field do we perceive more clearly the imprint of antiquity. Procopius imitated Herodotus and Thucydides; Agathias, more of a rhetorician, was inspired by the poets; Theophylact, a strangely pretentious author, was influenced by Alexandrine literature. Later, Nicephorus Bryennius took Xenophon for his model, while Anna Comnena strove to emulate Thucydides and Polybius; in the fifteenth century men like Chalcocondyles and Critobulus kept closely to the pattern of Herodotus and Thucydides. Close imitation of classical models gave many of these historians a cramped, involved, and mannered style and also inspired them with the ambition to make history a true work of art, rather than a bald recital of events.

They were something more than mere imitators, however; many of them showed real individuality in their work. Their material alone would have been enough to make them creative artists. The great figures of Justinian, Belisarius, and Heraclius, the splendid work of the Macedonian Emperors, the vigorous political and literary movement that marked the period of the Comneni, and the amazing expansion of Frankish conquest in the East may be reckoned among the finest themes in all the history of mankind. Byzantine authors brought exceptional gifts to their work; they were meticulous in gathering their material, conscious of their responsibility as historians, and intent on maintaining an objective point of view. Many of them, including Procopius, Psellus, Michael Attaliates, Cinnamus, Nicetas, Acropolites, and Phrantzes, being court dignitaries or officers of State, were closely concerned with the events they describe; while others, like Constantine VII, Nicephorus Bryennius, Anna Comnena, and John Cantacuzenus were of a princely line and had firsthand knowledge of government. Consequently, though they were perhaps less successful in their efforts to be impartial and less frank than they allege themselves to be, they always had matters of interest to relate, with plenty of telling detail, and could present vivid eyewitness accounts of contemporary events. To illustrate the prodigious wealth and variety of this literary *genre*—the *genre* that best testifies to the development of Byzantine civilization—we have only to recall the names of its most famous exponents: Procopius, Agathias, Menander, and Evagrius in the sixth century; Theophylact Simo-

catta in the seventh; Constantine Porphyrogenitus and Leo Diaconus in the tenth; Psellus and Michael Attaliates in the eleventh;
Nicephorus Bryennius, Anna Comnena, Cinnamus, and Nicetas
in the twelfth; Acropolites and Pachymeres in the thirteenth;
Nicephorus Gregoras and John Cantacuzenus in the fourteenth;
and finally Chalcocondyles, Ducas, Phrantzes, and Critobulus.
There were among them—Psellus is one example—those who, by
their observation, the precision of their descriptive passages, their
penetrating psychology, and the liveliness and humour of their
style, might stand comparison with the greatest literary figures
of any age or nation.

All Byzantines loved history, and besides historians proper
there were chroniclers, who compiled the countless résumés of
universal history so much in vogue throughout the mediaeval
Eastern world, from Malalas in the sixth century to George the
Syncellus, Theophanes, and Nicephorus at the end of the eighth.
In the ninth and tenth centuries there were George the Monk,
Symeon Magister, and their continuators, in the eleventh, Skylitzes, and in the twelfth, Cedrenus, Zonaras, Manasses, and
Glycas. Naturally there is little originality in these works, since
an author would often copy from his predecessors, and intellectual poverty is very marked. These chronicles were written as a
rule by monks for unsophisticated readers and had a pronounced
religious and popular bias. They consisted of anecdote and monastery gossip; there is much detailed narrative—above all, of a
miraculous order—while even more space is devoted to ready-
made opinions and tendentious bigotry. The critical spirit is entirely lacking, and often even concern for truth and accuracy.
Yet for all their crudeness, these chronicles hold an important
place in the history of Byzantine civilization. Historians wrote for
a select minority, but these lesser works circulated throughout the
East; they were translated into Syrian, Armenian, Bulgarian,
Serbian, and Russian, and thus contributed much to mediaeval
education. And although their authors were not concerned to
write well or to model themselves on the ancients, yet the vivid,
colloquial language they used was more important, more prom-
ising for the future, than the artificial style of the great historians. Despite their shortcomings, these works are of absorbing

interest and throw a revealing light on certain aspects of Byzantine mind and character.

The same taste for history—and stories—appears in the Byzantines' delight in scholarly research. Constantine Porphyrogenitus is an outstanding example of this. His book on *Ceremonies,* like the one on the *Administration of the Empire,* gives evidence of untiring curiosity and the fullest possible documentation; he gathered about him a series of encyclopaedias—historical, military, agricultural, medical, and hagiographic—in which was summarized all that the past had bequeathed to tenth-century Greeks. The lives of the saints—which despite their moral purpose and the pious legends they contain, are also historical documents of intense interest—were no less the fashion in the Byzantine world.

Lastly, a point worth remarking is that even those Byzantines for whom authorship was not a customary occupation were fond of recording the great events they witnessed. Cameniates described the capture of Thessalonica by the Arabs in 904, Eustathius, its capture by the Normans in 1185; and many wrote their memoirs and personal reminiscences, as did Psellus and John Cantacuzenus, and, above all, the enjoyable Cecaumenus.

Theology

Next to history, theology was certainly the branch of learning that most captivated the Byzantine mind; and here again there is no doubt that theological literature—at least until the twelfth century—was far superior to anything produced by the West in that field. There is an abundance of these writings, many of them prompted by the ceaseless battle against various heresies—Monophysitism, Monothelitism, and Iconoclasm—which troubled the Byzantine world from the fifth century to the ninth. Later there were polemics against paganism and Judaism, against the Moslems, and, above all, the Latins; there was the constant concern to defend Orthodoxy and establish dogma. The list of those who distinguished themselves in this field is long: Leontius of Byzantium in the sixth century; Maximus the Confessor in the seventh. In the eighth there were John of Damascus and Theodore of Studium; Photius in the ninth; Psellus in the eleventh; Euthymius Zigabenus, Nicholas of Methone, and Nicetas Acominatus in the twelfth century. Up to the last days of the Empire we find scholars attacking one another with great vigour. In the fourteenth century there were the champions of Eastern mysticism: Palamas, Cantacuzenus, and the two Cabasilas; while exponents of Western Scholasticism included Gregory Acyndinus, the translator of St. Thomas Aquinas, Demetrius Cydones, the translator of St. Augustine and St. Anselm, and Nicephorus Gregoras. In the fifteenth century came the friends and foes of the Latins: Marcus Eugenicus, George Scholarius, and Bessarion.

Innumerable works were devoted to scriptural commentary. The development of monastic life—especially in the famous religious houses of the Studium and Mount Athos—produced a mystical literature of which Symeon, known as "the new theologian," in the eleventh century and Nicholas Cabasilas in the fourteenth were the most famous exponents. Religious eloquence, directly inspired by classical rhetoric, was practised by orators far superior to most Western preachers of the day. The taste for edifying works called forth a rich hagiographic literature, of which the finest sixth-century examples were compiled by Cyril of Skythopolis and John Moschus; from the eighth to the eleventh century the *genre* blossomed into full flower, and the chief material of this period was gathered together in the huge collection of Symeon Metaphrastes in the tenth century.

Just as history was closely linked with the classical past, so Byzantine theology was dominated by the Christian past. After a period of creative activity inspired by the Fathers of the Church, from the ninth century onwards respect for tradition precluded all originality and freedom of thought in this great theological movement. A twelfth-century theologian noted that although the Greeks might be the "most courageous of men," they dared not depart from the principles laid down by the Fathers. Another in the fourteenth century explained that he had not included in his books the fruit of his own researches, but only what he had learnt from the Fathers and from sacred writings. John of Damascus, too, declared, "I will say nothing of my own." Thought was no longer the aim; men relied on the authority of bygone divines, and the circle of those consulted grew ever more restricted. Men mistrusted the powerful thought of Origen and set aside the ingenious doctors of the school of Antioch. Athanasius, Basil, Gregory of Nazianzus, Gregory of Nyssa, and Cyril of Alexandria were the masters of dogma; Chrysostom was the authority on exegesis, Basil on asceticism, and Maximus the Confessor on mysticism. These were supreme. Discussion was by quoted passages, and the main arguments were simply the affirmations of the Fathers. Scriptural commentaries were timid and devoid of breadth, criticism, or curiosity. For polemical purposes, *catenas* were compiled: extracts from the Fathers and from sacred writings. In the twelfth century, Nicholas of Methone in his fight against Neo-Platonism confined himself to copying an old treatise by Procopius of Gaza against Proclus. Western theology, which might have revived and regenerated Eastern thought, was quite unknown; not until the fourteenth century, when it was too late, do we find a few translations from St. Augustine or St. Thomas Aquinas, and this at a time when hatred of the West was so violent that sympathy with Latin ideas seemed treachery to Byzantium.

Consequently, despite certain great figures—Photius in the ninth century, Arethas of Caesarea in the tenth, Psellus in the eleventh, Eustathius of Thessalonica and Michael Acominatus in the twelfth—Byzantine theology began to stagnate from the ninth century onwards. Theologians went on attacking heresy in the old way, rebelling against the teaching of Western Scholasticism and bringing a strange narrow-mindedness to all they did. Religious eloquence and hagiography alone preserved some semblance of life, though the former became very wearisome, owing to abuse of rhetorical principles and to the cold, abstract, dogmatic turn given to it by so many of its exponents. Above all, notwithstanding the learning and industry of Greek divines and the beauty of some of their works, the strictly confessional cast of Byzantine thought in matters of religion militated against independent scholarship and the free spirit of discovery.

Trends in Philosophy

In this field too, however, the Byzantines tried at times to free themselves from the restrictions imposed by the Church. In all the mediaeval world, dominated as it was by Aristotelian philosophy, it was at the University of Constantinople that the doctrine of Plato first reappeared, in the eleventh century. It is to the eternal glory of Michael Psellus that he made room in the curriculum for the great Athenian. He has told us himself how, from Neo-Platonism and "the admirable Proclus," he rose little by little to "the pure light of Plato." He speaks of his enthusiasm for the man he considered both "the greatest of philosophers and a forerunner of Christianity." "He belongs to me," he cried; "he is mine!" By the warmth of his admiration and his zeal in spreading and defending this teaching he sometimes offended the strict Orthodoxy of the Patriarchs Xiphilinus and Cerularius. Yet he founded a school. His disciples, of whom John Italus in the twelfth century was the most famous, continued to study and to teach Platonism, and in the end this movement of free thought caused considerable anxiety to Church and government. Something resembling the Western struggle between nominalism and realism followed; but the Comneni restored order by anathematizing Italus and his adherents and commissioning the official theologians to oppose their doctrine. It is nevertheless true that Psellus, who has been justly described as "almost a man of the Renaissance," foreshadowed at a distance of a few hundred years the reawakening of Platonic philosophy that characterized the fifteenth century. Other Byzantines, such as Gennadius, Gemistus Plethon, and Bessarion, did much to make the doctrines of Plato known in the West.

Rhetoric and Eloquence

This trend of thought linked Byzantium with the ancients. Another bond was the love of eloquence and the antique forms in which this eloquence was expressed. Like the Greeks of old, the Byzantines took keen pleasure in the fair sequence of words and in fine, sonorous phrases; and though much of their utterance was bombastic and pretentious, yet a number of orators who formed their style on classical models—Photius, Eustathius, and Michael Acominatus, for instance—were equal to their masters, Isocrates, Libanius, and Themistius. From the ninth century to the fifteenth, and especially during the periods of the Comneni and Palaeologi, Byzantium was familiar with all forms of solemn oratory: panegyrics, funeral orations, harangues delivered on feast days at the imperial or patriarchal palace, and stylistic pieces (ἐκφράσεις) describing a work of art or a landscape. The authors, mostly professors at the University of Constantinople or at the school of St. Sophia, included Psellus, Michael Italicus, Nicephorus Basilaces, Basil of Achrida, Michael Acominatus, and Eustathius. During the period of the Palaeologi, there were Nicephorus Chumnos, Theodore Hyrtacenus, and Demetrius Cydones; and, like the philosophers who were their contemporaries, these men were the forerunners of the Renaissance humanists.

Variety in Byzantine Thought

These notes have given little indication of the varied nature of Byzantine thought. In mediaeval Greek literature we find works like the *Philopatris* of the tenth century, the *Timarion* of the twelfth, and the *Mazaris* of the fourteenth, as well as certain dialogues by Prodromus, whose salty, lively satire is undimmed by his obvious imitation of Lucian. We find elegant, witty essays— gay trifles, which, though their matter is slight enough, may be graceful, humorous, and well turned when the author is such a man as Psellus, Theodore Metochites, or Manuel Palaeologus, for example. We have already mentioned the work of the philologists; but we must not forget that there were poets in Byzantium, from George of Pisidia in the seventh century and Christopher of Mytilene in the tenth to Theodorus Prodromus in the twelfth and Manuel Philes in the fourteenth. Nevertheless it is not in the works of these men that we should seek the true Byzantine poetry, for it consisted largely of indifferent imitations of the classics, whether epic poems or romances, epigrams or lines written for some special occasion. We must look elsewhere; we must turn to the devotional poetry, certainly the most beautiful and personal outpouring of the Byzantine spirit, to the fervent hymns, so sincere, so powerfully dramatic in quality, composed in the new rhythmic manner at the dawn of the sixth century by Romanus, "prince of melodists," greatest and most original of Byzantine poets. We must turn to the folk-epos; to the eleventh-century cycle of *chansons de geste* of which the poem concerning Digenis Akritas is the noblest example. In epic poetry as in devotional, Byzantium owed nothing to the ancients. It was inspired by the greatness of the Christian faith, its triumphs and its sufferings, and by the sentiments and passions of the people. This poetry, of which the form and language were new, was deep-rooted in the Byzantine soul; it was indeed, as has been said, the blood and spirit of Christian Byzantium.

Characteristics of Byzantine Literature

Throughout its history—if we except the troubled period between the middle of the seventh century and the middle of the ninth—Byzantium remained in close touch with classical Greece. The fifth and sixth centuries are imbued with Hellenic influence, and from the ninth century onwards the awakening of ancient culture led to the renaissance of the tenth, eleventh, and twelfth centuries, which came into full flower in the period of the Palaeologi. It is true that this classical imprint, so deep and persistent, had its disadvantages. By too slavish adherence to antique forms, Byzantine literature acquired a stiff, conventional character; and notwithstanding the genuine merits of the writers, their work often lacked life and spontaneity. Moreover, the classical tradition developed some of the less attractive sides of the Byzantine mind: the taste for hair-splitting, affectation, love of fine-sounding, empty phrases and of ingenious experiments in form that took the place of thought. Above all, it turned literature into a scholars' preserve and made it less and less intelligible to the masses.

The result was a reaction that brought vernacular Greek into literature. Between the sixth and tenth centuries, writers like Malalas, Leontius of Neapolis, the chronicler Theophanes, and Emperor Constantine Porphyrogenitus had tried to reconcile the classical tradition with the spoken language; and perhaps if this form had been generally adopted, Greek might have evolved as did the Romance languages from Latin. But the classical influence was too strong; and as the gulf widened between the written and spoken language and the people became less and less able to understand the fine speeches and learned style of the scholars, there arose in the eleventh century a literature of the vulgar tongue. The epic songs from which grew the poem of *Digenis Akritas,* the stories, bestiaries, chronicles like the *Chronicle of the Morea,* and poems such as those by Theodorus Prodromus and Glycas, give sufficient evidence of the richness of this new art. Yet the consequences were unfortunate. From now on the intellectual life of the Greeks ran along two channels, and the popular tongue, so intolerant of grammatical rules, spelling, syntax, and morphology, never quite achieved the status of a literary language. The attempt is no less interesting; it proves that even in so classically minded a society as this, originality and creative force existed, and that alongside the high intellectual qualities of the few, a current of freshness and inspiration pervaded the whole race.

Another characteristic of this literature was its practical, utilitarian side. There was a precise and well-defined object in all this devotion to antiquity and to the study of its traditions and writings: namely, to use the knowledge and experience of the past for the benefit of the present. Such was the purpose of the countless encyclopaedias to whose compilation so much energy was devoted in the tenth century. The same realistic attitude appears in the passion for history and the taste for juridical studies that inspired not only the great legislative works of the sixth, eighth, and tenth centuries, but also many learned commentaries on common and ecclesiastical law. It appears in countless textbooks and treatises on tactics, ceremonial, political law, diplomacy, rural economy, and education, in which meticulous care is taken to foresee and solve all difficulties by the study of precedents and the formulation of rules of conduct.

Besides the literary aspect, we find abundant evidence of an intensely realistic approach to life and of practical political sense; and these characteristics are worthy of note, for they illustrate two very Byzantine traits: a resolute will to live and an aptitude for finding the ways and means of doing so.

Byzantine Civilization

During its thousand years of evolution, Byzantine art shows certain parallels with Byzantine literature. It followed the classical tradition and found unfailing inspiration and often renewal in antique models; it was strongly influenced by the Church and never quite escaped from its authority. It was an art of an official and wealthy order, which naturally deprived it of freshness and vitality. Yet it was not, as was long believed, monotonous and static, unsusceptible to change and without scope for originality or invention; it was not a stillborn art which, after a fleeting period of glory, survived in barren imitations of a few great masters.

In the history of Byzantine art we find variety, complexity, and flexibility. After a long period of preparation and experiment, during which artists ingeniously combined the Hellenistic tradition with the precepts of the ancient East, still vigorous in Syria, Egypt, and Asia Minor, there followed in Justinian's century a period of fine flowering. The Church of St. Sophia, a marvel of science and daring, marks the climax of the new style, which was characterized by splendour, ornamentation, strong, brilliant colours, and an atmosphere of pomp and dignity—all those features which went to make up the impressive beauty of the buildings of that period: St. Demetrius of Thessalonica, S. Apollinare Nuovo, and S. Vitale of Ravenna.

This was the first golden age of Byzantine art. But the great effort did not end here. The splendid renaissance that followed the Iconoclast revolution and flourished in the time of the Macedonian and Comnenian Emperors found sources of inspiration unknown to the previous age and revealed fresh qualities. Like contemporary literature, the art of this second golden age was dominated by the antique and secular tradition. Byzantium had returned to Hellenistic ideas, to sober simplicity and sculptural forms; and in both architecture and the mosaics that adorned the churches, as well as in the illuminated manuscripts of the day, the delicately worked ivory, and the shifting colours of the enamels, this highly developed art produced marvels of grace and beauty. Influenced as it was by theology, it often took an abstract

Ivory plaque of St. Constantine, the left wing of a triptych. Second half of 10th century.

Courtesy of the Dumbarton Oaks Collection

and symbolic form, and sacrificed much for the sake of the style, discipline, and regard for tradition on which the rules of iconography were based. Yet the creative impulse remained, and we find an emphasis on movement and expression, as well as keen and sometimes realistic observation; we find vitality and a constant search for renewal. Above all, we note a taste and feeling for

Robert L. Van Nice

St. Sophia. West façade.

colour, one of the most characteristic innovations of the period. It was the prelude to the evolution that was to lead by new paths to a second renaissance: that of the fourteenth and fifteenth centuries, perhaps the most brilliant in all the history of Byzantium.

The mosaics of Kariye-Jămĭ, the frescoes of Mistra, the churches of Athos, Macedonia, Serbia, and Russia bear witness to the marvellous blossoming that marked the period of the Palaeologi. Once more Byzantine art was changing: in returning to its most ancient sources—and in particular to the Alexandrian tradition that restored the humanists of the day to a place of honour—it lost its abstract character; it came to life; it became pictorial, dramatic, full of charm and feeling. Iconography was enriched and re-

Ivory triptych. Height: 4¾″. Second half of 10th century.

newed; it was now more emotional and passionate, and its technique, embodying a skilled and harmonious use of colour, had an almost impressionist character. Schools sprang up, differing from each other in style and inspiration; works were produced that bear comparison with the finest Italian primitives and yet owe little or nothing to them. And though indeed Byzantine art was often imitative and too apt to crystallize its most fertile discoveries into formulas, though it was too much the slave of tradition and too easily controlled by the Church, nevertheless it was remarkable for originality and creative force. At least twice during those thousand years it drew fresh vigour from ancient tradition.

But that was not its only source of greatness. Besides the Hellenistic cultural stream, a strong Oriental current ran through this art and inspired it. While the former perpetuated the taste for noble attitudes, measured gestures, simple, balanced composition, and a touch of idealism, the latter introduced a very different element: freer, more alive, less governed by rules, more concerned with movement, passion, and the picturesque, and a realism that never shrank from crude, lifelike detail. Throughout the history of Byzantine art these two traditions blended and clashed; one or the other predominated according to the age, and left its mark on the artistic trend of the day. Alexandria and Antioch ruled Constantinople by turns; and more than once, under Hellenic influence, the ancient East of Syria, Palestine, or Cappadocia—seemingly forgotten—made its sudden reappearance. As a result of this and of contact with Persians and Arabs, Byzantine art assumed an original aspect "matching the nation's own genius."

Time has destroyed many of the products of Byzantine art; yet how many have been spared! Besides the Church of St. Sophia, the most typical example, there are all the other churches, so varied in plan: basilicas like St. Demetrius or S. Apollinare Nuovo; centralized buildings like S. Vitale of Ravenna; cruciform ones like the Church of the Holy Apostles, whose pattern we find repeated in St. Mark's of Venice; and all those enchanting buildings dating from later centuries, constructed on the plan of the Greek cross and embellished with such imaginative grace and charm—the Theotokos in Constantinople and the Holy Apostles in Thessalonica, among others, are particularly exquisite examples. Rarely has architecture combined such science and variety of conception, such elegance and daring of execution, such skill and inventiveness in solving the most intricate technical problems; rarely has art been so fertile and free, drawing inspiration now from the grace and complexity of the Hellenistic tradition, now from the simplicity, the massive forms, firm lines, austerity, and gravity of the Oriental ideal.

Cyril Mango

Church of the Holy Apostles at Thessalonica.

Let us also remember the rich decoration of the churches: the walls faced with multicoloured marble; the mosaics with their blue or gold grounds sparkling in the curves of cupolas and arches, and the frescoes ranged one above the other round the walls. It is a complete system, incomparable in richness, splendour, and harmony; and we observe in it a marvellous under-standing in the use of colour and decoration. Everything about it is designed to produce an effect of brilliance and magnificence. Lastly, let us consider the arrangement and balance of these vast *ensembles*, the thought that must have gone into the composition of the subjects depicted, the rules of symbolical grouping—all the iconography that served the Church as a means of edification, by representing scenes from the Scriptures, by expounding dogma and interpreting the liturgical rites. These superlative works, which are at once artistic and theological, were one of the finest achievements of Byzantine genius. Iconography is the more note-worthy in that, within its traditional, immutable framework, we can discern a constant renewal, a vigilant, creative activity, which inspired and enriched the illustration of sacred themes. This is as true of the great iconography that arose with the ninth-century renaissance as of the equally vigorous movement of the fifteenth.

Another characteristic must be noted because it is typical of Byzantine civilization as a whole: the taste for gorgeousness and splendour so evident in all works of art. Everywhere in churches and palaces there were precious marbles, brilliant mosaics and work in gold and silver, and wonderful fabrics, all designed to enhance the beauty of the sacred offices and the majesty of im-perial persons. Byzantium sparkled with jewels and blazed with gold. Both in public and private life, there was a profusion of sumptuous stuffs of shot gold and purple, of finely carved ivory, bronzes inlaid with silver, richly illuminated manuscripts, cloi-sonné enamels of beautiful colours, gold and silver dishes, and precious jewellery—the finest that artists and craftsmen could create. Besides religious art to glorify God, there was a lesser-known secular art to glorify the majesty of the Emperor. The luxury of the imperial palaces equalled the splendour of the churches; in both, the decoration was superb. Surviving examples of this imperial art, which existed for the court and those of high rank, are few, but what we know of its derivation and tendency is well worth attention. Favourite subjects were those taken from classical history or mythology, scenes dear to Hellenistic artists; also representations of imperial victories and portraits of the sov-ereign in his glory. These themes were treated with remarkable realism and close observation; and in this field, too, by combining

Seated Christ. Mosaic in the lunette over the Imperial Door of St. Sophia. *Ca.* 900 A.D.

separate tendencies—a return to the antique, an Oriental love of colour and naturalistic execution—Byzantine art proved itself to be truly creative.

4. BYZANTINE LIFE

All that we know of Byzantine civilization as a whole is consistent with its literary development and the splendours of its art.

From a material point of view, Byzantine life was immensely elegant and sophisticated. The richness of private houses was no

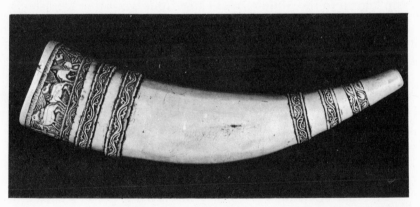

The Cleveland Museum of Art, John Huntington Collection
Ivory Horn of St. Blasius, from the "Guelph Treasure." 11th century.

less impressive than the magnificence of the imperial palaces. They were finely decorated; the interior walls were faced with marble; mosaics or paintings representing scenes from everyday life, mythological subjects, and historic events brightened the rooms, while the furniture was encrusted with mother-of-pearl and ivory and adorned with plaques of brilliant enamel. The same taste for ornament was displayed in carriages and harness, in jewellery and dress. Benjamin of Tudela describes the people of Constantinople as looking like "so many princes" in their gold-embroidered, brilliant silks, adorned with flowers, medallions and enamels, and religious and secular scenes. On their dining tables were dishes of silver and chased gold, glasses with inset plaques of gold and enamel, and other specimens of the goldsmith's art; and although Liutprand spoke disparagingly of the resined wine, the dishes cooked in oil, and certain sauces enjoyed by the Byzantines, he could not but praise the delicacy of the imperial table and in particular a roast kid stuffed with garlic, leeks, and onions, and dressed with the famous sauce known as *garon*. Indeed there seems to have been considerable refinement in the preparing and serving of food; and as in the East today, perfumes and flowers enhanced the delights of the meal.

These people loved festivals, receptions, and display, and were well versed in pageantry. All that we know of Byzantine industry is in keeping with this, and the finest and most delicate craftsmanship known to the Middle Ages came from Byzantine workshops.

In addition to the pre-eminence in material things for which Byzantium was famed and admired throughout the world, there was the even more striking intellectual superiority. We have already analysed the complexity of the Byzantine mind, its intelligence, subtlety, and lively curiosity, and the wide knowledge and full spiritual life that characterized the mediaeval Greeks. Compared with their barbarian neighbours, they seem of a higher order, a race of teachers and masters. They busied their minds with complicated matters and expressed their thoughts in fine language. They could examine and discuss abstruse problems, and in the ordering of their lives they displayed a graceful knack of avoiding unpleasantness. Above all, they never bothered themselves with needless scruples. It was therefore inevitable that Byzantium should make its influence felt throughout the mediaeval world. The outward brilliance of its civilization alone set a marvellous pattern for all who came near it, while the inner values made an even deeper impression on the young, crude, savage nations who found themselves in contact with the Greek Empire.

II. The Spread of Orthodoxy and the Formation of the Slavic World

1. BYZANTIUM AND THE SLAVIC WORLD

What papal Rome was to the mediaeval Germanic West, the Byzantium of the Christian emperors was to the Slavic world and the East: that is to say, the great educator and initiator, the bringer of religion and civilization to the still barbarous peoples that gravitated about the Empire.

All along the Byzantine frontiers there drifted a chaos of wild tribes, the remains of the great invasion that thundered against the Empire from the fifth to the seventh century and almost submerged it. In the northwestern part of the Balkan Peninsula there were the Croats and Serbs, whose domains extended to the Dalmatian coast of the Adriatic. To the northeast, between the Danube and the Balkans, there were the Bulgars, who had settled among the Slavic population and adopted their way of life. Beyond these states, which were founded on territory once belonging to the Empire, there was Great Moravia, on the other side of the Danube, another Slavic state which in the ninth century occupied what is now Hungary as far as Gran, but which was soon to be overrun by the Magyar hordes. Then in the central valley of the Dnieper, round Kiev, there were the Varangians who, with Rurik and his companions, brought to the Slavs of Russia the first beginnings of social organization. Further south, along the Black Sea from the Dnieper to the Caucasus, there were the Turkish race of Pechenegs on the lower Dnieper, the Khazars on the Don, as well as other races such as Uzes, Zichians, and Alans, and, on the Volga, the Black Bulgars.

The strong hands of Byzantium kneaded these barbarian tribes and shaped them into nations. "From these Slavic, Bulgarian, Magyar, and Varangian hordes, Byzantium made the Christian states of Serbia, Croatia, Bulgaria, Hungary, and Russia." Byzantium gave them the elements of survival—the elements of future greatness. It was Byzantine missionaries who, by propagating Orthodoxy, led these wild peoples to Christianity, and who, through religion, gradually taught them the things that go to make up an organized, civilized state. To the nations that Byzantium converted, it introduced the concept of government, the principles of law, a more civilized way of life, and an intellectual and artistic culture. Its engineers built towns for the Khazars; its architects built churches for the Russians; its chroniclers, whose works were translated into Bulgarian, Serbian, and Russian, provided models for Slavic annalists; and its folk tales captivated the imagination of all these childlike peoples. Most important of all, Byzantium gave the Slavs their alphabet and their literary language. Cyril and Methodius, "the Apostles of the Slavs," were commissioned by Emperor Michael III to evangelize the Moravians, and for the benefit of their new converts they translated the Scriptures into a Slavic dialect. For this they invented the Glagolitic script, derived from the Greek minuscule.

This was perhaps the greatest of all Byzantium's achievements and the chief factor in its success. For whereas Rome strove to impose the Latin language on all the races it converted, Byzantium, with a more astute and flexible political sense, soon perceived the advantage of addressing potential converts in their own language. At the end of the fourth century the Eastern Church encouraged Ulfila to create an alphabet for the Goths, to translate the Scriptures into their language, and to celebrate the Offices according to a Gothic liturgy. In the middle of the fifth century the imperial government similarly urged Sahak and Mesrob to translate the Bible from Greek into Armenian. In the sixth century the Gospel was translated into the Hunnish language for the Huns of the Caspian. From the seventh century onwards, Copts, Abyssinians, Syrians, Arabs, and Armenians used their own national languages in their liturgies. Cyril and Methodius did the same for the Slavs in the ninth century. They realized the futility of trying to explain already abstruse mysteries in a language difficult to understand. They were from Thessalonica and well versed in the customs and language of the Slavs who clustered about that great Hellenic city. They preached in Slavic, and to the Moravians they gave not only the Gospels translated into a dialect akin to the Moravian tongue, but also the Slavic liturgy, and at the same time did their utmost to recruit and train a Slavic clergy. Except in Moravia itself, where their work was soon undermined by the intrigues of the German clergy, they were successful, and their disciples spread the Orthodox faith through the Slavic world according to the same principles. Even today, in Serbia, Bulgaria, and Russia, millions of Orthodox believers use the Cyrillic alphabet and the Church Slavic invented more than ten centuries ago by the two brothers of Thessalonica.

That was not all. "The races of eastern Europe," says Rambaud, "would know hardly anything of their origins, had not the Byzantines taken care to edit the annals of these barbarians. But for this *corpus historiae Byzantinae,* the object of so much contempt —but for Procopius, Menander, and Theophanes, Porphyrogenitus, Leo Diaconus, and Cedrenus—how much would the Russians, Hungarians, Serbs, Croats, and Bulgars know of their own history?" [1] But for Byzantium, these peoples would be as ignorant of their past as for a long time they would have been of civilization.

[1] Rambaud, *op. cit.,* x.

There is no need to dwell on Byzantium's achievements among peoples who vanished from history centuries ago or among those upon whom its influence was transient. It is enough to recall what the Greek missionaries did in the plains of southern Russia, from the sixth century, when they converted the Goths and Huns of the Crimea and the Alans and Abasgians of the Caucasus, until the ninth century, when Cyril and Methodius brought Christianity to the Khazars, who in the eighth century had been profoundly influenced by Jewish propaganda and among whom Judaism flourished even in the tenth century. Nor will we say more than a word about the glorious apostolic mission that Cyril and Methodius conducted in Moravia for twenty years, including in its field of action the Slavs of Balaton and Bohemia. After the death of Methodius in 885, his disciples' retreat left the Church he had founded in disorder, and a few years later the Magyar invasion ruined the ephemeral Moravian empire forever. A more important and enduring work, whose historical importance it is impossible to exaggerate, was the conversion of the Bulgars, Russians, and Serbs. Byzantium's main purpose in this was, without doubt, to bring them under its influence. It did more: it brought them into history.

Byzantium and Bulgaria

By the eighth century, Byzantine influence had begun to penetrate into Bulgaria. In return for the support given to Emperor Justinian II, Khan Terbel had received the title of Caesar and assumed the crown of gold and the gold-threaded purple mantle. Later khans, haunted by the brilliant memory of their predecessor, played *Basileus* in their ancient capital of Pliska-Aboba. Although heathen, they proclaimed themselves "sovereigns by the grace of God." Christianity set the final seal of Byzantium upon them.

In about the year 864 Boris, Czar of Bulgaria, was converted to the Orthodox faith. Byzantine legend has shed a romantic light on this event. Theophanes tells us that the Bulgarian prince, who was a great hunter, wished to have scenes of his favourite sport painted in one of his houses. He approached a Byzantine monk named Methodius, but instead of giving him an exact description of what he wanted, he merely ordered him to paint "whatever he liked, so long as the subject was of a nature to inspire the viewers with fear and amazement." Impelled by divine inspiration, the Greek chose the tremendous scene of the Last Judgment, as pictured in Byzantine iconography. Boris was so appalled by this that, to escape the torments reserved for the damned, he allowed himself to be baptized.

The truth is somewhat different. Political rather than religious reasons influenced the barbarian's decision. Situated as he was between the Byzantine Empire and Great Moravia, into which Christianity was even then penetrating, the practical Boris realized that he could not remain heathen; the only question was, from which quarter to seek baptism. He hesitated between the Orthodoxy of his Greek neighbour and the Roman faith offered by Germany, of whom he had become the ally. The Byzantines could not allow Bulgaria to enter the Western sphere of influence and staged a demonstration of military force. This, together with the fact that his conversion was to be rewarded by an increase of territory, decided him, and it was from Constantinople that he begged baptism. He received the Christian name of Michael, and the Patriarch Photius, sensing the full importance of the event, greeted the neophyte as "the fairest jewel of our labours." However, the Bulgarian Czar soon quarrelled with the Greeks, and turning to Rome he asked Pope Nicholas I to establish the Latin ritual in his realm. This did not suit the Byzantines, who had no intention of losing Bulgaria. Rome yielded to Greek protests at the Council of 869, and Orthodox clergy were reinstalled on Bulgarian territory. After the death of Methodius in 885, his disciples had to leave Moravia, and in Bulgaria they found a refuge and completed the conversion of the country.

Thereafter Byzantine influence penetrated deeply into Bulgaria. The son and successor of Boris, Symeon, had spent many years of his youth as a hostage in the imperial city, and he had conceived a profound admiration for the intellectual capacity of the Greeks, among whom he had studied "the rhetoric of Demosthenes and the syllogisms of Aristotle." Once on the throne, the first concern of this "demi-Greek," as his contemporaries called him, was to model the barbarian court of Preslav the Great on the household of the *Basileus*. Writers of the day speak admiringly of the fine buildings, the lofty palaces and churches that arose in the Czar's city, the brilliance of gold and silver and the countless paintings that adorned them. The prince sat enthroned "in raiment embroidered with pearls, with necklaces of coins about his throat, bracelets on his wrists, and a girdle of purple," in the magnificent robes of the emperors of Byzantium. Around him sat his boyars, "bedecked with golden chains, girdles, and precious bracelets." The Czar's guard wore breastplates of shining brass and carried lances of silver and gold. Byzantine etiquette blended with barbaric splendour, and Symeon felt near enough to the *Basileus* to dream of winning the hegemony of the Balkans, of making Constantinople his capital and taking the title of "Czar of the Bulgars and Autocrat of the Romans."

His splendid dream faded in 924 at the gates of Byzantium. Yet thanks to him, Bulgaria was transformed. Symeon had a taste for letters and loved to surround himself with intellectuals. He had the most famous works of Byzantine literature translated into Bulgarian, and he compiled a collection of extracts from John Chrysostom. His flatterers compared him to "a diligent bee," because he "extracted nectar from every flower to distribute it among his boyars." Although he remained a barbarian in many ways and yielded to fits of cruelty and Asiatic despotism, Symeon did begin the task of turning Bulgaria into a civilized state. He adopted political maxims from Byzantium and imposed monarchical authority on the boyar aristocracy. He based his throne firmly on the Church which he subordinated to his will as did the Greek Emperor. By the time he died, Bulgaria had become a nation.

The Spread of Orthodoxy

The forty-year reign of his son, Peter, merely strengthened the Byzantine influence. This Czar married a Greek princess and was the steadfast ally and spiritual son, almost the vassal, of the *Basileus*. Relations between the two courts were close and cordial, and Constantinople showed marked consideration for its "Bulgarian friends." The imperial chancellery even allowed the Czar to take the title of *Basileus* and proclaimed his subjects "Most Christian People." Through these close relations, Byzantine literature and art penetrated into Bulgaria and transformed it. The Slavic kingdom became a satellite of the Greek Empire, which, at the end of the tenth century, was to conquer and annex it.

Beneath the Byzantine veneer, however, Bulgaria remained Bulgaria. The Bulgars never submitted willingly to the political authority of the emperors; they were continually in revolt, and Greeks who had the ill fortune to be exiled among them heartily cursed these evil-smelling, dirty boors, whose character seemed to them "the natural source of all wickedness."

It was owing to Byzantine influence, nevertheless, that Bulgaria entered the circle of socially organized states; and later, in the thirteenth century, the sovereigns of the new realm, like their tenth-century predecessors, were fascinated by Byzantium and meekly submitted to its influence.

Byzantium and Russia

Tsarigrad had an equal attraction for the Russian state that had sprung up on the Dnieper plains during the ninth century. By the tenth century, as we have seen, Russian merchants were coming in great numbers to trade in Constantinople; thousands of Russian mercenaries served in the imperial army and navy; and Greek influence began to penetrate as far as Kiev. Here, too, Christianity completed the work and brought civilization with it.

At the end of the ninth century, Basil I dreamed of converting the Russians, and a Russian diocese was created. However, Christianity had made but little headway in that country when in 957 the Grand Princess Olga came to Constantinople and there received baptism. Whatever significance Russian tradition may afterwards have attached to this event, we must not exaggerate its importance. It was not until forty years later, when Vladimir,

Olga's grandson, was converted to Orthodoxy, that Christianity really found a foothold in Russia.

The old Russian chronicle known as the *Chronicle of Nestor* gives a picturesque account of the approaches made to the Grand Prince by representatives of the different confessions—Roman Catholics, Orthodox Catholics, Jews, and Moslems—and of the enquiry Vladimir instituted into the merits of the various religions before making up his mind. Byzantium won the day. The Russian ambassadors returned from the Great City dazzled by the majesty and splendour of the Orthodox liturgy; and they declared: "In Rome, we admit, we saw beautiful things. But what we saw in Constantinople passes human understanding." Vladimir chose the Greeks. In 989, in the Cherson he had captured, he received baptism and married a princess of the imperial family. On his return to Kiev he commanded the mass conversion of his people. Russia was Christian.

In receiving Christianity, the Russian nation entered civilization; in receiving it at the hands of Byzantium, it prepared itself for yet higher destinies. During the sixty years that followed Vladimir's conversion, Russia maintained a close alliance with the Greek Empire. Churches were needed for the Orthodox priests whom Vladimir brought back with him to Kiev and for his newly converted subjects. He filled his capital with churches; he summoned Greek architects to build them and Greek painters to decorate them. He founded schools to instruct children in the new faith, and these schools were placed under the direction of Greek masters. It was from Byzantium that the first Metropolitan of Kiev arrived in 991, and with him the clerics who laboured to spread Orthodoxy throughout the country. But Christianity brought with it even more; it reformed society and strengthened family ties, while the political revolution it caused was more important still. Christianity introduced a new conception of sovereign authority. From being the chieftain of warrior bands, the Russian Grand Prince became a sovereign by divine right, in the image of the Byzantine Emperor; and the concept of the State was born. Christianity influenced legislation, too, and replaced personal rights and private vengeance with public trial and the idea of social protection. Lastly, as Byzantine literature pervaded Russia, it brought, besides the sacred books and patristic writings, those narratives that were to serve as models to Russian chroniclers, as well as philosophic and scientific works, romances, and many other things. This flood of new ideas transformed the whole social and moral life of Russia. The influence of Greek art was equally strong. Magnificent churches arose in all the Russian cities, and "in mud-walled towns, Vladimir erected churches with golden domes."

His son, Jaroslav (1015-1054), continued and completed the work. Jaroslav has been called the Charlemagne of Russia, and indeed, he reminds one of the great Frankish Emperor in his legislative work, his fondness for building, and his love of letters and the arts. Through him, eleventh-century Russia became what sixteenth-century Russia ceased to be: a European state. He wanted Kiev, his capital, to rival Constantinople, with its own Cathedral of St. Sophia, its own Golden Gate. He filled it with churches and religious houses, of which the most famous was the monastery of the Catacombs, on the side of the cliff above the Dnieper. Lying as it did between the Greek world and northern Europe, Kiev enjoyed tremendous commercial prosperity. Western writers called it "the emulator of Constantinople and the fairest ornament of Greece." To achieve this, Jaroslav, like his father, asked Byzantium for all he needed. Monks from Athos brought the monastic rule to Kiev, Greek cantors taught the Russian clergy, Greek craftsmen struck the first Russian coins, Greek architects and mosaicists built and decorated St. Sophia and made it a purely Byzantine church. The mosaics, with their Greek inscriptions, which even today strike fire from the curve of the cupola and from the "indestructible wall" of the apse, are, both in composition and style, one of the finest examples of eleventh-century Greek art. The curious frescoes adorning the tower stairs are plain evidence of the enchantment that the distant splendours of Byzantium had for the Russian world. For here is seen the whole pageant of the Byzantine court, with its ceremonial, its feasts and diversions, its chariot races and acrobats and the strange dances that entertained the Emperor and his people—everything, indeed, that awed and amazed the barbarians who visited Constantinople. Russian society followed the prince's example and took Byzantium for its pattern. As late as the sixteenth century it preserved the formal, complicated etiquette and Oriental customs made known to us by the *Domostroi,* as well as the dress, entertainments, and superstitions of Byzantium. Czarist Russia remained until the dawn of the twentieth century the continuator and most faithful likeness of the vanished Byzantine Empire, in its autocratic despotism, its Orthodoxy, its flexible diplomacy, and its conviction of having a religious and political mission to accomplish in the world.

Byzantium and Serbia

At the beginning of the seventh century the Serbs had settled in the northwest of the Balkan Peninsula and along the shores of the Adriatic. From the days of Heraclius, perhaps, and certainly towards the middle of the ninth century—the period of Basil I—these Serbs received Christianity from Byzantium and entered the Greek sphere of influence, which protected them from the Bulgars in the tenth century. Later, at the end of the twelfth, when Serbia led by Stephen Nemanja won its independence, and when under the successors of this prince—Stephen Dushan in particular—it became in the fourteenth century the chief state in the Peninsula, it was deeply pervaded by Byzantine influence.

Stephen Nemanja organized the Serbian State on the Byzantine model, and on the Byzantine model his son, St. Sava, founded a national Church, with a Slavonic liturgy and an independent head. It was towards the Greek world—towards holy Mount Athos— that father and son turned their eyes when St. Sava, full of mystic fervour, retired to Vatopedi, and Stephen Nemanja, after his abdication, founded the monastery of Chilandari and there died in the odour of sanctity. In the thirteenth and fourteenth centuries this influence was strengthened. The Nemanjas married Byzantine princesses and maintained close relations with the Byzantine world, often intervening in the internal affairs of the Empire. Stephen Dushan dreamed of winning the hegemony of the Balkans and in 1346 had himself crowned *Basileus* and Autocrat of Serbs and Romans, at Uskub.

The power of the Crown then became as absolute in Serbia as in Byzantium; the king, "Autocrat by the grace of God," wielded all power and authority in the State; he was the source of law; he reigned in Byzantine pomp, robed like the sovereigns of Constantinople. The dignitaries about him and the ministers who advised him bore the sonorous titles of the Greek court: they were Caesars, Despots, *Sebastocrators*, *Logothetes*, *Vestiarii* and *Strategi*. The laws were inspired by those of Byzantium, and at the end of the twelfth century the *Nomocanon* of Photius and the *Prochiron* of Basil I were translated into Serbian. Stephen Dushan also had the works of Byzantine lawyers translated, and the famous code promulgated by him in 1349 was imbued with the principles of Byzantine jurisprudence. Greek Orthodoxy became the State religion, and the Church was all-powerful, supporting the State that protected it.

The same influence was manifest in literature and art. The princes of the Nemanja family were great builders, and even today many works of theirs are to be seen in Serbia and Macedonia. It is true that the architecture and sculptured decoration of some of these buildings show Western influence, and certain *motifs* derive from the Georgian or Arab East. But the stamp of Byzantium predominates, especially in the work of the later Nemanjas, in the fourteenth century and the beginning of the fifteenth. The plans based on the Greek cross or the trefoil bear the mark of Oriental design; the paintings, of which some are quite certainly the work of Greek masters, show all the characteristics of the art that came into flower with the fourteenth-century Byzantine renaissance. We find the same realism and freedom of style, the same feeling for composition, the same movement, quaintness of detail, and grace. Portraits were numerous and executed with a great sense of truth. The Macedonian school, whose works filled Serbia, sprang directly from the school of Byzantium.

Byzantium and Rumania

The Byzantine influence made itself felt elsewhere in Eastern Europe. Though Croatia soon turned to the Latin West and Rome, it was from Byzantium that the country received its first Christian teaching. And although Hungary, on the other hand, was converted by the Roman Church, it maintained close ties with the Byzantine world and owed it much. And while it was principally through Bulgaria that Rumania came to know Byzantium, yet Rumania, too, from the fourteenth century onwards, based its religious and political organization, its ecclesiastical law, its liturgy, and its conception of sovereign authority on Byzantine models. From Byzantium it borrowed court titles, as well as juridical usage and social customs. Greek prelates were the first metropolitans of Wallachia and Moldavia. Even after the Empire had fallen, Greek influence persisted. It was an ex-patriarch of Constantinople who reorganized the Wallachian Church at the beginning of the sixteenth century. Sovereigns were enthroned according to Byzantine ceremonial, not only in the fifteenth century, but also during the Ottoman period; and it was as true successors to the emperors, arrayed in the same gorgeous robes, that they had themselves portrayed and, when they visited Constantinople, were received by the patriarch amid acclamations and *polychronia* formerly reserved for the Lords of Byzantium.

The earliest Rumanian chroniclers took the pattern for their writings from Byzantium; the earliest examples of Rumanian architecture were based on Byzantine plans and style. In the sixteenth century, and even in the seventeenth, Greek influence prevailed throughout the Danubian provinces. Princes took Greek brides, married their daughters to Greeks, spoke Greek, surrounded themselves with Greek officials, and installed Greek prelates in their churches. Greek books were translated and the Greek language taught in schools; and although this influence never reached the lower social strata, and often met with fierce hostility, it was powerful at court and in society. Indeed, in the seventeenth century the Wallachian court presented a most striking proof of the great Hellenistic revival that followed the fall of Byzantium.

The Spread of Orthodoxy

Traces of Byzantium are to be found outside the Balkan Peninsula.

Armenia, owing to its geographical position between the Eastern world—whether Persian or Arab—and Byzantium, was subjected to a dual influence. Throughout the long years preceding the Moslem conquest in the eleventh century, the country was in a continual state of vacillation—political, intellectual, and artistic—between its two powerful neighbours. However, its close political ties with Byzantium could not fail to have their effect. Some of the Armenian provinces formed part of the Greek Empire, while the regions that preserved their independence accepted the Emperor's suzerainty more or less willingly. From quite early times there was a continual coming and going of diplomats, generals, and merchants between Armenia and Byzantium. Armenian rulers visited Constantinople in the hope of pensions and titles; thousands of Armenian adventurers came to seek their fortunes in the capital. These sometimes attained the highest appointments—even the throne. Young men came to Constantinople to study, and many of the patriarchs who ruled the Armenian Church between the fifth and seventh centuries had been brought up within the Empire. The Armenians, even those most hostile to Byzantium, had a profound sense of its greatness, majesty, and sanctity, and, willingly or unwillingly, came fully under its influence.

"The princes of Armenia," writes Rambaud, "in their little courts of Ani, Van, and Moush, set themselves to imitate the splendours of the Sacred Palace." Armenian historians make continual mention of diadems, garments threaded with gold, eunuchs, and the solemn, intricate ceremonial by which the sovereign was made to appear as "more than mortal." All were proud of the Emperor's favour and the titles he conferred upon them. The Pagratid king of Armenia was the spiritual son of the *Basileus;* the king of Iberia bore the hereditary title of *Curopalates;* others boasted of being *Magister, Patrician,* or *Protospatharius.* Above all, being realists and poor, they joyfully welcomed the money bestowed upon them by the Empire. Despite all this, however, the Armenians long remained tenacious of their independence, and religious differences often set them at loggerheads with Byzantium. Yet they learned much from the Greeks, and while their civilization and their art remained their own, and their nationals abroad exerted widespread influence outside Armenia, while they contributed to the intellectual and artistic eminence of the Greek Empire, they received from it more than they gave.

Byzantine literary works were often translated into Armenian. The golden age of Armenian literature in the fifth century was characterized by the group of "first translators," so named because, following the example of Sahak and Mesrob, they translated the Scriptures into Armenian and with Byzantium's help gave the country its literary language. Later, the long series of Armenian historians often drew inspiration from Byzantine chronicles. Art, too, while preserving its Oriental character, was repeatedly influenced by Byzantium. Justinian's architects built a number of churches in Armenia. In the seventh century Armenian patriarchs often employed Greek architects, and in buildings of the tenth and eleventh centuries, many Byzantine characteristics appear alongside those of the Eastern tradition. It cannot be denied that both in its civilization and its art, Armenia had a character of its own, which gave it originality and interest; nevertheless it was Byzantium that brought Armenia within the circle of civilized nations in the fifth century and by its political activity within the country may be said to have created Armenia in its own image.

Lastly, the Arabs themselves owed much to Byzantium.

When in the seventh century the Moslems conquered Syria and Mesopotamia, great schools were flourishing in Antioch, Edessa, Nisibis, and Harran, and the masters who taught in them were steeped in Greek culture, in Aristotelian philosophy and ancient medicine. The Omayyad Caliphs applied to them for translations into Syriac and Arabic of the most important Greek and Byzantine works. The Abbasids were equally eager to collect Greek manuscripts and obtain translations of the most famous works of Greek science, medicine, and philosophy. Throughout the ninth century, scholars in Baghdad were busy translating Euclid, Archimedes, Ptolemy, Dioscorides, Hippocrates, Galen, Aristotle, and Theophrastus; and it has been justly said that but for Byzantium and the Byzantine traditions communicated to them by the schools of Syria, the Arabs, for all their brilliant gifts, would have remained what they were in the days of Mohammed: that is to say, semi-barbarians. It was through the Syrian translators that they learned the science and philosophy of Greece, and it was thanks to them that a great and fruitful intellectual movement arose throughout Islam, from Spain to India. Lastly, it was through the Arab schools in Cordova that the Christian West came to know Aristotle; and in this roundabout manner Scholasticism owes its origin, in part, to Byzantium.

The whole East, then, received intellectual benefit from the Empire: the Slavs, whom it ushered into history, and the Arabs, who owed it the intellectual glories of Baghdad and Cordova. It ruled them all, to a greater or lesser degree, through literature, art, law, and religion. Byzantium's contribution to the history of civilization is great indeed.

III. The Spread of Byzantine Civilization in the West

1. CAUSES OF BYZANTINE INFLUENCE

Byzantium also gave much to the West, for reasons which are not far to seek.

For centuries, as we know, the Greek Empire ruled parts of Italy; sometimes more, sometimes less. From the sixth century, when Justinian's armies reconquered the peninsula, to the eighth, when the exarchate of Ravenna fell beneath the Lombard assault, most of the country was a Byzantine province. In the second half of the ninth century, under the sovereigns of the house of Macedonia, Greek ambitions turned again to the West; and for another two centuries Byzantium extended its authority and its influence over the whole of southern Italy and as far north as Rome. During these two periods of Greek rule, a strong Hellenic current naturally swept the country. The imperial government, ever anxious to assimilate its new subjects, engaged in active propaganda to bring about the absorption of Latin elements, to make the peninsula an annex of the Empire and to create there a new Magna Graecia. Between the ninth and eleventh centuries, the Macedonian Emperors made tremendous efforts, both political and religious, to achieve this end, with such success that even after the collapse of Byzantine rule, Greek influence long survived under the Norman and Angevin kings. Between the sixth and eighth centuries the emperors pursued a similar plan, which it was the task of the exarchs of Ravenna to bring to fruition. This attempt clashed more than once with the national Roman tradition, represented by the Papacy and by the opposition of the Italian peoples. Yet wherever the State could intervene directly—that is to say, in administration or in the Church—or indirectly, as in society and the sphere of art, the exarchs largely succeeded in propagating Greek ideas, culture, language, and customs. Through them, Hellenism found firm foothold in Italy, until in the sixth and seventh centuries Ravenna had become Oriental in character, while Rome itself, being governed by Greek or Syrian Popes and full of Greek monks and Eastern colonists, was half Byzantine.[1]

We know something of the prestige enjoyed by the imperial city in the mediaeval West. It was to Constantinople that men turned for fine craftsmanship and high quality. It was from there that in the eleventh century the Italians sent for doors of bronze inlaid with silver for their churches; it was there that Didier, the abbot of Monte Cassino, commissioned the finely wrought images of repoussé silver gilt, the bronze candelabra, and the enamelled altar-front that adorned his basilica. From Constantinople, at the request of the Doge of Venice, came the celebrated retable of the Pala d'Oro. Merchants of Venice and Amalfi brought back from there the marvellous fabrics that were the glory of the Byzantine luxury trade. The West loved to model its buildings on the finest examples of Eastern architecture. The church that Charlemagne built at Aix-la-Chapelle was obviously inspired by S. Vitale of Ravenna; St. Mark's of Venice and St. Front of Périgueux are copies of the Church of the Holy Apostles built in Constantinople by Justinian.

Finally, it was from the East that people all over Italy and even as far away as Germany summoned the skilled master craftsmen: marblers, mosaicists, enamel-workers, and makers of miniatures, whose work was a revelation of beauty and skill such as had been forgotten by the West for centuries. We may easily

[1] In this connection, I venture to refer the reader to my book, *Études sur l'administration byzantine dans l'exarchat de Ravenne* (Paris, 1888), 241-288.

Virgin and Child. Ivory. Height: 9⅛″. 10th or 11th century.

imagine how much the Latins learned from these men, and consequently how great was the part played by Byzantium in the development of Western art.

And this was not all. Byzantium and the Latin West were in closer touch than is generally supposed. In early times, as we have seen, traders from Syria visited the western Mediterranean ports and settled in Italy, Africa, and even Gaul. Greek monks established numbers of religious foundations in the West, whether as a result of their flight from the Arab invasion in the seventh century, or from Iconoclastic persecution in the eighth, or because, as happened between the ninth and eleventh centuries, the emperors encouraged them to cover southern Italy with their monasteries.

Alongside this westward current there was another flowing east: pilgrims travelling to Jerusalem via Constantinople; merchants from Venice, Amalfi, or Pisa trading in eastern waters and often settling in the Greek capital; diplomats from every country and fortune-hunters of every race; travellers, laymen and religious, soldiers and civilians. Crowds of foreigners made their way to the great city. The Crusades increased the flow and added to the number of those who settled in the East. During the period of the Palaeologi, between the end of the thirteenth century and the middle of the fifteenth, traffic between Byzantium and Italy was livelier than ever. This constant exchange was bound to have its effect. Everyone coming from the East brought with him works of art, examples of superlative craftsmanship, ivories, illuminated manuscripts—all the pride of Byzantium; also, decorative *motifs* dear to the East, and perhaps even the plans of famous buildings; to say nothing of spices, purple dyes, new plants, and unknown fabrics. They brought ideas, too: echoes of the great intellectual, juridical, or philosophic movements current in Constantinople at that time; echoes of legends and folk tales from the remotest corners of the East.

There was no limit to what the West could learn; and these exchanges, which lasted as long as the Byzantine Empire itself, were of enormous consequence to the history of civilization.

Byzantium: Greatness and Decline

2. BYZANTIUM AND WESTERN ART

Few problems in the history of art have been more discussed than that of the Eastern influences on the Christian art of the West, or what is known as the "Byzantine Question." Byzantium's part has been by turns over- and understated. Some people, from a queer kind of patriotism, are hurt by the suggestion that the national art of Italy, France, or Germany may owe something to foreign influence; others, with equal prejudice and lack of critical sense, are determined to discover traces of the Orient everywhere.

To find an answer to this complex question, we must approach it with greater discrimination and consider it not as a whole, but in its separate aspects of place and period. But whatever reservations we may have to make in detail, in general it is safe to say that for centuries Byzantine art was the "regulating art of Europe."

During the fifth century its influence was all-powerful in Italy, Africa, and even Gaul. In Ravenna, the mosaics in the mausoleum of Galla Placidia and in the Orthodox baptistery are unquestionably the work—and the finest work—of Eastern artists, trained, perhaps, in the great school that flourished in Antioch at that time. In North Africa, religious buildings were inspired by Egyptian and Syrian models. Even in the buildings of the Trier region, we may detect ancient links with the East.

But when in the sixth century Byzantium regained its hold on Italy, the influence of its art became much more pronounced. S. Vitale of Ravenna is purely Byzantine in style, and its mosaics, like those of S. Apollinare Nuovo and S. Apollinare in Classe and

Madonna and Child. Italian. 13th century.

those of the Basilica of Parenzo, are reckoned among the finest
and most authentic creations of Graeco-Oriental art. The mosaics
in the seventh-century Roman buildings, which include St. Agnese
and the chapel of Pope John VII, are of the same pattern; while
the frescoes of St. Maria Antiqua, which were painted during
the period between the end of the seventh century and the middle of the ninth, are on the whole entirely Byzantine in composition, type, and style. The Iconoclast crisis, by banishing artists
to the West, reinforced the Oriental trend in Italy. In Rome, in
the Basilica of St. Praxedis, which dates from the first half of
the ninth century, the chapel of St. Zeno is a pure gem of the
Orient, brilliant with marble and golden mosaics. Either by way
of Italy or through direct communication with the East, the
Carolingian renaissance owed much to Byzantium. It is true that
other elements mingled in that highly composite art; but in buildings such as the dome of Aix-la-Chapelle or the church of Ger-
migny-les-Prés, and in the illumination of the beautiful ninth-
century Carolingian manuscripts, the general effect is entirely
Eastern.

In the period between the seventh and ninth centuries, as in
that between the fourth and sixth, the answer to the "Byzantine
Question" must be pronounced in favour of Byzantium.

But it was when the Greek Empire was at its apogee—during
that Macedonian renaissance which began in the middle of the
ninth century and continued until the twelfth—that Byzantium
played a really dominant part in the development of Western art.
Everywhere the buildings of the Christian East were copied; in
St. Mark's of Venice, in the many domed churches of Périgord
and in the Romanesque buildings of the Rhenish school. Everywhere their decoration was based on the *motifs* beloved of the
East, and Romanesque art in particular drew largely from this
treasury of form and composition. The interior of all basilicas
was adorned with sparkling mosaics. Venice, ever open to Eastern
influence, was almost a Greek city, and Byzantine mosaicists were
commissioned to decorate the basilica of Torcello as well as a
great part of St. Mark's. At the other end of Italy, in Norman
Sicily, Byzantine mosaicists worked at Cefalu, in the Martorana
and the Palatine Chapel, as well as in the palaces and pavilions
of the kings. Southern Italy, lying between these two provinces

of Oriental Christian art, owes no less than they to Byzantium. The great school of Monte Cassino was directed by masters summoned from Constantinople. At the gates of Rome, Greek artists decorated the monastery church of Grotta Ferrata; even Tuscany and northern Italy were full of artists working "in the Byzantine manner"; and if the scope of the Greek masters' work and the duration of their influence varied from region to region, still it is to them that Italy owed the basis for the glorious period at the end of the eleventh century and throughout the twelfth. Italy owed to Byzantium not only the models from which Italian artists worked, not only the bronze doors, gorgeous fabrics, enamels, richly illuminated manuscripts, that inspired them, but also the symbolic pattern of church decoration and the principles of iconography.

In France the problem of the origins of Romanesque art is closely bound up with the "Byzantine Question"; it may be that Romanesque architecture owes more to the East than we think, and that the decorative art of the eleventh and twelfth centuries drew inspiration from the same source. In Germany, from the tenth to the thirteenth century, we again detect Byzantine influence, no doubt connected with the marriage of Otto the Great's son to the Greek Theophano. In the great Germanic architectural works we find many imitations of the Byzantine manner, and even more in the manuscripts illustrated in the tenth century by the schools of Reichenau and Trier, and that of Ratisbon in the eleventh. This influence persisted until the thirteenth century, long after the Ottonian renaissance.

We must beware of exaggerating, however. It has been said that "the art of the East helped rather to awaken in Western artists the consciousness of their own qualities," and under the influence of other trends and traditions many of them soon broke free from the tutelage of their Greek masters. Nevertheless, the powerful Byzantine current never failed to renew itself, especially in Italy, after various checks, and to spread triumphantly through the West. Once more, this time from the tenth century to the twelfth, the "Byzantine Question" is resolved in favour of the East.

In the thirteenth and fourteenth centuries, Byzantine art continued to exercise a profound influence on Italy. In the South, in

the fourteenth century, the paintings in the churches were purely
Eastern both in style and iconography, even when executed by
Tuscan artists. In Tuscany, masters such as Giunta of Pisa, Mar-

Courtesy of the Fogg Art Museum, Harvard University

Nativity. Tuscan School. 13th century.

garitone d'Arazzo, and Guido of Siena were Byzantinists. The
creator of the mosaics of the tribune in the Baptistery in Florence
was a pupil of the Greeks, and so was the painter of the frescoes
in the Baptistery of Parma. Until the end of the thirteenth century and the dawn of the fourteenth, Byzantine art continued to
pass on to Italy its slowly garnered techniques, forms, concep-

tions of landscape, and rules of architecture and composition; also, through the countless icons distributed through Italy, it gave the country the new iconography, richer, more complex, more mystical, and full of feeling, which was being elaborated in the East at that time. The great primitives drank deep from this spring: Cimabue, Duccio, and Giotto himself; and although at times the Byzantine art of the thirteenth and fourteenth centuries received some rare flash of inspiration from Siena or Venice, *trecento* Italy owed far more to Byzantium, and at the beginning of the fourteenth century the great Tuscan masters were in many respects purely Byzantine in their genius.

3. BYZANTIUM'S INTELLECTUAL INFLUENCE ON THE WEST

The West owed more to Byzantium than artistic instruction; it owed ideas, and they lived long.

The Byzantine conception of imperial power as defined in the Code of Justinian was calculated to please any monarch. At the end of the tenth century, Emperor Otto III, Theophano's son, took pleasure in reviving the elaborate ceremonial of Byzantium and conferring on the dignitaries of his court the tremendous titles in use at the Sacred Palace. He arrayed himself in the robes of the *basileis* and like them exacted the adoration due to a god. Moreover, as the inscription on his seal indicates, he claimed to have revived the Roman Empire. These were merely the lofty dreams of a mystically inclined young prince in love with greatness. Byzantium was to provide a sounder foundation for theories of absolute monarchy.

It was not long before knowledge of the law of Justinian reached Italy, and by the middle of the eleventh century the law schools of Rome, Ravenna, and Bologna were flourishing. Both the *Institutes* and the *Digest* were known there. But when, towards the end of the eleventh century, Irnerius introduced a new system in Bologna and, instead of distorting Justinian's legislation as his predecessors had done, began to study it in its original form and expounded its sternly logical conclusions in his commentaries, the school of Bologna assumed enormous importance. Frederick Barbarossa, in the celebrated constitution of 1158, expressed his approval of the Bologna jurists, because he found in their teaching the best arguments for establishing imperial claims. At the end of the twelfth century students poured into Bologna in their thousands from all over the West, and the famous Glossators of the thirteenth century, Accursius, Odofredus, and Rolandino of Romanzi—whose curious tombs may still be seen in Bologna opposite the Church of St. Francis—gave the school a world-wide reputation. While for all Europe, Paris stood for dialectics, Bologna was the great university of jurisprudence. There the principles of Justinian law were annotated, and the learning that sprang from it was to "reign over all spheres of the mind, with the sovereignty of our own Scholasticism."

It was the imperialist traditions of the Bologna Glossators that inspired the lawmakers of Frederick II Hohenstaufen, when they proclaimed their Emperor "law incarnate upon earth" and acknowledged his right to order ecclesiastical affairs as freely as the secular interests of his empire. Bologna inspired the schools of Roman law in Alais and Montpellier, where the legislators of Philip the Fair were trained—Pierre Flote, Guillaume de Plaisians, and Guillaume de Nogaret—all those who formulated and defended the rights and claims of absolute monarchy, like the astute and crafty lawyers they were. The king of France, they declared, was "above the law," and need have no scruples in revoking the acts of his predecessors if it were in the public interest to do so. In the face of the papal claim to "command kings and kingdoms," they proclaimed the independence of the Crown; and the violence done to Pope Boniface VIII at Anagni, by Nogaret and Colonna, was in quite the Byzantine manner.

It was from Justinian law that legislators formed their conception of royal power and found arguments to justify the omnipotence of the Crown. Alongside the mediaeval, feudal idea of royalty there emerged a new spirit, from which evolved the modern State in its centralized and absolute form. The monarchy of Louis XIV proceeded from Justinian law; the Great King, like the *Basileus,* was invested by divine right with limitless authority. Distant Byzantium sowed many ideas that took root in the modern world, though their true origin is often forgotten.

Other things came to the West from Byzantium. Strange as it may seem, considering the hostility that existed between the Greek and Roman Churches, the unquestioned superiority of Byzantine theology up to the twelfth century gave the Eastern Church a certain ascendancy over that of the West. Scotus Erigena in the ninth century translated Dionysius the Areopagite and Maximus the Confessor; Peter Lombard and St. Thomas Aquinas were inspired by John of Damascus. Mediaeval France owed a number of its folk tales to Byzantium; they came through the Greek world from the distant East, and furnished material for the *fabliaux;* more than one of the devout and edifying legends of France, of which hagiographers and writers of adventure stories have taken advantage, were of Byzantine origin. More of mediaeval French literature comes from the Greek East than is commonly believed.

But the debt of fifteenth-century Italy was greater than any. While, as we have seen, the schools of the West wrote commentaries on Aristotelian philosophy only, the University of Constantinople, under the guidance of Psellus in the eleventh century, had restored Platonic doctrine to a place of honour. It was from Byzantium that Italy came to know Plato in the fifteenth century, thanks to Gemistus Plethon and Bessarion, and we know how Platonism flourished first in Florence and later throughout the West, and how great was its influence. The Greek language, which Italy relearned in the fourteenth century, and Greek authors, whose manuscripts were brought to the West by Greek scholars, were no less important factors in the intellectual revival.

As we know, a strong current of humanism pervaded the Byzantium of the Palaeologi, at the end of the thirteenth century and the beginning of the fourteenth, and the great professors of Constantinople—Planudes, Moschopulus, and Triclinius—were pioneers in the revival of classical studies. They inspired the men who were to carry the Hellenic tradition into Italy. At the end of the fourteenth century, Manuel Chrysoloras came to teach Greek in Florence, and after him his kinsman, John Chrysoloras, and George of Trebizond, who taught in Venice. With the fall of Constantinople the westward exodus of Byzantine scholars increased. Between the middle of the fifteenth century and the dawn of the sixteenth there arrived, among many other fugitives, John Argyopulus, Theodore Gaza, Demetrius Chalcocondyles, Andronicus Callistus, Marcus Musurus, and John and Constantine Lascaris. All brought precious manuscripts; they taught the West to admire the masterpieces of Greece once more, and made these accessible both through the teaching of Greek and by their translations of famous works. Besides the Greeks we have mentioned, there were of course others, poor people, indifferently educated and of dubious character, remote descendants of those *Graeculi* whom Rome had received and despised. Yet these, too, contributed something to the great humanist movement; and though it would be too much to say that but for Byzantium, there might never have been a Renaissance, there is no doubt that Byzantium helped in a most marvellous way to bring it about.

Conclusion. Byzantium's Heritage

In this book we have tried to show what Byzantium was, what part it played in the history of civilization, and finally what it did for the European world, during the thousand years of its existence. In the political field, Byzantium was for a long time the champion of Christianity against Islam. By its stubborn resistance it smashed the Arab assault between the eighth and eleventh centuries, later staving off and weakening that of the Turks. In the sphere of intellect, Byzantium defended civilization against barbarism. Within the boundaries of the Greek Empire the traditions of the ancient world were preserved and developed, and the civilization that flourished there was perhaps the most brilliant and advanced of any in the Middle Ages. Byzantium was the teacher of the Slav and Arab East. The West learned an incalculable amount from the same school, and in the fifteenth century the torch of the Renaissance was kindled from its flame.

Even after Byzantium had fallen and had ceased to exist as an Empire, it continued to influence the Eastern world very strongly and still does so. From the uttermost ends of Greece to the depths of Russia, all the peoples of Eastern Europe—Turks, Greeks, Serbs, Bulgars, Rumanians, and Russians—have preserved a living memory of it and garnered its traditions. Thus that old, old history, imperfectly known and partly forgotten, is no dead thing, as some would believe; it lingers on even in our own day, deeply imprinted in trends of thought and politics.

1. BYZANTIUM AND THE TURKS

When, by the capture of Constantinople, the Turks destroyed the Byzantine Empire, they inherited not only its territories and political power, but took possession of much else in the realm that they seemed to have annihilated.

Those rough warriors were neither administrators nor lawyers, and they understood little of political science. Consequently they modelled many of their state institutions and much of their administrative organization upon what they found in Byzantium. The pomp surrounding the Turkish sovereigns of the sixteenth and seventeenth centuries was as elaborate as the old Byzantine ceremonial, and the Sultan has been rightly called "a Moslem *Basileus.*" The hierarchy of his officials, as instituted by Mohammed II in the *Kanoun-Nameh,* is curiously reminiscent of the Greek Empire. A. Rambaud points out that the position of the two *Beylerbegs* of Anatolia and Roumelia was exactly that of the two *Domestics* of the *Scholae* of East and West, and that equal similarity existed between the *Grand Domestic* and the *Grand Vizier,* between the *Megadux* and the *Capitan-pasha,* and between the *Grand Logothete* and the *Rais-effendi. Logothetes* became *Defterdars,* while the *Nishanji* was the counterpart of the former imperial secretary (ἐπὶ τοῦ κανικλείου). There is every reason to believe that in the provinces the Ottoman *sanjaks* corresponded fairly exactly to the old Byzantine *themes,* while the *Beg* of the *sanjak* was the equivalent of the *Logothete* of the *theme;* and it would seem that in their administration the Ottomans preserved the framework bequeathed to them by the Empire.

We may wonder how much of the Turkish system of military fiefs was borrowed from Byzantium. Certainly the *timars* and *ziams,* the fiefs of the *spahis,* were counterparts of the old domains. As Zachariae of Lingenthal so well said, "It would be quite erroneous to consider the official institutions in the Ottoman Empire as specifically Turkish in origin." There is no doubt that in the systems and usages of Islam there survived far more of Byzantine tradition than is commonly believed.

The Turks also needed administrators and diplomats, and these they found in plenty among the conquered. Not, indeed, that Christians were allowed to take any part in government or public affairs so long as they remained Christians; but if they adopted the Moslem faith, their future was assured. The Sultan liked to choose his highest officers of state from among young men forcibly converted to Islam and enrolled in his household. "It was a state maxim," says Hammer, "that to attain the senior appointments in the Empire, a man had to be the son of a Christian." It has been noted that out of 48 *Grand Viziers*, only 12 were of Moslem parentage; the rest were Albanians, Bosnians, Dalmatians, Croats, and Greeks; and in this, too, the Turks were carrying on the traditions of the Byzantines, who had been so eager to convert, absorb, and employ the conquered races. Soon certain branches of the Ottoman administration were open even to Christians. The Sultan invited those who remained of the ancient Byzantine families—members of the clever, timeserving Phanariot aristocracy—to supply him with *Grand Dragomans;* these held almost the rank of minister, and their influence in the palace was at times predominant. Later from the same source he chose the *Hospodars,* who were charged with the government of Wallachia and Moldavia, and who in the ceremonies of their investiture and the methods of their administration preserved all the elaborate ritual of Byzantine etiquette.

Byzantium and Hellenism

In these ways conquered Byzantium maintained its influence over its conquerors. Even more strongly, and with far-reaching consequences, this influence survived among the Balkan peoples who had been subjects of the Empire and were now under the sway of Islam. The preservation of Hellenic culture and the Hellenic language in the territories conquered by the Turks, and the survival of the sense of nationality among the Christians of the Peninsula, were due entirely to the Orthodox Church, heir to and guardian of the traditions of Byzantium.

When the Empire collapsed, the Turks made little attempt to draw nearer to their Christian subjects. Mohammed II promised them freedom to practise their religion and to retain their property, but barred them from any share in public life or office. Provided they paid the extremely heavy taxes he imposed, he took little notice of them. Christians in the Moslem state lived like foreigners; they formed what the Turkish administration called the *Roum-milletti*, the Byzantine nation, and were governed by the Oecumenical Patriarch, who was appointed by the Sultan. By the *firman* given to Gennadius, Mohammed II allowed the Orthodox Church to retain its hierarchy and the privileges formerly accorded it by the Byzantine emperors; thus, in reorganizing his Church on the basis of the old law, the Patriarch became at once the religious and the political leader of his people. The Church had its own courts of justice, in which all lawsuits among the Christians soon came to be tried. It had its own schools which, according to Ottoman law, the Patriarch and his bishops alone had the right to open and direct. And although the Patriarch was largely in the hands of the Sultan, and Turkish authorities often gave the Christians rough treatment, nevertheless the gathering of all Christians into one huge community was of immense importance. For, thanks to the Church, they kept their ancient traditions, and their leader, the Patriarch, seemed to take the place of the vanished Emperor. He inherited from him not only outward prestige, but also something of his effective power, and from his palace in the Phanar district of Istanbul he governed all the Christian churches, Greek or Slavic, that existed in the Ottoman Empire.

Thus in the half of Christendom that lay under the yoke of Islam the Church played an essential part; it was the holy Ark in which, with the Christian faith, the Hellenic language, tradition, and nationality were preserved. The Church opened schools; immediately after the conquest the Patriarch Gennadius made haste to found "the great school of the nation" in the Phanar. The bishops opened other places of learning in their dioceses, at the instigation of the Holy Synod; and elementary and indifferent though the teaching may sometimes have been, yet it was given in Greek; and this was to be of untold importance for the future. When in the course of the seventeenth and eighteenth centuries this great scholastic effort was strengthened and developed, the Orthodox Church found it a powerful instrument for the perpetuation of Hellenism in the Empire of the sultans and for the preservation in the Greek people of the consciousness of their nationality.

Cyril Mango

St. Catherine, Thessalonica. Probably early 14th century.

It was not the Greeks alone who benefited, but also the Serbs, Bulgars, and Rumanians, who were equally under the rule of the Orthodox Church, and who in this great community of religion found a refuge for their nationhood. It is true that the Phanariot prelates had their faults; often they were tyrants, lovers of in-

· 293 ·

trigue, greedy and corrupt. At times they were extraordinarily clumsy in handling the non-Greeks in their charge; and the gross ignorance of the minor clergy aggravated the effects of their superiors' shortcomings. Nevertheless, in spite of the well-justified hatred often felt for Phanariot bishops, in spite of the too exclusively Hellenic tendencies in their government—especially in the seventeenth and eighteenth centuries—the Orthodox Church did immense service to the Christian nations of the Balkans. It maintained for them a framework wherein they could survive, it gave them cohesion in the face of their Turkish masters, and above all it enabled them to retain the memory of their origins and the sense of nationality. For four centuries the Orthodox Church kept Christian patriotism alive in the Balkan East, and beneath its shadow the first impulse was given, in the course of the eighteenth century, to the great movement through which, in the dawn of the nineteenth, the oppressed nations awoke and found their independence. On April 4, 1821, it was the Archbishop Germanus of Patras who proclaimed the revolt against the Turks and made the assembled people swear to fight for their country and their faith. The Ottoman government saw so clearly how much of this unexpected rising was due to the Orthodox Church that it chose as its first victims the Patriarch of Constantinople—who was hanged on April 22, 1821, at the door of his cathedral—and a number of his metropolitans.

In bygone times the Balkan peoples were born into political life through the influence of Byzantium; and to Byzantium, as represented by the Orthodox Church, they owed their resurrection. For this Church, being even more concerned to serve the national cause than the cause of faith, closely linked the two ideas of nationality and religion in the popular mind, and made them fruitful.

Byzantium's Heritage

2. BYZANTIUM AND RUSSIA

It was not only in the Balkans that Byzantine influence survived the Turkish conquest by so many centuries. It was preserved perhaps even more strongly beyond the boundaries of the Greek realm, in that Russia of which, in the eleventh century, Byzantium had been the tutor, and in which the Byzantine tradition remained the basis of the State and of national life.

When the Byzantine Empire collapsed, Greeks poured into Moscow as they did into Italy. Ivan III opened his realm to all the émigrés from the Greek world; they supplied him with statesmen, diplomats, engineers, artists, and theologians. They, too, brought with them Greek manuscripts, the precious heritage of the ancient civilization; and parallel to the great Western Renaissance, there followed a renaissance in the North. But it was mainly through the marriage of Ivan III to Sophia, the last of the Palaeologi, in 1472, that Russia became the political heir of Byzantium. By taking the Byzantine double-headed eagle as the new arms of his kingdom, the Grand Prince of Moscow proclaimed himself the heir of the Greek Emperors and announced his intention of making his capital succeed Byzantium, as Byzantium had succeeded Rome. Within the walls of the Kremlin as within those of the Sacred Palace, churches and monasteries arose alongside barracks and palaces, and what remains of the princely residence built in 1487 is strangely reminiscent of the Greek imperial palace. Again, the curious book entitled the *Domostroi*, compiled towards the end of the fifteenth century, shows us a society greatly resembling that of Byzantium and propounds a wisdom much like the wisdom of Cecaumenus.

A century later, in 1589, when Boris Godunov created the Patriarchate of Moscow, Russia seemed to be claiming the religious heritage of Byzantium and assuming the leadership of Orthodoxy in place of Constantinople, now desecrated by the Moslems. Czarist Russia never afterwards forgot these ambitions or allowed the stamp of Byzantine education to be effaced from the national character. Even in comparatively recent years, had we wanted to form some idea of what the Byzantine world was like, we should have turned our eyes to the court of St. Petersburg and to the Kremlin in Moscow. Nowhere more faithfully than in Czarist Russia was the living image of vanished Byzantium preserved.

The Czarist concept of imperial power was that of Byzantium. "The Czar," says A. Leroy-Beaulieu, "is the Lord's anointed, appointed by the divine hand to guard and guide the Christian people." [1] In the eyes of his subjects he was God's lieutenant on earth; and when he was anointed with holy oil in the Kremlin by the authority of the Church and according to Byzantine ritual, he became both absolute lord and highest representative of Orthodoxy. The elaborate formality surrounding the person of the Autocrat reminds us of the old Byzantine ceremonial. In sixteenth- and seventeenth-century Russia the stiff receptions and the audiences granted to ambassadors had all the magnificence of the Greek court and took place amid a similar display of luxury; there were even the mechanical roaring lions. Uniforms blazed about the imperial throne, and there were the same prostrations before the sovereign and the same formulas of abject submission. The Russian court retained much of this etiquette until the twentieth century, and the banquets held in the setting of the Kremlin preserved a strictly Byzantine character. In this realm, as in the old Greek Empire, everything depended on the sovereign's favour; therefore the court took and held a dominant position and exercised a powerful attraction on all seekers after position, wealth, or influence.

---

[1] This passage and those that follow are quoted from Anatole Leroy-Beaulieu's fine book, *L'Empire des Tsars et les Russes* (Paris, 1881), Vols. 1, 3.

The relationship between Church and State was the same in Russia as in Byzantium, though the Czar was in no sense a sort of national Pope, as is sometimes thought. Unlike the *basileis* the Czars were seldom theologians and did not as a rule interfere in questions of dogma or discipline. Nevertheless the Church, "beside an omnipotent Czar, grown up in the shadow of limitless power," could not but be "a State Church of an Autocratic State." "Happy in being honoured by the Orthodox Czar," it accepted its subordinate position gladly. "So far from rebelling . . . it accounted it a merit to show humility and submission." The Czar's authority over the Church increased still further when Peter the Great abolished the Patriarchate. He declared that "the people had begun to pay less heed to the Autocrat than to the supreme pastor, even to the point of siding with the latter against the former, in the belief that in so doing they were embracing the cause of God Himself." Peter would have none of this. "There was no room beside the imperial throne for the throne of a Patriarch." In this matter "the Czar went further than the Byzantine Autocrat."

It was not only in its close association with the State that the Russian Church resembled the Church of Byzantium. It also attached great importance to rites and ceremonies. Here too, the Russians outdid the Byzantines. They loved and venerated wonder-working icons and attributed great virtues to them. "Russia is perhaps richer in them than Italy or Spain." And here as in the Greek world we may observe the important position occupied by monks, the number and wealth of the monasteries, and the superior status of the black clergy, who alone are qualified to attain episcopal rank. Lastly, this Church, like the Byzantine, was an ardent propagator of Orthodoxy, and in the huge Czarist Empire that embraced so many different nations, it converted many dissidents: people of Turkish or Mongol origin in Siberia, and in Russia the Finns and many others. The Church proselytised from the Black Sea to the Pacific. Russian Orthodoxy "no more confined itself to one race than to one state"; by the profession of a single faith it helped the Czarist Empire to establish a measure of unity, as the Byzantine Church had once helped the Byzantine realm to do.

Imperial administration performed the same task by the same

methods as those once used by Byzantium. The Russian nobility welcomed families of foreign origin to its ranks, and Czarist governments were eager to attract and employ the ablest men of the peoples they had subjugated. Like the *basileis,* the Czars took Georgians and Armenians into their service, as well as Balts, Poles, and Turcomans, whose barely Russianized names gave plain evidence of their origins. Russians were as eager as Greeks to assimilate the conquered, and equally successful. Bureaucracy was as important here as in the Greek Empire, and Russian administration seemed an exact copy of the Byzantine pattern. The fourteen degrees of the *chin,* by which Peter the Great established the ranks of his officials, might almost be mistaken for the system in use at the Sacred Palace. It was the same scheme of social hierarchy based on appointment, service, and rank; there was also the same system of promotion, which went by favour of the Emperor.

Many more such examples could be given. But in one respect Byzantine influence was especially strong and far-reaching. In proclaiming themselves heirs of the *basileis,* the Czars undertook a dual task: that of protecting all Christians throughout the East and of taking revenge on Islam for the defeat of 1453. In neither task did they fail. As Tsarigrad once attracted the Varangians of Kiev, Constantinople became the goal of Czarist ambitions from the eighteenth century onwards. The famous will of Peter the Great is certainly apocryphal, yet it indicates the trend of Russian policy. Anna Ivanovna, Catherine II, Alexander I, Nicholas I, and Alexander II all dreamed of restoring the Byzantine Empire and assuming the imperial crown in the once-more Orthodox Church of St. Sophia. "From the dawn of Russian history," says a Russian writer, "Russia's ideal, greatness, and glory have been in Constantinople." "The Cathedral of St. Sophia," writes another, "gives our national life its true direction." To replace the Crescent by the Cross on the dome of the Great Church and relight the candles extinguished by the Turks was the ideal and the aim that Russia cherished for centuries, and with it the dream of liberating Christian peoples from the Ottoman yoke and taking possession of Tsarigrad, which was "indissolubly bound up with the idea of Christian Czarism." On the day when Moscow became Byzantium's heir, the policy of the Empire of the Czars was determined for centuries to come.

Byzantium's Heritage

3. BYZANTIUM AND BALKAN AMBITIONS

It was not upon Russia only that the Cathedral of St. Sophia exerted so powerful an attraction. All the Balkan races that found rebirth in the nineteenth century—Greeks, Serbs, Bulgars, and even Rumanians—turned their eyes to the Great Church as to the Metropolis of Orthodoxy. These young nations, too, claimed Byzantium's heritage and traced their title to it through history.

Throughout the Middle Ages, as we know, each of the Balkan states that grew up in turn alongside Byzantium dreamed of winning the hegemony of the Peninsula and, as a means to that end, of gaining possession of Constantinople. Such was the ambition of the first Bulgarian Empire, which under the powerful leadership of the Czars Symeon and Samuel in the tenth century extended from the Danube to the shores of the Adriatic, Epirus, and Thessaly. In 924 Byzantium very nearly became its capital. In the thirteenth century the second Bulgarian Empire, extending from the Black Sea to the Adriatic and the Aegean, had the same ambition, and in 1228 it seemed as if a Bulgarian Czar would reign in Constantinople. In the fourteenth century it was the turn of the Serbian Empire, founded by Stephen Dushan—that Great Serbia which at one time possessed the whole of western Macedonia, Albania, Epirus, Thessaly, Bosnia, and the Adriatic seaboard; and in 1355 a Serbian Czar seemed likely to march into Constantinople as conqueror.

The memory of these cherished dreams, these ambitions that so nearly found fulfilment, was never lost. Though Serbia renounced all claim to Constantinople and demanded little more than the western half of the Balkan Peninsula, Bulgaria after its revival always secretly aimed at the Bosphorus. Czar Ferdinand dreamed of setting the imperial crown upon his head beneath the vaulted roof of St. Sophia and, like Symeon, his remote predecessor, of proclaiming himself "Czar and Autocrat of the Bulgars and Greeks." In the Balkan war of 1912-1913, Constantinople was certainly the true goal of Bulgarian ambitions, and though the Bulgars were halted at the Chatalja lines by the Russian menace, and their way to Constantinople was barred, it is safe to say—and the events of 1915 are sufficient evidence—that the vindictive Czar Ferdinand did not forget this disappointment nor pardon those who were its cause.

Greece is the last claimant, and indeed considers herself a more legitimate heir than the Slavs could ever be. Greece has Thessalonica, which in Byzantine times was the second city of the Empire. Greece dreams of vast expansion into Asia Minor, once Byzantium's strength. (We may recall here the memoirs presented to King Constantine at the end of 1914 by Mr. Venizelos.) Greece has not forgotten the famous legend that foretells the day when, in liberated St. Sophia, a Greek priest will complete the celebration of the Mass so tragically interrupted by the Turks in 1453.

Byzantine history offers titles, rights, and promises for all these dreams, all these hopes and ambitions; and so throughout Eastern Europe, Byzantium remains strangely alive. Constantine Dragases, who fell heroically on the breached walls of his capital, Symeon and Samuel, who came near to establishing the Bulgarian hegemony in the Balkans, and the great Serbian Czar, Stephen Dushan. . . . To us these are scarcely more than names—unfamiliar names—in the history books. But to the people of Athens, Sophia, and Belgrade, they are great ancestors, whose memory is green, whose deaths must be avenged, whose labours must be resumed and completed. It is because they lived that their descendants lay claim to the heritage of Byzantium and so many splendid hopes are centred about the Great Church of St. Sophia. Five centuries have passed since Byzantium fell; but its memory persists, and for the many peoples who have received and treasured its heritage, its history, that to us seems dead, is full of promise and of pledges for the future.

Bibliographical Note

The bibliographical note which follows is an addition to the original French work, made in order to help a reader who wishes to study further the history and civilization of Byzantium. In drawing up this note we have made no attempt at completeness. Anyone well versed in the literature about Byzantium will be able to point to numerous omissions. We are very much aware of this. Nevertheless, this note does introduce the student to some fundamental works on Byzantium.

There is, however, one omission, which the compiler of this note regrets profoundly. With the aid of friends and colleagues, he has at times used books written in Russian and other Slavic languages, but unfortunately he does not read these languages. For this reason he thought it best not to include in this note works written in these languages.

Peter Charanis

I. General Histories of the Byzantine Empire:

Since Diehl wrote his book, a number of general histories of Byzantium have made their appearance, but the following are the most important: K. Amantos, *History of the Byzantine Em-*

pire (in Greek), 2 vols., Athens, 1939, 1947, second edition of Vol. 1, Athens, 1953; L. Bréhier, *Vie et mort de Byzance,* Paris, 1947; C. Diehl, and G. Marçais, *Le Monde oriental de 395 à 1081,* Paris, 1936; C. Diehl, R. Guilland, L. Oeconomos, and R. Grousset, *L'Europe orientale de 1081 à 1453,* Paris, 1945; G. Ostrogorsky, *Geschichte des Byzantinischen Staates,* Munich, 1940, second edition, Munich, 1952. An English translation, reviewed and revised by the author, is now in preparation. A. A. Vasiliev, *History of the Byzantine Empire,* 2 vols., Madison, Wisconsin, 1928-29, French edition, Paris, 1932, second English edition, Madison, Wisconsin, 1952; *The Cambridge Medieval History. 4. The Eastern Roman Empire (717-1453),* Cambridge, 1923. Among the older works one may still consult with profit the appropriate volumes of G. Finlay, *A History of Greece from its Conquest by the Romans to the Present Time, B.C. 146 to A.D. 1864,* ed. by H. F. Tozer, 7 vols., Oxford, 1887; and E. Gibbon, *The Decline and Fall of the Roman Empire,* J. B. Bury edition, 1896 and later. In reading Gibbon, care should be taken to guard against his anti-religious prejudices.

II.   General Works on Limited Periods and Monographs on Individual Reigns of Emperors:

On the fourth and fifth centuries in general, the work of Otto Seeck, *Geschichte des Untergangs der antiken Welt,* 6 vols., Stuttgart, 1920-23, is fundamental. Important, also, for its scholarship is the work of E. Stein which covers the period from 284 to 476: *Geschichte des Spätrömischen Reiches. 1. Vom Römischen zum Byzantinischen Staates,* Vienna, 1928. The most comprehensive account in English is the first volume of *The Cambridge Medieval History: The Christian Roman Empire and the Foundation of the Teutonic Kingdom,* Cambridge, 1911. Also, there is F. Lot, *The End of the Ancient World and the Beginning of the Middle Ages,* tr. from the French by P. Leon and M. Leon, New York, 1931.

On Constantine the Great and his period, the following may be cited for their scholarly basis and the different views they represent: A. Alföldi, *The Conversion of Constantine and Pagan Rome,* tr. by H. Mattingly, Oxford, 1948; N. H. Baynes, "Constantine," in *The Cambridge Ancient History,* 12, Cambridge, 1939. More fundamental is an earlier study by Baynes, "Constantine the Great and the Christian Church," *Proceedings of the British Academy,* 15 (1929), 341-442; H. Grégoire, *Les Persécutions dans l'empire romain* (= *Mémoires de l'académie royale de Belgique. Classe des lettres et des sciences morales et politiques,* 46, 1), Brussels, 1951; K. Hönn, *Konstantin der Grosse, Leben einer Zeitwende,* Leipzig, 1940; A. H. M. Jones, *Constantine and the Conversion of Europe,* London, 1948; A. Piganiol, *L'Empereur Constantin,* Paris, 1932; E. Schwartz, *Kaiser Constantin und die Christliche Kirche,* Leipzig, 1913; J. Vogt, *Konstantin der Grosse und sein Jahrhundert,* Munich, 1949. There is now an English translation by M. Hadas of J. Burckhardt, *The Age of Constantine the Great,* New York, 1949. For a discussion of the latest literature, see A. Piganiol, "L'état actuel de la question Constantinienne 1930/49," *Historia,* 1 (1950), 82-96; Pio Franchi de'Cavalieri, *Constantiniana* (= *Studi e Testi, 171*), Rome, 1953. One may also consult the *Life of Constantine* by Eusebius, which is available in English: Eusebius, "The Life of Constantine," tr. by E. C. Richardson in P. Schaff and H. Wace, eds., *A Select Library of Nicene and Post-Nicene Fathers of the Christian Church,* 2nd ser., 1 (New York, 1890), 481-559. This work should not be used, however, without some reference to the literature concerning its authenticity. Of this literature, the following are important: H. Grégoire, "Eusèbe n'est pas l'auteur de la 'Vita Constantini' dans sa forme actuelle et Constantin ne s'est pas converti en 312," *Byzantion,* 13 (1938), 561-583; *Id.,* "La vision de Constantin liquidée," *Byzantion,* 14 (1939), 341-351 (cf. N. H. Baynes in *Byzantinische Zeitschrift,* 39 [1939], 466-469); J. Vogt, "Berichte über Kreuzeserscheinungen aus dem 4. Jr. n. Chr.," *Mélanges H. Grégoire*, 1 (= *Annuaire de l'institut de philologie et d'histoire orientales et slaves*, 9), Brussels, 1949, 593-606; A. Piganiol, "Sur quelques passages de la *Vita Constantini*," *Mélanges H. Grégoire*, 2 (= *Annuaire de l'institut de philologie et d'histoire orientales et slaves*, 10), Brussels, 1950, 513-518; G. Downey, "The Builder of the Original Church of the Apostles at Constantinople. A Contribution to the Criticism of the *Vita Constantini* Attributed to Eusebius," *Dumbarton Oaks Papers*, No. 6 (1951), 51-80; P. Orgels, "Apropos des erreurs historiques de la 'Vita Constantini,' " *Mélanges H. Grégoire*, 4 (= *Annuaire de l'institut de philologie et d'histoire orientales et slaves*, 12), Brussels, 1953, 575-611; A. H. M. Jones, "Notes on the Genuineness of the Constantinian Documents in Eusebius's Life of Constantine," *Journal of Ecclesiastical History*, 5 (1954), 196-200. For a comprehensive and critical review of the documents transmitted under the name of Constantine, one may now consult H. D. Dörries, *Das Selbstzeugnis Kaiser Konstantins* (= *Abhandlungen der Akademie d. Wissenschaften zu Göttingen, Phil.-Hist. Kl.*, 3, F., No. 34), Göttingen, 1954. Further, there is J. Moreau, "Zum Problem der 'Vita Constantini,' " *Historia*, 4 (1955), 234-245. On the reign of Constantine as a whole, there is now the bibliographical study of J. Vogt and W. Seston, "Die Konstantinische Frage," *Relazioni del X Congresso Internazionale di Scienze Storiche. VI. Relazioni Generali e Supplementi*, Florence [1955], 731-799.

On the fourth century as a whole, the best general work for its scholarship and readability is A. Piganiol, *L'empire chrétien*, 325-395 (= G. Glotz, *Histoire générale. Histoire romaine*, Vol. 4, Pt. 2), Paris, 1947. There is now an English translation of the Theodosian Code, which is a capital source for the study of the internal conditions of the Empire during the fourth and early fifth centuries: Clyde Pharr, *The Theodosian Code and Novels and the Sirmondian Constitutions*, Princeton, 1952.

On Julian, important is the work of J. Bidez, *La Vie de l'empereur Julien*, Paris, 1930; also, P. D. Labriolle, *La Réaction païenne. Étude sur la polémique antichrétienne du Ier au VIe siècle*, Paris, 1934, 369-437.

On the period between 395 and 410, a period which saw the practical division of the Roman Empire, there is now the com-

Bibliographical Note

prehensive account, with detailed bibliography, of E. Demougeot, *De l'unité à la division de l'empire romain, 395-410,* Paris, 1951.

For the fifth century as a whole, the most comprehensive account is the first volume of J. B. Bury's *History of the Later Roman Empire,* second edition, London, 1923. On the Huns, there is E. A. Thompson, *A History of Attila and the Huns,* Oxford, 1948; also, J. Harmatta, "The Dissolution of the Hun Empire. I. Hun Society in the Age of Attila," *Acta Archaeologica Academiae Scientiarum Hungaricae,* Vol. 2, Pt. 4, Budapest, 1952, 277-304.

On the Sassanids of Persia, the fundamental work is that of A. Christensen, *L'Iran sous les Sassanides,* Copenhagen, 1936, second edition, 1944.

A number of historical sources of the fourth and fifth centuries are available in English. These include: Lactantius, "Of the Manner in Which the Persecutors Died," tr. by W. Fletcher, in A. Roberts and J. Donaldson, eds., *The Ante-Nicene Fathers,* 7, New York, 1888, 301-323. A new edition of this important work, with a French translation and notes, has just appeared: Lactantius, *De la mort des persécuteurs,* ed. and tr. by J. Moreau, 2 vols. (= *Sources chrétiennes,* 39), Paris, 1955; Eusebius, *The Ecclesiastical History,* tr. by K. Lake, 2 vols., London, 1926-32, Loeb Classical Library; Ammianus Marcellinus, *The Surviving Books of the History of Ammianus Marcellinus,* tr. by J. C. Rolfe, 3 vols., London, 1935-39, Loeb Classical Library (The third volume also contains the excerpts of Valesius); Sozomen, *Church History from A.D. 323-425,* an English translation revised by C. D. Hartranft, in P. Schaff and H. Wace, eds., *A Select Library of Nicene and Post-Nicene Fathers of the Christian Church,* 2nd ser., 2, New York, 1890, 179-427; Socrates, *Church History from A.D. 305-439,* tr. by E. Walford and revised by A. C. Zenos, in *ibid.,* 1-178; Theodoret, *The Ecclesiastical History, Dialogues and Letters,* tr. by B. Jackson, in P. Schaff and H. Wace, *A Select Library of Nicene and Post-Nicene Fathers of the Christian Church,* 2nd ser., 3, New York, 1892, 33-348. There are: Julian, *Works,* tr. by W. C. Wright, 3 vols., London, 1913-23, Loeb Classical Library; Saint Basil, *The Letters,* tr. by R. J. Deferrari, 4 vols., London, 1926-34, Loeb Classical Library; Synesius of Cyrene, *The Letters of Synesius of Cyrene,* tr. by A. Fitzgerald, London, 1926, and *The Essays and Hymns of Synesius of Cyrene,* 2 vols.,

London, 1930; Zacharias Scholasticus, *The Syriac Chronicle, Known as that of Zachariah of Mitylene,* tr. by F. J. Hamilton and W. W. Brooks, London, 1899; "Joshua the Stylite," *The Chronicle,* tr. by W. Wright, Cambridge, 1882; E. W. Brooks, tr., *The Sixth Book of the Select Letters of Severus, Patriarch of Antioch,* Vol. 2, Pts. 1, 2, London, 1903, 1904.

The age of Justinian has been the subject of numerous books. The following are important for their scholarship and general comprehensiveness: *The Cambridge Medieval History. 2. The Rise of the Saracens and the Foundation of the Western Empire,* Cambridge, 1926; J. B. Bury, *A History of the Later Roman Empire from the Death of Theodosius I to the Death of Justinian* (395-565), second edition, London, 1923, 2; C. Diehl, *Justinien et la civilisation byzantine au VIe siècle,* Paris, 1901; W. G. Holmes, *The Age of Justinian and Theodora,* 2 vols., London, 1905-07; E. Stein, *Histoire du bas empire. 2. De la disparition de l'empire d'occident à la mort de Justinien* (476-565), Paris, Bruxelles, Amsterdam, 1949; A. A. Vasiliev, *Justin the First. An Introduction to the Epoch of Justinian the Great,* Cambridge, Mass., 1950.

On the position of the Empire in the period immediately following the death of Justinian, especially for the reign of Maurice, there is now the detailed account of P. Goubert, *Byzance avant l'islam: 1. Byzance et l'Orient sous les successeurs de Justinien. L'Empereur Maurice,* Paris, 1951; 2. *Byzance et l'Occident sous les successeurs de Justinien.* Pt. 1. *Byzance et les Francs,* Paris, 1956.

Important sources of the sixth century are also available to the English reader. These include: all the works of Procopius, the most comprehensive contemporary historian of the age of Justinian (Loeb Classical Library, *Procopius with an English Translation,* by H. B. Dewing, 7 vols., London, New York, Cambridge, Mass., 1913-40); the ecclesiastical history of Evagrius, a work of some significance, especially for the last quarter of the sixth century during which the author lived (Bohn's Ecclesiastical Library, *History of the Church by Theodoret and Evagrius,* London, 1854); *The Christian Topography* of Cosmas Indicopleustes, a curious geographical treatise of the sixth century, written in order "to refute the theory that the earth was round, and to prove that Moses' tabernacle in the wilderness was a model of the universe," but containing invaluable information on the commerce with the regions of the Red Sea and the Indian Ocean (J. W. McGrindle, tr., *The Christian Topography of Cosmas, An Egyptian Monk,* The Hakluyt Society, 1st ser., 98, London, 1897). There exists also an English translation of important-parts of the Slavic version of the chronicle of John Malalas, a curious work of the sixth century, interesting for its language, an interest, however, which is lost in a translation, and also as an example of the literary tastes of the lower classes (*Chronicle of John Malalas,* Books VIII-XVIII, translated from the Church Slavic by Matthew Spinka in collaboration with Glanville Downey, Chicago, 1940). Available also are the legal enactments of Justinian: S. P. Scott, tr., *The Civil Law,* 17 vols., Cincinnati, 1932; also John of Ephesus, *The Third Part of the Ecclesiastical History,* tr. by P. Smith, Oxford, 1860; and John of Nikiu, *Chronicle,* tr. by H. Charles, London, 1916.

For the seventh and eighth centuries, the most comprehensive, though somewhat old, account, is still J. B. Bury, *History of the Later Roman Empire from Arcadius to Irene (395 A.D. to 800 A.D.),* 2, London, 1889. The most authoritative monograph on Heraclius is A. Pernice, *L'Imperatore Eraclio, saggio di storia bizantina,* Florence, 1905. On Justinian II, there is the interesting essay by Charles Diehl, "L'Empereur au nez coupé" in his *Choses et gens de Byzance,* Paris, 1926. The standard work on Constantine V is the monograph by A. Lombard, *Études d'histoire byzantine: Constantin V empereur des Romains,* Paris, 1902. For the invasions of the Arabs, there are the appropriate chapters in *Cambridge Medieval History,* 2; M. Canard, "Les expéditions des Arabes contre Constantinople dans l'histoire et dans la légende," *Journal asiatique,* 208 (1926), 61-121. For a re-evaluation of the reforming activity of the Isaurian Emperors, see G. Ostrogorsky, "Über die vermeintliche Reformatätigkeit der Isaurier," *Byzantinische Zeitschrift,* 30 (1929-30), 394-400. On the invasion of the Balkan Peninsula by the barbarians, especially the Slavs, the most recent authoritative survey is by P. Lemerle, "Invasions et migrations dans les Balkans depuis la fin de l'époque romaine jusqu'au VIIIe siècle," *Revue historique,* 211 (1954), 265-308. See further H. Grégoire, "L'origine et le nom des Croates et des Serbes," *By-*

zantion, 17 (1944-45), 88-118; P. Charanis, "The Chronicle of Monemvasia and the Question of the Slavonic Settlement in Greece," *Dumbarton Oaks Papers,* No. 5 (1950), 139-166. Important for the study of the history of the Balkan Peninsula in the seventh century is the capital work on the *Miracula Sancti Demetrii* by F. Barišić, *Miracles de St. Démétrius comme source historique* (in Serbian with a long French résumé)(= *Académie Serbe de Sciences. Monographie 219. Institut d'Études Byzantines,* No. 2), Belgrade, 1953. On the foundation of the Bulgarian kingdom, the best account in English is by S. Runciman, *A History of the First Bulgarian Empire,* London, 1930.

Two important legal documents, one belonging definitely to the eighth century, the other possibly so, are available in English. The eighth-century document is the *Ecloga,* the code of laws which, issued by the Isaurian Leo III, remained the basic law in Byzantium until the revival of the codes of Justinian toward the end of the ninth century (*A Manual of Roman Law. The Ecloga,* tr. by H. Freshfield, Cambridge, 1926); the other is *The Farmer's Law,* a document of great importance because it reflects the transformation that the Byzantine agrarian society underwent in the seventh century (W. Ashburner, "The Farmer's Law," commentary and translation, *The Journal of Hellenic Studies,* 32 [1912], 68-95). On "The Farmer's Law" the latest studies are: F. Dölger, "Ist der Nomos *Georgikos* ein Gesetz des Kaisers Justinian II?" *Festschrift für Leopold Wegner II* (= *Münchener Beiträge zur Papyrusforschung und antiken Rechtsgeschichte,* 35 [1945]), 18-48; J. de Malafosse, *Les lois agraires à l'époque byzantine. Tradition et exégèse,* offprint from *Recueil de l'Académie de Législation,* 29), Toulouse, 1949.

On the ninth century, the best general account is J. B. Bury, *A History of the Eastern Roman Empire from the Fall of Irene to the Accession of Basil I* (802-867), London, 1912. The standard monograph on Basil I is A. Vogt, *Basile I, empereur de Byzance et la civilisation byzantine à la fin du IXe siècle,* Paris, 1908. Important, also, for the history of Basil I, are the studies by N. Adontz, "L'âge et l'origine de l'empereur Basile I," *Byzantion,* 8 (1933), 475-500; 9 (1934), 223-260. On the reign of Michael III, significant studies have been made by H. Grégoire: "Inscriptions historiques byzantines. Ancyre et les Arabes sous Michel

Bibliographical Note

l'Ivrogne," *Byzantion*, 4 (1927-28), 337-346; *Id.*, "Michel III et Basile le Macédonien dans les inscriptions d'Ancyre," *Byzantion*, 5 (1929-30), 327-346; *Id.*, "Études sur le neuvième siècle," *Byzantion*, 8 (1933), 515-550. On the wars with the Arabs in the ninth century, the fundamental work is by A. A. Vasiliev, *Byzance et les Arabes*. 1. *La dynastie d'Amorium* (820-867), French edition prepared by H. Grégoire and M. Canard, Brussels, 1935. On the appearance of the Russians and their attacks on Constantinople, there exist now two important monographs with detailed bibliographical notes by A. A. Vasiliev: *The Russian Attack on Constantinople in 860*, Cambridge, Mass., 1946; "The Second Russian Attack on Constantinople," *Dumbarton Oaks Papers*, No. 6 (1951), 161-225; A. Stender-Petersen, "Das Problem der Ältesten Byzantinisch-Russisch-Nordischen Beziehungen," *Relazioni del X Congresso Internazionale di Scienze Storiche*. III. *Storia del Medioevo*, Florence [1955], 165-188. On the problem of the conversion of the Slavs to Christianity by Byzantine missionaries, there are two important books by Father F. Dvornik: *Les Slaves, Byzance et Rome au IXe siècle*, Paris, 1926; *Id.*, *Les Légendes de Constantin et de Méthode vue de Byzance*, Prague, 1933. On the significance of the ninth century in the separation of Byzantium and the West, there is now the important survey by F. Dölger, "Europa Gestaltung im Spiegel der frankisch-byzantinischen Auseinandersetzung des 9. Jahrhunderts," in his *Byzanz und die Europäische Staatenwelt*, Speyer am Rhein, 1953; also W. Ohnsorge, "Byzanz und das Abendland im 9. und 10. Jahrhundert. Zur Entwicklung des Kaiserbegriffs und der Staatsideologie," *Saeculum*, 5 (1954), 194-220; *Id.*, *Das Zweikaiserproblem im früheren Mittelalter. Die Bedeutung des byzantinischen Reiches für die Entwinklung der Staatsidee in Europa*, Hildesheim, 1947. See farther G. P. Bognetti, "I rapporti etico-politici fra oriente e occidente dal sec. V al sec. VIII," *Relazioni del X Congresso Internazionale di Scienze Storiche*. III. *Storia del Medioevo*, 3-65, and F. Dölger, "Byzanz und das Abendland vor den Kreuzzügen," *Ibid.*, 67-112. On the knowledge of Greek during the early Middle Ages, see now E. Delarnelle, "La connaissance du grec en occident du Ve au IXe, siècle," *Société Toulousaine d'Études Classiques*, *Mélanges*, 1 (Toulouse, 1946), 207-226.

Byzantium: Greatness and Decline

On Leo VI, the following works should be taken into account: V. Grumel, "La Chronologie des événements du règne de Léon VI," *Échos d'Orient,* 35 (1936), 5-42; R. J. H. Jenkins, "The Flight of Samonas," *Speculum,* 23 (1948), 217-236; G. Kolias, *Léon Choerosphactès,* Athens, 1939; A. Vogt, "La jeunesse de Léon VI le Sage," *Revue historique,* 174 (1934), 389 ff. On the Hungarians, see C. A. Macartney, *The Magyars in the Ninth Century,* Cambridge, 1930. The *Novels* of Leo VI, important sources for the internal history of the Empire during his reign, are available in French translations, as for instance, that of P. Noaille and A. Dain, *Les Novelles des Léon VI le Sage,* Paris, 1944.

The best and most detailed general treatment of the tenth century is offered by the following books: S. Runciman, *The Emperor Romanus Lecapenus and his Reign,* Cambridge, 1929; A. Rambaud, *L'Empire grec au Xe siècle: Constantin Porphyrogénète,* Paris, 1870 (this is a brilliant book which, despite its age, remains fundamental); G. Schlumberger, *Un empereur byzantin au Xe siècle: Nicéphore Phocas,* Paris, 1890, reprint, 1923; *Id., L'Épopée byzantin à la fin du Xe siècle,* 3 vols., Paris, 1896, 1900, 1905, reprint, 1925.

On the wars with the Arabs from 867 to 959, the fundamental work is by A. A. Vasiliev, but only a part of the Russian original has appeared in the French edition supervised by H. Grégoire: A. A. Vasiliev, *Byzance et les Arabes.* 2. *La dynastie macédonienne* (867-959), French edition prepared by H. Grégoire and M. Canard, Pt. 2, *Extraits des sources arabes,* tr. by M. Canard, Brussels, 1950. On the wars with the Bulgarians, see: S. Runciman, *A History of the First Bulgarian Empire;* N. Adontz, "Samuel l'Arménien, roi des Bulgares," *Mémoires de l'académie royale de Belgique. Classe des lettres,* 38 (1938), 1-63. On the conversion of the Russians, there is G. Laehr, *Die Anfänge des russischen Reiches* (*Historische Studien,* E. Ebering, ed., *Heft* 189), Berlin, 1930. Very important is the study by E. Honigmann, "Studies in Slavic Church History. A. The Foundation of the Russian Metropolitan Church According to Greek Sources," *Byzantion,* 17 (1944-45), 128-163. Honigmann's study disposes neatly of the thesis that the early Russian church was at the beginning organized under the auspices of Rome. For this thesis, see N. de Baumgarten, *Saint Vladimir et la conversion de la Russie*

Bibliographical Note

(= *Orientalia Christiana,* Vol. 27, No. 79), Rome, 1932. For a plausible explanation of the Latin influences in the early Russian church, see F. Dvornik, "Les Bénédictins et la christianisation de la Russie," *1054-1954: L'Église et les églises* (Collection Irenikon, Chevetogne, 1954), 323-349.

On Armenia and its relations to Byzantium, there are: J. Laurent, *L'Arménie entre Byzance et l'Islam depuis la conquête arabe jusqu'en 886,* Paris, 1919; S. Der Nersessian, *Armenia and the Byzantine Empire,* Cambridge, Mass., 1945; R. Grousset, *Histoire de l'Arménie des origines à 1071,* Paris, 1947. Further, see J. J. M. de Morgan, *Histoire du peuple arménien depuis les temps le plus reculés de ses annales jusqu'à nos jours,* Paris, 1919; Fr. Tournebize, *Histoire politique et religieuse de l'Arménie depuis les origines des Arméniens jusqu'à la mort de leur dernier roi* (*l'an 1393*), Paris, 1900. The emphasis of Tournebize's book is on religious history and his point of view is Roman Catholic.

On Georgia, the fundamental account in English is that by W. E. D. Allen, *A History of the Georgian People from the Beginning down to the Russian Conquest in the Nineteenth Century,* London, 1932. On the Khazars, there is now D. M. Dunlop, *The History of the Jewish Khazars,* Princeton, 1954.

Several important sources bearing upon the tenth century are now available to the English reader. These include: the *De administrando imperio* of Constantine Porphyrogenitus, a work of capital importance as a source not only for Byzantium, but for the history of eastern Europe in general (Constantine Porphyrogenitus, *De administrando imperio,* ed. by G. Moravcsik and translated into English by R. J. H. Jenkins, Budapest, 1949); the works of Liutprand of Cremona, the Italian ecclesiastic who visited Constantinople in 949 as the ambassador of Berengar, King of Italy, and again in 968 as the ambassador of Otto I, and recorded his impressions of the Byzantine capital. Particularly interesting for its description of social life in Constantinople and the light that it throws on the attitude of the Greeks toward the Latins and that of the Latins toward the Greeks is his report of the embassy of 968, the famous *Legatio* (F. A. Wright, tr., *The Works of Liutprand of Cremona,* New York, 1930); *The Primary Chronicle,* known also as the *Chronicle of Nestor,* the most important single source on the early history of the Russians and very valuable for the study of the relations between Byzantium and the Russians (*The Russian Primary Chronicle, Laurentian Text*, tr. by S. H. Cross and ed. by O. P. Sherbowitz-Wetzor, Cambridge, Mass., 1953). There exists also a French translation, though not yet complete, of the *De ceremoniis* of Constantine Porphyrogenitus, one of the most important sources for the study of Byzantine civilization (Constantin VII Porphyrogénète, *Le Livre des cérémonies*, ed. and tr. by A. Vogt, 2 vols., Paris, 1935, 1939). Several documents of the tenth century relating to monastic properties in Byzantium are also available in English (P. Charanis, "The Monastic Properties and the State in the Byzantine Empire," *Dumbarton Oaks Papers*, No. 4 [1948], 51-118).

For the first half of the eleventh century, the most detailed account is still A. Schlumberger, *L'Épopée byzantine à la fin du dixième siècle: 2. Basile II, le tueur de Bulgares; 3. Les Porphyrogénètes Zoé et Théodora, 1025-1057*. For Theodora and her immediate successors, there is also the work of H. Mädler, *Theodora, Michael Stratiotikos, Isaak Comnenos*, Plauen, 1894. The two general accounts in western languages covering the eleventh century are: C. Neumann, *Die Weltstellung des byzantinischen Reiches vor den Kreuzzügen*, Leipzig, 1894 (French translation by E. Renauld, *Revue de l'Orient latin*, 10 [1905], 57-171); P. Charanis, "The Byzantine Empire in the Eleventh Century," in K. M. Setton and M. W. Baldwin, eds., *A History of the Crusades. 1. The First Hundred Years*, Philadelphia, 1955. For an interpretive account, see R. J. H. Jenkins, *The Byzantine Empire on the Eve of the Crusades*, London, 1953 (a pamphlet—General Series: G24—of the Historical Association); also J. M. Hussey, "The Byzantine Empire in the Eleventh Century: Some Different Interpretations," *Transactions of the Royal Historical Society*, 4th ser., 32 (1950), 71-85. For the portraits of the emperors, the best account in English is that by J. B. Bury, "The Roman Emperors from Basil II to Isaac Komnenos," *English Historical Review*, 4 (1889), 41-64, 251-285, reprinted in *Essays*, ed. by H. Temperley, Cambridge, 1930; also C. Diehl, *Byzantine Portraits*, tr. by H. Bell, New York, 1927. For the period 1067 to 1081, there is B. Leib, "Jean Doukas, César et moine, son jeu politique à Byzance de 1067 à 1081," *Mélanges P. Peeters*, 2 (= *Analecta Bollandiana*, 68, 1950), 163-180. For Alexius Comnenus, the principal work is still that by F. Chalandon, *Essai sur le règne d'Alexius I Comnène, 1081-1118*, Paris, 1900. On the Normans in Italy and their relations to Byzantium, the fundamental work is still F. Chalandon, *Histoire de la domination normande en Italie et en Sicile*, 2 vols., Paris, 1907. For a critique of the sources concerning the establishment of the Normans in Italy, consult E. Joranson, "The Inception of the Career of the Normans in Italy: Legend and History," *Speculum*, 23 (1948), 353-397. On Bohemond, the principal monograph in English is by R. B. Yewdale, *Bohemond I, Prince of Antioch*, Princeton, 1917.

On the Seljuk Turks, the following are the principal publications: J. Laurent, *Byzance et les Turcs seljoucides dans l'Asie occidentale jusqu'en 1081*, Nancy, 1913; P. Wittek, "Deux chapitres de l'histoire des Turcs de Roum," *Byzantion*, 11 (1936), 285-319; C. Cahen, "La Première pénétration turque en Asie Mineure," *Byzantion*, 18 (1948), 5-67; C. Cahen, "The Turkish Invasion: The Selchükids," in Setton and Baldwin, *A History of the Crusades*, 1, 135-176. The reader is also referred to the articles "Turks" and "Seldjuks" in the *Encyclopaedia of Islam*. As an introduction to the various Turkish tribes which made their appearance in the history of Byzantium from the earliest times to the Ottoman Turks, and as a guide to the literature, the fundamental work is G. Moravcsik, *Byzantinoturcica*, 2 vols., Budapest, 1942-43.

Two important Greek sources bearing upon the eleventh century are now available to the English reader. One is the *Chronographia* of Michael Psellus, the famous Byzantine scholar of the eleventh century, whose work, which covers the period from 976 to 1077, is justly known for its lifelike portrayal of the emperors and its brilliant analysis of life in Byzantium in the eleventh century (Michael Psellus, *Chronographia*, tr. by E. R. A. Seuter, London, 1953; the French translation of the same work by E. Renauld, is Michel Psellos, *Chronographie ou histoire d'un siècle de Byzance (976-1077)*, 2 vols., Paris, 1926-28). The other is the *Alexiad* of Anna Comnena, the remarkable daughter of the Emperor Alexius Comnenus, whose work, which covers the reign of her father, 1081-1118, is one of the most interesting literary legacies of Byzantium (Anna Comnena, *The Alexiad*, tr. by A. S. Dawes, London, 1928; the French translation of the same work, by B. Leib, is Anne

Comnène, *Alexiade. Règne de l'empereur Alexis I Comnène 1081-1118,* 3 vols., Paris, 1937-45). Available also in an English translation is the supposed letter of Alexius to the Count of Flanders: E. Joranson, "The Problem of the Spurious Letter of Emperor Alexius to the Count of Flanders," *American Historical Review,* 55 (1950), 811-832.

For the Comneni in the twelfth century, the most important work is F. Chalandon, *Les Comnènes. 2. Jean II Comnène (1118-1143) et Manuel I Comnène (1143-1180),* Paris, 1912. On the western policy of Manuel, there is also the accurate monograph of H. von Kap-Herr, *Die Abendländische Politik Kaiser Manuels,* Strasbourg, 1881. Very important now is the work of P. Lamma, *Comneni e Staufer. Ricerche sui Rapporti fra Bisanzio e l'Occidente nel Secolo XII (= Instituto Storico Italiano per il Medioevo Studi Storici,* fasc. 14-18), Rome, 1955. On the party strife which followed the death of Manuel, the most important work is that by F. Cognasso, *Partiti politici e lotte dinastiche in Bizanzio alla morte di Manuele Comneno* (Reale Accademia delle scienze di Torino, 1911-1912), Turin, 1912. On Andronicus Comnenus, see the essay by C. Diehl, "Les romanesques aventures d'Andronic Comnène," in his *Figures byzantines,* 2nd ser., Paris, 1908. See, further, the important work by J. Danstrup, "Recherches critiques sur Andronicos Ier," *Yearbook of the New Society of Letters at Lund,* 1944, 71-101. On Isaac II Angelus, the principal work is F. Cognasso, "Un imperatore bizantino della decadenza: Isacco II Angelo," *Bessarione,* 31 (1915), 29-60, 247-289, reprinted separately, Rome, 1915. On the Normans of Southern Italy, there is E. Caspar, *Roger II (1011-1154) und die Gründung der normannisch-sicilischen Monarchie,* Innsbruck, 1904. For a brilliant analysis of Byzantine society during the period of the Comneni, see C. Diehl, *La société byzantine à l'époque de Comnènes,* Paris, 1929. On the kingdom of Serbia, the rise of which dates from the twelfth century, the work of K. Jireček is still standard: *Geschichte der Serben,* Vol. 1 (to 1371), Gotha, 1911; Vol. 2 (to 1538), Gotha, 1918. On the revival of the Bulgarian Empire, there are: N. Bănescu, *Un Problème d'histoire médiévale. Création et caractère du second empire bulgare,* Bucharest, 1943; R. L. Wolf, "The Second Bulgarian Empire: Its Origin and History to 1204," *Speculum,* 24 (1949), 167-206.

Bibliographical Note

On Venice, see H. Kretschmayr, *Geschichte von Venedig*, 2 vols., Gotha, 1905, 1920; C. Diehl, *Une République patricienne. Venise,* Paris, 1915.

On the Venetians in Constantinople, there is H. F. Brown, "The Venetians and the Venetian Quarter in Constantinople to the Close of the Twelfth Century," *The Journal of Hellenic Studies,* 40 (1920), 68-88. One may still consult the old work of J. Armingaud, *Venise et le Bas-Empire. Histoire des relations de Venise avec l'empire d'Orient* (= *Archives des missions scientifiques et littéraires,* 2nd ser., 4), Paris, 1867.

The Crusades: The most comprehensive and detailed account of the Crusades in English is S. Runciman, *A History of the Crusades:* 1. *The First Crusade and the Foundation of the Kingdom of Jerusalem,* Cambridge, 1951; 2. *The Kingdom of Jerusalem and the Frankish East, 1100-1187,* Cambridge, 1952; 3. *The Kingdom of Acre and the Later Crusades,* Cambridge, 1954. Also detailed and comprehensive is the French work by R. Grousset, *Histoire des croisades et du royaume franc de Jerusalem,* 3 vols., Paris, 1934-36. A group of American and European scholars are now engaged in the writing of a five-volume work which will cover the entire crusading movement. The first volume of this work has already appeared: *A History of the Crusades.* 1. *The First Hundred Years,* ed. by M. W. Baldwin, Philadelphia, 1955. Also, see P. Alphandery and A. Dupront, *La Chrétienté et l'idée de croisades. Les premières croisades,* Paris, 1954. Still useful is the brief general survey by L. Bréhier, *L'Église et l'Orient au moyen âge. Les croisades,* Paris, 1907, fifth edition, Paris, 1928. Very important for the light that it throws on the motives for the diversion of the Fourth Crusade is the work of L. Usseglio, *I marchesi di Monferrato in Italia ed in Oriente durante i secoli XII e XIII,* 2 vols., Milan, 1926; also H. Grégoire, "The Question of the Diversion of the Fourth Crusade," *Byzantion,* 15 (1941), 158-166; and A. Frolow, *Recherches sur la déviation de la 4ᵉ croisade vers Constantinople,* Paris, 1955. On the origin of the idea of the Crusade, the capital work is that by C. Erdmann, *Die Entstehung des Kreuzzugsgedankens* (= *Forschungen zur Kirchen- und Geistesgeschichte, Band 6*), Stuttgart, 1935. For the attitude of the Byzantines toward the Crusades in general, see P. Charanis, "Aims of the Medieval Crusades and How They

Were Viewed by Byzantium," *Church History*, 21 (1952), 123-135; P. Lemerle, "Byzance et la Croisade," *Relazioni del X Congresso Internazionale di Scienze Storiche*. III. *Storia del Medioevo*, Florence [1955], 595-620; and S. Runciman, "The Byzantine Provincial Peoples and the Crusades," *Ibid.*, 621-624. For the waning of the crusading spirit, see S. Runciman, "The Decline of the Crusading Idea," *Ibid.*, 637-652; also, P. A. Throop, *Criticism of the Crusade: A Study of Public Opinion and Crusade Propaganda*, Amsterdam, 1940.

A number of the western sources relating to the Crusades are now available to the English reader. These include in full or in part those that bear directly on the First Crusade (A. C. Krey, *The First Crusade. The Accounts of Eye-Witnesses and Participants,* Princeton, 1921; Fulcher of Chartres, *Chronicle of the First Crusade,* tr. by M. E. McGinty, Philadelphia, 1941); the account of the Second Crusade as recorded by Odo of Deuil who accompanied Louis VII to the East (Odo of Deuil, *de profectione ludovici VII in orientem,* tr. by V. G. Berry, New York, 1948); the work on Frederick Barbarossa by Otto of Freising, a work which also contains an account of the Second Crusade (Otto of Freising, *The Deeds of Frederick Barbarossa,* tr. by C. C. Mierow, 1953); the general history of the Crusades which William of Tyre completed about 1183 (William of Tyre, *A History of Deeds Done Beyond the Sea,* tr. and annotated by E. H. Babcock and A. C. Krey, 2 vols., New York, 1948); and the two accounts of the Fourth Crusade, one by Villehardouin, one of the principal leaders of the expedition, the other by Robert of Clari, who, as a simple knight, had also participated in the expedition (Sir Francis Marzials, tr., *Memoires of the Crusades by Villehardouin and De Joinville*, New York, Everyman's Library, 1933; Robert of Clari, *The Conquest of Constantinople,* tr. by E. H. McNeal, New York, 1936).

Available also is the *Voyage* of Benjamin of Tudela, particularly interesting for the information that it gives about the Jews in the Byzantine Empire and for its description of the commercial activity of Constantinople in the twelfth century (M. N. Adler, *The Travels of Rabbi Benjamin of Tudela,* with a critical Hebrew text, London, 1907. An old English text, published by T. Wright in *Early Travels in Palestine*, Bohn Library, 1848, was reprinted by M. Komroff in his *Contemporaries of Marco Polo,* New York, 1928).

The Breakup of the Empire: For the Empire of Nicaea, see A. Gardner, *The Lascarids of Nicaea, The Story of an Empire in Exile,* London, 1912; A. Meliarakes, *History of the Kingdom of Nicaea and the Despotat of Epirus (1204-1261)* (in Greek), Athens, 1898. Rather superficial is the work of J. B. Pappadopoulos, *Theodore II Lascaris, empereur de Nicée,* Paris, 1908. The emphasis is on the literary activity of Theodore Lascaris in J. Dräseke, "Theodore Lascaris," *Byzantinische Zeitschrift,* 3 (1894), 498-515. On the despotat of Epirus, an important work is I. Romanos, *Historical Dissertation on the Despotat of Epirus* (in Greek), Corfu, 1895. On the Empire of Trebizond, see J. P. Fallmerayer, *Geschichte des Kaiserthums von Trapezunt,* Munich, 1827; W. Miller, *Trebizond, the Last Greek Empire,* London, 1926; A. A. Vasiliev, "The Foundation of the Empire of Trebizond," *Speculum,* 11 (1936), 3-37.

The most comprehensive account of the history of the Latin empire of Constantinople is that by J. Longnon, *L'Empire latin de Constantinople et la principauté de Morée,* Paris, 1949. Detailed, since it covers only the period from 1204 to 1216, is E. Gerland, *Geschichte der Frankenherrschaft in Griechenland. 2. Geschichte des lateinischen Kaiserreiches von Konstantinopel,* Hamburg, 1905. Detailed also are the several studies by R. L. Wolff: "The Organization of the Latin Patriarchate of Constantinople, 1204-1261. Social and Administrative Consequences of the Latin Conquest," *Traditio,* 6 (1948), 33-60; "A New Document from the Period of the Latin Empire of Constantinople: the Oath of the Venetian Podestà," *Mélanges H. Grégoire,* 4 (= *Annuaire de l'institut de philologie et d'histoire orientales et slaves,* 12), (1953), 539-573; "Politics in the Latin Patriarchate of Constantinople, 1204-1261," *Dumbarton Oaks Papers,* No. 8 (1954), 223-303.

The Period of the Palaeologi: For the period of the Palaeologi there is as yet no overall, detailed general account. For a brilliant appreciation of the Empire under the Palaeologi, there is the work of C. Diehl, "L'empire byzantin sous les Paléologues," *Études byzantines,* Paris, 1905, 217-240. For the reign of Michael Palaeologus, there is the rather sketchy monograph of C. Chapman,

Byzantium: Greatness and Decline

Michel Paléologue, restaurateur de l'empire byzantin (1261-1282), Paris, 1926. On John Cantacuzenus, there is the old, but for its day good, study of V. Parisot, *Cantacuzène, homme d'état et historien*, Paris, 1845; also, J. Dräseke, "Zu Johannes Kantakuzenos," *Byzantinische Zeitschrift*, 9 (1900), 72-84; F. Dölger, "Johannes VI. Kantakuzenos als dynastischer Legitimist," *Annales de l'Institut Kondakov*, 10 (1938), 19-30. On John V Palaeologus, the only important study, though it deals with only one episode of his reign, is that by O. Halecki, *Un empereur de Byzance à Rome*, Warsaw, 1930. On the establishment of the Turks in Europe, see N. Jorga, "Latins et Grecs d'Orient et l'établissement des Turcs en Europe (1342-1362)," *Byzantinische Zeitschrift*, 15 (1906), 179-222. There are two important studies dealing with the period 1370 to 1400: R. J. Loenertz, "Manuel Paléologue et Démetrius Cydonès. Remarques sur leurs correspondances," *Échos d'Orient*, 36 (1937), 271-287, 474-487; 37 (1938), 107-124; P. Charanis, "The Strife among the Palaeologi and the Ottoman Turks, 1370-1402," *Byzantion*, 16 (1942-43), 286-315. Very important is the work of M. Silberschmidt, *Das orientalische Problem zur Zeit der Entstehung des türkischen Reiches nach venezianischen Quellen. Ein Beitrag zur Geschichte der Beziehungen Venedigs zu Byzanz, Ungarn und Genua und zum Reiches von Kiptschak (1381-1400)*, Leipzig, 1923. On the social strife, especially in Thessalonica, see O. Tafrali, *Thessalonique au XIVᵉ siècle*, Paris, 1913; P. Charanis, "Internal Strife in Byzantium in the Fourteenth Century," *Byzantion*, 15 (1940-41), 208-230. For important chronological data of the fourteenth century, P. Charanis, "An Important Short Chronicle of the Fourteenth Century," *Byzantion*, 13 (1938), 335-362. The best work on Manuel Palaeologus is still that of Berger de Xivrey, *Mémoire sur la vie et les ouvrages de l'empereur Manuel Paléologue (= Mémoires de l'Institut de France. Académie des inscriptions et belles-lettres,* Vol. 19, Pt. 2), Paris, 1853. On John VII, the best monograph is that by F. Dölger, "Johannes VII, Kaiser der Rhomaer 1390-1408," *Byzantinische Zeitschrift*, 31 (1931), 21-36. On the fall of Constantinople in 1453, the best account is still that of E. Pears, *The Destruction of the Greek Empire and the Story of the Capture of Constantinople by the Turks,* London, 1903. There is now an English translation of Kritovoulos, one of the Greek historians who described the last days of the Byzantine capital: Kritovoulos, *History of Mehmed the Conqueror,* tr. by C. T. Riggs, Princeton, 1954.

The five-hundredth anniversary of the destruction of the Byzantine Empire was the occasion for the appearance of a number of studies on the fall of Constantinople in 1453 and its consequences. *Byzantinoslavica,* 14 (1953) was devoted to this subject, and the review *L'Hellénisme contemporain* brought out a special number on it: *1453-1953. Le cinq-centième anniversaire de la prise de Constantinople,* Athens, 1953. Also, see *The Fall of Constantinople. A Symposium held at the School of Oriental and African Studies, 29 May, 1953,* London, 1955.

On the Latins in Greek lands, there are the important studies of W. Miller: *The Latins in the Levant: A History of Frankish Greece (1204-1566),* London, 1908; *Essays on the Latin Orient,* Cambridge, 1921; also, J. M. Rodd, *The Princes of Achaia and the Chronicles of Morea. A Study of Greece in the Middle Ages,* 2 vols., London, 1907. Still very important, though somewhat old, is the history of Greece by K. Hopf, *Geschichte Griechenland vom Beginne des Mittelalters bis auf die neuere Zeit* (in J. S. Ersch and J. G. Gruber, *Allgemeine Encyclopädie der Wissenschaften und Künste,* 85, 86), Leipzig, 1867-68. For a general picture of the expansion of the French in the Mediterranean, including Greece, see J. Longnon, *Les Français d'outre-mer au moyen-âge. Essai sur l'expansion française dans le basin de la Méditerranée,* Paris, 1929. On the establishment of feudal institutions in Greece, there is P. W. Topping, *Feudal Institutions as Revealed in the Assizes of Romania, the Law Code of Frankish Greece,* Philadelphia, 1949. Topping's work includes an English translation of the *Assizes of Romania.*

On the Catalans in Greece, the basic studies are those of A. Rubió y Lluch. For a listing of Rubió's works on the Catalans in Greece, see pages 61-63 of G. P. Cicellis' French translation of one of these works: *La compagnie catalane sous le commandement de Thibaut de Chepoy (Campagne de Macédoine et de Thessalie 1307-1310),* Athens, 1955 (*Extrait de L'Hellénisme contemporain,* 2nd ser., eighth year, fasc. 4-6; ninth year, fasc. 1); also, G. Schlumberger, *Expédition des "Almugavares" ou routiers catalans en Orient,* Paris, 1902. On the relations of the Catalan

Company with the West, see R. I. Burns, S.J., "The Catalan Company and the European Powers, 1305-1311," *Speculum,* 29 (1954), 751-771. The deeds of the Catalan Company in Greek lands, as recorded by the *Chronicle of Muntaner,* can be read in an English translation (*The Chronicle of Muntaner,* tr. from the Catalan by Lady Goodenough, 2 vols., The Hakluyt Society, 2nd ser., Nos. 47, 50, London, 1920-21). On the Catalan State in central Greece, there is now the substantial monograph with detailed bibliography by K. M. Setton, *Catalan Domination of Athens 1311-1388,* Cambridge, Mass., 1948.

On the Ottoman Turks, the fundamental work is J. von Hammer-Purgstall, *Geschichte des osmanischen Reiches,* 10 vols., Pest, 1827-34, French translation by J. J. Hellert in collaboration with the author, 18 vols., Paris, 1843, English abridgment by E. S. Creasy, *History of the Ottoman Turks,* new edition, London, 1877. Important also, despite some errors in the details, is the work of N. Jorga, *Geschichte des osmanischen Reiches nach den Quellen dargestellt,* 5 vols., Gotha, 1908-13. Still useful, though old, is the work of J. W. Zinkeisen, *Geschichte des Osmanischen Reichs in Europa,* Hamburg, 1840. Significant for its point of view concerning the origin of the Ottoman State is the work of H. Adams Gibbons, *The Foundation of the Ottoman Empire. A History of the Osmanlis up to the Death of Bayezid I (1300-1403),* London, 1916. Further, there is R. Tschudi, *Von alten Osmanischen Reich,* Tübingen, 1930; also, W. L. Langer and R. P. Blake, "The Rise of the Ottoman Turks and its Historical Background," *American Historical Review,* 37 (1932), 468-505; Mehmed Fuad Köprülü, *Les Origines de l'empire ottoman,* Paris, 1935. Useful also is the work of K. Amantos, *Relations of Greeks and Turks from the Eleventh Century to 1821. 1. The Wars of the Turks for the Conquests of the Greek Lands 1071-1571* (in Greek), Athens, 1955. For an analysis of the factors which led to the foundation of the Ottoman State, see P. Wittek: *Das Fürstentum Mentesche, Studien zur Geschichte Westkleinasiens im 13-15 Jahrh.,* Istanbul, 1934; *The Rise of the Ottoman Empire,* London, 1938; "De la défaite d'Ankara à la prise de Constantinople," *Revue des études islamiques,* Année (1938), 1-34. Very good is the book of G. G. Arnakis, *The Early Osmanlis. A Contribution to the Problem of the Fall of Hellenism in Asia Minor*

Bibliographical Note

(*1282-1337*) (in Greek with an English summary), Athens, 1947. On the expansion of the Ottomans in the eastern part of the Balkan Peninsula, F. Babinger, *Beiträge zur Frühgeschichte der Türkenherrschaft in Rumelien* (*14.-15. Jahrhundert*) (= *Südosteuropäische Arbeiten*, 34), Brünn, 1944. On Mehmed, the conqueror of Constantinople, there is now a detailed study: F. Babinger, *Mehmed der Eroberer und seine Zeit; Weltenstürmer einer Zeitenwende*, Munich, 1953, French translation by H. E. del Medico, *Mahomet II, le Conquérant, et son temps, 1432-1481. La grande peur du monde au tournant de l'histoire*, Paris, 1954. For a study of the Ottoman dynasty itself, see now the important work of A. D. Alderson, *The Structure of the Ottoman Dynasty*, Oxford, 1956.

On the later Crusades, there is now the comprehensive work of A. S. Atiya, *The Crusade in the Later Middle Ages*, London, 1938; also, by the same author, *The Crusade of Nicopolis*, London, 1934. On the Crusade of Varna, there is O. Halecki, *The Crusade of Varna. A Discussion of Controversial Problems*, New York, 1943. On the negotiations between the Papacy and Michael VIII Palaeologus (1258-1282) for a crusade, there are the studies of V. Laurent: "Grégoire X (1271-1276) et le projet d'une ligue anti-turque," *Échos d'Orient*, Nos. 191-192 (1938), 257-273; "La croisade et la question d'Orient sous le pontificat de Grégoire X (1272-1276)," *Revue historique du Sud-Est européen*, 22 (1945), 105-137. Also, see M. H. Laurent, "Georges le Métochite, ambassadeur de Michel VIII Paléologue auprès du B. Innocent V," *Miscellanea Giovanni Mercati*, 3 (= *Studi e Testi*, 123), Vatican, 1946, 136-153. Very important, still, is the work of J. Delaville Le Roulx, *La France en Orient au XIVᵉ siècle. Expéditions du maréchal Boucicaut*, 2 vols., Paris, 1886. Also, there is N. Jorga, *Philippe de Mézières 1327-1405. La croisade au XIVᵉ siècle*, Paris, 1896. See, too, J. Gay, *Le Pape Clement VI et les affaires d'Orient* (*1342-1352*), Paris, 1904; C. Marinescu, "Philippe le Bon, duc de Bourgogne, et la croisade (Première partie 1419-1453)," *Actes du VIᵉ Congrès Intern. d'Études Byzantines*, 1 (1950), 147-168.

A number of travel accounts falling within the period of the Palaeologi are available in English. Ibn Battuta, the Moroccan Moslem, transmitted his impressions of Constantinople, which he visited during the second quarter of the fourteenth century in the course of his travels, which took him as far as China (Ibn Battuta, *Travels in Asia and Africa 1325-1354*, tr. and selected by H. A. R. Gibb, London, 1929). Then there is the description of Constantinople and other information about Byzantium which the Spaniard Clavijo gives in the account of his travels to the court of Tamerlane in Samarkand and, where he had been sent in 1403 on an embassy by Henry III, King of Castile and Leon (Clavijo, *Embassy to Tamerlane 1403-1406*, tr. from the Spanish by G. Le Strange, London, 1928). Another Spaniard, Pero Tafur, recorded his impressions of Constantinople, which he visited in the course of his travels in the years 1435-1439 (Pero Tafur, *Travels and Adventures, 1435-1439*, tr. by M. Letts, London, 1926). Finally, there is the account of the Bavarian, Johannes Schiltberger, who, captured by the Ottoman Turks at the battle of Nicopolis in 1396, passed a number of years in captivity and survived to relate his experience (Johannes Schiltberger, *Bondage and Travels . . . In Europe, Asia, and Africa 1396-1427*, tr. by J. Buchan Telfer, Hakluyt Society, 1st ser., No. 58, London, 1879.)

III.   Regional Studies with General Significance:

For Byzantine Italy, very important are: C. Diehl, *Études sur l'administration byzantine dans l'exarchat de Ravenne* (568-751), Paris, 1888; L. M. Hartmann, *Untersuchungen zur Geschichte der byzantinischen Verwaltung in Italien* (540-750), Leipzig, 1889; J. Gay, *L'Italie méridionale et l'empire byzantine depuis l'avènement de Basile I jusqu'à la prise de Bari par les Normands 867-1071*, Paris, 1904. Detailed references to Byzantine Italy can also be found in the important work of L. M. Hartmann, *Geschichte*

Italiens im Mittelalter, 4 vols., Gotha, 1897-1915. Also G. Pochettino, *I Langobardi nell' Italia meridionale (570-1080),* Caserta, 1930.

Concerning the Hellenization of Southern Italy during the Middle Ages, see P. Charanis, "On the Question of the Hellenization of Sicily and Southern Italy during the Middle Ages," *American Historical Review,* 52 (1946), 74-87. On Greek civilization in Southern Italy in the later Middle Ages, see the richly documented paper of R. Weiss, "The Greek Culture of South Italy in the Later Middle Ages," *Proceedings of the British Academy,* 37 (1951), 23-50.

On Byzantine Africa, the capital work is C. Diehl, *L'Afrique byzantine. Histoire de la domination byzantine en Afrique (533-709),* Paris, 1896.

On Byzantine Spain, the most detailed account is P. Goubert, "Byzance et l'Espagne," *Revue des études byzantines,* 2 (1944), 5-98; 3 (1945), 127-142; 4 (1946), 71-134.

On the Peloponnesus before the Frankish conquest, there is now the comprehensive work by A. Bon, *Le Péloponnèse byzantin jusqu' en 1204,* Paris, 1951. For the period after 1204, the best study on Byzantine Peloponnesus is the work of D. A. Zakythinos, *Le Despotat grec de Morée. 1. Histoire politique,* Paris, 1932; *Le Despotat grec de Morée. 2. Vie et institutions,* Athens, 1953.

For Athens, the most comprehensive work is still that of F. A. Gregorovius, *Geschichte der Stadt Athen im Mittelalter von der Zeit Justinians bis zur türkischen Eroberung,* Stuttgart, 1889, Greek translation with additional documentation by S. Lampros, 3 vols., Athens, 1904-06. Important, also, for the history of Athens is the excellent work of G. Stadtmüller, *Michael Choniates Metropolit von Athen (ca. 1138-ca. 1222) (= Orientalia Christiana,* Vol. 33, No. 2), Rome, 1934. On Greece during the sixth, seventh, and eighth centuries, see P. Charanis, "Hellas in the Greek Sources of the Sixth, Seventh, and Eighth Centuries," *Late Classical and Mediaeval Studies in Honor of Albert Mathias Friend, Jr.,* ed. by K. Weitzmann, Princeton, 1955, 161-177.

On Thessalonica and Macedonia, there are the two works of O. Tafrali, *Thessalonique au quatorzième siècle,* Paris, 1913; *Thessalonique des origines au XIVe siècle,* Paris, 1919. More fundamental for Macedonia is the monumental work of P. Lemerle,

Byzantium: Greatness and Decline

Philippe et la Macédoine orientale à l'époque chrétienne et byzantine. Recherches d'histoire et d'archéologie, Paris, 1945. On Thessalonica under the Venetians, there is P. Lemerle, "La domination venetien à Thessalonique," *Miscellanea G. Galbiati,* 3 (= *Fontes Ambrosiani,* 27) (1951), 219 ff. For the latest general survey, see the article "Salonique," by Leclercq in *Dict. d'archéologie chrétienne et de liturgie,* 15 (1950), 624 ff.

On Thessalonica as a center of art, especially for the period of the Palaeologi, there is now the important work of André Xyngopoulos, *Thessalonique et la peinture macédonienne,* Athens, 1955.

On the topography and fortifications of Constantinople, see: A. D. Mordtmann, *Esquisse topographique de Constantinople,* Lille, 1892; A. Van Millingen, *Byzantine Constantinople. The Walls of the City and Adjoining Historical Sites,* London, 1899; A. M. Schneider, *Byzanz. Vorarbeiten zur Topographie und Archäologie der Stadt* (= *Istanbuler Forschungen,* 8), Berlin, 1936; B. Meyer-Plath and A. M. Schneider, *Die Landmauer von Konstantinopel,* Pt. 2 (= *Denkmäler Antiker Architektur,* 8), Berlin, 1943; A. M. Schneider, "Mauern und Tore am Goldenen Horn zu Konstantinopel," *Nachrichten d. Akad. d. Wiss. in Göttingen, Phil. Hist. Klasse* (1950), 65-107; R. Janin, *Constantinople byzantine. Développement urbain et répertoire topographique,* Paris, 1950; also the articles, "Byzantion," by E. Oberhummer and W. Kubitschek in A. F. von Pauly-G. Wissowa, *Real-Encyclopädie,* 3:1116-1158, and "Constantinoplis," by E. Oberhummer, in *Real-Encyclopädie,* 4:963-1013. On the churches and monasteries of Constantinople, the latest study is R. Janin, *La géographie ecclésiastique de l'empire byzantin. 3. Constantinople, les églises et les monastères,* Paris, 1953. Still important are: A. Van Millingen, *Byzantine Churches in Constantinople: Their History and Architecture,* London, 1912; J. Ebersolt and I. Thiers, *Les Églises de Constantinople,* Paris, 1913. For the Great Palace, still fundamental is J. Ebersolt, *Le grand palais de Constantinople et le livre des cérémonies,* Paris, 1910.

For Cyprus, the best study is the monumental work of Sir George Hill, *A History of Cyprus: 1. To the Conquest by Richard Lion Heart,* Cambridge, 1944; 2. *The Frankish Period, 1192-1432,*

Bibliographical Note

Cambridge, 1948; 3. *The Frankish Period, 1432-1571*, Cambridge, 1948.

On Byzantine Egypt, see: J. G. Milne, *A History of Egypt under Roman Rule*, third edition, London, 1924; *Id.*, "Egyptian Nationalism under Greek and Roman Rule," *Journal of Egyptian Archaeology*, 14 (1928), 226-234; H. I. Bell, "The Byzantine Servile State in Egypt," *Journal of Egyptian Archaeology*, 4 (1917), 86-106; *Id.*, "Egypt and the Byzantine Empire," in *The Legacy of Egypt,* ed. by S. R. K. Glanville, Oxford, 1942, 332-347; *Id., Egypt from Alexander the Great to the Arab Conquest*, Oxford, 1948. For the Byzantine administration of Egypt, the best studies are: M. Gelzer, *Studien zur byzantinischen Verwaltung Ägyptens* (= *Leipziger Historische Abhandlungen, Heft* XIII), Leipzig, 1909; G. Rouillard, *L'Administration civile de l'Egypte byzantine*, second edition, Paris, 1928. See also L. Valentin, "La réorganisation de l'Égypte byzantine au temps de Justinien Ier," *Bulletin de l'Association Guillaume Budé. Supplément: Lettres d'Humanité*, 11 (1952), 55-71. For the military organization of Byzantine Egypt, see J. Maspero, *Organisation militaire de l'Égypte byzantine*, Paris, 1912. On ecclesiastical organization and opposition to the Greeks, there is J. Maspero, *Histoire des patriarches d'Alexandrie*, Paris, 1923. On the Arab conquest of Egypt, the standard work is that of A. L. Butler, *The Arab Conquest of Egypt and the Last Thirty Years of Roman Dominion*, Oxford, 1902.

For Roman and Byzantine Palestine, there is now the comprehensive work of P. F. M. Abel, *Histoire de la Palestine depuis la conquête d'Alexandre jusqu'à l'invasion arabe. 2. De la guerre juive à l'invasion arabe*, Paris, 1952.

On the eastern frontier of the Byzantine Empire down to 1071, the standard study is that of E. Honigmann, *Die Ostgrenze des byzantinischen Reiches von 363 bis 1071*, Brussels, 1935. Still fundamental for the historical geography of Asia Minor is the work of Sir William Ramsay, *Historical Geography of Asia Minor*, London, 1890.

Byzantium: Greatness and Decline

IV.   The Byzantine Church:

There is really no comprehensive and detailed history of the Byzantine Church covering all its aspects and the entire span of its history. The nearest to it is the work of Gennadios, the Metropolitan of Helioupolis and Theiroi, only the first volume of which has appeared: *History of the Œcumenical Patriarchate* (in Greek), 1, Athens, 1953. However, a number of brief, but useful, general accounts do exist: H. F. Tozer, *The Church and the Eastern Empire*, London, 1888; W. F. Adeney, *The Greek and Eastern Churches*, New York, 1908; A. Fortescue, *The Orthodox Eastern Church*, London, 1927 (the treatment is from the Roman Catholic point of view); B. J. Kidd, *The Churches of Eastern Christendom from A.D. 451 to the Present Time*, London, 1927; R. M. French, *The Eastern Orthodox Church*, London, 1951; J. Pargoire, *L'Église byzantine de 527 à 847*, third edition, Paris, 1923.

For the conciliar period, the accounts are numerous. The following may be cited as standard: L. Duchesne, *Early History of the Christian Church, From its Foundation to the End of the Fifth Century*, rendered into English from the fourth French edition, 3 vols., London, 1909, 1912, 1924. B. J. Kidd, *A History of the Church to A.D. 461*, Oxford, 1922; A. Fliche and V. Martin, eds., *Histoire de l'Église*: 3. J. R. Palanque, G. Bardy, and P. de Labriolle, *De la paix constantinienne à la mort de Théodose*, Paris, 1936; 4. P. de Labriolle, G. Bardy, G. de Plinval, and L. Bréhier, *De la mort de Théodose à l'élection de Grégoire le Grand*, Paris, 1937; 5. L. Bréhier and R. Aigrain, *Grégoire le Grand, les états barbares et la conquête arabe 590-737*, Paris, 1938. On the Church Councils themselves, the great work remains, K. J. Hefele—C. Leclercq, *Histoire des conciles*, Paris, 1907—.

On the religious policy of Zeno, there is B. Schwartz, *Die Kirchenpolitik Kaisers Zenons*, Würzburg, 1950 (= *Würzburg, Phil. Fak. Diss. V.* 17, May, 1950). (The editor did not see this book.)

On Church-State relations during the reign of Anastasius I, the most detailed study, with bibliography, is P. Charanis, *Church and State in the Later Roman Empire. The Religious Policy of Anastasius the First, 491-518*, Madison, Wisconsin, 1939. Also, there is P. Peeters, "Hypatius et Vitalien. Autour de la succession de l'empereur Anastasé," *Annuaire de l'institut de philologie et d'histoire orientales et slaves*, 10 (1950), 5-51. On the diffusion of Monophysitism in the sixth century and the organization of the Monophysitic Church in the eastern provinces outside of Egypt and Palestine, fundamental is the work of E. Honigmann, *Évêques et évêchés monophysites d'Asie antérieure au VIᵉ siècle*, Louvain, 1951. On the sixth century as a whole, there is L. Duchesne, *L'Église au VIᵉ siècle*, Paris, 1925. On the ecclesiastical legislation of Justinian I, see H. Alivisatos, *Die Kirchliche Gesetzgebung des Kaisers Justinian I*, Berlin, 1913. See now also the richly documented study, E. H. Kaden, "L'église et l'état sous Justinien," *Mémoires publiés par la Faculté de Droit de Genève*, 9 (1952), 109-144. (Not Caesaropapism but close and intimate cooperation between Church and State characterized the policy of Justinian, according to Kaden.) The literature on the Council of Chalcedon and its repercussions has been greatly enriched by the publication of three monumental volumes on the occasion of the fifteen-hundredth anniversary of that Council: A. Grillmeier and H. Bacht, eds., *Das Konzil von Chalkedon. Geschichte und Gegenwart: 1. Der Glaube von Chalkedon*, Würzburg, 1951; 2. *Entscheidung um Chalkedon*, Würzburg, 1953; 3. *Chalkedon Heute*, Würzburg, 1954. While virtually every contribution contained in the first two volumes has some bearing on the Byzantine Church, a number contained in the second volume are particularly important: R. Haacke, "Die Kaiserliche Politik in den Auseinandersetzungen um Chalkedon (451-553)," 95-177; P. Goubert, "Les successeurs de Justinien et le Monophysisme,"

179-192; H. Bacht, "Die Rolle des orientalischen Mönchtums in den kirchenpolitischen Auseinandersetzungen um Chalkedon (431-519)," 193-314; T. O. Martin, "The Twenty-Eighth Canon of Chalcedon: A Background Note," 433-458; E. Herman, "Chalkedon und die Ausgestaltung des Konstantinopolitanischen Primats," 459-490; A. Michel, "Der Kampf um das politische oder petrinische Prinzip der Kirchenführung," 491-562; L. Ueding, "Die Kanones von Chalkedon in ihrer Bedeutung für Mönchtum und Klerus," 569-676; S. Salaville, "La fête du concile de Chalcédoine dans le rite byzantin," 677-695. Also on the Council of Chalcedon, there is R. V. Sellers, *The Council of Chalcedon: A Historical and Doctrinal Survey*, London, 1953.

On the Papacy and its relations with Byzantium to the eighth century, see E. Caspar, *Geschichte des Papsttum*, 2 vols., Tübingen, 1930-33.

For the period after the sixth century, the Iconoclastic Controversy and the final break with Rome have been the two aspects of the Byzantine Church that have received the greatest attention.

On the Iconoclastic Controversy the most important among the older studies, and still standard, is the work of K. Schwarzlose, *Der Bilderstreit, ein Kampf der Griechischen Kirche um ihre Eigenart und ihre Freiheit*, Gotha, 1890; also, L. Bréhier, *La Querelle des images, VIIIᵉ-IXᵉ siècle*, Paris, 1904; *Id.*, "Les caractères généraux et la portée de la réforme iconoclaste," *Revue des cours et conférences*, April 11, 1901, 226-235. Very important are the two works of G. Ostrogorsky: *Studien zur Geschichte des byzantinischen Bilderstreites*, Breslau, 1929; "Les débuts de la querelle des images," *Mélanges Charles Diehl*, 1, Paris, 1930, 235-255. The best general survey in English is E. J. Martin, *A History of the Iconoclastic Controversy*, London, 1930. There exists also an English study on Theodore of Studium, the champion of images: A. Gardner, *Theodore of Studium. His Life and Times*, London, 1905. Significant contributions have also been made by G. B. Ladner: "Der Bilderstreit und die Kunstlehren der byzantinischen und abendländischen Theologie," *Zeitschrift für Kirchengeschichte*, 3rd ser., 1 (1931), 1 ff.; "Origin and Significance of the Byzantine Iconoclastic Controversy," *Mediaeval Studies*, 2 (1940), 127-149; "The Concept of the Image in the Greek Fathers and the Byzantine Iconoclastic Controversy," *Dumbarton Oaks Papers,* No. 7 (1953), 1-34. On the theological setting of the controversy, see especially P. Lucas Koch, "Zur Theologie der Christus-ikone," *Benediktinische Monatsschrift,* 19 (1937), 375 ff.; 20 (1938), 32 ff., 168 ff., 281 ff., 437 ff.; also, G. Florovsky, "Origen, Eusebius, and the Iconoclastic Controversy," *Church History,* 19 (1950), 77-97. Other important studies include: N. H. Baynes, "The Icons before Iconoclasm," *Harvard Theological Review,* 44 (1951), 93-106, reprinted in N. H. Baynes, *Byzantine Studies and Other Essays,* London, 1955, 226-239; *Id.,* "Idolatry and the Early Church," *Ibid.,* 116-143; P. J. Alexander, "Hypatius of Ephesus. A Note on Image Worship in the Sixth Century," *Harvard Theological Review,* 45 (1952), 177-184; *Id.,* "The Iconoclastic Council of St. Sophia (815) and its Definition (Horos)," *Dumbarton Oaks Papers,* No. 7 (1953), 35-66; E. Kitzinger, "The Cult of Images in the Age before Iconoclasm," *Dumbarton Oaks Papers,* No. 8 (1954), 83-150; M. V. Anastos, "The Ethical Theory of Images Formulated by the Iconoclasts in 754 and 815," *Ibid.,* 151-160; *Id.,* "The Argument for Iconoclasm as Presented by the Iconoclastic Council of 754," *Late Classical and Mediaeval Studies in Honor of Albert Mathias Friend, Jr.,* Princeton, 1955, 177-188. On the position of the Patriarch Nicephorus, there is A. Visser, *Nikephoros und der Bilderstreit; eine Untersuchung über die Stellung des Konstantinopeler patriarchen Nikephoros innerhalb der iconoklastischen Wirren,* The Hague, 1952. For a new point of view concerning the attitude of the Iconoclastic Emperors toward the Papacy, see V. Grumel, "Cause et date de l'annexion de l'Illyricum oriental, de la Sicile et de la Calabre au patriarcat byzantin," *Mélanges J. Lebreton,* 2 (= *Recherches de science religieuse,* 60 [1952], 191-200.

On the relations with Rome, there are now two general surveys: M. Jugie, *Le Schisme byzantin: Aperçu historique et doctrinal,* Paris, 1941; G. Every, *The Byzantine Patriarchate,* London, 1947. For the period between 737 and 1057, see A. Fliche and V. Martin, eds., *Histoire de l'Église:* 6. E. Amann, *L'époque carolingienne,* Paris, 1937; 7. E. Amann and A. Dumas, *L'Église au pouvoir des laïques (888-1057),* Paris, 1942. On Photius and the schism with Rome, the fundamental study now is F. Dvornik, *The Photian*

Schism, History and Legend, Cambridge, 1948. Still useful, though in some of its aspects outmoded by Dvornik's book, is J. Hergenröther, *Photius, Patriarch von Konstantinopel,* 3 vols., Regensburg, 1867-69. For the period between Photius and Cerularius, there is A. Michel, "Von Photius zu Kerullarios," *Römische Quartalsschrift für christliche Altertumskunde und für Kirchengeschichte,* 41 (1933), 125-162. (Cf. V. Laurent, "Notes critiques sur de récentes publications," *Échos d'Orient,* 35 [1932], 97-110. On the same period, but with a new approach to the problem is V. Grumel, "Les préliminaires du schisme de Michel Cérulaire ou la question romaine avant 1054," *Revue des études byzantines,* 10 (1953), 5-23. On the schism of 1054, see L. Bréhier, *Le Schisme oriental du XIe siècle,* Paris, 1899; A. Michel, *Humbert und Kerullarios,* 2 vols., Paderborn, 1925, 1930; P. Charanis, "The Byzantine Empire in the Eleventh Century," in K. M. Setton and M. W. Baldwin, *History of the Crusades,* 1, Philadelphia, 1955, 207 ff. On the role of Michael Psellus in the affair of 1054, there is now the basic work of A. Michel, "Schisma und Kaiserhof in Jahre 1054. Michael Psellos," *1054-1954. L'Église et les églises,* 1 (Collection Irenikon, Chevetogne, 1954), 351-440. For the second half of the eleventh century, see: B. Leib, *Rome, Kiev, et Byzance à la fin du XIe siècle,* Paris, 1924; W. Holtzmann, "Die Unionsverhandlungen zwischen Kaiser Alexios I und Papst Urban II," *Byzantinische Zeitschrift,* 28 (1928), 38-67; B. Leib, "Les patriarches de Byzance et la politique religieuse d'Alexis Ier Comnène (1081-1118)," *Mélanges Jules Lebreton,* 2 (= *Recherches de science religieuse,* 40, 1952), 201 ff. Important for its summary analysis of the factors involved in the estrangement of the churches and for its bibliographical references is the work of Y. M. J. Congar, "Neuf cents ans après: Notes sur le 'Schisme oriental,'" *1054-1954. L'Église et les églises,* 1:3-95. One may now also consult the interpretive essay of S. Runciman, *The Eastern Schism. A Study of the Papacy and the Eastern Churches during the XIth and XIIth Centuries,* Oxford, 1955.

On relations with the Papacy after 1054, the most important and comprehensive work is W. Norden, *Das Papsttum und Byzanz. Die Trennung der Beiden Mächte und das Problem ihrer Wiedervereinigung bis zum Untergangs des byzantinischen Reichs*

(*1453*), Berlin, 1903. For the thirteenth century, there is now the work of M. Roncaglia, *Les Frères mineurs et l'église grecque orthodoxe au XIIIe siècle (1231-1274)*, Cairo, 1954. On the Council of Lyons, see V. Grumel, "Le IIe Concile de Lyon et la réunion de l'église grecque," *Dictionnaire de théologie catholique* (Paris, 1926), 1391-1410. For a good analysis of the papal attitude toward the Greek Church some years after the Council of Lyons, see D. J. Geanakoplos, "On the Schism of the Greek and Roman Churches. A Confidential Papal Directive for the Implementation of Union (1278)," *The Greek Orthodox Theological Review*, 1 (1954), 16-24. See also *id.*, "Michael VIII Palaeologos and the Union of Lyons (1274)," *Harvard Theological Review*, 46 (1953), 79-89. Further, there is M. H. Laurent, *Le bienheureux Innocent V (Pierre de Tarentaise) et son temps* (= *Studi e Testi*, 129), Vatican, 1947. On the attempt at Union during the reign of John V, there is O. Halecki, *Un empereur de Byzance à Rome. Vingt ans de travail pour l'union des églises et pour le défense de l'empire d'orient, 1355-1375*, Warsaw, 1930. On the question of the Union of the Churches after the Council of Lyons, see M. Viller, "La question de l'union des églises entre grecs et latins depuis le concile de Lyons jusqu'à celui de Florence (1274-1438)," *Revue d'histoire ecclésiastique*, 17 (1921), 260-305, 515-532; 18 (1922), 20-60; also, R. Loenertz, "Les dominicains byzantins Théodore et André Chrysobergès et les négociations pour l'union des églises grecque et latine de 1415 à 1430," *Archivum FF. Praedicatorum*, 9 (1939), 5-61; and H. Rees, *The Catholic Church and Corporate Reunion. A Study of the Relations between East and West from the Schism of 1054 to the Council of Florence*, Westminster, 1940. On the Council of Florence and some of its repercussions, see further D. J. Geanakoplos, "The Council of Florence and the Problem of Union between the Greek and Latin Churches," *Church History*, 24 (1955), 324-346; M. Cherniavsky, "The Reception of the Council of Florence in Moscow," *ibid.*, 347-359; I. Ševčenko, "Intellectual Repercussions of the Council of Florence," *ibid.*, 291-323. All three studies contain important bibliographical references.

There is as yet no comprehensive account of the crisis in the Byzantine Church provoked by the Hesychast movement. But there are some studies. For the sources of Hesychasm, there is the excellent work of K. Holl, *Enthusiasmus und Bussgewalt beim griechischen Mönchtum. Eine Studien zum Symeon dem Neuen Theologen*, Leipzig, 1898; also, I. Hausherr, *Vie de Syméon le nouveau Théologien* (= *Orientalia Christiana*, Vol. 22, No. 45), Vatican, 1928. Also on Symeon the New Theologian, see: Hieromonk Basil Krivoshein, "The Most Enthusiastic Zealot. St. Symeon the New Theologian as Abbot and Spiritual Instructor," *Ostkirchliche Studien*, 4 (1955), 108-128; *Id.*, "The Brother-Loving Poor Man," *The Christian East*, 2 (1953-54), 216-227; *Id.*, "The Writings of St. Symeon the New Theologian," *Orientalia Christiana Periodica*, 20 (1954), 298-328. The best study of the Hesychast doctrine is Father Basil (Basil Krivoshein), "The Ascetic and Theological Teachings of Gregory Palamas," *Eastern Churches Quarterly*, 3 (1938), 26-33, 71-84, 138-156, 193-214. On Gregory Palamas and the Palamite controversy, there are also the studies of M. Jugie, "Palamas et controverse palamite," *Dictionnaire de théologie catholique*, 11 (1932), 1735-1818; *Id.*, "La controverse palamite (1346-1368). Les faits et les documents conciliaires," *Échos d'Orient*, 30 (1931), 397-421. There is the more recent J. Meyendorff, "Les débuts de la controverse hésychaste," *Byzantion*, 23 (1954), 87-120. See also the brief bibliographical note by V. Laurent in *Byzantinische Zeitschrift*, 48 (1955), 225. On Byzantine monasticism in general, including the Hesychasts, see H. Delehaye, "Byzantine Monasticism," in N. H. Baynes and H. St. L. B. Moss, eds., *Byzantium. An Introduction to East Roman Civilization*, Oxford, 1948, 136-165. For an analysis of recent works on the spiritual life of Byzantine monasticism, including Hesychasm, see A. Wenger, "Bulletin de spiritualité et théologie byzantines," *Revue des études byzantines*, 13 (1955), 140-195. See farther I. Hausherr, "L'hésychasme étude de spiritualité," *Orientalia Christiana Periodica*, 22 (1956), 5-40.

Bibliographical Note

V.   Imperial Government and Administration:

There is now a comprehensive, overall, general account of Byzantine institutions, including imperial government and administration: L. Bréhier, *Les institutions de l'empire byzantin*, Paris, 1949. For an analysis of the practices and usages which made up the "constitution" of the Byzantine Empire, the best general account is J. B. Bury, *The Constitution of the Later Roman Empire*, Cambridge, 1910, reprinted in *Selected Essays of J. B. Bury*, ed. by H. Temperley, Cambridge, 1930. The most recent survey on the Emperor and imperial administration is that by W. Ensslin, "The Emperor and the Imperial Administration," in N. H. Baynes and H. St. L. B. Moss, eds., *Byzantium. An Introduction to East Roman Civilization*, Oxford, 1948, 268-307. On the imperial administrative system during the middle Byzantine period the best study is that of J. B. Bury, *The Imperial Administrative System in the Ninth Century with a Revised Text of the Kletorologion of Philotheos* (= *British Academy Supplemental Papers I*), London, 1911. For the last centuries of the Empire, there is E. Stein, "Untersuchungen zur spät-byzantinischen Verfassungs- und Wirtsschaftsgeschichte," *Mitteilungen z. Osmanischen Geschichte*, 2 (1925), 1-62.

On the origin and nature of imperial power, see W. Ensslin, "Das Gottesgnadentum des autokratischen Kaisertums der frühbyzantinischen Zeit," *Studi Bizantini e Neoellenici*, 5 (1939), 154-166; *Id.*, "Gottkaiser und Kaiser von Gottes Gnaden," *Sitzungsberichte der Bayerischen Akademie der Wissenschaften, Philosophisch-historische Abteilung, Jahrgang 1943, Heft 6*, Munich,

1943; *Id.*, "Der Kaiser in der Spätantike," *Historische Zeitschrift*, 177 (1954), 449-468; L. Bréhier and P. Batiffol, *Les Survivances du culte impérial romain*, Rome, 1920; J. Straub, *Vom Herrscher-ideal in der Spätantike* (= *Forschungen zur Kirchen- und Geistes-geschichte*, ed. by E. Seeberg, W. Weber, and R. Holtzmann, 18), Stuttgart, 1939; N. H. Baynes, "Eusebius and the Christian Em-pire," *Annuaire de l'institut de philologie et d'histoire orientales et slaves*, 2 (1933), 13-18, reprinted in N. H. Baynes, *Byzantine Studies and Other Essays*, London, 1955, 168-172; *Id.*, "The By-zantine State," *Byzantine Studies* . . . , 47-66; F. E. Granz, "Kingdom and Polity in Eusebius of Caesarea," *Harvard Theo-logical Review*, 45 (1952), 47-66; R. Guilland, "Le droit divin à Byzance," *Commentaria societatis philologae polonorum EOS*, 42 (1947), 142-168; F. Dölger, "Die Kaiserurkunde der Byzantiner als Ausdruck ihrer politischen Anschauungen," *Historische Zeit-schrift*, 159 (1938-39), 229-250, reprinted in F. Dölger, *Byzanz und die Europäische Staatenwelt*, Speyer am Rhein, 1953, 9-33; M. Mitard, "Le pouvoir impérial au temps de Léon VI le Sage," *Mélanges Charles Diehl*, 1 (Paris, 1930), 217-223; N. G. Svoronos, "Le serment de fidélité à l'empereur byzantin et sa signification constitutionnelle," *Revue des études byzantines*, 9 (1951), 106-142; L. Bréhier, "L'origine des titres impériaux à Byzance," *By-zantinische Zeitschrift*, 15 (1906), 161-178; V. Laurent, "Notes de titulature byzantin," *Échos d'Orient*, 38 (1939), 355-370, es-pecially important for tracing the use of the title, *Basileus Rhômaeôn;* E. H. Kantorowicz, *Laudes Regiae. A Study in Litur-gical Acclamations and Mediaeval Ruler Worship* (= *University of California Publications in History*, 33) Berkeley, 1946. Kan-torowicz's work deals primarily with western Europe, but there are numerous references to Byzantium in it. Also, see E. Stein, "Post consulat et autokratoria," *Annuaire de l'institut de phi-lologie et d'histoire orientales et slaves*, 2 (1933-34), 869-912; and the long review of this work by F. Dölger, *Byzantinische Zeit-schrift*, 36 (1936), 123-145. For the penetration into Russia of the Byzantine ideas on the character of imperial power, an im-portant work is I. Ševčenko, "A Neglected Byzantine Source of Muscovite Political Ideology," *Harvard Slavic Studies*, 2 (1954), 141-179.

On the imperial idea as expressed in ceremonial and in art,

Bibliographical Note

see: O. Treitinger, *Die oströmische Kaiser- und Reichsidee nach ihrer Gestaltung im höfischen Zeremoniell,* Jena, 1938; J. Ebersolt, "Mélanges d'histoire et d'archéologie byzantines. I. Étude sur la vie publique et privée de la cour byzantine," *Revue de l'histoire des religions,* 76 (1917), 3-105; A. Grabar, *L'Empereur dans l'art byzantin. Recherches sur l'art officiel de l'empire d'Orient,* Paris, 1936.

On the coronation ceremony, see: F. E. Brightman, "Byzantine Imperial Coronations," *Journal of Theological Studies,* 2 (1901), 359-392; R. M. Wolley, *Coronation Rites,* Cambridge, 1915, 7-31; A. E. R. Boak, "Imperial Coronation Ceremonies of the Fifth and Sixth Centuries," *Harvard Studies in Classical Philology,* 30 (1919), 37-47.

On the significance of coronation, important for the different points of view which they represent are the following: W. Sickel, "Das byzantinische Krönungsrecht bis zum 10. Jahrhundert," *Byzantinische Zeitschrift,* 7 (1898), 511-557; P. Charanis, "Coronation and its Constitutional Significance in the Later Roman Empire," *Byzantion,* 15 (1940-41), 49-66; W. Ensslin, *Zur Frage nach der ersten Kaiserkrönung durch den Patriarchen und zur Bedeutung dieses Aktes im Wahlzeremoniell,* Würzburg, 1948. See further H. E. del Medico, "Le couronnement d'un empereur byzantin vu par un juif de Constantinople," *Byzantinoslavica,* 16 (1955), 43-75.

On the power of the Emperor in the Byzantine Church, an important work is A. Michel, "Die Kaisermacht in der Ostkirche (843-1204)," *Ostkirchliche Studien,* 2 (1953), 1-35, 89-109; 3 (1954), 1-28, 131-163; 4 (1955), 1-42.

On Rome as an element in the political thinking of the Byzantines, the basic study is F. Dölger, "Rom in der Gedankenwelt der Byzantiner," *Zeitschrift für Kirchengeschichte,* 56 (1937), 1-42, reprinted in Dölger, *Byzanz und die Europäische Staatenwelt,* 70-115. Also, see: W. Hammer, "The Concept of the New and Second Rome in the Middle Ages," *Speculum,* 19 (1944), 50-62; E. Bach, "Imperium Romanum, étude sur l'idéologie politique du XIIe siècle," *Classica et Mediaevalia,* 7 (1945), 138-145.

On the senate as a constitutional element, there are the following: C. Lécrivain, *Le sénat romain depuis Dioclétien à Rome et à Constantinople,* Paris, 1888; C. Diehl, "Le sénat et le peuple

Byzantium: Greatness and Decline

byzantin au VIIe et VIIIe siècle," *Byzantion*, 1 (1924), 201-213; and A. A. Christophilopulu, *The Senate in the Byzantine Empire* (in Greek), Athens, 1949.

On the people of Constantinople as a factor in the constitutional and political life of the Empire, the fundamental study is that of M. Manojlovič, "Le peuple de Constantinople de 400 à 800 après J. C. Etude spéciale de ses forces armées, des éléments qui le composaient et de son rôle constitutionnel pendant cette période," tr. from the Croatian by H. Grégoire, *Byzantion*, 11 (1936), 1-91. Also, G. I. Bratianu, *Privilèges et franchises municipales dans l'empire byzantin*, Paris, 1936; *Id.*, "La fin du régime des partis à Byzance et la crise antisémite du VIIe siècle," *Revue historique du Sud-Est européen*, 18 (1944), 49-67; F. Dvornik, "The Circus Parties in Byzantium. Their Evolution and their Suppression," *Byzantina-Metabyzantina*, 1 (1946), 119-133; and especially A. Maricq, "La durée du régime des partis populaires à Constantinople," *Académie royale de belgique. Bulletin de la classe des lettres et des sciences morales et politique*, 5th ser., 35 (1949), 63-74; *Id.*, "Factions du cirque et partis populaires," *Ibid.*, 37 (1950), 396-421.

On the aristocracy as a factor in the administration of the Empire, R. Guilland, "La noblesse de race à Byzance," *Byzantinoslavica*, 9 (1948), 307-314; P. Charanis, "The Aristocracy of Byzantium in the Thirteenth Century," in P. R. Coleman-Norton, ed., *Studies in Roman Economic and Social History in Honor of Allan Chester Johnson*, Princeton, 1951, 336-356. On the granting of titles of nobility, R. Guilland, "La collation et la perte ou la déchéance des titres nobiliaires à Byzance," *Revue des études byzantines*, 4 (1946), 24-69. Further, R. Guilland, "La noblesse byzantine à la haute époque (IVe-Ve siècles). Observations diverses," *Prosphora eis Stilpona P. Kyriakiden* (= *Hellenika. Supplement 4*), Thessalonica, 1953, 255-266.

Concerning the final fate of Byzantine emperors, see R. Guilland, "La destinée des empereurs de Byzance," *Epeteris Hetaireias Byzantinôn Spoudôn*, 24 (1954), 37-66.

On the different offices in the administration of the Empire there is yet no comprehensive overall account. But there are a number of important monographs: E. Stein, "Zum frühbyzantinischen Staatsrecht," in Stein, *Studien zur Geschichte des*

Bibliographical Note

byzantinischen Reiches vornehmlich unter den Kaisern Justinus II u. Tiberius Constantinus, Stuttgart, 1919, 161-185; A. E. R. Boak, *The Master of the Offices in the Later Roman and Byzantine Empires (University of Michigan Studies, Humanistic Series, 14),* New York, 1924; J. E. Dunlap, *The Office of the Grand Chamberlain in the Later Roman and Byzantine Empires (University of Michigan Studies, Humanistic Series, 14),* New York, 1924; J. Ebersolt, "Sur les fonctions et les dignités du vestiarium byzantin," *Mélanges Charles Diehl,* 1 (Paris, 1930), 81-89; C. Diehl, "Un haut fonctionnaire byzantin: le logothète," *Mélanges offerts à M. Nicolas Jorga* (Paris, 1933), 217-227 (cf. *Byzantinische Zeitschrift,* 34 [1934], 373-379); J. R. Palanque, *Essai sur la préfecture du prétoire du Bas-Empire,* Paris, 1933 (cf. *Byzantion,* 9 [1934], 327-353; *Byzantion,* 9 [1934], 703-713); A. Vogt, "Le protospathaire de la phiale et la marine byzantine," *Échos d'Orient,* 39 (1940-41), 328-332; N. Banescu, "La signification des titres *praetor* et de *pronoetes* à Byzance aux XIe et XIIe siècles" (*Miscellanea Giovanni Mercati,* 3 (= *Studi e Testi,* 123), Rome, 1946, 387-398. Very important contributions for an administrative history of Byzantium are the various studies of R. Guilland: "Le grand domesticat à Byzance," *Échos d'Orient,* 37 (1938), 53-64; "Les eunuques dans l'empire byzantin. Étude de titulature et de prosopographie byzantines," Études byzantines, 1 (1943), 196-238; 2 (1944), 185-225; 3 (1945), 179-214; "Études sur l'histoire administrative de l'empire byzantine. Le Césarat," *Orientalia Christiana Periodica,* 13 (1947), 168-194; "Études sur l'histoire administrative de l'empire byzantin: le grand connétable," *Byzantion,* 19 (1949), 99-111; "Études de titulature et de prosopographie byzantines. Le protostrator," *Revue des études byzantines,* 7 (1950), 156-179; "Contribution à l'histoire administrative de l'empire byzantin. Le drongaire et le grand drongaire de la veille," *Byzantinische Zeitschrift,* 43 (1950), 340-365; "Études sur l'histoire administrative de Byzance. Le domestique des scholes," *Revue des études byzantines,* 8 (1950), 5-63; "Études de titulature et de prosopographie byzantines. Les chefs de la marine byzantine: Drongaire de la flotte, grand drongaire de la flotte, duc de la flotte, mégaduc," *Byzantinische Zeitschrift,* 44 (1951), 212-240; "Les chapitres relatifs aux fonctions des dignitaires du traité du Pseudo-Codinos: chapitres 5, 6, 7 et 16. Traduction française," *Byzantinoslavica,* 13 (1952-53), 233-251; "Sur les dignitaires du palais et sur les dignités de la grande église du Pseudo-Codinos: chapitres 1-4, 8-13," *Byzantinoslavica,* 15 (1954), 214-229; "chapitres 14-15, 17-22," *Ibid.,* 16 (1955), 97-112; "Études sur l'histoire administrative de l'empire byzantin. Le stratopédarque et le grand stratopédarque," *Byzantinische Zeitschrift,* 46 (1953), 63-90; "Observations sur la liste des dignitaires du Pseudo-Codinos," *Revue des études byzantines,* 12 (1954), 58-68; "Études de titulature byzantine. Les titres auliques réservés aux eunuques," *Revue des études byzantines,* 13 (1955), 50-84. On the principal minister of imperial administration, there is now the important study of H. G. Beck, "Der byzantinische Ministerpräsident," *Byzantinische Zeitschrift,* 48 (1955), 309-338. Further, see J. Verpeaux, "Contribution à l'étude de l'administration byzantine: *o mesazōn," Byzantinoslavica,* 16 (1955), 270-296.

On the provincial organization known as the theme system, the following are the important studies: H. Gelzer, *Die Genesis der byzantinischen Themenverfassung* (= *Abhandlungen der Kgl. Sächsischen Gesellschaft der Wissenschaften, Philol.-hist. Klasse,* Vol. 18, No. 5), Leipzig, 1899; F. W. Brooks, "Arabic Lists of Byzantine Themes," *Journal of Hellenic Studies,* 21 (1901), 67-77; C. Diehl, "L'Origine du régime des thèmes dans l'empire byzantin," in his *Études byzantines,* Paris, 1905, 276-292; E. Stein, "Zur Entstehung der Themenverfassung," in his *Studien zur Geschichte des byzantinischen Reiches vornehmlich unter den Kaisern Justinus II u. Tiberius Constantinus,* Stuttgart, 1919, 117-140; *Id.,* "Ein Kapitel vom persischen und vom byzantinischen Staats," *Byzantinisch-Neugriechische Jahrbücher,* 1 (1920), 70-87; E. Darko, "La militarizzanione dell' impero bizantino," *Studi Byzantini e Neoellenici,* 5 (1939), 88-99; S. P. Kyriakides, *Byzantine Studies,* 2-5 (in Greek), Thessalonica, 1939, 29-232; D. A. Zakythinos, "On the Administrative Division of the Byzantine Empire" (in Greek), *Epeteris Hetaereias Byzantinôn Spoudôn,* 17 (1941), 202-274; 18 (1948), 42-62; 19 (1949), 1-25; A. Pertusi, *Constantino Porfirogenito De Thematibus* (= *Studi e Testi,* 160), Rome, 1952. Pertusi's book is a critical edition of the *De Thematibus* of Constantine Porphyrogenitus, but his commentary is an invaluable contribution to the history of the theme system.

Bibliographical Note

Concerning what he says about the origin of the themes, one should also consult W. Ensslin, "Der Kaiser Herakleios und die Themenverfassung," *Byzantinische Zeitschrift*, 46 (1953), 362-368; and G. Ostrogorsky, "Sur la date de la composition du livre des thèmes et sur l'époque de la constitution des premiers thèmes d'Asie Mineure," *Byzantion*, 23 (1954), 31-66. But see A. Pertusi, "Nuova ipotesi sull' origine dei temi bizantini," *Aevum*, 27 (1954), 126-150.

On the Byzantine army, the only comprehensive overall account covering the entire span of the history of the Empire is that given by L. Bréhier, *Les institutions de l'empire byzantin*, 335-403. For the period before Heraclius, the fundamental work is that by R. Grosse, *Römische Militärgeschichte von Gallienus bis zum Beginn der byzantinischen Themenverfassung*, Berlin, 1920. Also, see: T. Mommsen, "Das römische Militärwesen seit Diocletian," *Hermes*, 24 (1889), 195-279; C. Lécrivain, "Étude sur le Bas Empire. III. Les soldats privés au Bas Empire," *Mélanges d'archéologie et d'histoire*, 10 (1890), 267-283; F. Aussaresses, *L'Armée byzantine à la fin du VIᵉ siècle*, Paris, 1909; J. Maspero, *Organization militaire de l'Egypte byzantine*, Paris, 1912; W. Ensslin, "Zum Heermeisteramt des spätrömischen Reiches," *Klio*, 23 (1929), 306-325; 24 (1930), 102-147, 467-502; D. Van Berchem, *L'Armée de Dioclétien et la réforme constantinienne*, Paris, 1952; N. H. Baynes, "Two Notes on the Reforms of Diocletian and Constantine," *Byzantine Studies and Other Essays*, 173-186. For the eleventh century, there is the account given by G. Buckler in her *Anna Comnena: A Study*, Oxford, 1929, 353-381. On the system of the military estates as the basis of the Byzantine army after Heraclius, see R. Gaignero, *Des Bénéfices militaires dans l'empire romain et spécialement en Orient et au Xᵉ siècle*, Bordeaux, 1889. On the later military institution known as *pronoïa*, the fundamental work is now that of G. Ostrogorsky, *Pour l'histoire de la féodalité byzantine*, tr. from the Serbian by H. Grégoire, Brussels, 1954.

On the Byzantine navy, the principal accounts are: J. de la Gravière, "La Marine des Byzantins," *Revue des Deux Mondes*, 65 (1884), 130-158; K. Neumann, "Die byzantinische marine," *Historische Zeitschrift*, new ser., 45 (1898), 1-23; L. Bréhier, "La marine de Byzance du VIIIe au XIe siècle," *Byzantion*, 19 (1949), 1-16; *Id., Les institutions de l'empire byzantin*, 404-429 (cf. *Byzantion*, 20:375-377); G. Buckler, *Anna Comnena: A Study*, 381-386; also J. B. Bury, "The naval policy of the Roman Empire in relation to the western provinces from the seventh to the ninth century," *Centenario della Nascita di Michele Amari*, 2 (Palermo, 1910), 21-34.

On the art of war in Byzantium, the two best general accounts are given by C. W. C. Oman, *The Art of War in the Middle Ages A.D. 378-1515*, revised and ed. by J. H. Beeler, Ithaca, New York, 1953, 31-56; and F. Lot, *L'Art militaire et les armées au moyen âge en Europe et dans le Proche Orient*, 2 vols., Paris, 1946 (Vol. 1, 19-73, is devoted to Byzantium). Also, see G. Buckler, *Anna Comnena: A Study*, 387-418.

On Greek fire, see G. Schlumberger, "Le feu grégeois dans les luttes au Xe siècle entre Byzantins et Sarrasins," in his *Récits de Byzance et de Croisade*, 2nd ser., Paris, 1922, 37-48; C. Zenghelis, "Le feu grégeois," *Byzantion*, 7 (1932), 265-286; N. D. Cheronis, "Chemical Warfare in the Middle Ages. Kallinikos' 'Prepared Fire,'" *Journal of Chemical Education*, 15, 8 (1937), 360-365; and now the important work of M. Mercier, *Le feu grégeois. Les feux de guerre depuis l'antiquité. La poudre à canon*, Paris, 1952.

On the theory of the "family of princes" presided over by the Emperor as a technique of diplomacy, see G. Ostrogorsky, "Die byzantinische Staatenhierarchie," *Seminarium Kondakovianum*, 8 (1936), 41-61; F. Dölger, "Die 'Familie der Könige' in Mittelalter," *Historische Jahrbuch*, 60 (1940), 397-420, reprinted in his *Byzanz und die Europäische Staatenwelt*, 34-69; A. Grabar, "God and the 'Family of Princes' Presided over by the Byzantine Emperor," *Harvard Slavic Studies*, 2 (1954), 117-124. For a general account of Byzantine diplomacy, see L. Bréhier, *Les institutions de l'empire byzantin*, 281-323.

Bibliographical Note

VI.   Finances:

On the coinage of the Byzantine Empire, see J. Sabatier, *Description générale des monnaies byzantines,* 2 vols., Paris, 1862; W. Wroth, *Catalogue of the Imperial Byzantine Coins in the British Museum,* 2 vols., London, 1908; A. Andréadès, "De la monnaie et de la puissance d'achat des métaux précieux dans l'empire byzantin," *Byzantion,* 1 (1924), 75-115; H. Mattingly, "The monetary system of the Roman Empire from Diocletian to Theodosius I," *Numismatic Chronicle,* Vol. 6, Pt. 6 (1946), 111-120; D. A. Zakythinos, *Crise monétaire et crise économique à Byzance du XIIIe au XVe siècle,* Athens, 1948; R. S. Lopez, "The Dollar of the Middle Ages," *The Journal of Economic History,* 11 (1951), 209-234; *Id.,* "Harmenopoulos and the Downfall of the Bezant," *Tomos Constantinou Harmenopoulou,* Thessalonica, 1951, 111-125; *Id.,* "La crise du besant au Xe siècle et la date du livre du préfet," *Annuaire de l'institut de philologie et d'histoire orientales et slaves,* 10 (1950), 403-418. With reference to the last work of Lopez, one should consult A. P. Christophilopoulos, "Concerning the Book of the Prefect" (in Greek), *Epeteris Hetaereias Byzantinôn Spoudôn,* 23 (1953), 152-156; and P. Grierson, "The Debasement of the Bezant in the Eleventh Century," *Byzantinische Zeitschrift,* 47 (1954), 379-394.

On the purchasing power of Byzantine money as it can be inferred from prices, see, in addition to the work of Andréadès cited above, G. Ostrogorsky, "Löhne und Preise in Byzanz," *Byzantinische Zeitschrift,* 32 (1932), 293-333; G. Mickwitz, "Ein Goldwertindex der römisch-byzantinischen Zeit," *Aegyptus,* 13

(1933), 95-106; also A. Segré, "Inflation and its Implication in Early Byzantine Times," *Byzantion*, 15 (1940-41), 249-279.

Very important for the economy of the fourth century is G. Mickwitz, *Geld und Wirtschaft in römischen Reich des vierten Jahrhunderts n. Chr.*, Helsingfors, 1932.

On the finances and financial administration of the Empire, important are the following: A. M. Andréadès, "Les finances byzantines," *Revue des sciences politiques*, 3rd ser., 26th year (1911), reprinted in his *Oeuvres*, 1 (Athens, 1938), 423-450; *Id.*, "Le montant du budget de l'empire byzantin," *Revue des études grecques*, Vol. 34, No. 156 (1921), reprinted in his *Oeuvres*, 1:451-492; *Id.*, "Deux livres récents sur les finances byzantines," *Byzantinische Zeitschrift*, 28 (1928), reprinted in his *Oeuvres*, 1:563-597; *Id.*, "Public Finances [of the Byzantine Empire]: Currency, Public Expenditure, Budget, Public Revenue," in Baynes and Moss, *Byzantium*, 71-85; E. Stein, "Zur byzantinischen Finanzgeschichte," in his *Studien zur Geschichte des byzantinischen Reiches* . . . , 141-160; *Id.*, "Vom Altertum im Mittelalter. Zur Geschichte der byzantinischen Finanzverwaltung," *Vierteljahrschrift für Sozial- und Wirtschaftsgeschichte*, 21 (1928), 158-170; (also, Stein's remarks in *Byzantinische Zeitschrift*, 24 [1924], 377-387); F. Dölger, *Beitrage zur Geschichte der byzantinischen Finanzverwaltung besonders des 10. und 11. Jahrhunderts* (= *Byzantinisches Archiv, Heft* 9), Leipzig, 1927; G. Ostrogorsky, "Die ländliche Steuergemeinde des byzantinischen Reiches im X. Jahrhundert," *Vierteljahrschrift für Sozial- und Wirtschaftsgeschichte*, 20 (1927), 1-108. For an appreciation of the finances of the Byzantine Empire as the source of its power, see L. M. Hartmann, *The Early Mediaeval State. Byzantium, Italy and the West*, London, 1949 (Historical Association Publication: G14). This is a translation by H. Liebeschütz of Hartmann's *Ein Kapitel vom spätantiken und frühmittelalterlichen Staate*, which was published in Stuttgart in 1913.

On the Byzantine taxation system, besides the works on public finances and financial administration, the following should be consulted: A. Déléage, *La Capitation du Bas-Empire*, Macon, 1945 (this work on the *capitatio* is of fundamental importance; it includes a discussion of all the significant previous studies, but see now F. Lot, *Nouvelles recherches sur l'import foncier et la capitation personnelle sous le Bas-Empire*, Paris, 1955); L. M. Hartmann, *Untersuchungen zur Geschichte der byzantinischen Verwaltung in Italien 540-750*), Leipzig, 1889, 74-104, 165-175 for the notes; F. Dölger, "Das Aerikon," *Byzantinische Zeitschrift*, 30 (1930), 450-457; G. Rouillard, "Les taxes maritimes et commerciales d'après des actes de Patmos et de Lavra," *Mélanges Charles Diehl*, 1 (Paris, 1930), 277-289; J. Danstrup, "Indirect Taxation at Byzantium," *Classica et Mediaevalia*, 8 (1946), 139-167; F. Dölger, "Zum Gebührenwesen der Byzantiner," *Études dediées à la mémoire d'André Andréadès* (Athens, 1939), 35-59.

On the *epibolè* the fundamental work is that by H. Monnier, "Études de droit byzantin: L'epibolè," *Nouvelle revue historique de droit français et étranger*, 16 (1892), 125-164, 497-542, 637-672; 18 (1894), 433-486; 19 (1895), 59-103. On the question whether the *epibolè* continued after the reign of Romanus III Argyrus (1028-1034), see G. Rouillard, "L'epibolè au temps d'Alexis Comnène," *Byzantion*, 10 (1935), 81-89; F. Dölger, "Das Fortbestehen der Epibole in mittel- und Spätbyzantinischer Zeit," *Studi in Memoria di Aldo Albertoni*, 2 (Padova, 1934), 1-11 (also, *Byzantinische Zeitschrift*, 35:14; 36:157 ff.).

On the relation of taxation, the *capitatio* in particular, to the evolution of the agrarian society of the Empire, M. Pallasse, *Orient et Occident à propos du colonat romain au Bas-Empire*, Lyon, 1950 (the latest work on the colonate; it has full references to the important studies); A. Segré, "The Byzantine Colonate," *Traditio*, 5 (1947), 106-133; A. Constantinescu, "Réforme sociale ou réforme fiscale? Une hypothèse pour expliquer la disparition du servage de la glèbe dans l'empire byzantin," *Bulletin de la section historique de l'acad. roumaine*, 11 (Bucharest, 1924), 94-109.

VII.   Economic Life:

No comprehensive, overall, and detailed economic history of the Byzantine Empire exists. For a brief summary, see A. M. Andréadès, "The Economic Life of the Byzantine Empire," in Baynes and Moss, *Byzantium. An Introduction to East Roman Civilization*, 51-70.

On agriculture and agrarian conditions, fundamental are the works of G. Ostrogorsky: "Agrarian Conditions in the Byzantine Empire in the Middle Ages," in J. H. Clapham and E. Power, *The Cambridge Economic History of Europe from the Decline of the Roman Empire. 1. The Agrarian Life of the Middle Ages*, Cambridge, 1941, 194-223; "Die wirtschaftlichen und sozialen Entwicklungsgrundlagen des byzantinischen Reiches," *Vierteljahrschrift für Sozial- und Wirtschaftsgeschichte*, 22 (1929), 129-143; *Les praktika byzantins* (this work, originally published in Russian in *Byzantinoslavica*, 9 [1948], 203-306, was translated into French by M. C. de Grünwald, and was included in Ostrogorsky's work, *Pour l'histoire de la féodalité byzantine* [Brussels, 1954], 259-368); and now *Quelques problèmes d'histoire de la paysannerie byzantine* [Brussels, 1956]; also, P. Charanis, "On the Social Structure of the Later Roman Empire," *Byzantion*, 17 (1944-45), 39-58; *Id.*, "On the Social Structure and Economic Organization of the Byzantine Empire in the Thirteenth Century and Later," *Byzantinoslavica*, 12 (1951), 94-154; L. Bréhier, "Les populations rurales au IXe siècle d'après l'hagiographie byzantine," *Byzantion*, 1 (1924), 177-190. For an overall picture of rural life in Byzantium, see G. Rouillard, *La Vie rurale dans l'empire by-*

zantin, Paris, 1953. On the economic life of Macedonia, especially in the eleventh and twelfth centuries, there is D. A. Xanalatos, *Beiträge zur Wirtschafts- und Sozialgeschichte Makedoniens im Mittelalters, hauptsächlich auf Grund der Briefe des Erzbischofs Theophylaktos von Achrida*, Munich, 1937. For a summary general account of land tenure to 1204, there is K. M. Setton, "On the Importance of Land Tenure and Agrarian Taxation in the Byzantine Empire, from the Fourth Century to the Fourth Crusade," *American Journal of Philology*, 76 (1953), 225-359.

On large estates and the problem of protecting the small, independent peasant proprietors, in addition to the above, see: A. Ferradou, *Les Biens de monastères à Byzance*, Bordeaux, 1896; G. Testaud, *Des Rapports des puissants et des petits propriétaires ruraux dans l'empire byzantin au Xᵉ siècle*, Bordeaux, 1898; G. M. Platon, "Observations sur le droit de *protimesis* en droit byzantin," *Revue générale du droit de la législation et de la jurisprudence en France et à l'étranger*, 27-29 (1903, 1904, 1905); F. Zulueta, "De patronis vicorum," *Oxford Studies in Social and Legal History*, 1 (Oxford, 1909); A. Constantinescu, "La communauté de village byzantin et ses rapports avec le petit traité fiscal byzantin," *Bulletin de la section historique de l'académie roumaine*, 13 (1927), 160-174; F. Martroye, "Les patronages d'agriculteurs et de vici au IVᵉ et au Vᵉ siècle," *Revue historique de droit français et étranger*, 4th ser., 7 (1928), 202-248; E. R. Hardy, *The Large Estates of Byzantine Egypt*, New York, 1931; F. Dölger, "Die Frage des Grundeigentum in Byzanz," *Bulletin of the International Committee of Historical Sciences*, 5 (1933), 5-15; A. Andréadès, "Floraison et décadence de la petite propriété dans l'empire byzantin," *Mélanges offerts à Ernest Mahaien*, 1 (Paris, 1935), 261-266; G. Stadtmüller, "Oströmische Bauern- und Wehrpolitik," *Neue Jahrbücher für deutsche Wissenschaft*, 13 (1937), 421-438; E. Stein, "Paysannerie et grands domaines dans l'empire byzantin," *Recueil de la société Jean Bodin*, Brussels, 1937, 123-133; P. Collinet, "La Politique de Justinien à l'égard des colons," *Studi Byzantini e Neoellenici*, 5 (1939), 600-611; A. N. Diomedes, "The Policy of the Macedonian Dynasty Against the Large Estates" (in Greek), *Hellenika*, 11 (1939), 246-262; E. Bach, "Les Lois agraires byzantines du Xᵉ siècle," *Classica et Mediaevalia*, 5 (1942), 70-91; G. Danstrup, "The State and Landed

Byzantium: Greatness and Decline

Property in Byzantium to 1250," *Classica et Mediaevalia*, 8 (1946),
221-267; G. Ostrogorsky, "The Peasant's Preemption Right," *Journal of Roman Studies*, 37 (1947), 117-126; *Id.*, "Les grands domaines dans l'empire byzantin," *Recueil de la Société Bodin*. 4.
Le Domain (1949), 35-50; P. Charanis, "The Monastic Properties
and the State in the Byzantine Empire," *Dumbarton Oaks Papers*,
No. 4 (1948), 51-118; D. A. Zakythinos, "Processus de féodalité,"
L'Hellénisme contemporain, 2nd ser., second year (1948), 499-
534; *Id.*, Étatisme byzantine et expérience hellénistique," *Annuaire de l'institut de philologie et d'histoire orientales et slaves*,
10 (1950), 667-680; *Id.*, "La Société dans le despotat de Morée,"
L'Hellénisme contemporain, 2nd ser., fifth year (1951), 7-28;
E. E. Lipsič, *Byzanz und die Slaven. Beiträge zur byzantinischen
Geschichte des 6-9. Jahrhunderts*, tr. from the Russian by E.
Langer, Weimar, 1951. The editor has not yet seen the study of
J. de Malafosse, "Le droit agraire au Bas-Empire et dans l'empire
d'orient," *Rivista di diritto agrario*, 1 (1955), 35-73.

On slavery in Byzantium, see A. Hadjinicolaou-Marava,
Recherches sur la vie des esclaves dans le monde byzantin, Athens,
1950.

On the equipment for yoking horses and oxen, there is Ct.
Lefebure des Noëttes, "Le system d'attelage du cheval et du
boeuf à Byzance et les conséquences de son emploi," *Mélanges
Charles Diehl*, 1 (Paris, 1950), 182-190.

On the commerce and industry of Byzantium, no systematic
and exhaustive study exists. The latest general survey is that by
S. Runciman, "Byzantine Trade and Industry," in M. Postan and
E. E. Rich, eds., *The Cambridge Economic History of Europe*.
2. *Trade and Industry in the Middle Ages*, Cambridge, 1952, 86-
118. The chapter by R. S. Lopez in the same publication (257-
354) entitled, "The Trade of Medieval Europe: the South," also
bears upon the commerce of Byzantium. Useful also is the general
survey of R. S. Lopez, "East and West in the Early Middle Ages:
Economic Relations," *Relazioni del X Congresso Internazionale di
Scienze Storiche. III. Storia del Medioevo*, 113-164. On the commerce of the Orient in general, including the Byzantine Empire,
the fundamental work is still that of W. Heyd, *Histoire du commerce du Levant au moyen-âge*, 2 vols., French translation by F.
Raynaud, Leipzig, 1885 (last reprint, Leipzig, 1936). For the

Bibliographical Note

trade in the Mediterranean in general, see: A. Schaube, *Handels-geschichte der Römanischen Völker bis zum Ende der Kreuzzüge*, Munich, 1906, especially 223-275. On the commerce with the West at the beginning of the Middle Ages, see: L. Bréhier, "Les colonies d'Orientaux en Occident au commencement du moyen-âge," *Byzantinische Zeitschrift*, 12 (1903), 1-39; R. S. Lopez, "Mohammed and Charlemagne: A Revision," *Speculum*, 18 (1943), 14-38; *Id.*, "Le problème des relations anglo-byzantines du VIIe au Xe siècle," *Byzantion*, 18 (1948), 139-162. For the silk trade and industry, very important is R. S. Lopez, "Silk Industry in the Byzantine Empire," *Speculum*, 20 (1945), 1-42; also R. Hennig, "Die Einführung der Seidenraupenzuch ins Byzantiner-reich," *Byzantinische Zeitschrift*, 33 (1933), 295-312. On the provisioning of Constantinople, important is the work of G. I. Bratianu, "Études sur l'approvisionnement de Constantinople et le monopole du blé à l'époque byzantine et ottomane," in his *Études byzantines d'histoire économique et sociale*, Paris, 1938, 129-181. On Constantinople as a center of industry and commerce, see E. Gren, *Kleinasien und der Ostbalkan in der wirtschaftlichen Entwicklung der römischen Kaiserzeit* (= *Uppsala Universitets Årsskrift*, 1941, No. 9), Uppsala, 1941. On the population and wealth of Constantinople, there are: A. M. Andréadès, "On the population and wealth of Constantinople during the Middle Ages" (in Greek), *Oeuvres*, 1, Athens, 1938, 387-421; P. Charanis, "A Note on the Population and Cities of the Byzantine Empire in the Thirteenth Century," *The Joshua Starr Memorial Volume* (= *Jewish Social Studies, Publication Volume* 5), New York, 1953, 135-148. Other works on commerce and industry are: L. Brentano, "Die byzantinische Volkswirtschaft," *Schmollers Jahr-buch*, 41 (1917), 1-50; K. Dieterich, "Zur Kulturgeographie und Kulturgeschichte des byzantinischen Balkan-handels," *Byzan-tinische Zeitschrift*, 31 (1931), 37-57, 334-350; A. M. Andréadès, "L'Empire byzantin et le commerce international," *Annali della R. Scuola Normale Superiore di Pisa. Lettere, Storia e Filosofia*, 2nd ser., 4 (1935), 139-148; G. Mickwitz, "Un problème d'in-fluence: Byzance et l'économie de l'Occident mediéval," *Annales d'histoire économique et sociale*, 8 (1936), 21-28; J. Ebersolt, *Orient et Occident. Recherches sur les influences byzantines et orientales en France avant et pendant les croisades*, second edition,

Byzantium: Greatness and Decline

Paris, 1954 (important for the commerce in relics and objects of art); G. I. Bratianu, *Recherches sur le commerce génois dans la Mer Noire au XIIIᵉ siècle*, Paris, 1929; R. S. Lopez, *Genova marinara nel ducento, Benedetto Zaccaria*, Messina, 1933; A. R. Lewis, *Naval Power and Trade in the Mediterranean A.D. 500-1100*, Princeton, 1951; P. Charanis, "Piracy in the Aegean during the Reign of Michael VIII Palaeologus," *Annuaire de l'institut de philologie et d'histoire orientales et slaves*, 10 (1950), 117-136. There are now available in English a number of Venetian and Genoese commercial documents relating to Byzantium: *Medieval Trade in the Mediterranean World. Illustrative Documents*, tr. with introduction and notes by R. S. Lopez and I. W. Raymond, New York, 1955.

On interest, there is G. Cassimatis, *Les intérêts dans la législation de Justinien et dans le droit byzantin*, Paris, 1931.

On the regulation of trades and professions, still fundamental for the early period is the work of J. P. Waltzing, *Étude historique sur les corporations professionnelles chez les Romains depuis les origines jusq' à la chute de l'empire d'Occident*, 2 vols., Brussels, 1895-96; also F. M. de Robertis, *Il diritto associativo romano. Dai collegi della repubblica alle corporazioni del basso impero*, Bari, 1938. Very important for the early period and also for the tenth century is the study of G. Mickwitz, *Die Kartellfunktionen der Zünfte und ihre Bedeutung bei der Entstehung des Zunftwesen; eine Studie in spätantiker und mittelalterlicher Wirtschaftsgeschichte*, Helsingfors, 1936. For the tenth century, the following are fundamental: A. Stökle, *Spätrömische und byzantinische Zünfte, Klio*, Beiheft 9 (1911); A. Christophilopoulos, *The Book of the Prefect of Leo the Wise and the Guilds in Byzantium* (in Greek), Athens, 1935. Somewhat superficial, but useful are: C. M. Macri, *L'Organisation de l'économie urbaine dans Byzance sous la dynastie de Macédoine*, Paris, 1925; G. Zoras, *Le corporazioni byzantini: Studio sull'eparchiko biblion dell imperatore Leone VI*, Rome, 1931. Also, see A. Andréadès, "Byzance, paradis du monopole et du privilège," *Byzantion*, 9 (1934), 171-181. For the thirteenth century, there is P. Charanis, "On the Social Structure and Economic Organization of the Byzantine Empire in the Thirteenth Century and Later," *Byzantinoslavica*, 12 (1951), 149-152.

Bibliographical Note

The Book of the Prefect, issued by Leo VI and the most important single source of the organization of urban economy in Byzantium in the tenth century, is available in English: A. E. R. Boak, "The Book of the Prefect," *Journal of Economic and Business History,* 1 (1929), 597-619; and E. H. Freshfield, *Roman Law in the Later Roman Empire. Byzantine Guilds, Professional and Commercial,* Cambridge, 1938.

On the Jews in the Byzantine Empire, the most comprehensive work is J. Starr, *The Jews in the Byzantine Empire 641-1204* (= *Texte und Forschungen zur byzantinisch-neugriechischen Philologie,* No. 30), Athens, 1939; *Id., Romania. The Jewries of the Levant after the Fourth Crusade,* Paris, 1949; *Id.,* "Byzantine Jewry on the Eve of the Arab Conquest," *Journal of the Palestine Oriental Society,* 15 (1935), 280-293; B. N. Nelson and J. Starr, "The Legend of the Divine Surety and the Jewish Moneylender," *Annuaire de l'institut de philologie et d'histoire orientales et slaves,* 7 (1939-44), 289-338. Also, see: A. M. Andréadès, "Les juifs et le fisc dans l'empire byzantin," *Mélanges Charles Diehl,* 1 (Paris, 1930), 7-29; *Id.,* "The Jews in the Byzantine Empire," *Economic History,* 3 (1934), 1-23; F. Dölger, "Die Frage der Judensteuer in Byzanz," *Vierteljahrschrift für Sozial- und Wirtschaftsgeschichte,* 36 (1933), 1-24; D. Browe, "Die Judengesetzgebung Justinians," *Analecta Gregoriana,* 8 (1935), 109-146; P. Charanis, "The Jews in the Byzantine Empire under the First Paleologi," *Speculum,* 22 (1946), 75-78; A. Sharf, "Byzantine Jewry in the Seventh Century," *Byzantinische Zeitschrift,* 48 (1955), 103-115.

For an analysis of the economic factors in the decline of the Byzantine Empire, see P. Charanis, "Economic Factors in the Decline of the Byzantine Empire," *Journal of Economic History,* Vol. 13, fasc. 4 (1953), 412-425. For analysis of factors in addition to the economic in the decline of the Byzantine Empire, see F. Dölger, "Politische und geistige Strömungen im sterbenden Byzanz," *Jahrbuch der Österreichischen Byzantinischen Gesellschaft,* 3 (1954), 3-18.

Byzantium: Greatness and Decline

VIII. Civilization:

The latest, most comprehensive and detailed treatment of Byzantine civilization as a whole is L. Bréhier, *La Civilisation byzantine,* Paris, 1950. Also, see N. H. Baynes and H. St. L. B. Moss, *Byzantium. An Introduction to East Roman Civilization,* Oxford, 1948. Other useful general accounts are: D. C. Hesseling, *Essai sur la civilisation byzantine,* Paris, 1907; N. H. Baynes, *The Byzantine Empire,* London, 1926 (last printing, 1946); *Id., Byzantine Studies and other Essays,* London, 1955, especially pages 1-46, 67-82; S. Runciman, *Byzantine Civilization,* London, 1933; N. Jorga, *Histoire de la vie byzantine. Empire et civilisation,* 3 vols., Bucharest, 1934.

The most detailed and thorough treatment of daily life in Byzantium is the work of P. Koukoules, *The Private Life of the Byzantines* (in Greek), 5 vols., Athens, 1948-52. For the twelfth century, there is L. Oeconomos, *La Vie religieuse dans l'empire byzantin au temps des Comnènes et des Anges,* Paris, 1918.

On Byzantine law, still fundamental is K. E. Zachariä von Lingenthal, *Geschichte des griechisch-römischer Rechtes,* third edition, Berlin, 1892, reprinted, 1955. Important also is G. A. Petropoulos, *History of Roman Law* (in Greek), Athens, 1944.

For a general history of Byzantine philosophy, see B. Tatakis, *La philosophie byzantine* (= E. Bréhier, *Histoire de la philosophie. Deuxième fascicule supplémentaire*), Paris, 1949. Important also is J. Hussey, *Church and Learning in the Byzantine Empire, 867-1185,* London, 1937.

For individual studies on Byzantine intellectuals and men of letters, there are the following: On Michael Psellus as philosopher, C. Zervos, *Un philosophe néoplatonicien du XIe siècle: Michel Psellos*, Paris, 1919; on Psellus as man and politician, A. Rambaud, "Michel Psellos. Philosophe et homme d'état byzantin au XIe siècle," published first in April, 1877, in *Revue historique* and reprinted in A. Rambaud, *Études sur l'histoire byzantine*, Paris, 1922, 111-171; on Psellus as historian, J. Hussey, "Michael Psellus, the Byzantine Historian," *Speculum*, 10 (1935), 81-90; on the family of Psellus, C. Diehl, "Une famille de bourgeoisie à Byzance au XIe siècle," *Figures byzantines*, 1st ser., 11th printing, Paris, 1930, 291-316.

On John Italus, P. E. Stephanou, *Jean Italos, philosophe et humaniste* (= *Orientalia Christiana Analecta*, 134), Rome, 1949.

On Anna Comnena, G. Buckler, *Anna Comnena: A Study*, Oxford, 1929. This is actually a study of Byzantine civilization during the reign of Alexius Comnenus.

On Maximus Planudes, C. Wendel, "Planudes," A. F. von Pauly-G. Wissowa, *Real Encyclopädie, Neue Bearbeitung*, 20 (1930), 2202-2253.

On Theodore Metochites, Hans-Georg Beck, *Theodoros Metochites. Die Krise des byzantinischen Weltbildes im 14. Jahrhundert*, Munich, 1952.

On Nicephorus Gregoras, R. Guilland, *Essai sur Nicéphore Grégoras. L'homme et l'oeuvre*, Paris, 1926; *Id., Correspondance de Nicéphore Grégoras*, Paris, 1927.

No comprehensive monograph yet exists on Demetrius Cydones, but considerable material concerning him is offered by the following publications: G. Cammelli, *Démétrius Cydonès. Correspondance*, Paris, 1930; G. Mercati, *Notizie di Procoro e Demetrio Cidone, Manuele Caleca e Teodoro Meliteniota ed altri appunti per la storia della teologia e della letteratura bizantina del secolo XIV* (= *Studi e Testi*, 56), Rome, 1931; R. J. Loenertz, *Les recueils de lettres de Démétrius Cydonès* (= *Studi e Testi*, 131), Rome, 1947; M. Jugie, "Démétrius Cydonès et la théologie latine à Byzance au XIVe et XVe siècles," *Échos d'Orient*, 27 (1928), 385-402; Hans-Georg Beck, "Die 'Apologia pro vita sua' des Demetrios Kydones," *Ostkirchliche Studien*, 1 (1952), 208-225, 264-282.

On Manuel Calecas, fundamental is the publication of his letters with a French résumé of each and an introduction by R. J. Loenertz, *Correspondance de Manuel Calecas* (= *Studi e Testi*,

152), Rome, 1950. Also, see: J. Gouillard, "Les influences latines dans l'oeuvre théologique de Manuel Calecas," *Échos d'Orient*, 37 (1938), 36-52; R. J. Loenertz, "Manuel Calecas, sa vie et ses oeuvres d'après ses lettres et ses apologies inédites," *Archivum FF. Praedicatorum*, 17 (1947), 195-207.

For a summary account on the intellectuals of the fifteenth century, see D. A. Zakythinos, *Le Despotat grec de Morée. 2. Vie et institutions*, Athens, 1953, 311-376. On Pletho, there is M. V. Anastos, "Pletho's Calendar and Liturgy," *Dumbarton Oaks Papers*, No. 4 (1948), 183-269; *Id.*, "Pletho and Islam," *ibid.*, 270-305. Anastos gives full bibliographical references on Pletho. But see now the excellent book of F. Masai, *Plethon et le Platonisme de Mistra*, Paris, 1956. On Bessarion, fundamental is the work of L. Mohler; *Kardinal Bessarion als Theologe, Humanist und Staatsmann*, 1, Paderborn, 1923. Still useful is the older work of H. Vast, *Le Cardinal Bessarion (1403-1472). Étude sur la Chrétienté et la renaissance vers le milieu du XVe siècle*, Paris, 1878. Also, see E. Candal, "Bessario Nicaenus in Concilio Florentino," *Orientalia Christiana Periodica*, 6 (1940), 417-466; R. J. Loenertz, "Pour la biographie du cardinal Bessarion," *Orientalia Christiana Periodica*, 10 (1944), 116-149. On George Scholarius, see M. Jugie, "Scholarios, Georges," *Dictionnaire de Théologie Catholique*, 14, 2 (1941), 1521-1570; *Id.*, Georges Scholarios, professeur de philosophie," *Studi Bizantini Neoellenici*, 5 (1939), 482-494; also, the introduction to the first volume of L. Petit, X. A. Siderides, M. Jugie, eds., *Oeuvres complètes de Georges Scholarios*, 8 vols., Paris, 1928-36.

On the Byzantine intellectuals and the origin of Humanism, G. Cammelli, *I dotti bizantini e le origini dell' umanesimo. 1. Manuele Crisolora*, Florence, 1941; *2. Giovanni Argiropulo*, Florence, 1941; *3. Demetrio Calcondila*, Florence, 1954. See also the general account of K. M. Setton, "The Byzantine Background to the Italian Renaissance," *Proceedings of the American Philosophical Society*, 100 (1956), 1-76. Setton's study has important bibliographical references.

On Byzantine literature in general, the most important account is still that of K. Krumbacher, *Geschichte der byzantinischen Litteratur von Justinian bis zum Ende des oströmischen Reiches (527-1453)*, second edition, Munich, 1897. Less comprehensive,

Bibliographical Note

but useful, is G. Montelatici, *Storia della letteratura bizantina (324-1453)*, Milan, 1916. Also, see F. H. Marshall, "Byzantine Literature," in Baynes and Moss, *Byzantium*, 221-251. On the Christian Greek literature to the end of the fourth century, there is A. Puech, *Histoire de la littérature grecque chrétienne depuis les origines jusqu' à la fin du IVe siècle*, 3 vols., Paris, 1930. On Byzantine hagiography, P. Peeters, *Orient et Byzance. Le tréfonds oriental de l'hagiographie byzantine* (= Société des Bollandistes, *Subsidia Hagiographica*, 26), Brussels, 1950. As an example of Byzantine hagiography, one may consult three important biographies of saints in E. Dawes and N. H. Baynes, tr., *Three Byzantine Saints. Contemporary Biographies of St. Daniel the Stylite, St. Theodore of Sykeon, and St. John the Almsgiver*, Oxford, 1948.

On Byzantine hymnography there is now the important book by E. Wellesz, *A History of Byzantine Music and Hymnography*, Oxford, 1949. Important also for Byzantine music is R. Palikarova Verdeil, *La musique byzantine chez les Bulgares et les Russes du IXe au XIVe siècle* (= *Monumenta Musicae Byzantinae, Subsidia*, III), Copenhagen, 1953.

On the question as to whether there was a religious drama in Byzantium in the sense of the passion play of the West, see: G. La Piana, *Le Rappresentazioni sacra nella letteratura bizantina delle origini al sec. IX con rapporti al teatro sacro d'Occidente*, Grottaferrata, 1912; V. Cottas, *Le Théâtre à Byzance*, Paris, 1931 (but see the devastating review of this book by G. La Piana, "The Byzantine Theatre," *Speculum*, 11 [1936], 171-211); A. Vogt, "Études sur le théâtre byzantin. Un mystère de la Passion," *Byzantion*, 6 (1931), 37-74; M. Carpenter, "Romanos and the Mystery Play of the East," *The University of Missouri Studies. Philological Studies in Honor of W. Miller*, Vol. 11, No. 3 (1936), 21-51; S. Baud-Bovy, "Sur un 'Sacrifice d'Abraham' de Romanos et sur l'existence d'un théâtre religieux à Byzance," *Byzantion*, 13 (1938), 321-334; E. Wellesz, "The Nativity Drama of the Byzantine Church," *The Journal of Roman Studies*, 37 (1947), 145-151. For an English translation and study of the "Cyprus Passion Cycle," see A. C. Mahr, *The Cyprus Passion Cycle*, Notre Dame, Indiana, 1947. Also on the Byzantine theater, see A. Vogt, "Le théâtre à Byzance et dans l'empire du IVe au XIIIe siècle. I. Le théâtre profane," *Revue des questions historiques*, 59 (1931), 257-

296; *Id.*, "Études sur le théâtre byzantin. II," *Byzantion*, 6 (1931), 623-640.

On the Byzantine epic, basic are the studies of Henri Grégoire: "L'épopée byzantine et ses rapports avec l'épopée turque et l'épopée romane," *Académie royale de Belgique, bulletin de la classe des lettres et des sciences morales et politiques,* 5th ser., 17 (1931), 463-493; *Id.*, "Les sources poétiques, et littéraires de Digenis," *Actes du IIIe congrès international des études byzantines* (1932), 280-294; H. Grégoire and R. Goossens, "Autour de Digenis Akritas: les cantilènes et la date d'Andros-Trébizonde. Cantilènes grecques et romans arabes," *Byzantion*, 7 (1932), 287-317; H. Grégoire and R. Goossens, "Les recherches récentes sur l'épopée byzantine," *Antiquité classique*, 1 (1932), 419-439; H. Grégoire, "Études sur l'épopée byzantine," *Revue des études grecques,* 46 (1933), 29-69; *Id.*, "L'Âge héroique de Byzance," *Mélanges offerts à M. Nicolas Jorga* (Paris, 1933), 382-397. Finally, there is the important book by H. Grégoire, *Digenis Akritas, The Byzantine Epic in History and Poetry* (in Greek), New York, 1942. Other works on the Byzantine epic include: A. Rambaud, "Une épopée byzantine au Xe siècle. Les exploits de Digenis Akritas," in his *Études sur l'histoire byzantine*, third edition, Paris, 1922, 65-108 (Rambaud's article was first printed in 1875 in the *Revue des deux mondes*); C. Diehl, "Le roman de Digenis Akritas," in his *Figures byzantines,* 2nd ser., 8th printing, (Paris, 1927), 291-319; S. Kyriakides, *Digenis Akritas* (in Greek), Athens, 1926; A. Adontz, "Les fonds historiques de l'épopée byzantine," *Byzantinische Zeitschrift,* 29 (1929-30), 198-227; R. Goossens, "Les recherches récentes sur l'épopée byzantine," *Antiquité classique,* 2 (1933), 449-472; H. Grégoire and H. Luedeke, "Nouvelles chansons épiques des IXe et Xe siècles," *Byzantion,* 14 (1939), 235-263; A. Frantz, "A Byzantine Epic and its Illustrators," *Byzantion,* 15 (1940-41), 87-91; S. Impellizzeri, *Il Digenis Akritas, L'Epopea di Bisanzio*, Florence, 1940 (very important); *Id.*, *"La morte di Digenis Akritas"* (*Estratto dagli Atti del Museo Pitres,* 1), Florence, 1950; also H. Grégoire, "La problème de la version originale de l'épopée byzantine de Digenis Akritas," *Revue des études byzantines,* 6 (1948), 27-35.

For a translation of the poem in English with a commentary

and a critical introduction, there is now J. Mavrogordato, *Digenes Akrites,* Oxford, 1956.

There is a French translation of the Trebizond version of Digenis Akritas by C. Sathas and E. Legrand, *Les exploits de Digenis Acritas,* Paris, 1875; there is also an Italian translation made from the Grottaferrata version by S. Impellizzeri, *Il Digenis Akritas, L'Epopea di Bisanzio,* Florence, 1940.

On the question of the language in general, see H. Zilliacus, *Zum kampf der weltsprachen in oströmischen Reich,* Helsingfors, 1935.

On Byzantine education, see: L. Bréhier, "L'enseignement supérieur à Constantinople dans la dernière moitié du XI° siècle," *Revue internationale de l'enseignement,* 38 (1899), 97-112; *Id.,* "Notes sur l'histoire de l'enseignement supérieur à Constantinople," *Byzantion,* 3 (1926), 73-94; *Byzantion,* 4 (1927-28), 13-28; *Id.,* L'enseignement classique et enseignement religieux à Byzance," *Revue d'histoire et de philosophie religieuse de la faculté protestante de l'université de Strasbourg,* 21 (1941), 34-69; F. Fuchs, *Die höheren Schulen von Konstantinopel im Mittelalter* (= *Byzantinisches Archive,* 8), Leipzig, 1926; G. Buckler, "Byzantine Education," in N. H. Baynes and H. St. L. B. Moss, *Byzantium,* 200-220; F. Dvornik, "Photius et la réorganisation de l'académie patriarcale," *Mélanges P. Peeters,* 2 (= *Analecta Bollandiana,* 68), 1950, 108-125. In addition, there are the appropriate chapters in the more general books on Byzantine civilization: G. Buckler, *Anna Comnena,* 165-225; F. Dvornik, *Les légendes de Constantin et de Méthode vue de Byzance,* Prague, 1933, 25-45; J. M. Hussey, *Church and Learning in the Byzantine Empire, 867-1185,* 51-116; L. Bréhier, *La civilisation byzantine,* 446-503.

On Byzantine art in general, see: C. Diehl, *Manuel d'art byzantin,* 2 vols., second edition, Paris, 1925-26; O. M. Dalton, *Byzantine Art and Archaeology,* Oxford, 1911; *Id., East Christian Art,* Oxford, 1925; O. Wulff, *Altchristliche und byzantinische Kunst,* Berlin, 1914; G. Millet, *Recherches sur l'iconographie de l'Évangile,* Paris, 1916; L. Bréhier, *L'art byzantin,* Paris, 1924; A. Grabar, *La peinture religieuse en Bulgarie,* Paris, 1928; *Id., L'art byzantin chez les Slaves. Les Balkans,* 2 vols., Paris, 1930; D. Talbot Rice, *Byzantine Art,* Oxford, 1935 (Pelican edition, revised, 1954).

Byzantium: Greatness and Decline

On Byzantine architecture in general, there are: J. A. Hamilton, *Byzantine Architecture and Decoration,* London, 1934; E. H. Swift, *Hagia Sophia,* New York, 1940; A. Grabar, *Martyrium, Recherches sur le culte des reliques et l'art chrétien antique,* 2 vols., Paris, 1946 (Volume 1 deals with architecture).

On St. Sophia, there are the following: E. M. Antoniades, *St. Sophia* (in Greek), 3 vols., Athens, 1907-09; W. R. Lethaby and H. Swainson, *The Church of Sancta Sophia, Constantinople: A Study of Byzantine Building,* London, 1894; A. M. Schneider, *Die Hagia Sophia zu Konstantinopel,* Berlin, 1939.

On Byzantine mosaics, see: E. Diez and O. Demus, *Byzantine Mosaics in Greece,* Cambridge, Mass., 1931; T. Whittemore, *The Mosaics of St. Sophia at Istanbul,* 1-4, London, 1933-52; O. Demus, *Byzantine Mosaic Decoration. Aspects of Monumental Art in Byzantium,* London, 1949; *Id., The Mosaics of Norman Sicily,* London, 1950; A. Xyngopoulos, *The Decoration in Mosaic of the Church of the Holy Apostles at Thessalonica* (in Greek), Thessalonica, 1953. For brilliant illustrations of Byzantine paintings, including mosaics, see A. Grabar, *Byzantine Painting,* Geneva, 1953 (Edition Albert Skira).

On Byzantine miniatures, there are: N. Kondakov, *Histoire de l'art considéré principalement dans les miniatures,* French edition by M. Trawinski, 2 vols., Paris, 1886, 1891; J. Ebersolt, *La Miniature byzantine,* Paris, 1926; K. Weitzmann, *Die byzantinische Buchmalerei des IX. und X. Jahrhunderts,* Berlin, 1935; *Id., Illustrations in Roll and Codex,* Princeton, 1947. Important, too, are the studies of A. M. Friend, Jr., "The Portraits of the Evangelists in Greek and Latin Manuscripts," *Art Studies* (1927), 118-147; (1929), 1-29.

On the minor arts, consult: J. Ebersolt, *Sanctuaires de Byzance. Recherches sur les anciens trésors des églises de Constantinople,* Paris, 1921; *Id., Les arts somptuaires de Byzance. Étude sur l'art impérial de Constantinople,* Paris, 1923.

On the continuation of Byzantine cultural influences after the fall of the Empire, see N. Jorga, *Byzance après Byzance,* Bucharest, 1935.

Bibliographical Note

IX. Bibliographical Aids and Periodicals:

Two important summaries of official Byzantine Acts exist. The imperial Acts from the death of Justinian (565) to 1282 are summarized by F. Dölger, *Regesten der Kaiserurkunden des oströmischen Reiches*, 3 parts, Munich, 1924, 1925, 1932; those of the Byzantine Patriarchs to 1206 by V. Grumel, *Les Regesten des actes du patriarchat de Constantinople*, Vol. 1, fasc. 1-3, Socii Assumptionistae Chalcedonenses, 1932, 1936, 1947.

Important as a guide to the Byzantine historians is G. Moravcsik, *Byzantinoturcica*, 1, Budapest, 1942.

An important bibliographical guide for the literature on Byzantium which appeared during the years 1938-1950 is F. Dölger and A. M. Schneider, *Byzanz*, Bern, 1952. Useful, also, is the bibliography published under the auspices of UNESCO: *Dix années d'études byzantines. Bibliographie internationale 1939-1948*, Paris, École des Hautes Études, 1949.

Six periodicals currently published are devoted almost exclusively to Byzantine studies: *Byzantinische Zeitschrift*, 1892—; *Epeteris Hetaereias Byzantiôn Spoudôn*, 1924—; *Byzantion*, 1924—; *Byzantinoslavica*, 1929—; *Études byzantines* (*Revue des études byzantines* since 1946), 1943—; *Jahrbuch der Österreichischen Byzantinischen Gesellschaft*, 1951—. All these periodicals carry bibliographical notes, but particularly detailed are those of *Byzantinische Zeitschrift* and *Byzantinoslavica*.

Index

Index

Index

Index

Index

Index

Magyars (*see* Hungarians)
Mainotes, 73
Maiphergat, 156
Malalas, 243, 249
Malik-Shāh, 208
Manasses, 243
Manfred Hohenstaufen, King, 222
Maniakes, General George, 115, 135
Maniakes family, 114
Mantzikert, 15, 121, 208
Manuel Comnenus, Emperor, 16, 19, 38, 42, 47, 126, 171, 181-184, 187, 192, 208, 218, 220
Manuel II Palaeologus, Emperor, 20, 224, 248
Marmara, Sea of, 96, 191
Marseilles, 83, 89, 196
Mardaites, 71, 72
Martin I, Pope, 213, 214
Maximus, Abbot, 214
Maximus the Confessor, 244, 246, 287
Meander River, 208
Mediterranean Sea, 51, 83, 178
Melisseni, the, 162
Melitene, 76, 208
Menander, 241, 242, 263
Menas, 34
Mesopotamia, 164, 238, 274
Mesrob, 262, 274
Methodius, St., 11, 215, 262-265
Metochites, Theodore, 233, 248
Michael III, Emperor, 136, 262
Michael V, Emperor, 130
Michael VIII Palaeologus, Emperor, 194, 197, 205, 223
Miletus, 164
Mistra, 21
Mleh (Melias), 75
Mocenigo, Doge, 196
Modon, 194
Mohammed II, Sultan, 21, 290-292
Moldavia, 272, 291
Montaner, Ramon, 202
Montpellier, 196
Moravia, 215, 264
Morea, 162, 194, 210
Morosini, Roger, 194
Moschopulus, 234, 287
Moschus, John, 245

Moslems (*see* Arabs)
Murad II, Sultan, 210
Musurus, Marcus, 288
Myriocephalon, 208

Narbonne, 83, 196
Narses, 47
Naupactus, 77
Nauplia, 81, 161
Naxos, 194
Negropont, 81, 194
Neo-Caesarea, 208
Nicaea, 157, 208, 210
Nicaean Emperors, 19
Nicephorus I, Emperor, 168
Nicephorus II Phocas, Emperor, 13, 38, 47, 51, 115, 117, 131-136, 155, 169-172, 180
Nicephorus, Patriarch, 243
Nicetas Acominatus, 35, 56, 144, 149, 171, 192, 193, 219, 221, 234, 241-244
Nicholas I, Pope, 215, 265
Nicholas I, Czar, 298
Nicholas, Patriarch, 172, 173
Nicholas of Methone, 244, 246
Nicomedia, 210
Nicopolis, 224
Nile Valley, 80, 83
Nineveh, 9
Nisibis, 274
Nogaret, Guillaume de, 286
Normans, 15, 18, 41, 44, 57, 160, 184, 203, 221
North Africa, 9

Odo of Deuil, 18
Odofredus, 286
Olga, Grand Princess, 57, 267
Omayyad Caliphs, 51, 274
Opsikion, 41
Orkhan, Sultan, 202, 204
Orthodox Church, 7, 11, 35, 59, 73, 77, 102, 128, 141-143, 163-175, 182, 186, 211-224, 236, 262-275, 291-294
Ostrogoths, 6, 43, 44, 177, 178
Othon de la Roche, 162
Otranto, 77

Index

Otto I the Great, Emperor, 63, 180, 283
Otto III, Emperor, 285
Ottomans (*see* Turks)

Pachymeres, 193, 201, 243
Palaeologi, the, 19, 31, 37, 107, 193, 194, 200, 206, 209, 222, 234, 253, 279
Palaeologus (*see* individual names)
Palamas, 245
Palestine, 164
Pankalia, 157
Papacy, 7, 8, 11, 15, 19, 20, 34, 57, 126, 168, 173, 180-184, 211-224, 277, 287
Paphlagonia, 115, 208
Paris, 83, 286
Patmos, 92, 194, 232
Patras, 81, 86
Pechenegs, 53, 60, 81, 97, 105, 138, 262
Peloponnesus, 71, 81, 191
Pepin the Short, King, 214
Pera, 195
Persia, 238
Persian Empire, 44
Persians, 9, 53, 73, 178
Peter, Czar (Rumania), 267
Peter the Great, Czar, 298
Phanariots, 29, 293
Philadelphia, 191, 206-210
Philes, Manuel, 248
Philip the Fair, King, 286
Philippopolis, 77, 191
Phocaea, 118, 194, 195
Phocas, General, 115, 135
Phocas (centurion), Emperor, 127
Phocas family, 154
Phoenicia, 81
Photius, Patriarch, 11, 150, 174, 215, 216, 230, 232, 244, 246, 247, 265, 271
Phrantzes, 242, 243
Pillars of Hercules, 51, 178
Pindus Mountains, 71
Pisa, 84, 88, 105, 183, 193, 196, 279
Pisans, 51, 55, 82, 194

Plaisians, Guillaume de, 286
Planudes, 234, 287
Pliska-Aboba, 265
Polyeuctes, Patriarch, 131, 172
Pontus, 82, 86
Preslav the Great, Czar, 266
Princes' Islands, 194
Proclus, 246
Procopius, 49, 56, 62, 102, 177, 234, 241, 246, 263
Prodromus, Theodorus, 248, 249
Propontis, 105
Psellus, Michael, 130, 147, 158, 173, 233, 234, 241, 244, 246, 248, 287

Ragusa, 196
Ravenna, 83, 178, 180, 214, 276, 286
Red Sea, 80
Renaud de Châtillon, 218
Rhodes, 191, 209
Robert of Clari, 18, 83, 196
Rodosto, 82, 210
Roger de Flor, 203, 204
Rolandino of Romanzi, 286
Roman Church (*see* Papacy)
Roman Empire (Western), 176-179, 214
Romanus I Lecapenus, Emperor, 115, 155, 186
Romanus IV Diogenes, Emperor, 15, 115, 148, 208
Roum, 121, 208
Roumelia, 290
Roussel de Bailleul, 203
Rumania, 271
Rumanians, 21, 289, 293, 299
Rurik, 261
Russia, 191, 261, 263, 267-270, 295-298
Russians, 14, 51-53, 60, 79, 81, 97, 105, 187, 263, 289

Sacred Palace, 8, 31, 99, 136, 230
Sahak, 262, 274
St. Sophia, Church of, 7, 59, 102, 199, 251, 299
Samarkand, 79

Index

Samos, 114
Samosata, 76
Samuel, Czar, 14, 74, 186, 299, 300
Santa Severina, 77
Santorini, 194
Sardinia, 7, 178
Sava, St., 270
Scandinavians, 61, 73
Scholarius, George, 245
Sebaste, 208
Seljuks (*see* Turks)
Selymbria, 82, 210
Septum, 178
Serbia, 126, 263, 270, 299
Serbs, 9, 18, 21, 53, 60, 138, 186, 189, 197, 200, 201, 206, 261, 263, 289, 293, 299
Sergius, Patriarch, 172
Seville, 196
Sicily, 53, 57, 178
Sinai Peninsula, 164
Sinope, 118
Skleros, General, 115
Skleros family, 114
    (*see also* individual names)
Skylitzes, 243
Slavs, 53, 71, 73, 178, 186, 187, 261-278
    (*see also* individual peoples)
Smyrna, 118, 208
Sophia (city), 300
Sophia Palaeologus, Grand Princess, 295
Spain, 83, 88, 178
Spaniards, 73, 210
Stephen II, Pope, 214
Stephen Dushan, Czar (Serbia), 20, 186, 209, 270, 271, 299, 300
Stephen Nemanja, King, 186, 208, 270
Struma, 86
Strymon River, 71
Studium, 168, 232, 245
Symeon, Czar, 14, 186, 266, 299, 300
Symeon Ampelas, 117
Symeon Magister, 243, 245
Symeon Metaphrastes, 245
Symmachus, Pope, 212

Syria, 9, 14, 18, 79, 80, 83, 86, 164, 184, 187, 190, 207, 238
Syrians, 71, 263, 274, 279

Tana, 194
Taranto, 77
Taron, 76
Tarsus, 118
Taurus Mountains, 117
Tenedos, 194
Terbel, Khan, 264
Thebes, 81, 86
Theodora, Empress (wife of Justinian), 8, 32, 130
Theodora, Empress (wife of Theophilus), 93
Theodora, Empress (sister of Zoë), 37
Theodore of Studium, 168, 244
Theodoric, 6, 177, 178
Theodosius I the Great, Emperor, 5
Theodosius II, Emperor, 96, 97, 105
Theophanes, St., 243, 249, 263, 265
Theophanes Continuatus, 37
Theophano, Empress, 136, 283
Theophilus, Emperor, 11, 93
Theophylact Simocatta, 242
Thessalonica, 20, 71, 77, 81, 86, 191, 194, 199, 204, 206, 209, 210, 219, 221, 300
Thessaly, 71, 204, 210, 299
Thrace, 41, 71, 79, 93, 115, 178, 189, 191, 200, 204, 209, 210
Tinos, 194
Trajan Gate, 47
Trani, 77
Trebizond, 21, 79, 82, 86, 118, 194, 208, 209
Triclinius, 234, 287
Tughril-Beg, 208
Tunisia, 49
Turkestan, 79
Turkey, 210
Turks, 15, 16, 41, 57, 73, 94, 138, 160, 187-190, 197, 200-205, 206-210, 223, 230, 262, 289, 290-294
Tuscany, 107, 283
Tzetzes, John, 232, 234

· 365 ·

Index

Ulfila, 262
Uskub, 270
Uzes, 262

Vandals, 41, 43, 44, 53, 178
Varangian Guard, 42, 109
Varangians, 261, 298
Vardar River, 71
Varna, 224
Vatopedi, 270
Venetians, 18, 51, 82, 193-199, 209, 210, 221
Venice, 53, 57, 84, 88, 90, 105, 183, 191-196, 209, 220, 222, 277, 282
Villehardouin, Geoffroi de, 18, 83, 162

Visigoths, 6, 53
Vladimir I, Czar, 59, 267-269
Volga River, 262

Wallachia, 272
Wallachians, 71, 291
Western Church (*see* Papacy)
William of Tyre, 221

Xiphilinus, Patriarch, 247

Zealots, 162
Zeno, Emperor, 7, 213
Zichians, 262
Zoë, Empress, 32, 37, 130
Zonaras, 243